The Beginnings of Behavioral Economics

Perspectives in Behavioral Economics and the Economics of Behavior

The Beginnings of Behavioral Economics

Katona, Simon, and Leibenstein's X-Efficiency Theory

Roger Frantz

Series Editor
Morris Altman

ELSEVIER

ACADEMIC PRESS
An imprint of Elsevier

Academic Press is an imprint of Elsevier
125 London Wall, London EC2Y 5AS, United Kingdom
525 B Street, Suite 1650, San Diego, CA 92101, United States
50 Hampshire Street, 5th Floor, Cambridge, MA 02139, United States
The Boulevard, Langford Lane, Kidlington, Oxford OX5 1GB, United Kingdom

Notices
Knowledge and best practice in this field are constantly changing. As new research and experience broaden our understanding, changes in research methods, professional practices, or medical treatment may become necessary.

Practitioners and researchers must always rely on their own experience and knowledge in evaluating and using any information, methods, compounds, or experiments described herein. In using such information or methods they should be mindful of their own safety and the safety of others, including parties for whom they have a professional responsibility.

To the fullest extent of the law, neither the Publisher nor the authors, contributors, or editors, assume any liability for any injury and/or damage to persons or property as a matter of products liability, negligence or otherwise, or from any use or operation of any methods, products, instructions, or ideas contained in the material herein.

Library of Congress Cataloging-in-Publication Data
A catalog record for this book is available from the Library of Congress

British Library Cataloguing-in-Publication Data
A catalogue record for this book is available from the British Library

ISBN 978-0-12-815289-8

Publisher: Candice Janco
Acquisition Editor: Candice Janco
Editorial Project Manager: Susan Ikeda
Production Project Manager: Debasish Ghosh
Cover Designer: Matthew Limbert

Typeset by SPi Global, India

Dedication

This book is dedicated to the first seven inductees into my Mount Rushmore—Behavioral Economics Hall of Fame. Listed chronologically by year of birth: George Katona (1901–81), Herbert Simon (1916–2001), Harvey Leibenstein (1922–94), Daniel Kahneman (1934-present), Amos Tversky (1937–96), George Akerlof (1940-present), and Richard Thaler (1945-present).

Contents

Acknowledgments **xi**

1 Introduction **1**
- I What this book is about and what it is not about **1**
- II Two beginnings, one door **3**
- III Leibenstein's writings, 1950–66 **5**
- IV Empirical studies on X-efficiency **7**

2 Two beginnings **9**
- I The door **9**
- II Homo economicus **17**
- III Behavioral economics. What is it? **19**
- IV Final comments on this chapter and looking ahead to Chapter 3 **24**

3 The "Big 3." Simon, Katona, Leibenstein **25**
- I Herbert A. Simon **25**
- II George Katona **30**
- III Harvey Leibenstein **38**
- IV Behavioral economics or speculation? **45**
- V Final comments on this chapter, and looking ahead to Chapter 4 **45**

4 It didn't just happen overnight **47**
- I Gabriel Tarde **48**
- II James March **50**
- III Richard Nelson and Sidney Winter **52**
- IV Kenneth Boulding **53**
- V James Duesenberry **54**
- VI Reinhard Selten **57**
- VII G.L.S. Shackle. The paradox of rationality **59**
- VIII Tibor Scitovsky **61**
- IX Final comments on this chapter, and looking ahead to chapters **64**
- Appendix: Full rationality and the new behavioral economics 64

5 Leibenstein before X-efficiency theory **71**
- I Efficiency wages **72**
- II Similarities in Akerlof's and Leibenstein's behavioral economics **77**
- III Social preferences. The psychology and sociology of demand **79**

	IV	The nature of human knowledge	**82**
	V	Organizational analysis and economic theory	**83**
	VI	Final comments on Chapter 6, and looking ahead to Chapter 6	**94**
6	**X-efficiency. An intervening variable**		**95**
	I	In the beginning…	**95**
	II	X vs. allocative efficiency	**97**
	III	Final comments on this chapter, and looking ahead to Chapter 7	**108**
	Appendix: Dual-selves, herding, gift exchange, framing and the new behavioral economics		109
7	**Empirical research on XE: c.1967–1990**		**117**
	I	Some issues surrounding X-efficiency	**117**
	II	Early studies on X-efficiency using questionnaires and/or interviews	**121**
	III	Early studies not using questionnaires and/or interviews	**123**
	IV	Ownership form	**124**
	V	Protection	**126**
	VI	Level of competition	**127**
	VII	Government (regulations)	**129**
	VIII	Management	**133**
	IX	Final comments on this chapter, and looking ahead to Chapter 8	**135**
8	**XE among US financial institutions: c.1991–2017**		**137**
	I	Parametric and non-parametric approaches	**137**
	II	Frontier analysis	**140**
	III	Bank studies	**141**
	IV	Non-bank studies	**151**
	V	Final comments on this chapter, and looking ahead to Chapter 9	**155**
9	**XE among financial firms in Asia: c.1991–2017**		**157**
	I	China	**157**
	II	Korea and Japan	**165**
	III	Other Asian nations	**166**
	IV	Final comments on this chapter, and looking ahead to Chapter 10	**169**
10	**XE among Asian non-financial institutions: c.1991–2017**		**171**
	I	China	**171**
	II	Taiwan	**171**
	III	India	**176**
	IV	Indonesia	**177**
	V	Final comments on this chapter, and looking ahead to Chapters 11 and 12	**177**

11 XE in Europe: c.1991–2017 **179**
I Eastern Europe and post-communist **179**
II EU members **183**
III Individual nations **184**

12 XE in Australia and New Zealand, Latin America, the Middle East, Africa, and the world: c.1991–2017 **189**
I XE in Australia and New Zealand **189**
II XE in Latin America **192**
III XE in Middle East and Africa **194**

13 Conclusions **203**
I Two beginnings and the door **203**
II Homo economicus **203**
III Overlaps between the first and other generations **204**
IV X-efficiency theory **204**
V Leibenstein and the empirical studies of X-efficiency theory **205**

References **207**
Index **233**

Acknowledgments

I want to thank several people for their help and assistance with this project. Morris Altman, editor of this Series who asked me to write this book. People who read part of the text and/or discussed the text with me are Michelle Baddeley, Richard Curtin, Shabnam Mousavi, Roberta Muramatsu, Mark Pingle, Joe Sabia, E.M. Sent, Shosh Shahrabani, and John Tomer. Susan Ikeda of Elsevier kept me on track. My wife Nancy read parts of the text, and helped with the graphics. Three people contributed in a different way and I very much appreciate their assistance. Taylor Mackay, a Ph.D. student at the University of California Irvine, and an M.A. student of mine at SDSU, wrote the material on the econometrics of parametric and non-parameric techniques which is part of Chapter 8. Michael Mitzkewitz of the University of Luxembourg, and Rosemarie Nagel of ICREA and the University Pompeu Fabra-Barcelona, wrote the material on Reinhard Selten which appears in Chapter 4. Finally I want to acknowledge and thank Zachary Zhu. Zachary emailed me "out of the blue" when he was a junior in high school in San Diego; he is about to graduate high school. Zachary asked if he could be an R.A. on a behavioral economics project. He was a very good research assistant, helping to find materials I needed, and writing some of the citations which became part of the references. I really appreciated his assistance. If he chooses, one day Zachary will be getting emails from high school students wanting to be his R.A.

Introduction

1

The Boston Celtics of the National Basketball Association won NBA titles in 1959–66, 8 years in a row. They also won the title in 1968 and 1969. They were led by their 6′9″ Center, Bill Russell, a man considered the greatest defensive player in his or any time. But he hardly ever shot the ball more than 10 or 12 ft from the basket; he wasn't a good shooter. And, he wasn't very good at "free throws" 15 ft from the basket. Most tall players of his day weren't good at either of those skills. The Celtics' starting line-up was Russell, 6′9″, K.C. Jones, point guard, 6′1″, Sam Jones, shooting guard, 6′4″, Tom Sanders, power forward, 6′6″, and Tom Heinsohn, shooting forward, 6′6″. Average height 6′5″. Consider the current Golden State Warriors. They have won NBA championship is 2015, 2017 and 2018. Their starting line-up averages almost 6′7 1/2″. Their 6′11″ center, and their 6′9″ shooting forward both shoot well from 25′ to 30′ from the basket. With the possible exception of their power forward, the other four starters all shoot "lights out" from 25 to 30 ft. They are good "free throw" shooters.

Current NBA players are taller, in better physical condition, they jump higher, they run faster, and they "fly through the air with the greatest of ease," spin around 360 degrees while in the air and jam the ball into the basket. There are 6′10″ point guards in today's NBA. Watch some NBA games from the late 1950s and the 1960s and if think that you are watching a high school basketball game then it would be understandable. The game is that different in 2019 from "back-in-the-day." But regardless of how different it looks, the Celtics then, and the Golden State Warriors today are playing the same game: basketball. The Celtics were the best in their day: 10 championships in 11 years. Today, they probably would not make the playoffs.

Even when things look different, there are similarities among them. Basketball is basketball. And, behavioral economics is behavioral economics. The 1950s and 1960s version, "old" behavioral economics, may look different from the 1974–2019 version, "new" behavioral economics, just as the 1965 Celtics look different from the 2019 Golden State Warriors. But along with the rather obvious differences there are similarities. This book is about some of the obvious differences and some of the important similarities. Maybe more than this, this book will try to get more well-deserved recognition for those who came before the truly momentous years in the history of (behavioral) economics: 1974 and 1979.

I What this book is about and what it is not about

This book is about the pre-Kahneman and Tversky behavioral economists, and the relationship between their behavioral economics and that of the behavioral economics beginning with Kahneman and Tversky. These two groups are the "old" and "new" behavioral economics, respectively. Or, if you prefer, the first generation behavioral

The Beginnings of Behavioral Economics. https://doi.org/10.1016/B978-0-12-815289-8.00001-0

economics and the generations which came after. The "old" group includes Herbert Simon, George Katona, Harvey Leibenstein, who I refer to as the "big 3" of the "old" group. It also includes Boulding, March, Cyert, Scitovsky, Shackle, Nelson, Winter, Duesenberry, Rheinhard Selten, and an early 20th century French Judge and sociologist Gabriel Tarde. Tarde is a forerunner of behavioral economics because he wrote about behavioral economics in the early years of the 20th century. The others are first gen behavioral economics because they started writing about it in the 1940s.

Paul Samuelson in 1949 wrote about the "sophisticated-anthropomorphic sin." This "sin" is not realizing that the content of those who came before is equivalent to those who came later because the earlier group does not use the same terminology or symbols as the later group. Equivalent is too strong a word in this case. But what I will try to show in this book is that the ideas and topics written about by the "old" group was also in the writings of the new behavioral economists, in substance if not in style.

One of the most important aspects, if not the most important aspect of their common interest/substance was to show that homo economicus was, to use a term used by Richard Thaler, a unicorn. So long as homo economicus, the unicorn, was the model human, behavioral economics would not exist. Homo economicus is a fully rational maximizer. His behavior is based on certain rules, similar with the way gravity "behaves" according to certain rules. He can't act in any other way because he does not have free will. Homo economicus is, therefore, a robot, a machine which acts according to the "software" programs placed in its "hardware." Kahneman, Tversky, and Thaler wrote about the gap between full rationality and human rationality, but Katona, Simon, and Leibenstein wrote about this gap as much as 30 years before Kahneman, Tversky, and Thaler. The other first gens also wrote about this gap.

Below is a quote from each of Katona, Simon, and Leibenstein. The quotes indicate their research agenda. The quotes do not sound similar with the "new" behavioral economists. They do sound more the way economists wrote in the 1950s and 1960s.

> *Unlike pure theorists, we shall not assume at the outset that rational behavior exists or that rational behavior constitutes the topic of economic analysis. We shall study economic behavior as we find it*
>
> *Katona (1951, p. 16).*

> *...replace the global rationality of economic man with a kind of rational behavior that is compatible with the access of information and the computational capacities that are actually possessed by organisms, including man, in the kinds of environments in which such organisms exist*
>
> *Simon (1955, p. 99).*

> *At the core of economics is the concept of efficiency. Microeconomic theory is concerned with allocative efficiency. Empirical evidence... suggests that... allocative efficiency is trivial...microeconomic theory focuses on allocative efficiency to the exclusion of other types of efficiencies that, in fact, are much more significant in many instances*
>
> *Leibenstein (1966, p. 392).*

The "old" group developed larger themes, they did not do experiments. The larger themes included the nature of human rationality and non-allocative efficiency. The new behavioral economists do experiments about the nature of human rationality, to name but one theme. Both the old and the new behavioral economists reject the characterization of human rationality being that of homo economicus. The styles of the "old" and the "new" differ from each other, but the substance, I assert, is very similar with respect to perhaps the most important topic in behavioral economics: the nature of human rationality.

This book is not a platform for whining. Whining is making a sad, often nasally sound, expressing discontent, disappointment or unhappiness. There will be no whining in this book. What would I whine about? First, an opinion piece published in the New York Times on February 11, 2001. The authors is Louis Uchitelle, the title, "Some Economists Call Behavior a Key." The sentence which sent many behavioral economists of my age group, 55 in 2001, into a total tizzy was, "In the histories of economics still to be written, the spring of 1994 will almost certainly be flagged as momentous. That is when... David Laibson... received his Ph.D. in economics" (Uchitelle, 2001). The tizzy followed a sense of being diminished, rejected, and ignored. Some number of these behavioral economists of my age never accepted the changing nature of behavioral economics, from the approach of Katona, Simon, and Leibenstein, and others, to that of Kahneman, Tversky, Thaler, and others who came after them. The complaint was that behavioral economics seemed to have begun with a set of big ideas which ran contrary to neoclassical economics. It then shifted into a newer version of neoclassical economics which "captured" every aspect of human nature and behavior which seemed contrary to neoclassical economics. Many members of the "old guard," those around age 55 in 2001, were furious, saying, "You can't turn neoclassical economics into behavioral economics by adding a parameter to your model."

With hindsight, it was naïve to think that as behavioral economics became more intriguing to economists that it would not be incorporated as much as possible into neoclassical economics. At the same time, the "old" groups, the first gen behavioral economics—Simon, Katona, Leibenstein, Boulding, March, Cyert, Scitovsky, Shackle, Nelson, Winter, Duesenberry, Rheinhard Selten, Gabriel Tarde, and others—have to various degrees been discounted, under-appreciated, forgotten by the "new" behavioral economists. I am not going to whine about this. I am only going to try to explain why the "old" group laid some of the ground-work for the "new" group. And hence why they deserve a better treatment than they have received. Kahneman and Tversky, and Thaler all deserved the Nobel Prize, so did Herbert Simon and Reinhard Selten.

II Two beginnings, one door

Behavioral economics had two beginnings. The famous beginning, the truly revolutionary beginning, was in the years 1974 and 1979. The first year, 1974, was when Tversky and Kahneman published their article in *Science*, "Judgment Under Uncertainty: Heuristics and Biases." The second year, 1979, was when Kahneman and Tversky published their article in Econometrica, "Prospect Theory: An Analysis of Decisions Under Risk." Shortly after was the beginning of a long "train" of important publications by Richard Thaler. The other beginning started in the 1940s with several publications by George Katona and Herbert Simon, followed in 1950 and then 1966 by Harvey Leibenstein. There was also Shackle beginning in the early 1940s, Duesenberry in 1949, March and Simon in 1958, Selten in the mid-1960s, and others. There can be two beginnings in behavioral economics because the first one, the one beginning in the 1940s, was been discounted. Some believe that there was only one beginning, but it is a major contention of this book that there were two.

As a way of thinking about the beginnings and the "old" and the "new" behavioral economics, I divide behavioral economists into three groups. The first gens consist of those who began writings before 1974 and include Katona, Simon, Leibenstein, and the other names already mentioned. The second group, includes Kahneman, Tversky, Thaler, and Akerlof. The third group, also part of the "new" behavioral economists consists of those who began publishing beginning around 1985 or later. This group is also a very illustrious group, including George Lowenstein, Andrei Shleifer, Colin Camerer, David Laibson, Mathew Rabin, Sendhil Mullainathan, and Raj Chetty. To illustrate what each group did in the history of behavioral economics, I use the metaphor of a door. The first gens built a door and on the front placed a sign, "Behavioral Economics. Enter Here." The second group opened the door. The third group walked into the room. The first and second group had two and three Nobel Prize winners, respectively. Many would not be surprised if this third group has at least three winners. The topic of the two beginnings, and the door are part of Chapter 2.

Chapter 3 is about the "Big 3"—Simon, Katona, and Leibenstein. Simon, the polymath, Nobel Laureate, received his PhD in political science from the University of Chicago at age 27. Katona received his PhD in psychology at the University of Gottingen at age 20. He then studied with the founders of Gestalt psychology before moving to the United States, eventually to Ann Arbor, Michigan where he spent the remainder of his professional life at the University of Michigan. In 1951 his book, *Psychological Analysis of Economic Behavior*, was published. It was an early major statement about economics and psychology, a.k.a., behavioral economics. Rabin (2002) said that Katona's emphasis on empirical research/observations is the appropriate foundation for economic science, and the approach which has persisted for most behavioral economists who followed Katona.

Leibenstein not only discussed a non-allocative form of efficiency, but also wrote about (other) limitations to neoclassical theory, e.g., marginal productivity theory, independence in consumer decision making, full human rationality. He received his PhD in economics in 1951 from Princeton. He went on to teach at Berkeley before moving to Harvard where he spent the remainder of his life, dying prematurely in 1994 from the results of an auto accident. The three of them wrote about subjects that the other two did not. However, they all rejected homo economicus. Simon called it bounded rationality, Leibenstein called it selective rationality, and Katona called it habitual, routinized, impulsive or nonunderstandable behavior. Leibenstein and Katona agreed that a lack of pressure reduces rational decision making.

Chapter 4 is about the other first gen behavioral economists, including Boulding, March, Cyert, Scitovsky, Shackle, Nelson, Winter, Duesenberry, Rheinhard Selten, and Gabriel Tarde. I refer to these first gen economists as the "it didn't happen overnight gang." This refers to the fact that the behavioral revolution didn't just suddenly appear in 1974. The modern version began around 1940, almost 35 years before Kahneman and Tversky's article in *Science*. These first gen behavioral economists wrote about framing, imitation or herding behavior, multiple selves, the firm as black box, social norms, interdependence among consumer behaviors, satisficing, asymmetric information, non-allocative efficiency, arousal and performance, and illusions about money, effort, and time. What they agreed about is a rejection of homo-economicus. The Appendix to Chapter 4 discusses the limits to human rationality, doubts about homo-economicus, written about both the "old" and the "new" behavioral economists.

III Leibenstein's writings, 1950–66

Chapters 5 and 6 are about Leibenstein's writings. Chapter 5 is about his writings from 1950 to 1960. Chapter 6 is about X-efficiency theory, the original article which was published in 1966. The pre-1966 writings I will focus on are "Bandwagon, Snob, and Veblen Effects in the Theory of Consumer Demand" (1950); *A Theory of Economic Demographic Development* (1954); *Economic Backwardness and Economic Growth* (1957); *Economic Theory and Organizational Analysis* (1960).

Bandwagon, Snob, and Veblen Effects in the Theory of Consumer Demand (1950)

His 1950 paper is about the implications of consumer interdependence on the demand curve. One implication is that the elasticity of demand changes, in one case—bandwagon effect—becoming more elasticity, and in the other—snob effect—becoming less elastic. In the case of the Veblen effect, the demand curve can slope upward to the right. Another implication is that price changes can affect quantity demanded and demand. A large role in determining the demand curve is not objective data, but subjective beliefs about data and subjective reactions to subjective beliefs. Leibenstein's methodology for estimating demand curves with interdependence was an experiment, not an experiment of the kind done by "new" behavioral economists, but a gedankenexperiment, a thought experiment. Einstein used a gedankenexperiment in developing the theory of relativity. Jonas Salk used it in discovering the cure for polio.

A Theory of Economic Demographic Development (1954)

In his 1954 book, *A Theory of Economic Demographic Development*, Leibenstein says that maximizing behavior can not adequately explain changes in either fertility or family size. Optimum population theory is also inadequate because the idea of an optimum can satisfy "idle curiosity but can hardly be of any real use" (Leibenstein, 1954, p. 182).

Economic Backwardness and Economic Growth (1957), and; Investment Criteria, Productivity, and Economic Development (1955)

According to George Akerlof and Janet Yellen, Harvey Leibenstein wrote the original article on efficiency wage models and development economics (Akerlof & Yellen, 1986, p. 2). The article appeared in Akerlof & Yellen's (1986) book, *Efficiency Wage Models of the Labor Market*. The article, "The Theory of Underemployment in Densely Populated Backward Area," is a chapter in Leibenstein's (1957) book. In this article/chapter Leibenstein shows the relationships between wages, nutrition, and health problems, and; between labor productivity and real wages. Akerlof and Yellen assert that research has also shown the relevance of Leibenstein's theory for more developed economies.

In his 1957 book, Leibenstein says that rational behavior is not relevant to all fertility decisions but only to decisions about the *n*th child. In his 1955 article with Walter Galenson, Leibenstein challenges the use of the (social) marginal productivity principle for allocating investment and for increasing economic growth and development. Economic theory says that the efficient use of investment funds is achieved when the social marginal product in each alternative use is the same. This will maximize the value of the national product. The principle implies that a less developed economies should use technologies and choose industries which require a lower capital/labor ratio than that used in more developed economies. Leibenstein (and Galenson) argue that the best path uses the best technology on as large a scale of operation possible, and a high capital/labor ratio.

Economic Theory and Organizational Analysis (1960)

Leibenstein's last book before the publication of his X-efficiency article was *Economic Theory and Organizational Analysis (ETOA)*. Reading ETOA is both confusing and enlightening at the same time. The confusion comes from the fact that the book is more organizational theory than economic theory, and so the topics seemed somewhat "foreign" to me. The writing seemed to be "all over the place," and amorphous. Then there is the enlightening part, the part which came to me in a kind-of "ah ah" experience, that ETOA was a precursor of XE theory. This 1960 book, 6 years before his seminal article on XE theory, is actually a discussion of X-efficiency theory before there was X-efficiency theory. I do not believe that Harvey was consciously writing a precursor to X-efficiency theory. The book was part of the evolution of his writing. Since his dissertation in 1951 Harvey was challenging the orthodoxy. It all led to 1966. What appears again and again in the 1960 book are discussions about effort discretion, imperfect knowledge, non-marketed inputs, and multiple equilibria and inert areas, all of which are foundational concepts for X-efficiency theory. In ETOA these concepts are presented within a theory of how to make a firm more efficient, i.e., organizational theory. In X-efficiency theory the concepts are used to explain a non-allocative form of efficiency, how it affects the firm's performance relative to their frontiers, i.e., economic theory. There is one other aspect of ETOA, one based on working closely with Harvey over many years. Still it is a conjecture on my part; ETOA was Harvey's attempt to follow Herbert Simon into the world of organizational analysis.

Chapter 6 is about X-efficiency theory. Harvey told me this story about his "aha" moment which led to X-efficiency theory. At the Univ. of California, Berkeley, one of his graduate assistants worked with varying degrees of effort. One day this graduate student would work with great effort, and the next day he would, as if, sleep walk through the day. After observing this for some time Leibenstein had his aha moment. He wondered whether this pattern of behavior was the pattern expressed by many people other than his graduate assistant. Thus began X-efficiency theory. That was "observation # 1." "Observation # 2" was that firms are not always the highly organized and closely and excellently managed firms of orthodox economic theory, firms which efficiently transform inputs into maximum outputs. Or, if you prefer, produced the output rate with the minimum number of inputs. Leibenstein's observations were in part from nations in lesser developed countries about which he did much research. What characterized firms? Employees have a certain freedom of how much effort to expend. Second, labor contracts are incomplete, meaning that not every action which employees are to do can be written done in complete detail. Third, the firms production and costs functions are not complete. There isn't a fixed relationship between inputs and outputs, and between outputs and costs. The output and cost functions are bands rather than thin lines. Fourth, rationality is selective, sometimes it may be 100%, at other times it may be at 50%. Fifth, we have a dual self. Our superego thrives to do as well as possible. Our id thrives not to thrive. On average, each individual is influenced by both functions in a way that leads to a compromise between the two. That is, each of us forges a compromise between the way we feel we must behave and the way we would like to behave were it not for a sense of obligation to duty or to a set of standards. In other words, each individual strikes a compromise that provides them with a sense of (psychological) "comfort." The compromise helps determine the degree of rationality used when making decisions. Leibenstein put more emphasis on procedural rationality than substantive rationality. He discussed the components, including avoiding procrastination, and herding behavior. Between inputs and output is the degree of X-efficiency. X-efficiency is an intervening variable between inputs and output. X-efficiency closes the gap between input and outputs. This idea of a gap is something Leibenstein wrote about in his theory of entrepreneurship (Leibenstein, 1968).

IV Empirical studies on X-efficiency

Chapters 7–12 discuss approximately 200 empirical studies in X-efficiency. Chapter 7 looks at the studies published between 1967 and circa 1990. Some of the earliest studies gathered data from interviews and questionnaires. The topics of these studies on the causes of X-efficiency varied: ownership forms, protection from international trade, market power, government regulations, and the role of management. Some of the industries studied are, manufacturing, airlines, railroads, restaurants, health care, agriculture, cement, textiles, sugar, water utilities, gas, electricity, education, steel, plastics, communication equipment, and cocoa. The nations included Spain, United States, Tanzania, Australia, Canada, Sweden, France, W. Germany, Latin America, Thailand, India, Taiwan, England, India, Korea, Malaysia, and Brazil.

Chapters 8–12 cover studies published from c. 1991–2014. These five chapters cover the following: US financial sector; Asian financial sector; Asian non-financial sector; Europe, and; Australia, New Zealand, Middle East, Africa, and Latin America. These studies used both parametric and non-parametric measuring techniques. Most of these studies used either stochastic frontier analysis (parametric), and data envelope analysis (non-parametric). Whereas before 1991 very few studies were on the financial sector, beginning in 1991 a large number of the studies were on the financial sector of firms world-wide. Not all of the studies estimated X-efficiency. Those that did, report that on average, a firm is about 20% off their frontier. That makes X-efficiency an important concept.

Two beginnings

2

I The door

"Man is a rational animal — so at least I have been told."
(Russell, 2009, p. 45; The Basic Writings of Bertrand Russell (Routledge Classics. Routledge: New York.))

One of the 10 tweets I sent in 2017 was to Richard Thaler. It was the day before he was named winner of the Nobel Prize in Economics. I told him that I hoped that we would be named the 2017 winner of the Nobel Prize in Economics. Has anyone done more since the late 1970s or 1980s to advance behavioral economics? A good case can be made that no one else has done more. However, if he is not the number one reason for the advancement of behavioral economics he is certainly very close to being # 1. Even more than Kahneman's Nobel Prize, Thaler's Nobel Prize represents, in my opinion, the greater recognition of a larger, deeper, and wider view of economics.

In an interview with National Public Radio (October 23, 2017) Richard Thaler said that for 50 or 60 years—beginning between 1957 and 1967—economists have been studying a fictional creature, what he calls ECONS, a perfectly rational individual who doesn't succumb to cognitive errors. But, as other-worldly, non-HUMAN, as ECONS may be, economists have been studying ECONS using "very fancy models." In some economic circles that has been known to be enough to treat them as this-worldly, HUMAN. Economists might as well, said Thaler, study unicorns. Thaler's statement about studying unicorns, i.e., ECONS, is particularly revealing about the beginnings of behavioral economics. The x-istence[a] of ECONS eliminates the need for behavioral economics. ECONS don't make mistakes, they are completely rational, they are not limited by cognitive limits or errors. Complete rationality, no cognitive limits or errors, and no errors in decision making makes behavioral economics irrelevant or impossible, or meaningless, or all three. Hence, disparaging ECONS showed one way to behavioral economics. It was a point of view that Thaler could have learned from Katona, or Leibenstein, or Simon.

Behavioral economics has combined economics with psychology (sociology, neuroscience) in order to better understand the behavior of HUMANS. But ECONS aren't real humans; as Thaler said, why not study unicorns. ECONS or unicorns, either makes behavioral economics irrelevant or unnecessary.

One of the purposes of psychology is to change or improve behavior. Why would anyone need to change or improve the behavior of ECON(S)? They wouldn't. You want to change or improve the behavior of a being who doesn't make mistakes in judgment? Getting an ECON, or economic-man "on the couch" would be hilariously

[a] The spelling of existence as x-istence comes from George Stigler's famous 1976 retort about X-Efficiency theory. Throughout this book I will spell the word as x-istence.

The Beginnings of Behavioral Economics. https://doi.org/10.1016/B978-0-12-815289-8.00002-2

boring. On or off the couch, ECONS are boring because they always do the right thing. Their behavior is predictable. HUMANS are not boring; our behavior is not always predictable. Thaler didn't spend time studying unicorns. And neither did George Katona, Harvey Leibenstein, Herbert Simon, and others, who began replacing ECONS with HUMANS while working on their green blackboards with white chalk in the 1940s.[b] There are others, and they will appear in this book along with the others mentioned in this paragraph. Leibenstein, Simon, and Katona are three of a larger group who began writing about real human beings before Kahneman or Tversky. Hence they are "old" or "first generation" behavioral economists. If Thaler is the "father" of behavioral economics, then these others who were writing about 30 years before Thaler are the "grandfathers."[c] But others refer to them simply as economists who discussed the importance of psychological variables. Were they behavioral economists? The answer is most often, No. That answer is most often, incorrect.

Two beginnings

Behavioral economics is believed to have begun in the 1970s with Kahneman and Tversky. It is a major contention and purpose of this book to argue that behavioral economics has two beginnings, one in the 1940s and the other in the mid 1970s. Kahneman and Tversky represents a major advancement of behavioral economics, but they were not the beginning. I have no problem thinking of Kahneman and Tversky, and Thaler as *a* beginning of behavioral economics, but not *the* beginning. My contention is that the two beginnings are Beginning 1 and 1a. How can their be two beginnings? In the case of the history of behavioral economics there are two beginnings because for the most part the Beginners of Beginning 1a have not recognized the Beginners of Beginning 1. So from the point of view of the Beginners of Beginning 1a, the beginning started in the 1970s.

Beginning 1 began in the 1940s with the writings of Katona (or the 1930s with Hayek). Beginning 1a began in 1974 with Kahneman and Tversky. In 1940 Katona published a book about learning, *Organizing and Memorizing: Studies in the Psychology of Learning and Teaching*. Learning would become important in behavioral economics. Other pre-1950s publications by Katona are "The Role of Frame of Reference in War and Post-War Economy" (1944), and in 1947 he published "Contribution of Psychological Data to Economic Analysis." In 1953 he published, "Rational Behavior and Economic Behavior." His major work on behavioral economics in the 1950s was *Psychological Analysis of Economic Behavior* (1951). His other major work was in 1975, *Psychological Economics*. Harvey Leibenstein's major publication on behavioral economics was, "Allocative Efficiency and X-Efficiency" (1966). Herbert Simon's were in 1954, on "Bandwagon and Underdog Effects and the

[b] Friedrich Hayek began writing about ECONS and real humans in the 1930s without using those names. Hayek will be discussed in later chapters.

[c] Thaler was declared to be the "Father of Behavioral Economic" in the funny, and informative movie, The Big Short. Soon after being so declared Thaler is seen driving through the Las vegas Strip with Selena Gomez. A Nobel Prize and a date with Selena Gomez!

Possibility of Election Predictions"; 1955, "A Behavioral Model of Rational Choice"; 1956, "Rational Choice and the Structure of the Environment"; 1957, *Models of Man*, and; 1959, "Theories of Decision-making in Economics and Behavioral Science." Ken Boulding, not a member of the "Big 3" but a first generation behavioral economist nonetheless, published *There is a Spirit*, in 1945; *A Reconstruction of Economics* in 1950; and *The Image* in 1956. Boulding's concept of an image is a precursor of Kahneman and Tversky's concepts of framing and mental accounting.

In "Contemporary Economic Research," an article by Kenneth Boulding which appeared in a 1961 book, Trends in Social Science, edited by Donald Ray, Boulding says that economics can take one of two paths in the future. One is the traditional view, the view that economics is about traditional time series economic variables, prices, outputs, and inputs. The point of time series is to discover their "laws of motion." The other path is "moved by and concerned with men... which might be called 'behavioral economics'" (Boulding, 1961, p. 21). Behavioral economics does not attempt to refine traditional economic analysis as much as it introduces a new set of variables related to the human organism. These new variables include "men's images, or cognitive and affective structures" (Boulding, 1961) most related to economic decision making.

A second group includes "new" behavioral economists. The "new" behavioral economics was composed of a very impressive group, including Tversky, Kahneman, Akerlof, and last but not least Richard Thaler. Kahneman and Tversky's important papers which revolutionized economics were in 1974 and 1979. And Richard Thaler began publishing in the mid 1970s. In 1975 his publication with Sherwin Rosen, his PhD dissertation advisor, was "The Value of Saving A Life: Evidence From The Labor Market." in 1980, "Toward a Positive Theory of Consumer Choice"; "Judgment and Decision Making Under Uncertainty: What Economists Can Learn from Psychology," and; "Interpreting Alpha Rationality in Hierarchical Games" (with H.M. Shefrin). And, In 1981, "Maximization and Self-Control," and; "An Economic Theory of Self-Control" (with H.M. Shefrin). The Nobel Prize was won by Akerlof, in 2001; Kahneman, in 2002, and; Thaler, in 2017. Simon won the Nobel Prize in 1978.

A third group consists of new behavioral economists who began publishing around 1985. In this group I include George Lowenstein, Andrei Shleifer, Colin Camerer, David Laibson, Mathew Rabin, Sendhil Mullainathan, and; Raj Chetty. Some believe that this latter group contains two or three future Nobel Laureates. Three have won the John Bates Clark metal for the most promising economist under the age of 40, the award won by Shleifer (1999), Rabin (2001), and Chetty (2013). Ken Boulding won in 1949. Two have won the "genius award," The MacArthur Fellowship—Rabin, in 2000, and; Mullainathan, in 2003.

The "new" group, the second and third group, criticized neoclassical theory but wanted to fix it, not reject and replace it. And they used mathematical models, adding a few new assumptions and/or variables of Neoclassical Models 1.0, thereby creating Neoclassical Models 2.0, a.k.a. behavioral economics. Mullainathan and Thaler (2000) added that Neoclassical Models 1.0 differed from Neoclassical 2.0 in that the latter recognizes that humans have limited cognitive abilities, limited willpower, and their self-interest was bounded. In Advances in Behavioral Economics, the editors,

Camerer, Loewenstein, and Rabin (2004) say that increasing the realism of the assumptions of neoclassical models improves economics on its own term, rather than by replacing it. Neoclassical 2.0 is useful because it gives economists a framework from which they can analyze all types of human economic behavior. And it makes falsifiable predictions. But even the new behavioral economics was out of the mainstream, at first. Why would young faculty members engage in out-of-the-mainstream research, i.e., engage in a risky career move? Whatever the threat was, it has long since disappeared as behavioral economics has become the mainstream, and the research agenda has become advantageous to the researcher.

The new group may not have wanted to replace neoclassical theory, but some behavioral economists "back in the day" wanted to completely replace it. The most anti-neoclassical group among the people researching behavioral economics beginning in the 1970s was led by Benjamin, Benny, Gilad, the first President of SABE. Benny rejected positivism and deductive reasoning, and considered neoclassical theory as simplistic, and anti-science.

At the opening of the first behavioral economics conference which was held at Princeton in the fall of 1982, Benjamin Gilad, said that the goal of SABE and behavioral economics in general was to totally and unequivocally destroy neoclassical theory, brick by brick, mind by mind. It was a declaration of "war." I was sitting in the balcony with Harvey Leibenstein and Benny's voice seemed to never fall below 75 dB. Harvey said that he was having flashbacks to being at Berkeley in the early 1960s. Most of the first generation behavioral economists found Benny to be too radical for their tastes. Times have changed. Benjamin, or Benny as he was known, has left academia and the goal of SABE is economics which yields both heat and light about human economic and non-economic behavior.

The door

My image of the history of behavioral economics is that of a door. The first group, the first gen people, built a door and on it placed a sign, "Behavioral Economics, Enter Here." The second group opened the door. The third group walked into the room just at the other side of the door, sat down and continued their research on their ipads and (desk-top and lap-top) computers. The second group followed the third group into the room. The first group couldn't enter the room because they didn't know the secret handshake.

Group 2 "giants" of behavioral economists "stood on the shoulders" of Group 1 giants, even if they didn't know it. And Group 3 giants stood on the shoulders of Group 2 giants. Group 1 giants stood on the shoulders of some really old giants.

Nothing in the paragraph(s) above, and nothing in the paragraphs below or chapters to follow are to be interpreted to mean that I deem Richard Thaler's contributions to (behavioral) economics to be anything other than of the highest order. Add Daniel Kahneman, and Amos Tversky to the previous sentence. Add the names of the new behavioral economists in the third group as well. The point of this book is not to "put down" anyone. It is to point out the contribution to behavioral economics of the first generation behavioral economists.

The (sophisticated) anthropomorphic sin

The first gens began writing about ECONS and HUMANS, not necessarily using those words, for as much as 35 years before Kahneman and Tversky published their revolutionary articles in *Science*, and then *Econometrica*. Why have they not received more recognition? Below is one possible answer.

One reason for this has been, I believe, what Paul Samuelson calls the anthropomorphic sin of reading modern analysis into older writers' works (Samuelson, 1949, p. 373). When the post-Kahneman and Tversky behavioral economists read the *pre*-Kahneman and Tversky economists they didn't read much of modern or new behavioral economics in their writings. The "sophisticated-anthropomorphic sin" is that some individuals do not realize that the content of those who came before is equivalent to those who came later because the earlier group does not use the same terminology or symbols as the later group. Equivalent is too strong a word in this case. But what I will try to show in this book is that what the "old" group wrote about appeared in the writings of the new behavioral economists. One of the most important things the "old" group did was to show that homo economicus was a unicorn. Without that, behavioral economics would never exist. Thaler wrote about unicorns, but Katona and Simon wrote about the implausibility of homo economicus about 30 years or more before Thaler. Leibenstein came late to that party, writing about it maybe 15 years before Thaler.

This "sophisticated-anthropomorphic sin" spreads, not so much by a conscious process from person to person, but by a unconscious "herding" process. In his *Principles of Economics*, Marshall said it very well. Discussing the concentration of firms in a particular locality/neighborhood, Marshall said that when people in the same profession work closely with one another that the skills required are "as it were in the air." People learn skills as if unconsciously (Marshall, 1890, p. Book 4, Chap. 10, paragraph 7). In *Economic Backwardness and Economic Growth* Leibenstein says that some of our professional training comes almost "imperceptibly" from the environment in which we work. It happens when we "talk shop." The result is that we can't pinpoint the source(s) of our "intellectual indebtedness." We borrow from others, at times not even realizing it (Leibenstein, 1957, p. viii). Even before the Internet, our "neighborhood" covered many parts of the world through journals, books, conferences, visiting positions and the like. With the Internet the neighborhood is virtually the entire world and virtually instantaneously via all of the above and email, on-line journals and journals available on-line, Skype, Twitter, and many other ways we communicate via social media.

1994. A momentous year in the history of behavioral economics?

On February 12, 2001 I received a large number of emails. It was the day after the New York Times published the article which made the people I knew feel unappreciated. They were so angry. The title of the article was "Some Economists Call Behavior a Key" (February 11, 2001). The author, Louis Uchitelle, says that "In the histories of economics still to be written, the spring of 1994 will almost certainly be flagged as momentous. That is when... David Laibson... received his Ph.D. in economics." Now, Laibson is a very good economist, and many economists, including myself, would not be surprised if he receives the Nobel Prize one day. But, my friends and colleagues screamed through their emails: "flagged as momentous"?

I have listed below a few years which occurred before, and in one case in 1994, and which I believe are about as momentous, if not more momentous. They are, 1972, Founding of the Journal of Behavioral Economics (at Western Illinois University, Richard Hattwick, editor); 1974, Frederick Hayek wins Nobel Prize, and, Tversky and Kahneman's article in Science; 1978, Herbert Simon wins Nobel Prize; 1979, Kahneman and Tversky's article in Econometrica; 1980, Founding of Journal of Economic Behavior and Organization; 1981, Founding of Journal of Economics and Psychology; 1982. Founding of Society for the Advancement of Behavioral Economics (SABE); 1987. Founding of Journal of Economic Perspectives, and, vol. 1, # 1 of Anomalies; 1992, Gary Becker wins Nobel Prize; 1994, Reinhard Selten wins Nobel Prize.

Frederick Hayek's behavioral economics

For the history of behavioral economics it is unfortunate that Hayek's contribution are overlooked. This is in part because of his association with Austrian economics, a group which everyone "knows" have nothing to do with behavioral economics. But what everyone knows may be distorted by cognitive errors, following others' misperceptions in order to get along with others, our own misunderstandings, personal experience, or social norms.

Hayek's behavioral economics include his theories of rationality, and his belief that economics cannot and should not try to mimic physics. Hayek believed that human rationality was limited because humans have cognitive limits. Herbert Simon said that Hayek was vital in the development of the concept of bounded rationality. Hayek's theory of limited rationality led him to write that no one person or group can design society to their liking. Hence, Hayek's well-known statement that the economy, among other institutions, is "the result of human action but not the result of human design" (Hayek, 1945).

One of Hayek's definitions of rationality stems from his distinction between individualism true and individualism false. Individualism false is the rationalist philosophy of Descartes. Descartes explains it when he says that, "a single human mind can comprehend as much as a much larger group and use their knowledge to organize society" (Hayek, 1945, p. 9). Rationality is the ability to organize society with your level of knowledge. According to Descartes, humans have no cognitive limits. Hayek calls this philosophy the "fatal conceit" (Hayek, 1988).

Individualism true is the philosophy of Mandeville, Smith, Hume, Edmund Burke, and others. In this philosophy humans are neither highly rational nor highly intelligent, but is very irrational and fallible. Perhaps foretelling the behavioral economics of Kahneman and Tversky, Hayek says that "It may indeed prove to be far the most difficult and not the least important task for human reason rationally to comprehend its own limitations" (Hayek, 1979, p. 162).

A second aspect of hayek's behavioral economics is his belief that we should not try to mimic physics. The economy is a complex phenomena, and the number of causes of economic activity, and the number of variables necessary to comprehend the patterns of economic activity are "often insurmountable" (Hayek, 1979, p. 27). As compared with the complexity facing economists, physicists deal with simple phenomena. Prediction is physics is thus relatively doable, whereas in economics "the ideal of prediction and control must largely remain beyond our reach" (Hayek,

1979, p. 34). The conscious mind is thus not sufficient for adequately analyzing economic activity. Our use of our unconscious mind, what Hayek called our "supra-conscious," is, therefore, necessary. Other terms Hayek's used for the unconscious are intuition, know-how, tacit knowledge, and physiognomy perception.

Vernon Smith said of Hayek that "In our time it was Hayek who articulated forcefully the idea that there are two kinds of rationality" (Smith, 2008, p. 25). Constructionist rationality—Simon's concept of objective or substantive rationality. Ecological rationality, a.k.a., a "rational social order"—Simon's concept of subjective or procedural rationality—emerges from evolution, rules which people follow without knowing how to enunciate them. It is the order created by individualism true.

Hayek and Other First Gen Behavioral Economists. I am going to simply list similarities in the topics written about by Hayek and some of the other first gen behavioral economists. For the most part, Hayek's writing preceded he writings of the other behavioral economists. Simon: bounded rationality, cognitive limits to rationality; time and complexity reduces rationality; foresight, or "mind reading" necessary for equilibrium; natural sciences deal with fewer variables making predictions easier; necessity of utilizing the unconscious in decision making; explanation and prediction as goals of science. Leibenstein: methodological individualism; knowledge as subjective; explanation and prediction as goals of science; complexity and time reduce the ability to make correct predictions; rationality include the ability to be understood by others; unknown origin of convention and/or rules; existence and importance of tacit knowledge; the X-istence of X-efficiency. Nelson and Winter: humans are not homo economicus; rule or routine based behavior; knowledge includes scientific and tacit knowledge; tacit knowledge is a source of skills or human capital; the source of knowledge and skills are the habits we live by.

Even the best of us have been rejected

Those who thought that psychological factors were important in human behavior and should be part of economic theory and tested empirically, did not always have their ideas welcomed. But that list is far and wide. The list of economists whose submitted papers were rejected is a virtual whose-who in the economics profession. They include Gary Becker, Jagdish Bagwadi, Fisher Black, Myron Scholes, James Buchanan, Gerard Debreu, Roy Harrod, James Tobin, Tibor Scitovsky, Franco Modigliani, Paul Krugman, Milton Friedman, Edward Lazear, and Robert Lucas (Gans & Shepherd, 1994).

The experience of Thaler, Akerlof, and Leibenstein seem particularly relevant here. Richard Thaler was in his own words "only an average economist with rather modest prospects" (Sunstein, 2018, p. 54). Thaler said that "I began to have deviant thoughts about economic theory while I was a graduate student…I was never quite sure whether the problem was in the theory or in my flawed understanding of the subject matter" (Thaler, 2015, p. 12). His dissertation advisor at the University of Rochester, Sherwin Rosen, said that "We didn't expect much of him" (Thaler, 2015, p. 2). Merton Miller did not like the idea of Thaler being on the faculty at Chicago but did not block his appointment because "each generation has got to make its own mistakes" (Thaler, 2015, p. 7). Richard Posner said to Thaler, "You are completely unscientific" (Thaler, 2015). Thaler's first publication, "Toward a Positive Theory of Consumer Choice" was rejected by "six or seven major journals" (Thaler, 2015, p. 51). He finally got it published in a brand new journal, the Journal of Economic Behavior and Organization, a journal that "no one had ever heard of" (Thaler, 2015, p. 54). Daniel Kahneman said of Thaler with whom he co-authored papers early in Thaler's career that "Everybody knew that he was bright, that he was brilliant. But he wasn't doing anything that they considered to be economic research. He wasn't doing anything that was mathematical" (Cassidy, 2017). Lesser mortals may have given up and opened an investment advising firm, possible with the name 1/N. Professor Thaler stuck with it and helped to create the "new" behavioral economics.

Kahneman says of Thaler that "His story is the success story of behavioral economics. Going from the outside to the mainstream. And that was largely due to him" (Cassidy, 2017). In Misbehaving Thaler tells an interesting story about being on the "outside" and an interaction at a conference he had with a "well known economist" who said "If I take what you are saying seriously, what am I supposed to do? My skill is knowing how to solve optimization problems." To which Thaler commented in Misbehaving that the "well known" economist was worried that a change in the economic paradigm would make his "toolkit…obsolete" (Thaler, 2015, p. 43). It may be the darndest thing, bur another "well-known" economist, a colleague of Harvey's at Harvard told Harvey almost the same thing. His colleague said, "Harvey, you want me to learn new things, and I don't want to learn new things." Harvey said that "He was joking, but not entirely."[d]

George Akerlof, considering which colleges to apply said that he "heeded the assistant principal of Lawrenceville[High School] who admonished me that I should not wreck my life by even thinking about going to Harvard…" (Akerlof, 2001b). His 1970 paper, "The Market for 'Lemons' which is mentioned as a basis for his Nobel Prize had been rejected two or three times in the course of the year by editors who felt that the issues in the paper were too trivial to merit publication in a serious academic journal" (Akerlof, 2001a). And Herbert Simon, a polymath, was questioned as a Nobel Prize winner because he wasn't a real economist. He eventually left the Economics department at Carnegie Mellon for the department of Psychology at Carnegie Mellon because of his treatment by many economists.

Harvey Leibenstein was writing about the implications of individuals being less than fully rational. The fact is that most economists in the 1960s when Leibenstein wrote his seminal article on XE theory rejected the idea that individuals are not completely rational. Leibenstein was one of a small minority who did not reject the idea of incomplete or less than perfectly rational behavior. By 2017 a typical response about human rationality is, "Of course individuals are not completely rational. Does anyone believe anything else"? Yet, so many who respond in this way are not familiar with the name Harvey Leibenstein. Leibenstein wasn't a neoclassical "denier." He simply believed that neoclassical theory was not always the best explanation for all things economics. One of Leibenstein's purposes to assume less than complete rationality and investigate the implications for neoclassical theory.

The attitudes at Rochester, Chicago, and Harvard filtered down to San Diego State Univ. where I joined the faculty in 1978 after completing my PhD. One of the senior

[d] Leibenstein told me this in a private conversation.

faculty members introduced me to others saying "This is Roger, he thinks motivation is important in economic behavior." I thought to myself how odd it was that an economist would say such a thing. I just finished my dissertation where I showed that a young man's score on the Rotter Internal-External Locus of Control scale both affected their labor market outcomes and was affected by them. But even this aside, the idea that motivation is irrelevant seemed odd, even in the late 1970s. I had Amartya Sen on my side. In his article "Rational Fools" said that commitment "is central to the problem of work motivation, the importance of which for production performance can hardly be ignored" (Sen, 1977, p. 333).

From the point of view of economic theory, what my elder colleague said wasn't odd at all. Economic theory in those days was very restricted, little more than applied logic. A world inhabited by ECONS, and only ECONS. Output was maximized and costs minimized, in theory and assumed to happen in the real world. Everything fit together so perfectly, and so effortlessly. No HUMANS. No indeterminacy of output or costs. Pure perfection. It is one thing which made micro theory so attractive, and what was so wrong about it.

II Homo economicus

Maybe the most momentous event in the history of behavioral economics was when it was discovered that homo economicus was more Tom Hagen than Sonny Corleone, more Fredo Corleone than Michael Corleone. That discovery was written about many times, before and after 1974. As long as economists believed in Homo Corleone Economicus, the "old" behavioral economists had a big mountain to climb. Homo Corleone Economicus is a foundation, perhaps the foundation of modern economics. To reject it is to reject (orthodox) economics. And most (orthodox) economists found this unacceptable in the 1950s and 1960s. Katona, Leibenstein, and Simon, and other pre-Kahneman and Tversky researchers showed the true identity of homo economicus.

John Stuart Mill is believed to be the first to use the term economic-man. He was not. In his "On the Definition of Political Economy, and on the Method of Investigation Proper to It," Mill implies the x-istence of economic-man without using that term. Political economy, he says, does not analyze the entirety of human nature or the entirety of his behavior. It is concerned solely with the wealth gaining activities of people. It was Mill's critics who used the term economic man. During the late 19th century economic man was a derogatory term used by advocates of the Historical School and who were opposed to Mill's use of abstractions in his theory of political economics. In, A History of Political Economy (1888) John Kells Ingram says that Mill "dealt not with real but with imaginary men—'economic men' ... conceived as simply 'money-making animals'" (Persky, 1995, p. 218). John Neville Keynes in his 1890 book, the Scope and Method of Political Economy (2011) says that Mill's abstractions of human nature and behavior created his "principal subject-matter an 'economic man,'" whose behavior is determined only by a desire for wealth. Economic man is only an approximation of actuality, and cannot "suffice as an adequate basis upon which to construct the whole science of economics" (Keynes, 2011, p. 123).

For Mill's part, he believed that trying to create a single theory of human nature and behavior would be both unnecessary and hopelessly indeterminate. And, people's behavior are affected not only by a desire for wealth at the minimum amount of effort, but by the human institutions which humans work under. Mill's writings about the metayers (British and French sharecroppers) and cottiers (Irish tenant farmers) expressed this relationship between behavior and institutions. Leave it to say that Mill himself, and Thaler himself about 175 years later, did not believe that economic-man was a real human. Fritz Machlup, in his 1963 book, Essays on Economic Semantics, lists the following descriptions of economic-man since that concept was first used: a maxim, an a priori truth, an incontrovertible proposition, a useful invention, an unquestionable datum from experience, and a typical pattern of behavior under capitalism (Blaug, 1992, p. 74).

"Economic man" is completely rational, has complete knowledge of the relevant parts of the environment, and acted out of self-interest in order to maximize his well-being, or utility. And, economic-man had no history of cognitive errors, not because most of the writings of the above economists were in the pre-Internet/Twitter/Google era, and hence there was no email or Twitter trace on every breath they took, every move they made. There was no one telling homo economicus, "I'll be watching you." It was simply that homo economicus did not make cognitive errors. This perfection of decision making stemming from the perfection of human nature was a foundation, if not the foundation, of orthodox, neoclassical, economics.

The pre-eminence of homo-economicus in economics

Consider the names of economists whose works defined so much about economics in the 20th century: Edgeworth, Jevons, Walras, and Pareto. All of them built mathematically based economic models based on economic-man. The rational choice theory of Lionel Robbins was also based on economic-man and had a major impact on orthodox economic theory. And there was also Arrow, Debreu, Becker, Samuelson, Hicks, and Friedman to name but a few of the leading voices in economics whose works were based on economic-man. Milton Friedman's, in his famous article, "The Methodology of Positive Economics" (1953) attempted to protect economic-man and the rationality assumption from critics, and hence to rid psychology from economics by arguing that the testing of a theory is not the realism of assumptions but the theory's ability to correct predict. Hence (assumptions from) psychology is irrelevant in economics. Complete rationality, no errors in decision making makes behavioral economics irrelevant or impossible, or meaningless. We don't need psychology to help us predict human behavior.

For a long time homo economicus was kind of like the Mohammad Ai of economic concepts; undefeated, a knockout artist, taking on all challengers, quickly, one challenger after the other. Katona and Leibenstein wrote about how people are homo economicus if and only if the pressures to be homo economicus are high enough, certainly higher than the perceived benefits of remaining Tom Hagen or Fredo.

Daniel Kahneman doesn't believe in homo economicus. Akerloff and Thaler spoke about deviations from homo-economicus, calling it near and quasi rationality. Did they want to preserve homo-economicus's existence? After all, near and quasi rationality is close to perfect rationality, so, why are we arguing? In 2014 the New England Patrots beat the Seattle Seahawks in the Super Bowl, winning 28–24 when Seatlle had a near touch-down in the final seconds. The Patriots had a real, 100%, interception at the goal line and won the Super Bowl. Near and quasi only counts in a game of horse-shoes.

Dysrationalia

Keith Stanovich, in his 2009 book What Intelligence Tests Miss. The Psychology of Rational Thought, distinguishes intelligence from rational behavior. In the mid-1990s he coined the term "dysrationalia"—meaning the inability of a person possessing adequate intelligence to act rationally. Intelligence is what is measured by IQ tests. Among cognitive scientists there were two types of rationality: instrumental, and epistemic. Instrumental rationality means acting so you get what you want, given your intelligence and non-mental resources. It means the optimization or maximization of one's goals, or utility. Epistemic rationality means that our beliefs are consistent with the available evidence about the reality of the world. People may not be able to solve or care about solving logic problems as presented by Kahneman and Tversky but they do care about both instrumental and epistemic rationality.

Stanovich says that most people have been largely concerned with intelligence, what IQ tests measure, but have largely ignored our capacities for rational thought. Stanovich says that there was "enormous resistance" to taking seriously any abilities other than what is measured by an IQ test. And this was true as late as the late 1980s. Stanovich is a psychologist; if psychologists knew little about rationality vis-à-vis intelligence as late as the 1980s, then what did economists know about rationality? If rationality is always perfect then you need not know anything about rationality. In addition, assuming complete rationality makes economics simpler.

But then why didn't we assume that all humans have a high IQ? For one thing, we had data showing that we all don't have a high IQ. These days, 2019, when I speak with economists, they usually say that "of course" people aren't fully rational, i.e., homo economicus, "we all know that." And they say that "of course" people are affected by social factors when making consumption decisions, that is, we are not Robinson Crusoe. We may all know that now. But in the 1950s and 1960s when Leibensetin (Katona, Simon, and others) were writing, few people knew it or were willing to write about it as if they did know it. Katona, Leibenstein, and Simon knew it and wrote about it.

Leibenstein gave us a measure of rationality, specifically procedural rationality. There are some procedures which people follow which lead to rational decision making. If they don't, then they aren't. Fully rational people are maximizers, and firms which employ maximizers produce on their output and cost frontiers. Do they? As I will show in this book, almost ad nauseam, the answer is no. Leibenstein called it X-inefficiency. Stanovich calls it a "disability," an aptitude-achievement discrepancy. Firms have a frontier, an aptitude, but their achievement falls short of their frontier. Does that mean that the firm is X-disabled?

III Behavioral economics. What is it?

In, "Behavioral Economics: How Psychology Made Its (Limited) Way Back Into Economics," Esther-Mirjam Sent distinguished "old" from "new" behavioral economics, a distinction which will remain as part of the lore of the history of behavioral economics. The "old" guys include Katona, Leibenstein, and Simon, Cyert, March, Nelson, and Winter. To this I would add several others including Gabriel Tarde, Scitovsky, Duesenberry, Shackle, and Minsky. The "old" behavioral economics began when the "old" behavioral economists started publishing on topics which would be recognized later as topics in behavioral economics, such as herding, multiple selves, gift exchange and social norms, bounded rationality, and less than perfectly rational behavior. They wondered about the implications of a departure from perfect rationality on firms and organizations. Many of them wrote from the point of view of industrial organization, and organizational theory. They did not assume that the utility function had a particular shape but sought empirical evidence for it. Some had a distaste, some felt a revulsion for neoclassical economics. Some simply believed that neoclassical economics was a powerful tool but that it did not have the best answer for economic phenomena under all conditions. This was Leibenstein's position among other of the "old guard."

There is considered to have been four groups of "old" behavioral economists located in different Universities: Carnegie Mellon with Simon, Cyert, and March; the University of Michigan with Katona; Oxford with George Shackle, and; the University of Sterling with Peter Earl, and Brian Loasby. A different grouping views behavioral economics more as an "umbrella" term. It includes Simon and the Carnegie school; Katona and the Michigan school; psychological economics; Harvey Leibenstein and X-efficiency theory; George Akerlof and behavioral macroeconomics; Richard Nelson, Sidney Winter, and evolutionary theory; behavioral finance, and; Vernon Smith and experimental economics.

Articles written by Camerer and Lowenstein (2004), Thaler (2016), and Angner and Lowenstein (2012), list the following persons as being part of the historical roots of behavioral economics: Smith, Bentham, Edgeworth, Fisher, Pareto, and Keynes. Katona, Leibenstein, Scitovsky, and Simon, Pigou, J.M. Clark, Jevons, Cairnes, Sen, Veblen, Mitchell, Duesenberry, Easterlin, Boulding, Rabin, Kahneman and Tversky, Thaler, Fischoff, Laibson, and Zeckhauser. The fact remains that despite the contributions by the individuals and groups mentioned above, it was Kahneman, Tversky, and Thaler who truly revolutionized economics.

Behavioral economics is what behavioral economists do

Camerer and Lowenstein (2004) in "Behavioral Economics. Past Present and Future" state that behavioral economics means the inclusion of more realistic psychological foundations in economic theories and models. The result is greater explanatory power of those models. It is important to note that these authors categorically deny that behavioral economics means rejecting neoclassical theory outright. (Katona, Leibenstein, and Simon believed the same.) The reason is that neoclassical theory has a value because it can be applied to any type of human behavior. Rather than rejecting neoclassical theory the authors prefer that one or two assumptions in the models be altered for the sake of greater reality. Or, if you add one or two parameters to the standard models then the neoclassical model and the behavioral model become one and the same.

Camerer and Lowenstein state that behavioral economics is based on Behavioral Decision Research, which in turn classifies research into judgment, and choice. Judgment is about estimating probabilities, and choice studies processes people to choose action among alternatives. What are basic concepts and research findings in behavioral economics? I assert that it is identical with asking what do behavioral economists do? Part of the list they offer as to what behavioral economists do is research on heuristics, hindsight bias, base rate fallacy, law of small numbers, gambler's fallacy, preference reversals, context effects, loss aversion, endowment effects, and equity premiums. In other words behavioral economists do what Camerer and Lowenstein and their colleagues and others have done since Kahneman and Tversky gave a big push to the changing direction of economics.

Katona, Leibenstein, Simon and others writing before Kahneman and Tversky didn't do research on most if any of these concepts. It follows that they weren't considered to be behavioral economists. The roots of behavioral economics may include what these first gen behavioral economists did; but even so, they would be classified as forerunners. But they can't be classified as behavioral economists because they didn't do the same research as Kahneman and Tversky rocked the world of economics, and about 30 years before Thaler rocked it again. Camerer and Lowenstein seem to be saying that behavioral economics is what they and like minded economists do.

In 2016 Thaler published an article of the same title as Camerer and Lowenstein did 14 years earlier, "Behavioral Economics: Past, Present, and Future." In addition to the description of behavioral economics being equated with certain research topics listed by Camerer and Lowenstein, Thaler adds several including, other regarding preferences, present-biased preferences, and beta-delta models. He says that the integration of economics and psychology, a.k.a., behavioral economics has been "brewing for quite a while" (Thaler, 2016, p. 1577). He begins with Smith and ends with Simon and Katona. Not to be repetitive, but it is my contention that the acceptance of homo economicus makes behavioral economics unnecessary and irrelevant. The reason that I consider Leibenstein and the others to be behavioral economists is because they developed theories and models showing homo economicus to be unnecessary and irrelevant, and that it limited economics. Thaler would not have disagreed. Thus, Leibenstein and the others gave reasons for the need for what became known as behavioral economics.

Did Thaler and the other behavioral economists beginning with Kahneman and Tversky consciously know what the "older" group was writing about? Maybe, they knew some of their writing. But, as Kahneman wrote in Thinking Fast and Slow, what we know consciously and what we know are not the same thing. The ideas of the "older" group were "in the air."

Thaler says that homo economicus was never anything more than an idealized version of human behavior. The idea that people always optimize was always implausible. Why was economic models based on homo economicus so widely accepted even when most economists knew it was a fiction? Thaler says it is because the models based on homo economicus were the "easiest to solve" (Thaler, 2016, p. 1579). Convenience rather than psychological realism supported homo economicus.

How did economists defend homo economicus even when the evidence pointed against it? "Explainawaytions" (Thaler, 2016) is the delightful and brilliant word used by Mathew Rabin to describe economists' defense of homo economicus. What were these explainawaytions? One is Milton Friedman's "as if" explanations. Simply put, the billiards master may not know the physics of billiards, but she plays as if she does. Businesspeople may not know how to define or measure marginal costs and revenues, but they make decisions as if they do know these things. Consciously knowing how to maximize is unimportant. What matters is what they do. The other explainawaytions mentioned is that the empirical methods used in the research was not adequate. People were asked questions whether people preferred one of two options. For example, do you prefer a sure gain of $240, or a 25% chance to gain $1000 and a 75% chance to gain or lose nothing. People often choose the "wrong" answer. The problem was that the participants had nothing to gain or lose so there was no need to think seriously about the questions. Second, the questions were asked only once so learning was not possible. Third is the Invisible Handwave. In a real market setting, if the stakes are high enough then tendencies to misbehave will be "vanquished." Ironically, this is as good a short explanation of the existence of X-inefficiency as appears in the literature.[e]

Nicholas Barberis paper, "Richard Thaler and the Rise of Behavioral Economics" (Barberis, 2018), explains Thaler's role in the growth of behavioral economics to four major factors. First, documenting various "anomalies," many of which were published in the Journal of Economic Perspectives. Second, developing models which are based on assumptions which are more psychologically realistic. His intuitions decades ago have become central to the latest generations of behavioral economic models. Third, helping others make better decisions, perhaps largely through his efforts to increase the saving rate. And, fourth, attracting young talent many of whom he mentored. No arguments about these four points extolling Thaler's contributions to behavioral economics. In "The rise of behavioral economics: Richard Thaler's Misbehaving," Sunstein (2018) says that "It is not possible to appreciate Thaler's career without understanding that he was long viewed as a renegade (p. 56). His contributions to behavioral economics? Sunstein says that the emergence of behavioral economics in the 1980's was due mostly to Thaler's 'creative work' on the endowment effect, mental accounting, a concern for fairness, among others" anomalies (p. 53).

Angner and Lowenstein (2012) referenced extensively Gardner's (1985) book, The Mind's New Science: A History of the Cognitive Revolution (New York: Basic Books). They see behavioral economics as a branch of neuroscience/cognitive science. Doing so is "eminently useful for understanding both the historical origins, nature, strengths and weaknesses of behavioral economics" (Angner & Lowenstein, 2012, p. 2). Eric Wanner, President of the Russell Sage Foundation says that "The field is misnamed – it should have been called cognitive economics" (Angner & Lowenstein, 2012) Angner and Lowenstein don't define behavioral economics as what has occurred since Kahneman and Tversky. They simply review behavioral economics research, from pre-old behavioral economics through new behavioral economics.

[e] Crespo (2013) offers different conceptions of maximization: the metaphysical and the empirical conceptions.

Daniel Kahneman, in his 2003 article, "Maps of Bounded Rationality: Psychology for Behavioral Economics," said that many of the ideas he wrote about in this article were "anticipated informally decades ago" (Kahneman, 2003, p. 1449). However, placing these ideas in a "coherent" form about decision making has occurred only more recently. He goes on to discuss the endowment effect, framing, hot states, and many other concepts from the "new" behavioral economics. Kahneman recognizes the ideas put forth by others but which were not in a "coherent" form. Is this what Paul Samuelson called the "sophisticated-anthropomorphic sin" (Samuelson, 1949).

Rexford Tugwell. Forerunner of behavioral economics

One economist not named in any of the papers on the history of behavioral economics mentioned above is Rex(ford) Tugwell (1891–1979). Tugwell taught at Univ. of Chicago, Columbia, Univ. Cal., Santa Barbara, and the Univ. of Washington, among others. His books include The Trend of Economics, The Art of Politics, The Battle for Democracy, and The Industrial Discipline and the Government Arts. His articles include "The Principle of Planning and the Institution of Laissez Faire" (American Economic Review, Papers and Proceedings), "The New Deal in Retrospect (Western Political Quarterly)," and "The Significance of American Agricultural History" (Agricultural History). He was the recipient of the Veblen-Commons Award, for outstanding Contributions to institutional economics. He was part of F.D. Roosevelt's "Brain Trust," and Governor of Puerto Rico during WW 2. His publication which is of interest here is his 1922 paper in the Journal of Political Economy in 1922: "Human Nature in Economic Theory." The problem according to Tugwell is that human nature is not in economic theory, but without human nature economic theory is inadequate.

"Conscious" economic theory does not take into account a realistic account of human nature. The economic theory of human nature is "unreal," and it does not include all of the "irrational" elements within human nature. However conscious economic theory is still "a step beyond" the philosophy of homo economicus. These inadequacies of conscious economic theory are known by psychologists through research in their laboratories. For example, psychologists know that humans do not have a "clear-headed" control of behavior. Human action is controlled by instincts, what psychologists refer to as the "power plant" of behavior. Reason is not the cause of behavior. The role of reason is to repress undesirable behavior so we can gratify our instincts. In addition to instincts our behavior is also determined by "habit patterns." The three important factors in human behavior are instinct, habits, and finally reasoning.

Wesley Clair Mitchell (1874–1948) defined psychology as a "dark, subjective realm which a man without a lantern had better leave unexplored" (Tugwell, 1922, p. 321). Tugwell responds that economists cannot leave psychology unexplored because we are "thrust" into the dark realm. Regardless of how different they think Tugwell sees an overlap between economics and psychology. What psychologists have learned in their laboratories, economists see it in "fields and factories and are under an obligation to recognize and understand" the relevant aspects of human nature.

However says Tugwell, if economics is defined as the study of market phenomena, then there is a reason for avoiding psychology. If we do not care why we are willingness to pay a certain price for something but only are concerned with whether or not we do pay a certain price, then psychology is not important for economics. Without the inclusion of human nature the best forecasts will go "astray." Good forecasts must take into account the reactions of every individual in the market. Tugwell believes that knowledge of human reactions requires knowledge of human nature. Tugwell refers to those economists who limit economics to market phenomena as "price economists." Are non-price economists behavioral economists? Tugwell doesn't use the term; he might say "instinct economists."

Pick any field within economics and Tugwell's philosophy is "It is only the study of human nature that can force the great closed door of economic theory" (Tugwell, p. 332). Take the theory of consumption. Human nature is essential for a study of consumption because it helps explain human wants and their satisfaction. Welfare economics is also about human satisfaction and satisfaction is a psychological term. Welfare economics can't be limited to peoples' "transient appearances" in the market. Welfare theory without human nature is similar to studying a disease without first studying human physiology. Human nature is essential for the study of production because the joy of effort and the "humanity of production" is more "dignified" than the fact that production is the source of supply to the market. In addition, without human nature production must be confined to a "mechanistic" explanation of the production process. Others have also resisted the tendency to limit production to a mechanistic or engineering activity. Those people include Katona, Leibenstein, and Simon. Tugwell was a forerunner of these first generation behavioral economists.

IV Final comments on this chapter and looking ahead to Chapter 3

Economists, psychologists, and everyone in between, lend me your laptops. I come to praise those who built the door, to praise those who opened the door, and to praise those who walked through the door. In other words, I come here to praise behavioral economics. I cannot, but even if I could, I would not come here to bury anyone.

In Chapter 3 I will focus on three persons who helped build the door: George Katona, Harvey Leibenstein, and Herbert Simon. Then, in Chapter 4 I will discuss some of the many others who helped to build the door.

The "Big 3." Simon, Katona, Leibenstein

3

I am not overly concerned about crossing all my Is and dotting all my Ts. For example, Simon, Katona, and Leibenstein are called here the "Big 3" among the pre-Kahneman and Tversky behavioral economists. Why these three persons? My reasons are simple, and they are mine. Simon won the Nobel Prize in 1978. Katona was a psychologist who wrote extensively about psychological economics beginning in the 1940s; he also called it behavioral economics. Leibenstein was my mentor, and he wrote extensively about the limits of neoclassical theory since 1950. Other pre-Kahneman and Tversky behavioral economists are Gabriel Tarde, James March, James Duesenberry, G.L.S. Shackle, Tibor Scitovsky, Richard Nelson, Sidney Winter, and Reinhard Selten. These behavioral economists wrote before 1974 (the year of Kahneman and Tversky's first major publication in behavioral economics), which is why I have designated them first generation behavioral economics. They also wrote after 1974, but this signifies nothing about their behavioral economics status.

With respect to the Big 3's writings, Herbert Simon wrote about, among other things, bounded rationality, intuition (System 1) and logical thinking (System 2), ECONS vs HUMANS, satisficing, rejection of "as if" theorizing, learning theories in economics and psychology, rationality in economics and psychology, and the nature of human knowledge (tacit knowledge). Leibenstein wrote about, among other things, multiple-selves, gift exchange, social norms, consumer interdependence, and less than perfect rationality. Katona wrote about, among other things, ECONS vs HUMANS, expectations, aspirations, adaptive behavior, macro-behavioral theory, procedural rationality, and less than perfect rationality. Some of the core ideas in behavioral economics as developed after 1974/1979 were written about by the Big 3, beginning in the 1940s.

I Herbert A. Simon

The History of Economic Thought website says that Simon is a pioneer of behavioral economics. He has hastened a revolution in economics, a revolution in decision making under uncertainty in organizations. The result has been a view of human beings which is a far cry from homo economicus. Which, naturally or rationally, leads to the question, was Simon a hedgehog or a fox? The Greek poet and soldier Archilochus (c. 680–645 BC) said that the fox knows many things, but the hedgehog knows one important thing. This was later made popular by Isaiah Berlin in his book, The Hedgehog and the Berlin (1953). The hedgehog and the fox are representative of two different types of intelligence. The hedgehog has an all-embracing, all-encompassing idea, which all ideas are filtered through. The fox has ideas which apply to many different

The Beginnings of Behavioral Economics. https://doi.org/10.1016/B978-0-12-815289-8.00003-4

situations. Simon's (1916–2001) all embracing idea was human problem solving and decision making. Simon said that the Renaissance mind is not broader than other types of mind but it covers a "narrow swathe" which is applied to many fields. His own swathe, he says is "human problem solving and decision making" and "almost everything I have done lies in that quite narrow band" (Simon book, p. 2). He explained to his daughter Kathie how he made contributions in so many fields—economics, artificial intelligence, cognitive science, public administration, sociology, information processing, decision-making, problem-solving, organization theory, and complex systems. He said "I am a monomaniac. What I am a monomaniac about is decision making" (Roger & Marsh, 2016). Therefore, it does not seem to be out of bounds to say that Simon was both a hedgehog and a fox.

In 1949 he published an article in Econometrica with D. Hawkins, "Some Conditions of Macroeconomic Stability." This article demonstrated the "Hawkins-Simon" conditions for non-negative square matrices. In 1975 he won the Turing Award. The Turing Award is the "Nobel Prize of Computing," given annually to an individual(s) who has made significant advances in knowledge of technical importance in the computer field. The award is given by the Association for Computing Machinery. In 1978 he won the Nobel Prize in Economics. It may be the case that no one in the economics profession had the breath and depth of knowledge of so many fields as did Simon. Simon helped create chess playing computer programs, and more generally computer programs which can "think" and make decisions (Boden, 1990). For example, he developed the logic theorist (LT) in 1956. LT discovers proofs for the theorems in Principia Mathematica (Whitehead & Russell, 1910). Amazingly, LT begins with goals and works backwards to eliminate unproductive paths. In 1957 he developed the general problem solver (GPS), which uses heuristics to solve problems. The EPAM program, 1989, can mimic human learning. The MAPP program, 1989, mimics pattern recognition, and hence it can play chess with a high level of skill. The "adaptive production system" simulates learning-by-doing. Simon also developed programs which makes scientific discoveries, programs named BACON, BLACK, GLAUBER, and STAHL.

Yet, his first-class analytical mind was combined with a spiritual, even metaphysical, outlook. In Models of My Life (1996) Simon says that before taking a statistics exam as a graduate student at the University of Chicago, an exam created by Oscar Lange, Simon says that while taking his morning shower "it came to me with blinding and unaccountable certainty" that the exam would include a question on the chi-square. He studied extra and the exam did contain a question on chi-square. He goes on to say that "On no other occasion have I had such loving attention from my guardian angel" (Simon, 1996a, p. 84). Speaking about his colleague and co-author, Allen Newell, Simon said that through their long association they had somehow "developed an extraordinary capacity to communicate even our subtleties to one another" (Simon, 1996a, p. 206).

Simplicity is often the best approach

In 1956 Simon published a paper in the Psychological Review, "Rational Choice and the Structure of the Environment." Simon believes that decision making is a common ground for economics and psychology. While psychology focused on adaptive behavior or learning theories, economics focused on rational behavior. One difference between the approaches of psychology and economics is that the latter assume a much greater complexity in the decision making procedures, and a much greater capacity in the individual (referred to as an organism) for gaining and using information. Another difference is that the psychologists' learning theories are a better predictor of actual human behavior than are the economists' theories of rational behavior. Human behavior may be adaptive but it falls short of maximizing; it is closer to satisficing. One of the main points of the paper is that rational decision making processes depends on the complexity of the individual decision maker, and the complexity of the environment.

For example, Simon offers a simple way for an organism to deal with finding and consuming food, a simple way which is also a rational way. There are three stages: (a) explore the available surface and look for food; (b) when you find food, eat the food, and; (c) if the energy needed to find and eat the food is less than the energy contained in the food, then the organism spends the available time resting. Simon does not find this three stage process to be remarkable in any sense. However, it is rational, and it is much simpler than the models proposed by economists. Simon then discusses how the model of rational behavior changes when the person has multiple goals rather than simply the single goal of finding and consuming food. He also shows the effects of learning, as well as clues about where the different things are located which help satisfy her goals.

He demonstrates these things using many "fancy" algebraic equations. The conclusion derived from his model about rational behavior is that it doesn't require either a utility function or procedures for estimating marginal rates of substitution among various wants. Economic theories of rational behavior are less useful then psychological theories of perception and cognition. Finally, behavior observed in laboratory and field experiments are more useful than the results of "arm chair" or "blackboard" economics.

Simon's, 1956 academic article shows him as an early behavioral economist, challenging the rationality postulate, and discussing why economic explanations of rationality can be inefficient, and possible wrong. Simon followed this 1956 article with two other writings covering the same material. One is the "Parable of the Ant." It appears in Chapter 3, "The Psychology of Thinking: Embedding Artifice in Nature," in his book, The Sciences of the Artificial (Simon, 1996b). The idea of the parable is that a complex environment does not mean that the person, or animal, operating in that environment must also be complex. The person, or animal, can use a very simple set of rules for behaving rationally, and despite the complex environment those rules will produce rational behavior. The simplest set of rules is often the best set of rules.

The parable of the ant

The parable is about an ant making its way along a beach which has been affected by wind and waves. The beach is not composed of flat sand. It has mounds of sand and seaweed, rocks and pebbles. The ant can't move in a straight line because the mounds, rocks, and pebbles get in her way. The ant moves straight ahead, and then veers left and then right. The ant is not taking a "random walk" because although she is not walking in a straight line, the veers and turns are a necessary part of her reaching her goal amidst a complex environment. An ant as a behaving system is simple. The ebbs of flow in their walk is due to the complexity of the environment. Simon adds that a human being as a behaving system is simple. The apparent complexity of her behavior is due to the complexity of her environment. Humans, he says, are adaptive system and if we are successful at adapting it is because we adapt to the (complexity of our) outer environment. Engaging in rational behavior need not be the outcome of complex behavior, and the complexity of our mathematical models which try to explain the complexity. We are simple, economists tend to make us seem complex.

Tit-for-Tat. Tit-for-Tat means "equivalent retaliation." Tit-for-tat is an effective strategy in game theory if the game is an iterated prisoner's dilemma (PD) game. An iterated PD game is when two players play the PD game many times in succession, they remember what the other player did in their previous action, and they change their own strategy given their opponents previous actions.

Robert Axelrod (1976) created a PD tournament in which every participant sent their strategy for a 200 move game. Every strategy played against every other strategy. The tournament was described in Axelrod's book, The Evolution of Cooperation. On every move a player can either cooperate with the other player, or defect. Think of two firms who have agreed, explicitly or implicitly, about the price to charge. A cooperator will charge that price. A defector will lower their price in the hopes of selling more and increasing their profits. The winner of the tournament was Anatol Rapoport who submitted "Tit-for-Tat" (TFT). TFT is based on a few simple rules. First, TFT always cooperates with the other player on TFT's first move. Second, TFT will always match the other player's previous move. If the other player cooperates (defects) on move 1, TFT will cooperate (defect) on move 2. TFT reciprocates the other player's previous move. Third, TFT will never be the first to defect. In the Axelrod tournament, if both players cooperate then both get 3 points. If Player A cooperates and B defects, then B lowers their price alone and increases sales and profits. The defector gets 5 points and the cooperator gets 0 points. If both defect, then they both get one point. The strategy with the most points after 200 moves wins. The results of the second tournament was the same, TFT won.

The characteristics of TFT were as follows. First, TFT is nice: it cooperates at the beginning, and will never be the first to defect. Second, TFT reciprocates what the other player does on the previous move. Third, TFT is not envious. It doesn't try to maximize the number of 5–0 scores in their favor. It attempts to maximize their own score, which given the scoring means cooperating. Fourth, it isn't clever or tricky. It is simple, and becomes obvious to the other player than cooperating is in everyone's best interest. Most of the complicated, clever, and tricky strategies were submitted by economists. Those strategies lost. The simple strategy won, twice.

Bounded rationality and satisficing

Homo economicus, ECONS, has no limits to their rationality. HUMANS have limits due to the manageability of the decision problem, the cognitive limitations of their minds, and the time available to make the decision. HUMANS, therefore, are satisficers, seeking not an optimal/maximizing solution but a satisfactory solution. The Nobel Committee said of Simon that his medal is "for his pioneering research into the decision-making process within economic organizations." Simon's academic publications on bounded rationality and satisficing are too numerous to include here. Just a few: "A Behavioral Model of Rational Choice" (Simon, 1955), The Sciences of the Artificial (1968, 1996), "Theories of Bounded Rationality" (1972), Models of Bounded Rationality (1982), "Human Nature in Politics: The Dialogue of Psychology with Political Science" (1985).

In 1957 Simon wrote about these two topics from both his 1955 and 1956 papers, but in the form of a short story, "The Apple. A Story of a Maze." The story appears in Models of My Life, Chapter 11, "Mazes Without Minotaurs." The story is about a boy named Hugo who was born and lived alone in a large castle shaped like a maze. The rooms are windowless and are long in the shape of a rectangle. Going out one door does not allow you to return to the same room. Some rooms have food, most don't. Hugo is hungry so he looks for clues about recognizing which rooms have food. He learns that some paintings on the wall mean that there is food in that room. The paintings are abstract art, and Hugo learns to understand abstract relations. He learns that certain smells are associated with certain food, some of which he likes and others which he doesn't like. He learns about his tastes and preferences from how the food smells. He also learned to prefer the colors of the paintings in the rooms with the food he liked. He also learned that the process leading to preferences was mostly a subconscious process. Simon, similar to Leibenstein had connections with Austrian economics. The extreme complexity of his environment limited Hugo to being a satisficer, not a maximizer. In the end of the story Simon says that he is Hugo "journeying through the maze of my own life" (Simon, 1996a, p. 188). Simon's behavioral economics was explained with math and with short stories, and parables.

Volumes upon volumes have been written about Herbert Simon. Here I simply am going to present some of his ideas on rationality which he wrote about in his 1945 book, Administrative Behavior. First, the idea that humans are "always or generally rational" (Simon, 1997a, p. 72) is "decisively refuted" (Simon, 1997a) by research in psychology and sociology. Second, rationality in the sense of choosing the alternative which produces an ideal array of consequences is difficult because it requires an amount of knowledge which is restricted to the Creator: knowing all alternatives, knowing all the consequences of all alternatives, being able to compare the consequences of all the alternatives. Third, and perhaps the most interesting point. If we know the entire set of consequences which may occur in the long long long run then future consequences would in effect be determining current behavior! An individual would have to follow the consequences over unlimited time, space, and values. Therefore, an individual would have to know how the world will be changed into the long long long run by his every action today.

Fourth, an individual would to know not only the timeless consequences of his behavior but would also have to know the actions of others. Fifth, most skilled behavior is unconscious and automatic rather than conscious and deliberate, intuitive rather than analytical. We usually think of rational behavior as being guided by conscious analytical reason. According to Simon human rationality and creativity relies on information stored in our memory, our unconscious mind. That information Simon called tacit knowledge. Tacit knowledge is gained by learning from others rather than, in the example gives about using a crane, reading manuals. Experts make good use of their subconscious. For one thing experts are very good at pattern recognition, an ability which is known intuitively via the subconscious, rather than logically. Experts, including chess grandmasters, are very good at pattern recognition and have a well functioning intellect: they call it an educated hunch. Among chess grandmasters and experienced physicists, vis-à-vis, novices, Simon reports that the experts came to the correct solution in a shorter period of time by making fewer steps and spending less time or each step. The expert has more knowledge and makes better and quicker use of the information in their memory/subconscious. In short the expert demonstrates "the usual appearance of intuition," while the novices use more "conscious and explicit analysis" (Simon, 1996a, p. 136).

Sixth, homo economicus is presented as having "omniscient" rationality, a belief which Simon calls "preposterous" (Simon, 1996a, p. 87). Even though omniscient rationality is not real human behavior, Simon does say that humans are intendedly boundedly rational. Seventh, homo economicus is said to deal with the "real" world and its complexity. Simon says that the real world is a "buzzing, blooming confusion" while the perceived world is but a simplification.[a] In our perceived simplified world we use simple rules of thumb. Eighth, Simon defines rationality using several adverbs: objectively, subjectively, consciously, deliberately, organizationally, and personally.

Ninth, Simon rejects Friedman's "as if" explanation for rationality. In An Empirically Based Microeconomics (Simon, 1997b) he responds to Milton Friedman's theory of the "as if" perfect billiard player (Friedman, 1953; Friedman & Savage, 1948). Simon says that a theory of pool playing should be a theory based not on an expert but on a non-expert pool player and the heuristics used to try to make shots. Often, the attempts are unsuccessful. Furthermore, the heuristics used are based on "rules of thumb" rather than on solving differential equations. What we want to learn from the rules of thumb is the practical guides to behavior used by ordinary/average pool players. The problem with "as if" assumptions is that they ignore the limits of our knowledge and our computational power, and hence are not a good guide to understanding human economic behavior. Behavioral economics, by contrast attempts to change the core assumptions which are unsound, and to offer an empirically grounded theory of human economic behavior (Simon, 1997b).

Tenth, Simon developed his theory of bounded rationality in part by observing managers who did not seem to be equating marginal returns of different activities (Simon, 1997b, p. 500). Simon believes that the equations of rational expectations were the product of an economist sitting in a cozy armchair, not observing real people in the real world. Ouch!

II George Katona

George Katona's (1901–81) name does not appear in the History of Economic Thought website. But, an obituary of Katona in the New York Times ("the paper of record,"

[a] The term, buzzing blooming confusion, is a term originally used by William James in his 1890 book, Principles of Psychology.

"all the news that's fit to print") said that in integrating psychology and economics Katona is considered as the dean of behavioral economics. Harold T. Shapiro, the president of the University of Michigan, said that Katona's pioneering word integrating psychology and economics has left a "lasting imprint" on economic thinking (Bird, NY Times, June 19, 1981).

Katona's beginnings

His PhD was in psychology from the University of Gottingen; he was 20 years old. At the tender age of 20 he already had differences with economic theory. First, his view of rationality focused on the processes of decision making (procedural) and not on the outcomes (substantive) which was the focus of economists. Second, his focus was on disequilibrium adjustments, rather than equilibrium as the criteria for suitable outcomes. Economics' focus was equilibrium, while psychology focused on how people learn and adapt to a constantly changing environment. Economists also believe that people learn and approach the equilibrium solution which is both the rational and optimum solution. Psychologists believed that disequilibrium was not only a short run phenomenon. Third, Katona was concerned with solving real world problems. He was less oriented to theory, his research less abstract and mathematical. (The same basic view was expressed by Raj Chetty in his 2015 Ely Lecture.) Fourth, similar to Leibenstein, he studied the implications of human behavior being less than completely rational. He did not assume that humans are completely rational, or that economic models should be based on completely rational behavior. These would be conclusion of research not the assumption. Fifth, similar to Leibenstein's belief, science was about understanding and prediction. Sixth, assumptions are important. They are the best guide to directing research leading to advances in knowledge.

Katona went to Frankfurt where in 1923 he wrote a paper on the causes of German hyperinflation. He then moved to Berlin where he studies Gestalt psychology with Max Wertheimer. Wertheimer was one of the three founders of gestalt psychology along with Kurt Koffka and Wolfgang Köhler. Katona then immigrated to the United States in 1932, becoming a citizen in 1939. In 1947 he went to the University of Michigan where he helped begin the Survey Research Center. He was a Professor of Economics and Psychology and remained at Michigan for the remainder of his career, remaining active even after he retired in 1972. It was at the Survey Research Center that Katona did much of his work developing behavioral economics.

Why economics and psychology drifted apart

In his 1951 book, *Psychological Analysis of Economic behavior*, Katona gives reasons why economics and psychology drifted apart in the 20th century. In a footnote on page 4 he uses a term from Wesley Claire Mitchelle's 1914 paper in the *Quarterly Journal of Economics*, "Human Behavior and Economics: A Survey of Recent Literature"—"non-intercourse." Why the non-intercourse? First, psychologists rejected 19th century "rationalistic-hedonistic" decision making. They understood that human behavior was more complex than that which was part of the rationalistic-hedonistic theory.

Second, psychology separated itself not only from economics but all the social sciences. Psychologists studied abnormal behavior, the role of the unconscious, physiological processes, and the association among non-sense syllables. They weren't optimistic about how these topics could help understand activities such as saving and investment. Third, the belief among economists and others that psychological factors were not measurable and were uncertain and undefined. Economists were working toward economics being an exact science which contained laws which would be valid in various circumstances. One of those laws is the x-istence of economic-man, homo economicus, she who knows all, including knowing what everyone are going to do.

ECONS vs HUMANS

Richard Curtin of the Univ. of Michigan regarded Katona as having initiated behavioral economics in the 1940s. Katona, an empirical scientist, believed that the importance of the HUMAN factor, not the role of ECONS, in economic theory was a goal of behavioral economics. Economic theory has understood for a long time that economic outcomes depend on the behavior of both HUMANS and markets. However, the primary focus has been on markets. Katona sought to differentiate the behavior of HUMANS from that of markets. Katona believed that an important topic of the study of HUMANS was to understand the relationship between human beings and information, the study of expectations, uncertainty, and aspirations. And understanding the behavioral aspects of these things and others would lead to an enriched economic theory based on empirical findings and observations. Katona was not against orthodox economic theory, he was not a neoclassical "denier." He wanted to apply a better set of insights about HUMAN economic behavior to bolster neoclassical theory.

Characteristics of behavioral economics/psychological economics

Katona's philosophy about and the characteristics of behavioral economics/psychological economics (BE/PE) can be seen in two of his publications, Psychological Economics (1975), and Essays in Behavioral Economics (1980). Some of his beliefs about BE/PE comes from his work in Gestalt psychology. In the 1920s Katona studied with Max Wertheimer in Berlin. Wertheimer was one of the three founders of gestalt psychology along with Kurt Koffka and Wolfgang Köhler. Katona believes that Wertheimer "found" the basis of economic behavior in his book Productive Thinking (1945). Katona summarized Wertheimer "finding" in his book Psychological Economics. In his writing on BE/PE, and other subjects Katona admits that he wanted to write as if he were a very good journalist. About BE/PE, first, BE/PE relies on empirical research or controlled observations rather than "armchair speculation" (p. 42) and "dogmatic statements of pure reasonings" (Katona, 1975, p. 41). Second, they don't assume that people are rational or that rational behavior guides economic behavior. Before they assume anything, they gather data. Third, human behavior is distinguished by its plasticity. Machines do the same thing every time. The behavior of a machine is characterized by its repetitiveness. Human behavior is not repetitive or reflexive. Humans mature over time, and learn from experience with the result that human behavior changes. According to Wertheimer via Katona the effects of experience on behavior is at the heart of economic behavior. Fourth, in his book PE he says that the "aims and goals of economics are always macroeconomics" (Katona, 1975, p. 41). What we want to know about the economy is how the macro economy is performing. For example what is the total number of cars bought in 2018, not whether Cass Thaler bought a car. On the other hand, the individual is the beginning of psychology. The individual is the one who thinks, feels, learns and, occasionally, lies. This leaves us with a potential conflict between psychology and economics. Fifth, BE/PE is concerned with procedures affecting spending, saving, and investing, and; sixth, BE/PE studies the psychological forerunners of economic behavior, the motives, expectations, and attitudes which influence economic behavior (Katona, 1980, p. 3).

Together these six points annoyed many members of the economics profession (Tobin, 1972, p. 37). There is nothing in Katona's writings about natural experiments, base rate fallacy, the ikea effect, the confirmation bias, or any of the many biases common in the behavioral economics literature. Does this mean that Katona is not a behavioral economist? Does it mean that he is a forerunner of behavioral economics? My answers are no and no. It means that he is a first generation, pre-Kahneman and Tversky behavioral economist.

Katona takes on homo economicus, and discusses framing

Rationality

In an age in which economists believed almost as a religious belief in homo economicus, Katona maintained that people are neither completely rational nor completely capricious or impulsive (Katona, 1953). Years later Leibenstein would call it "selective rationality" (Leibenstein, 1976). Katona was interested in the process or procedures people use in decision making. Is the process a rational one? By contrast, economic theory emphasized the rationality of the outcome, e.g., did the decision maker equate at the margin. Herbert Simon called the process and outcome foci procedural and substantive rationality, respectively.

Katona described rational behavior as "purposive and understandable behavior" (Katona, 1963, p. 49). behavior leading to "genuine decision making-deciding according to the requirements of the situation" (Katona, 1963, pp. 49–50). Simon and Gigerenzer called this ecological rationality (Mousavi, 2017).

The alternative to rational behavior is not, says Katona, necessarily irrational behavior, it is habitual or routinized behavior. It is this type of behaviors which often guides human behavior. Habits result in our behavior being relatively inflexible, and hence not conducive to rational decision making. The product of habitual behavior is an automatic response without regard to relevance, motives or needs. Katona describes it as "emotional, haphazard, nonunderstandable" behavior (Mousavi, 2017), "impulsive, whimsical… even ununderstandable behavior" (1975, p. 217). It is non-genuine, non-rational, non-maximizing decision making. On the other hand, maximizing behavior reduces all human motives to a single motive—maximization of some function. Humans tend to have many motives.

Although habitual behavior is a common form of behavior and leads to inflexible behavior, breaking behavior habits does happen. Sometimes, a "bell" in our head sounds, we stop doing what we're doing, listen to the "voice" in our head which follows the bell, and reconsider our behavior (Katona, 1960, p. 140). Reconsidering our behavior is a feature of "genuine" decision making (Katona, 1975, p. 221). When does this happen? It is relatively rare. The pressure must be high enough to force a behavior change. But even in these situations the change is geared to meeting expectations and not to optimize an outcome (Katona, 1980, pp. 13–14). Katona estimates that only about 25% of major consumer purchases reflected careful planning. James Tobin in 1959 paper in the Review of Economics and Statistics said that the economics profession owes much to Katona's pioneering work in consumer attitudes and behavior (Hamid in HBE, p. 137).

Framing

Being a student of gestalt psychologists Max Wertheimer and Kurt Lewsin, Katona rejected the orthodox view of orthodox economic theory that the meaning of information is contained in the content of information. That is, information is an objective fact. And, the aggregation of the individual pieces of information equals the entirety of the information. By contrast Katona believed that the perception of information in its entirety, the field, gives the individual pieces of information their meaning, and hence the entirety of information is more than the sum of the individual pieces of information. In more current terms. it means that the meaning of information depends on its context, or how information is framed. Kahneman and Tversky's Prospect Theory (1979) were more successful than Katona in having economists realize that the framing and hence the meaning of a problem affects the perception of the problem and the decision made by humans in response to that problem.

Katona believed that framing, or frames of reference, was important in how people learned about the current stage of the business cycle and future developments of the cycle. Katona says that one form of learning is habituation, meaning becoming inured to events. People become inured, or accustomed, to inflation, unemployment, and/or good or bad news. However, although "only what's new is news," (Katona, 1975, p. 202), habituation to good news creates bad news. This is because too much good news creates diminishing marginal utility to more good news, while more bad news does not create as much diminishing marginal utility to more bad news. And, habituation to good news is stronger than to bad news. In other words, we become more tired of good news than bad news. Consider that among so-called serious journalists, "serious news" means "what is going wrong" (Pinker, 2018, p. 50).

About 30 years before Christopher Sims received much attention for his theory of "rational inattention" (Sims, 2003), Katona wrote about because our attention is limited we tend to put less attention to favorable economic news and more attention on bad news. People are, so to speak, "bad news averse."

All humans do not react to the same economic news in the same way because different people perceive information differently, depending on the context relevant to themselves. Katona explains this using a stimulus-response—intervening variables approach. (This may sound as if it is about econometrics, but it is NOT!) There is no direct deterministic connection between "stimulus" and "response." Katona used the term intervening variables to explain what connects changes in economic variables (income or prices)—the stimulus—and the response (spending) by individuals. The intervening variables are not necessarily observable, but they are things which go on inside the individual which produces a response from a given stimulus. Because we are individuals, different from each other, the response to a given stimulus can be different among people. And because we change over time, our response to a given stimulus can be different over time. He considered expectations, motives, and attitudes to be the three main intervening variables. These variables create our perceptions of the world and it is how these perceptions are organized which create our reactions to the stimuli. The "organized perceptions" is our frame or frame of reference. About 25 years after Katona wrote about this, Kahneman and Tversky published Prospect Theory. Akerlof (2007) considered social norms to be a very important intervening variable in explaining unemployment. Akerlof and Schiller (2009) identified "animal spirits" as an important intervening variable.

Katona's behavioral macro

Katona's first explicit concern with behavioral economics was his 1942 book, War Without Inflation. Katona began with the assumption that inflation was not caused only by economic factors, but also by psychological factors. Aggregate economic data doesn't cause inflation but serve as a precondition for inflation. What must exist for inflation to exist is a frame of reference creating inflationary expectations. In general Katona's observations in the early 1950s led him to believe that the frame of reference and the context in which information is received (perceived) determines its (Curtin, 2017, p. 20). One-half century later Katona's ideas about frames of references are widely accepted in behavioral economics circles. For example, Kahneman and Tversky theory about framing. The acceptance of Katona's ideas 50 years later makes Katona, not a forerunner of behavioral economics, but an early or "old" behavioral economist.

Consumer behavior

Katona took objection to Keynes' "fundamental psychological law," that in the aggregate, changes in income and changing in consumer expenditures are related such that the marginal propensity to consumer is greater than zero but less than 1.0. Keynes believed that business firms make investment decisions based on expectations about the future, they are forward looking, while consumers were backward looking. Business could, therefore, influence the economy's future, while consumers' backward approach could not. Consumers were considered passive automatons, mindlessly spending a certain percentage of their income on consumption regardless of the state of the economy (Curtin, 2017, p. 28). Katona challenged two assumptions made by Keynes' fundamental psychological law. First, investment spending by consumers, i.e., expenditures on cars, homes, and high priced consumer durables, is not enough to affect cyclical developments. Second, consumers do not have the financial resources to be able to vary the timing of their expenditures based on their expectations about the future. Katona gathered data for the 1920s and 1930s showing that investment spending by consumers exceeded that of business investment spending. And the cyclical pattern between the two were similar. Recall the saying, "it takes a theory to replace a theory."

Katona developed a theory of aspirations to explain economic growth. The orthodox view, according to Curtin, is supply-side, i.e., capital, technology, and labor productivity. And, people's aspirations are assumed to be insatiable. And, aspirations affect only the goods and services consumed by consumers. Katona asserted that aspirations can affect the demand for all goods and services, and have an independent and significant affect on the rate of economic growth. It also affects peoples' willingness to incur debt, participate in the labor force, and investment more in human capital.

Aspirations are not static. Economic success gives rise to new aspirations, but failure does not have the same sized reduction in aspirations. It takes a relatively long period of frustration and failure to reduce aspirations. It is kind of an asymmetric aspirations function. It was largely ignored in the economic literature because orthodox theory assumed that aspirations are expected only to increase. In effect, Katona added a demand-side to the orthodox supply-side theory of aspirations (and growth).

The economic literature as a whole may have ignored Katona, but Nobel Laureate James Tobin, winner of the Nobel Prize in 1981, didn't ignore him. The economics profession, he says, "owes a very considerable debt" to Katona and the other members of the Survey Research Center at University of Michigan, "for their imaginative and pioneering work in the collection and interpretation of buying intentions and attitudinal data" (Tobin, 1959, p. 44). Yet, Katona annoyed many members of the economics profession because of his rejection of utility and profit maximization, his rejection of the assumption of homo economicus, and his rejection of formal analytical "system-wide" models (Warneryd, 1982, p. 3).

The law of large numbers

According to Katona, the "principles of economic behavior" means "regularities persisting" in most or all cases studied. It does not mean individual circumstances which make each individual person or firm unique. Is the behavior of individual persons or firms irrelevant for the macro economy because individual differences will cancel each other out. The "regularities of large numbers" is what is of interest to economists. And this is accomplished without any regard to any of the inestimable and inconsequential details. But, this is correct if and only if what causes decisions among each of a large number of individuals is independent of all other individuals. In this case there is more certainty in what a large number of individuals will do than what a single individual will do. Hence, ignore the individual. If many, most, or all individuals are affected by the same factors then individual differences don't cancel each other out: they are add together. A wave of optimism or pessimism affects a large number of people the same way. The wave gets larger, not smaller. Changes in attitudes or expectations is similar to a contagious disease; the disease spreads and more people become ill. Individual temperatures don't cancel each other out so that the "macro" temperature is 98.6.

Is the behavior of a single individual more uncertain than that of millions of individuals? Only if the factors affecting each of millions is independent of all others. Is the future behavior of a single individual always uncertain? Katona says no. Individuals know or believe they know what they will do in the future. And social scientists, which includes both psychologists and economists can ask about their plans. And people are often able and willing to supply honest answers. Katona doubts that the behavior of a few is more uncertain than that of many. (Consumer) surveys can get information about individuals' expectations about future behavior and it is a "major methodological tool of psychological economics" (p. 57).

It is correct to say that what we are most interested in is identifying regularities in behavior. But, says Katona, regularities can be identified only be done by studying the behavior of individuals. By doing this individuals can be placed in groups of homogenous individuals at which point the law of large numbers can be used. Therefore, he concludes by saying that "a major requirement of present-day economics consists of the collection of microdata that serve to enrich our knowledge of microprocesses" (p. 58).

Intervening variables. Motives, attitudes, and expectations

The effect of experience—a stimulus or a change in the environment—is not the same for all people, or not the same for one person over time. The format is [stimulus—organism—response], or [change in the environment—intervening variables—overt behavior].

The intervening variables is the effects of the organism/person which affects the results of experience. Intervening variables are the motives, attitudes, and expectations of the person. Motives move the person in certain directions. Attitudes are what makes some things valuable and other things value-less. Expectations are also known as a "frame of reference," or the context within which the stimulus occurs. Katona gives an example of stimulus A within context X leads to response or behavior B, but the same stimulus within context Y leads to response or behavior C. The same stimulus leads to a different response or behavior because the intervening variables affect the "organization of perception" of, and our reaction to the environment. In this way they affect economic behavior. Behavior changes from B to C; perception changes, people do learn. Learning comes in two forms. The first is memorizing, repetition, conditioning. The second is problem solving, understanding. In the first form people learn from the *past*. Our expectations and habits are determined by what happened in the past; as it was yesterday so it will be tomorrow. I "learn" about tomorrow from yesterday. In the second form, we do not infer the future from the past. We reorganize our perceptions and this makes our habits dubious or misplaced. Katona discussed these two forms of learning in his 1940 book, *Organizing and Memorizing*. Under what conditions do we learn from the second form? Only when we see ourselves being at a "crossroad." Some 30 years later, Harvey Leibenstein called it *pressure* (from market competition). The pressure must be high enough for change to seem like the best option. Otherwise it is the status quo.

Prediction and understanding

Finally, Katona believed that prediction and understanding about phenomena are both important outcomes of research. Both are enhanced if the assumptions of the model are realistic. In *Beyond Economic Man* Leibenstein (1976) said that the prediction only matters is a matter of "faith or of taste" (p. 14), what he calls the "romantic" approach to economic theory. As much if not more than prediction is obtaining a coherent explanation of events. Hence Leibenstein said in Beyond Economic Man that explanation is enough, even if prediction is absent. However, prediction in the absence of explanation is devoid of science.[b]

III Harvey Leibenstein

Did Leibenstein do experiments on the endowment effect? No. On loss aversion? No. On present-bias preferences? No. On any other topics done by Thaler, Camerer, Rabin, or any other economist since Kahneman and Tversky published their ground breaking work? No. Did he use a lot of mathematics in his research papers. NO. Does that mean that he is not a behavioral economist? No. Did he go against the quickly moving "stream" of economic theory in the 1950s and 1960s, and beyond? YES. His work makes him a first generation behavioral economist, a pre-Kahneman and Tversky behavioral economist. Not a forerunner of behavioral economics, but an early or first generation behavioral economist.

The History of Economic Thought website said of Leibenstein that he was most famous for X-efficiency theory, and fertility theory. Leibenstein tried but did not succeed in replacing allocative or Pareto efficiency with X-efficiency. Yet, he is "hailed as a pioneer of behavioral economics." Why is Leibenstein hailed as a pioneer of behavioral economics?

First, he contributed to what was probably the most important step in the development of behavioral economics, showing that the homo economicus had no "bullets" in his gun. It turns out, homo economicus was more Fredo Corleone than Michael Corleone. He was more the "Wizard of Oz" than an all powerful Emperor who controls the Empire. More than that, Arrow (1986), in, "Rationality of Self and Others in an Economic System," said that economic theory can be based on assumptions other than rationality. So, homo economicus is not only Fredo, but he is not needed in the "movie." Leibenstein showed that homo economicus could, and should, be "cut down

[b] There is another book with the title Beyond Economic Man. This other book is Beyond Economic Man: Feminist theory and Economics (1993). It is edited by two outstanding economists, Farianne Ferber, and Julie Nelson. The editors say that there are several books criticizing economic theory, but without "feminist identification" (Ferber & Nelson, 1993, p. 13). Leibenstein's book was one of the several books mentioned. In contrast to the neoclassical analysis bases on individuals who are rational optimizers. Leibenstein uses a model where the behavior of humans interacting with other humans is determined by differences in personalities and market conditions. This, they say, has important implications for an analysis of households. But, they continue, X-efficiency theory has focused on firms, not households, and Leibenstein's analysis of intrahousehold consumption is "curiously gender free" (Ferber & Nelson, 1993). I find it curious that they think it is curious.

to size." He did this with his publications beginning in 1950. Of the approximately 200 empirical studies consistent with X-efficiency theory, Harvey authored none of these studies. He co-authored one with Shlomo Maital; it was a "silly" article about the goal and assist scoring of players on the Boston Bruins of the National Hockey League. He also used several ideas from Austrian economics.

Atoms and molecules. Individuals vs firms and households

Atoms are basic building blocks of everything. A grouping of atoms is a molecule. In Beyond Economic Man, Leibenstein (1976) distinguished the molecular from the atomistic level of the economy. The molecular level of the economic system consists of firms and households. The atomistic level consists of individuals who work for firms or live in households. Why make the distinction? Leibenstein was convinced that the economy suffers from waste, preventable waste. Conventional price theory is about the molecular level, i.e., the theory of the firm and the household. Waste doesn't exist in conventional theory; the misallocation of scarce resources exists when the market is affected by monopoly power. That is known as allocative inefficiency, which is a deadweight welfare loss.

Conventional price theory is inadequate for understanding preventable waste. Studying the atomistic level, individual behavior, was at least a necessary condition for understanding preventable waste, and inefficiency. The inefficiency from waste was not a misallocation of resources, it is a waste of resources. It is due, says Leibenstein, to sloth, habits, emulations, standard operating procedures, conventions, moral imperatives, and psychological inertia. Any of these elements, ex., habits, may be undertaken without careful calculation and, if so, they are categorized as non-maximizing behavior. If the firm was a black box, then Leibenstein made it gray. There were shades of gray for different people, but gray nonetheless.

Princeton, Notestein, and Morgenstern

At Princeton Leibenstein's two mentors were Frank Notestein (1902–83), the demographer, and; Oscar Morgenstern (1902–77), the co-author of Theory of Games and Economic Behavior. Notestein is known for his work on population change, specifically, the demographic transition (DT). DT is the change in population a country goes through from a pre-industrial to an industrial economic state, when population is characterized by high birth and death rates to lower birth and death rates. Notestein was more interested in problem solving than in engaging in analytical modes of research. Thus, he generalized more than he wrote mathematical papers. Leibenstein wrote his doctoral dissertation under Notestein's mentorship, and his dissertation became his 1954 book, A Theory of Economic-Demographic Development. It is a book of pure theory with a few simple equations and graphs.

Harvey the Austrian

Morgenstern's (Austrian) influence was felt in Leibenstein's, 1950 paper on consumer demand, and in his expressing certain beliefs which are part of Austrian economics:

the importance of the individual, methodological individualism; the role of science in understanding and prediction, and; subjective rationality vis-à-vis objective rationality.

How are his beliefs related to behavioral economics? They are part of understanding real human behavior. With respect to methodological individualism, Leibenstein says that it is virtually self-evident to non-economists and, at the time. The Austrian philosophy of methodological individualism is what Leibenstein considered self-evident. Focusing on the individual, Leibenstein sees that an organization's goals are the goals of the individuals in the firm because a firm is but a collection of individuals where each individual has a role to play. An organization has no will of its own, and will behave only as the individuals working in the firm behave. This implies that individuals have a certain amount of free will on-the-job. The only exception to his ideas of methodological individualism is when the organization is run by a "dictator with perfect control." But this rarely, if ever, exists. As a result, employees enjoy a certain amount of effort discretion, and this helps explain the firm's direction.

It also implies that more basic to an organization than production is activities, or "doing." John R. Commons said that "transactions" were the basic unit of analysis, and Oliver Williamson said that transactions are at the heart of transactions cost analysis. The Austrians called it "catallactics."

In Harvey's view both the market and the firm are a system of exchange. Interactions create benefits, and costs. However, in neoclassical theory the exchanges are based on full information, i.e., complete production and cost functions and complete labor contracts. Exchanges are effective because communications are effective, because the "market" for human interactions are effective. But incomplete information and imperfect markets creates a gap between the potential and the actual output and costs. And these give rise to X-inefficiency.

Prediction and understanding was the second belief. Leibenstein called the idea that prediction is the only criteria of scientific knowledge as the "romantic" view (Leibenstein, 1976, p. 12). The romantic view he held to be simply "a matter of faith or of taste." Leibenstein was an advocate for understanding, a coherent explanation of events, as being another criteria for scientific knowledge. He says that prediction without understanding is "worthless." Explanation without prediction is "sufficient" (Leibenstein, 1976, p. 13).

Leibenstein agrees with Hayek that prediction in economics is difficult because of too many interrelationships between a very large number of economic and non-economic variables. The non-economic variables are particularly troubling because they cannot be understood with (the then) existing knowledge of economics. And the future is truly unknown which makes prediction very difficult. What economists can do is to understand general trends or patterns. Hayek called this the "explanation of the principle."[c]

[c] In "The Use of Knowledge in Society," Hayek says that unorganized or tacit knowledge includes knowing how to make full use of different forms of capital, and full use of human skills. He also comments that inefficient managers can reduce profits by allowing costs to rise above necessary levels, and that with a given amount of capital, and output, costs can vary greatly. Leibenstein could not have stated it any better.

According to Hayek equilibrium is attained only when people have perfect foresight about their own behavior, but even more, about the behavior of others. This requires that peoples' behavior follow a pattern which can be understood by others. Correct foresight is the basic characteristic of equilibrium (Hayek, 1945, p. 42). According to Leibenstein, within a group setting, individual effort depends on the effort of others. And, the pattern of effort must be understandable by others. The effort equilibrium of an individual will be an effort level which conforms to the effort norms of others. Leibenstein refers to this norm as the "inert area." Why do individuals stay within the inert area? According to Leibenstein, and Carl Menger before him, people remain within the inert area if and only if the cost of changing the level of effort exceeds the benefits of changing the effort level. Here Leibenstein shows his neoclassical side.

The nature of rationality was the third belief. Leibenstein did not believe that objective rationality is the only form of rationality. Objective rationality is the rationality of economic man, the maximization of some function, substantive rationality, the equality of marginal costs and marginal benefits. His preference was what Simon called procedural rationality. In X-efficiency theory a rational decision was based on certain specific procedures. For now, the procedures include making non-reflexive decisions, independent decisions, not deferring decisions because you believe that decisions will be easier in the future, making decisions based on a realistic assessment of the environment. These will be discussed in Chapter 6.

Morgenstern's Influence on Leibenstein's Theory of Demand. Morgenstern's influence is easily seen in Leibenstein, 1950 article, "Bandwagon, Snob, and Veblen Effects in the Theory of Consumers' Demand." Leibenstein shows some implications of dropping the assumption of independent decision making, and assuming instead that decisions among consumers are interdependent. He did this by engaging in a thought experiment, in German, a gedankenexperiment. This experiment is a conceptual experiment rather than an actual experiment. It was used by Albert Einstein in creating his theory of relativity, and Jonas Salk's discovery of the Salk vaccine used to eradicate polio. Participants are asked at each hypothetical price how much would they buy. This gives a demand curve assuming independence among consumers. They were then asked, at each hypothetical price, how much they would buy if they knew that all others were buying Q1. Then they were asked how much would they buy if they knew all others were buying Q2, where Q2 > Q1. This will give a demand curve assuming interdependence. Leibenstein then shows that the two demand curves are not identical with each other, and this demonstrates either the bandwagon effect, the snob effect, or the Veblen demand curve. Leibenstein's iterative questioning may be seen as an anticipation of experimental economics, and inspired by game theory.

Leibenstein questions the marginal productivity theory

In the 1950s Leibenstein also worked with Walter Galenson on economic growth and development in lesser and more developed economies. The result was a catalog of inputs explaining differences in international productivity growth. Leibenstein's tendency for generalizations rather than a tight analytical model is expressed when he said that "We do not intend to advance a complete model" (p. 343). The paper is theoretical, utilizing mostly simple graphs and equations. Leibenstein challenges the use of the (social) marginal productivity principle for allocating investment, and for increasing economic growth and development. Economic theory says that the efficient use of investment funds is achieved when the social marginal product in each alternative use is the same. This will maximize the value of the national product. The principle implies that a less developed economies should use technologies and choose industries which require a lower capital/labor ratio than that used in more developed economies. Leibenstein (and Galenson) argue that the best path uses the best technology on as large a scale of operation possible, and a high capital/labor ratio. Why? Because given high rates of population growth, and; political and institutional instability which hinder technological change, time is of the essence in development. This requires a rapid rate of growth to escape the Malthusian trap, and that is achieved with the best technology, high capital/labor ratios, and large scales of operation. The capital/labor ratio is not the important thing for growth and development. The important thing is the output/labor ratio, the productivity of labor. And this is affected by several things, including capital per worker; the size of the labor force and the capital stock; the quality of the labor force, i.e., skills, knowledge, energy, adaptability, health, energy, and discipline, and; the organization of labor, a factor which would be central to X-efficiency theory. The list and in the context of economic growth and development sounds similar to the work of Edward Denisonin the 1960s and 1970s (1962, 1974).

X-efficiency theory

According to Mark Perlman, X-efficiency as a part of the history of economic thought has three underpinnings: Alfred Marshall, the Morgenstern-Austrian Subjectivism, and American institutionalism and the das Adam Smith Problem.

Marshall put formal analytics in footnotes, and his level of abstraction was relatively low, certainly lower than Samuelson, Pigou, and Solow. Marshall's main concern, and his definition of economics was about how humans in their everyday life made decisions. This led him to put great importance on learning, and to eschew "arm chair" economics. He thought of firms, not as a "black-box" but as an organization. In larger and older firms inertia is more likely to be alive and well, and this made it easier for smaller and younger firms to win customers and increase their market share. Marshall's successor at Cambridge, Arthur C. Pigou, did not share Marshall's thinking Style. However, the Oxford Economists' Research Group, especially P.W.S. Andrews, used questionnaires to gain information about the workings of managers.

Marshall believed that intangible factors played an important role in human decision making, but intangibles can't be clearly specified. His method, in addition to his use of abstraction and formal analytics, included episodic rather than "tight" formal model building and empiricism. Neither Marshall nor Leibenstein believed that a "reasonable" human is necessarily logical. A reasonable man lives in a dynamic world characterized by states of disequilibrium. Habits, conventions, subjective and incomplete perceptions of the external world, and his internal world of felt pressures are reasons why humans usually cannot and do not maximize. For whatever reasons humans don't maximize, Leibenstein was not interested in fitting the reasons into a maximizing model to make it appear that they actually are maximizing. But, increase pressure and humans move toward maximization.

The Morgenstern-Austrian tradition includes subjectivity or willfulness in (consumer) decision making. The consumer's subjective taste for goods decision making was considered by the Austrians von Weiser, and Bohm Bawerk as the "first cause" of economic activity. Neither von Weiser nor Bohm Bawerk tried to explain how the mind works. If subjectivity plays an important role, then how the mind works is an important question. The question how the mind works was expressed in Morgenstern and von Neumann's concept of the minimax. Leibenstein rejected the Walrasian tatonnement process leading to an equilibrium solution. Inside the firm there may be markets but these markets are not perfect, and disequilibrium is the norm. Finally, the Austrian tradition, notably Hayek believed that conventions are a signaling or communication devise. Conventions are a pressure which lead humans to act in a way which can reduce the firm's level of X-efficiency.

Das Adam Smith Problem. This refers to the presumed inconsistency between Smith's Theory of Moral Sentiments (1759), and his Wealth of Nations (1776). In the former, humans are gregarious, engaging in herding behavior, able to detach from his judgments so that they are objective. In the latter humans become economic-man, homo economicus, single minded toward the achievement of efficiency. Perlman believes that X-efficiency can identify the forces which create these two models of human behavior. X-efficiency theory talks about internal and external pressures which lead a person to make a decision about what they ought to do, ethical consideration, and what they want to do, self-interest. The ought was the focus of the Theory of Moral Sentiments, and the want the focus of the Wealth of Nations.

Das John Maynard Keynes's Rationality Problem. This refers to the presumed inconsistency between Keynes' Theory of Probability—TP—(1921), and his General Theory—GT—(1936) with respect to Keynes' philosophy of rationality. In TP, Keynes views humans as basically rational, because he assumes that humans use all available information to know the probability of relevant events. In GT he views humans as being basically irrational, because rather than using probabilities derived from a rational, objective, process they use social conventions to make decisions. The result is that humans are subject to unstable psychological forces, and are "poorly informed, quirky and downright fickle" (Gan, 2016, p. 2).

In TP Keynes characterizes probability as being an objective reality. People with the same information will come up with the same probability. All rational humans with the same information will come to the same conclusion. TP defines one end of the rationality continuum; a human with complete information will be perfectly rational. However, even if all individuals have the same information, an individual's frame of mind, and the personal way they interpret the information means that the individual's own perspective is what guides decision-making. Hence, rationality is more subjective than objective.

If only uncertainty ceased to exist. Humans would be at the end of the continuum described in TP. But we often are not at that end; we are at neither end. We lack enough information to correctly calculate probabilities. Perfect information is an economist's most pleasurable illusion. Uncertainty, and selective rationality, are "cold" realities.

When Keynes uses the word uncertainty he means that science cannot help us in making probability judgments. "We simply do not know" (Gan, 2016, p. 4). GT discussed how humans cope with uncertainty. Humans simple assume that the future will look like the present, unless information indicates otherwise. The best guess about what tomorrow will be like is what today looks like. Except we know that tomorrow will not look like today. But we don't know how it will differ because the information we have is uncertain. If it weren't uncertain then we would know how tomorrow will be different. No wonder Keynes said that we are influenced by unstable psychological cogencies.

Misguided by uncertainty, we decide to be guided by a (social) convention. The convention we follow is the judgment of others. Specifically, we try to anticipate "what average opinion expects average opinion to be" (Gan, 2016, p. 6). We engage in herding behavior. But if everyone else uses a social convention then it is rational to use it as well. The fact is that conventions, such as driving on the right hand side of the street or road, need not be either efficient or optimal. Opinions can and do change, sometimes violently. The result are waves of optimism and pessimism, neither of which may be based on facts. The absence of facts means that the waves are not necessarily irrational, not even unreasonable. But it does suggest that the assumption of complete rationality is in serious doubt. We have rational impulses and where possible we are rational. But "where possible" is not often available. Hence mathematical expectations for calculating probabilities is not going to be the norm. We fall back on "whim or sentiment or chance" (Gan, 2016, p. 8). In GT Keynes says that "I accuse the Classical economic theory of being itself one of those pretty, polite techniques which tries to deal with the present by abstracting from the fact that we know very little about the future" (Gan, 2016, p. 7). All of this sounds similar to Katona's outline of human decision-making (Katona, 1951, 1975).

Gan says that "By allowing for the economic mind to be capable of both irrationality and rationality, Keynes may seem inconsistent in his theorizing, but in fact he has opened up the possibilities for rethinking our conceptions of rationality" (Katona, 1951, 1975, p. 8). The das John Maynard Keynes Problem is solved by postulating that individuals may be both (perfectly) rational and irrational. Keynes did help economists rethink rational, but Katona, Leibenstein, and Simon, and others, before Kahneman and Tversky, also worked out some of our conceptions about rationality, including the idea that people can be both rational and irrational.

Jennifer Hapern, in her 1998 article "Bonded Rationality: The Rationality of Everyday Decision Making in a Social Context" (Halpern, 1998) says that social interactions show that people are "generally reason rationally" when it comes to their own perceptions of alternatives. Of course, she says, personal perceptions may not be objectively correct. But, regardless of being correct or not, personal perceptions encompass "shared ways of misperceiving the world" (p. 225). So, we are generally rational, but when we are not it is because we are following others' misperceptions in order to get along with others, or our own misunderstandings, or personal experience, or social norms (p. 219). Other factors are cognitive limits and illusion, using heuristics, social and cultural factors (p. 231). The term for this is bonded rationality. Bonded rationality deviates from rationality which occurs when we make an "independent assessment" of alternatives. An independent assessment was exactly one of the procedures Leibenstein (1976) said results in a greater level of rationality (and a higher degree of X-efficiency), 22 years prior to Halpern using the same term for the same purpose. Getting along requires that we must know do certain things. First, how others personalize their alternatives. Second, we must personalize ours so others understand us. Third, we must reason rationally when it comes tour own understandings of things. Fourth, we must assume that others will reason rationally (Leibenstein, 1976, p. 226).

IV Behavioral economics or speculation?

Economic research has been said to have four stages: explore including define the problem, develop a theory and/or a hypothesis, empirical testing of the theory, and the conclusions of the research including an assessment of their importance (Ruggles, 1952, p. 409). The "Big 3" limited their work to the first two. They presented empirical evidence, but it (mostly) wasn't their evidence. And more importantly, it wasn't econometric evidence. When the Big 3 were writing, the results of an experiment was *hoc est gratum* (not acceptable). It is said that when the methodology of economic research does not include econometrics, and/or statistical analysis, such as probability analysis, there are only two things left. One is institutional analysis. But institutional analysis has been "positively irritating" because it "attempts to explain economic phenomena in ways other than those consecrated by the customs, habits, and usages of the guild of economists" (Ruggles, 1952, p. 427).

That leaves speculation. Speculation is a residual in that if it is not the other methodologies then it is, by definition, speculation. Synonyms for speculation include gossip, guesswork, hearsay, and opinion: definitely not part of science. Most definitely not part of the science of behavioral economics. Samuelson might call this conclusion that the first generation is speculation an example of the sophisticated anthropomorphic sin. The Big 3 were first gen behavioral economists, writing in the style of "old" behavioral economics, not the "new" variant.

V Final comments on this chapter, and looking ahead to Chapter 4

In Chapter 5 we will look at concepts discussed by Katona, Leibenstein, Simon, and other first generation behavioral economists, have been the subject of research efforts by the "new" behavioral economists. One thing each of the "Big 3" did was challenge homo economicus. With homo economicus there isn't any behavioral economics, because humans in a sense do not have free will: we MUST maximize. Without free will there isn't any real human behavior, there is only a divinely ordained set of divinely engineering blueprints which is us. The "Big 3" helped to "knock homo economicus down to size," and in doing so, they helped build the door. In Chapter 4 I will look at some of the other first generation behavioral economists.

It didn't just happen overnight

4

The announcement for Daniel Kahneman winning the Nobel Prize in 2002 said in part that Kahneman and Tversky discovered how human decision-making deviates from homo economicus's perfect rationality. Without parsing words, and without taking anything away from Kahneman's much deserved Nobel Prize, economists and economic psychologists have been writing about deviations of human rationality from traditional economic theory since at least the 1930s. While none of these first gen behavioral economists were responsible for creating a revolution in economics, all of them helped create the intellectual foundation for the behavioral revolution to occur. This chapter discusses some of the writings of these first generation—pre-Kahneman and Tversky—behavioral economists. The focus is mainly on their writings about homo-economicus/human rationality.

We have discussed the "Big 3" in the previous chapter: Katona, Leibenstein, and Simon. From that discussion it seems clear that the "behavioral economics revolution" didn't just happen overnight. Before we could look inside the black box of the firm, study individual consumer and producer behavior, and other things human, certain beliefs had to be left by the wayside. In this book my emphasis is on three such beliefs. First, humans are fully rational. Second, and concomitant with the first, humans are maximizers. And third, the only form of (in)efficiency is allocative. The third makes it unnecessary/counterproductive to look inside the black box, because the only inefficiency is outside the firm—market (allocative) inefficiency. But it is inside the black box is where a whole host of non-allocative (in)efficiencies take place. The economists whose work is discussed in this and the previous chapter will be referred to as the "it didn't just happen overnight gang." The parts of their work which will be the focus is that relating to rationality, and maximization. Beginning in Chapter 5 (non) allocative (in)efficiency will be added.

Finally, there are economists who have written on topics within the orbit of behavioral economics but who are not included in this chapter. Of course there is our "father"—Adam Smith. Nava Ashraf, Colin F. Camerer and George Lowenstein published an article in 2005 titled, "Adam Smith. Behavioral Economist." There is also John Maynard Keynes who spoke about rationality, the role of animal spirits, cognitive illusions such as the money illusion and how they affect decision making.[a] Others who have been included in a list of economists contributing to the history of behavioral economics include Bentham, Edgeworth, Fisher, Pareto, J.M. Clark, Cairnes, Wesley Claire Mitchell, and Veblen. In this chapter we are limiting ourself to a smaller set but a more recent set and those who seem to have a more direct connection with modern behavioral economics. We begin with a French sociologist and Judge from late 19th and early 20th centuries, Gabriel Tarde.[b]

[a] A book on the money illusion is, The Money Illusion (1928), written by Irving Fisher.

[b] Articles about Tarde, Duesenberry, Shackle, Minsky, Scitovsky, and Leibenstein (and Becker, and Thaler) were published in the Journal of Behavioral Economics for Policy, vol. 2, # 1.

The Beginnings of Behavioral Economics. https://doi.org/10.1016/B978-0-12-815289-8.00004-6

I Gabriel Tarde

Tarde (1843–1904) was a French sociologist and Judge who coined the term "economic psychology" in his two volume book La Psychologie Economique (1902); he is a forerunner of behavioral economics. He wrote about the effects of herding or imitation in decision making. Tarde was very critical of economic-man, including the assumption that humans have "unrestricted" rationality. He rejected the idea that rational behavior must be devoid of emotions, devotion, or passions. He accepted the idea that people have a dual-self, the materialistic-egoistic and the spiritual. He rejected the idea that humans are concerned almost exclusively about satisfying their materialistic-egoistic desires. He believed that the economic-man was a "mutilation" of a real human. And he considered economic-man as neither necessary nor sufficient to explain economic behavior. Ken Arrow agreed with him. Arrow (1986), in, "Rationality of Self and Others in an Economic System," said that economic theory can be based on assumptions other than rationality. In terms of individual behavior is concerned, what is required is a coherent theory of how stimuli create reactions to the stimuli. In the case of consumer demand, an acceptable theory is that of habit formations and habits affecting the reactions to stimuli. This could be worded to sound identical to utility maximization, but it would not be the same. For example, under utility maximization a change in prices affects the utility maximizing bundle of commodities. If prices and income return to their initial levels, then the utility maximizing bundle would return to its initial bundle. Under a model of habit formation, if prices and income return to their initial levels the bundle consumed would likely not return to the initial bundle.

Tarde was also critical of economists' desire to "dominate" all of the social sciences. He, this French Judge and sociologist, accused us of being academic imperialists. He was critical that most economists ignored (economic) psychology (Ajdukovic, Sylvain, Rodolphe, & Spiegelman, 2018; Warneryd, 2008).

The exceptions among economists who did not ignore psychology which he mentioned were Smith, Schmoller, Adolph Wagner, and Menger (Warneryd, 2008, p. 1690). He was critical about economics containing too much mathematics, i.e., Cournot, and not enough psychology. His book, Psychologie Economique, can be summarized with this statement: "The tendency to mathematize economic science and the tendency to psychologize it, far from being irreconcilable… lend each other mutual support" (Layour & Lepinay, 2009, p. 1).

He was critical about the static nature of economics, and the focus on equilibrium rather than dynamic non-equilibrium processes. Finally, he rejected economists' belief that value was objective, insisting that it is subjective. Value has three forms: utility value, truth value, and beauty value; he also called them the value of utility, the value of truth and the value of beauty.

Utility value he called desire, and is the primary force behind human action. Truth value he called belief. This is the degree of certainty about a given condition of the world. And this degree of certainty or belief is subjective. Savage (1954) decision theory is similar to Tarde's in its reliance on subjective psychological belief.

Very little was said about beauty value. All three forms of utility are involved in every aspect of human judgment, and each of the three, plus power and glory, are quantities. All people, as a return for their effort, seek the growth of wealth, glory, truth, power, or artistic excellence. The problem with economics is that it limits itself to wealth.

Competition as a mental conflict

Tarde believed that competition was about a conflict within an individual, a conflict within the human mind. The conflict is between belief (truth value), and desire (utility value); truth and utility are the two main determinants of value. The outcome of this conflict between belief and desire is the degree of price stability. This conflict between truth and desire is means that our inner self is not unified, but dual. The desire to purchase a commodity was to be measured by the excess of desire over the regret of having less money after the purchase. Resolving the conflict creates demand; summing over individuals creates a demand curve.

Economic inputs

Economic inputs are not the classical land, labor, and capital, but repetition, opposition, and adaptation. The three economic inputs are also the three parts of any evolutionary system; one evolutionary system is the economic system. Repetition, imitation what you previously did, resemblances or similarities, is what creates knowledge and the accumulation of knowledge. The function of science is the accumulation of resemblances and hence knowledge. Opposition, a lack of imitation, is about conflict, a.k.a., competition, as well as price and commercial wars. Adaptation is about harmony. Harmony or the resolution of conflict increases the acceptance of inventions, imitating others' technology. These inventions either increase the satisfaction of existing needs or satisfies new needs. For social sciences, including economics, the three inputs are felt through imitation.

Imitation

In Tarde philosophy about the economy, imitation plays a leading role. Fads, crazes, fashion, crime, and (the wisdom of) crowds are understandable from understanding "suggestion and imitation" (Warneryd, 2008, p. 1693). He distinguished logical from "extra-logical" imitation, and relates both to rationality. Logical imitation is imitation based on a reasoned, rationale, analysis of the ideas being imitated. Extra-logical imitation results in *herding* as people talk about the ideas. Tarde says that herding is part of "inter-spiritual actions," individual minds interacting with other minds. Tarde calls this "inter-psychology." This is how one person is influenced by other people. It shows that his theory of social change makes him both an associate of evolutionary and institutional economics. He is also a forerunner of behavioral economics. Warneryd says that he is also a forerunner of social psychology.

II James March

March received a PhD from Yale in 1953 in political science. Until 1964 he was a faculty member at the Carnegie Institute of Technology, later renamed as Carnegie Mellon, where he was a colleague with Herbert Simon, whose PhD was from the University of Chicago, in political science in 1943. With Simon he co-authored Organizations in 1958. March was a core member of the Carnegie School, along with Simon and Richard Cyert. With Cyert he coauthored A Behavioral Theory of the Firm (1963). The concept of rationality was an important one for members of the Carnegie School.

Rationality, stories, myths, and guesses

In, The Ambiguities of Experience (March, 2010), March talks about stories and myths of organizational experience. Stories help members of an organization to interpret and share their histories and experiences. Stories also help members to place new experiences within an existing frame. Stories of organizational experience are affected by themes called myths. A myth expresses a cultural ideal or emotions powerfully felt by many organization members. A myth can reduce the confusions felt in life.

The four main mythic themes are hierarchy, the significance individual leaders, historical efficiency, and the myth of rationality. Rationality is a myth. The myth of rationality is that the human spirit expresses itself by basing actions on future consequences. Our actions reflect our choices which in turn are based on consequences. Rationality is an axiom of proper behavior and a prophet of behavior. It is an omnipresent myth in stories of management, and the core of the answer to the question "why did you do that" (March, 2010, p. 57). The answer involves expectations of consequences: "consequential sense" (March, 2010).

In his 1978 article, "Bounded Rationality, Ambiguity, and the Engineering of Choice," March says that rational choice involves two guesses, one about future consequences and another about future preferences. About future consequences, the rational choice theory states that humans can consider all relevant alternatives, and work accurately with all relevant information. By contrast March says that there are limits on both, and these call into question rational choice theory. About future preferences, March says that rational choice theory is questionable because in contrast to that theory, preferences are not stable, neither consistent nor precise, and not exogenous (March, 1991, pp. 98–99).

Simon's theory of bounded rationality deals with the future consequences. Simon's theory of bounded rationality was a substitution for omniscient rationality. But there were other types of rationality which can become substitutes for omniscient rationality. Some of these other types of rationality (March, 1978) are discussed immediately below.

Forms of rationality

First, limited rationality. Rationality is limited because of, for example, our limited ability to deal with the necessary amount of information required to solve a problem. Second, contextual rationality. This form of rationality places rationality within a social context. Third, game rationality emphasizes the intelligent interaction of self-interested individuals in one or more institutions in pursuit of individual goals. Fourth, process rationality emphasizes the process of decision making (procedural rationality) rather than the outcome of decision making (substantive rationality). Fifth, adaptive rationality emphasizes learning through experience. Sixth, selected rationality emphasize the process by which individuals and/or organizations are selected to survive and/or grow. Seventh, posterior rationality emphasize the discovery of intentions after actions have been taken.

Procedural and substantive rationality

In *Organizations*, with Herbert Simon, the authors say that procedural rationality is a "logic of consequences" (March & Simon, 1958, p. 8). By contrast substantive rationality is a "logic of appropriateness" (March & Simon, 1958). Appropriate procedures (procedural rationality) does not necessarily result in good outcomes (substantive rationality). March and Simon express this by saying that procedural rationality does not always lead to "intelligent" actions (March & Simon, 1958). And without perfect information/knowledge about available alternatives, about the consequences of each alternative, about the probability distribution of future events, a human can "at best" (March & Simon, 1958, p. 159) be "subjectively" rational not "objectively" rational. What happens when people do not have perfect information/knowledge? What happens when the complexity of the problems we are working with exceeds our intellectual/cognitive capacity? Humans become satisficers, they search for satisfactory alternatives rather than optimal alternatives. The conclusion that human rationality is "qualified," limited, or bounded. March and Simon refer with approval to von Mises and Hayek about the benefits of decentralization over central planning. The argument is "simple." When the complexity of the problems we are working with exceeds our intellectual/cognitive capacity, the problem is too much for a single individual or a bunch of central planners. The knowledge needed to solve such problems is available through the competitive price system.

The same argument about perfect knowledge and limited rationality was made by March and his co-author Richard Cyert in their 1963 book, A Behavioral Theory of the Firm (Cyert & March, 2013). In addition they also discuss how limited rationality leads firms to deal with uncertainty by using standard operating procedures, and rules of thumb for making decisions rather than equating at the margin. Firms are not an omnisciently rational system, but rather an adaptively rational system (Cyert & March, 2013, p. 99). The latter means that firms and individuals learn from experience. But, full homo economicus rationality is a myth, a false story.

In a chapter on managerial rationality Cyert and March sound similar to Leibenstein when he discusses XE. Cyert and March say that under conditions of "vigorous" competition the assumption of the goal of profit maximization will lead to correct predictions of human behavior. However when competition is weakened by, say, monopoly power, then the assumption of profit maximization is also weak. Similar to Leibenstein, Cyert and March state that market pressure from vigorous competition leads firms to strive for maximize profits, i.e., minimize costs and obtain higher levels of XE. On the other hand, monopolies do not strive for minimum costs, i.e., maximum XE. In addition, and again similar to Leibenstein, Cyert and March state that absentee ownership also creates a divide between the self-interest of the owners from the managers and as a result lowers the levels of XE.

III Richard Nelson and Sidney Winter

Richard Nelson and Sidney Winter are known as evolutionary theorists. Although their writings date to the early 1960s they are perhaps best known for their 1982 book, An Evolutionary Theory of Economic Change. In Winter's (1964) article, "Econ Natural Selection & the Theory of the Firm" he says that the theory of the firm is not a theory of the firm. The theory of the firm cannot and does not predict the answers to questions about how the firm's decision makers define their objectives, or how they reach their decisions (Winter, 1964, p. 231). The theory of the firm is a theory of how a (representative) firm reacts to market conditions.

Maximization vs reality

The theory that the survival of the fittest are the profit maximizers is a defense of the theory of the firm against those who argue that the theory does not correspond to reality (Winter, 1964, p. 225). In Winter's (1971) article, "Satisficing, Selection, and the Innovating Remnant," he says that the suggestion that firms act "as if" they rationally pursued maximum profits is part of the professions ideology (Winter, 1971, p. 240). The "as if" argument is used when the assumptions of perfect and costless information, among other assumptions, are challenged (Winter, 1971, p. 243). It also provides "relief" for feelings of "intellectual discomfort" when the theory of maximizing behavior is challenged (Winter, 1971, pp. 243–244). The fact is that most people who have studied organizational behavior assert that at least in the short run firms make decisions based on time-honored rules, procedures and policies, and not necessarily on rational procedures. Rational and/or irrational behavior are both is based on rules, procedures, and policies (Winter, 1971, pp. 240–241).

In Nelson and Winter (1973) article, "Toward an Evolutionary Theory of Economic Capabilities," they state matter-of-factly that models of maximization and equilibrium do not correspond to economic reality. Firms often use decision rules which are not based on maximizing behavior (Nelson & Winter, 1973, p. 441).

The black box

Inside the "black box" is where people use the procedures leading to decisions. Do the procedures always result in optimizing or maximizing decisions and behavior? They say, no. Do they ever optimize or maximize? Yes. Humans are selectively rational, and satisficers. Nelson and Winter took the idea of satisficing from Simon and used it as an alternative to the maximization postulate. Why bounded or selectively rational? Because the environment is too complex relative to our level of knowledge and other constraints. These other constraints are scarcity of time, limited communications channels, and limited assistance for "organizing, analyzing, and thinking about the available information" (Nelson & Winter, 1982, p. 67). Nelson and Winter refer to it as a "severe information-processing constraints" (Nelson & Winter, 1982, p. 66). The information processing constraints means that managers cannot maximize profits even if they were inclined to try to do. However, Nelson and Winter deny that they are so inclined. More important is that they can't maximize, i.e., minimize costs. So, the firm is going to be (X) inefficient.

Examining the black box they find that it is neither one big machine or a set of engineering blueprints. Workers have effort discretion because no one can completely control their behavior. Behavior is guided not by optimizing behavior but by rules which are tacit. People observe rules which are "not known as such to the person following them" (Nelson & Winter, 1982, p. 77). Behavior is also guided by "skills" which are also often tacit. The individual can't explain them, their origin, or even when they are being used. Skills are used in making choices which are made "automatically and without awareness that a choice is being made" (Nelson & Winter, 1982, p. 73). Winter calls it "unteachable knowledge" (Winter, 1986). It is knowledge which is impossible to communicate.

IV Kenneth Boulding

Boulding saw the future of economics, and it was behavioral economics. In "Contemporary Economic Research" (1961) he said that "There will be movement toward behavioral economics... which involves study of those aspects of men's images, or cognitive and affective structures that are more relevant to economic decisions" (Boulding, 1961, p. 21). Boulding compares the attitude of economists toward behavior and astronomer's attitude toward gravity. Astronomers, at least before Einstein, did not pay attention to the behavior of gravity because gravity's behavior was so perfect that, in effect, it did not have any behavior. Likewise, economist have not really been interested in human behavior because it is assumed to be perfectly rational (Boulding, 1961, p. 82).

Boulding's (1956) book, The Image, provides an alternative theory of human behavior from that of behaviorism, and orthodox economic theory. Behaviorism states that behavior is the outcome of conditioning, while thoughts or feelings of an individual play no part. Boulding theory is that behavior is affected by the image a person has of the world they live in. The image is the totality of a person's subjective knowledge of the world, a person's worldview or view of the world. It consists of all past experiences, all of the concepts, assumptions, both conscious and unconscious, relations, myths, and beliefs which a person "carries" with them in their mind. An image is one's subjective knowledge, not the truth, but what I believe to be true. It is how they see the world. It determines our perceptions and thoughts. It defines our reality. It is our frame of reference. Why we need an image is because, contrary to orthodox economic theory, Boulding considered humans to be boundedly rational. This leads us to look at the world and try to get a picture of it. This picture is the image.

In 2011, Daniel Kahneman, in Thinking, Fast and Slow, said that events are constructed in our mind and there is an image of the outcome of the event in our mind (Kahneman, 2011, p. 328). Because we are boundedly rational, have limited cognitive abilities, and live in a world of uncertainty, the image helps us frame things so that the world is manageable.

On page 57 of The Image, Boulding says that "We have… defined an organization as a structure of roles." On pages 119–120 he says that "Our basic unit of analysis will be the role. We shall look upon and attempt to analyze organizations in terms of the relations between the roles that make up the organization." (Kahneman, 2011, pp. 119–120).

V James Duesenberry

In Duesenberry's (1949) classic, Income, Saving and the Theory of Consumer Behavior, he asks whether a consumer acts rationally, i.e., according to preference and marginal utility theories. Specifically, does the consumer have a list of all prices for all goods and services, and then on the basis of that information choose how much of each to consume? Does the consumer act according to a systematic budgeting procedure. Duesenberry says that no one actually believes this. But, even if he doesn't go through the steps required of rational behavior, does he act as if he does? Duesenberry says that it is possible but "extremely doubtful" (Duesenberry, 1949, p. 23). Humans are not rational consumers, at least not always rational consumers.

Dual selves

How do humans decide how much to save, other than the fact that savings = income − consumption. Each person has, as it were, two selves. One self wants to increase their current standard of living, and the other self wants to improve their future standard of living by saving now. The two-selves are in a conflict, or struggle with each other. The actual level of saving is the result of whatever compromise the person makes. In 1981, more than 30 years after Duesenberry wrote about the two-selves, Thaler and Shefrin developed a model of intertemporal choice and self-control. Their multiple-self individual consists of a farsighted planner and a myopic doer. In 1976 Leibenstein's two self-human consisted of the superego and the id.

Duesenberry gets Leibensteined, and vice-versa

In a 2005 New York Times editorial, "The Mysterous Disappearance of James Duesenberry," Robert Frank says that most economists simply did not want to believe Duesenberry's relative income hypothesis, perhaps because it implies the existence of wasteful spending (Frank, 2005). And, waste implies irrational behavior. Thus, most economists over 50 ignore Duesenberry and most economists under 50 are not familiar with his name. Substitute the name Harvey Leibenstein for James Duesenberry and these last few sentences about ignoring and not knowing Leibenstein's name applies as well. Consider that both men were Professors at Harvard. Both men made contributions in the way we view consumer and producer behavior, yet both men either largely ignored or forgotten. (There is a cost to being a renegade, especially when you deny the basic assumption(s) which are the foundation for the profession's beliefs, and research agenda.)

The desire to make economics a science, or to insist that it is a science led economists after 1920 to remove socially based consumption from economic theories and models. It was called eradicating economics from any tinge of "psychologizing." Paul Samuelson's 1947 landmark Foundations of Economic Analysis made him the "eradicator-in-chief." Yet, Duesenberry received acknowledgment from both Arrow and Shackle (Mason, 2000) for his contribution to understanding human behavior expressed in his 1949 book, Income, Saving and the Theory of Consumer Behavior. But there was also Friedman's (1957) permanent income hypothesis which became Duesenberry's chief competitor in the 1950s.

Social norms

Duesenberry's theory is about the social influences on human behavior, specifically, savings and consumption behavior. In order to understand consumption one must understand the social character of consumption. However, Robinson Crusoe lives virtually alone on an island. There is no social character when you are alone. Therefore, the economics profession either gives up Robinson Crusoe or ignores Duesenberry; Duesenberry lost to a fictitious character.

Duesenberry called the social influence on consumption the "demonstration effect," or the relative income hypothesis. The demonstration effect is the effect on savings and consumption which are independent of both income and price influences. The demonstration is seeing what others are consuming, and wanting to emulate them as much as possible. Veblen discussed this in his Theory of the Leisure Class. But Veblen's work was marginalized because it represented "trivial sociological observations…" Duesenberry argued that consumer goods which are otherwise completely useless are in high demand because it provides self-esteem (Duesenberry, 1949, p. 29).

Interdependence

The demonstration effect implies interdependence of consumer preferences. Interdependent preferences contradicts the orthodox assumption of independent preferences, i.e., the consumption decisions of "Robinson Crusoe." And it contradicts the assumption of the (horizontal) additivity of individual demand curves into the market demand curve. Psycho-logical and sociological reasoning raises serious doubts about both the independence assumption, and the belief in homo economicus. This itself makes Duesenberry an early behavioral economist. There are other connections with behavioral economics. In Chapter 3 of *Income, Saving and the Theory of Consumer*

Behavior he says that "The level of saving actually achieved by anyone represents the outcome of the conflict between his desire to improve his current standard of living and his desire to obtain future welfare by saving" (Duesenberry, 1949, p. 22). In other words, our saving is affected by our dual-self, one part which is attached to the here and now and the other which is attached to the future. Duesenberry uses data from the Office of Public Opinion Research which shows that people's desired income is a function of income aspirations, not maximum income. People are satisficers, to use Simon's term. Finally, Duesenberry argues that consumption behavior as being the outcome of habits, genetics, and learning, but not rational planning (Duesenberry, 1949, p. 24). Duesenberry was a "very bad man."

Duesenberry's "demonstration effect" is based in part on the preservation of self-esteem which is assumed to be a fundamental drive of human beings. Self-esteem is assumed to be part of one's status and measured as the consumption/display of high quality status goods. Seeing others consuming high quality goods leads others to emulate them in order to maintain self-esteem.

Despite both Duesenberry and Leibenstein analyzing interdependent preferences Leibenstein's work was different from Duesenberry in two ways. First, Leibenstein's was micro oriented while Duesenberry was more macro oriented. Second, Leibenstein attempted to integrate inter-dependence into conventional demand theory while Duesenberry sought a more far-reaching revision of demand theory. In his 1949 book Duesenberry said that "In the last few years economists have had to take a somewhat schizophrenic attitude toward the theory of consumption" (Duesenberry, 1949, p. 1). This is because the theory of consumption was inconsistent with the empirical results about consumption behavior. The inconsistency between theory and evidence involved three data sets on consumption which Duesenberry tried to reconcile with the theory.

Consumption: Theory and evidence

First, cross-section data shows that savings rises with income. Second, long run savings behavior shows that savings does not rise with income due to economic growth. Third, short-run savings behavior shows that savings rises with income but at a different rate as the cross-section data.

First, the cross section data. Cross section data shows that the saving rate rises with income. This is because as income rises there are fewer people consuming higher quality goods and hence there are fewer people to impress and use for the purpose of maintaining self-esteem. Hence savings rises with higher income. Second, the long run data. Long run data shows that the savings rate does not rise with income. This is because income is relative, and when income grows due to economic growth everyone's income rises (more or less) and everyone is in the same "place" as before. The demonstration effect is neither motivating savings nor motivating spending.

Third, the short run data. During a recession income falls. People do not want their consumption to fall below its "normal" level. As a result they save less and spend more.

However, when income rises during an upturn people don't increase their spending much because they do not have to spend much more to maintain their "normal" level In other words, increases in consumption is not as important as is decreases in consumption.

Consistent with Kahneman and Tversky's prospect theory, losses (of consumption) are felt more strongly than gains because we are loss averse. Using the current situation as the normal situation or a reference point is the situation to which people are attached. Hence deviations are looked upon with suspicion. This is an example of the status quo bias. The demonstration effect assumes that people are paying attention to what we are doing. Yet. Gilovich, Medvec, and Savitsky (2000) claim that people don't pay as much attention to us as we believe. This is the spotlight effect. And, of course, following others in consumption is called herding, a form of a bandwagon effect. The data is consistent with Duesenberry's theory yet most economists didn't pay much attention to his behavioral economics.

VI Reinhard Selten

Written by Michael Mitzkewitz (University of Luxembourg) and Rosemarie Nagel (ICREA Universitat Pompeu Fabra-Barcelona GSE).

Reinhard Selten, born in 1930, studied mathematics in the Goethe University, Frankfurt (West Germany), with a minor in physics. Describing himself as unfocused, he attended many lectures of different faculties, e.g., in sociology and philosophy by Theodor W. Adorno, or in psychology by Gestalt psychologist Edwin Rausch. Selten participated as a subject in experiments in perceptual psychology which helped him later in applying experimental method in economics.

Selten discovered game theory reading a popular science article in Fortune. He wrote his master thesis in 1957 and PhD thesis in 1961 in the field of cooperative game theory under the supervision of the mathematician Ewald Burger. In 1957 Selten obtained an assistantship under Heinz Sauermann in economics in the Frankfurt University until 1967, finishing his habilitation in the area of price theory (Selten, 1970). Inspired by Ricciardi's (1957) book containing the first computerized experiment designed for training management, Selten conceived the idea of using experiments in economics as a research method, Also, the articles on the first experiments on characteristic function games impressed him greatly (Kalisch, Milnor, Nash, & Nering, 1954). Selten's first publication ("An oligopoly experiment," Sauermann & Selten, 1959) initialized experimental economics in Germany. Only in 1983 he opened the first European experimental economics computerized laboratory with his new position at Bonn University, Under Sauermann's official and Selten's intellectual leadership a team of young economists started to develop this new field of research. The group published several papers in "Beiträge zur experimentellen Wirtschaftsforschung" ("Contributions to Experimental Economics," Sauermann, 1967–1978) and organized in German international experimental economics conferences from the late 1960s, including early experimenters from the United States, like James Friedman, Austin Hoggatt, Charles Plott, Al Roth, and Andrew Schotter. Some of them also published in the "Contributions."

An important inspiration was "Models of Man" by Herbert A. Simon (Simon, 1957a) which convinced Selten immediately of modeling human economic decision making as boundedly rational behavior. Sauermann and Selten (1962) developed an "aspiration adaptation theory of the firm," built on Sauermann's personal accounts of his management activities as a textile manufacturer. A firm is not modeled as a profit-maximizing entity, but rather as an adaptor of different targets (aspiration levels). If the goals can be simultaneously reached at an operational level, the aspiration levels can be increased. If the goals produce a conflict or the targets are not met, either special measures must be taken or aspiration levels should be lowered through "adjustment steps," one target variable at a time. Later Selten classified this theory as a "purely speculative approach." He had come to the conclusion that theories of bounded rationality must be based on the results of experimental research. "Armchair reasoning is no substitute for empirical research" (Selten, 1990, p. 653). It was a characteristic of the Selten School of Behavioral Economics that experiments serve to develop new theories, not confirm or reject existing theories.

Selten (1967) constructed an oligopoly experiment with single firms represented by groups of subjects, who should protocol the reasons for their joint decisions. Based on these protocols Selten developed "causal diagrams," characterizing the qualitative reasoning prior to quantitative decisions. Causal diagrams are a precursor of cognitive maps as they were introduced later by Robert Axelrod in the social sciences (Axelrod, 1976).

Selten realized early that aspects such as fairness and distributive justice significantly influence decisions. This led to his "theory of equal division payoff bounds" (Selten, 1973, 1978b, 1983), which predicts the outcomes of experiments on three-person games in characteristic function form. Roughly speaking, players within a specific coalition cannot be pushed below payoffs they would get in alternative coalitions with equal split outcomes. Also presentation effects (later introduced independently by Kahneman and Tversky as framing) play a role in the decision-making process as in oligopoly experiments in continuous time (Selten & Berg, 1970). Strategically irrelevant features such as changing fixed costs led to different behavior. Later Selten wrote to these first observations of framing effects: "These results alone should have been sufficient to destroy confidence in the optimization approach as the explanation of economic behavior" (Selten, 1990, p. 649).

Selten's most famous contribution to normative game theory, the subgame perfect equilibrium, was actually a by-product of his experimental research. He conducted experiments of an oligopoly with demand inertia in the early sixties with several strategic variables. To compare the observed behavior with rational behavior, Selten determined the set of Nash equilibria for a simplified model of the original experiment. After elimination of implausible equilibria Selten identified the "natural" solution: The subgame perfection was born (Selten, 1965). "Thus, in an oblique way an experiment on a dynamic game motivated a theoretical analysis of a highly simplified version of it and as a side of this analysis a basic game theoretic concept was introduced," explained Selten later (see Svorencík & Maas, 2016).

The mutual fertilizing of theoretical analysis and experimental research was typical for Selten. He described himself as a "methodological dualist." "The little coherence in my work is due to a desire to understand both fully rational and boundedly rational economic behavior, especially in the context of game situations" (Selten, unpublished autobiographical note). Let us also add that at the time, in the sixties, not only experimental work was unknown to most economists, but also theoretical work on non-cooperative game theory was not "en vogue." The 1965 paper led to the game theoretical revolution in economics and a wave of refinements of Nash equilibria.

Another example of Selten's dualistic approach is the famous chain store paradox (Selten, 1978a), "Even game theoretically untrained persons understand the backwards induction argument without difficulty. Nevertheless, the conclusion is behaviorally unacceptable, The author was so worried about this contradiction that he felt three weeks of physical discomfort. Logically, the backwards induction argument is absolutely compelling but emotionally the author could not accept it as a guide to behavior. He experienced the motivational limits of his own rationality"(Selten, 1990, p. 651). Therefore, he proposed in the same paper a three tier hierarchical theory of decision making. At the lowest level, the "routine level," decisions are based on experience in similar situations without cognitive effort. At the "level of imagination" possible consequences of alternative decisions are simulated. The "level of reasoning" analyzes consciously and rationally a model of the decision-making situation. Not always the decision is made at the highest level activated. "To what extent the three levels of decision making can be trusted to yield adequate decisions is a matter of experience" (Selten, 1990, p. 652). The "routine level" corresponds largely to Kahneman's System 1 and the "level of reasoning" to Kahneman's System 2. The "level of imagination" cannot be assigned clearly in Kahneman's dichotomy.

Selten and Stoecker (1986) run an experiment on repetitions of 10-periods prisoner's dilemma super-games. They observed that subjects must first learn cooperation and then a special end effect behavior from one super-game to the next. If a subject observes that he himself stops cooperation before the other player, there is a behavioral tendency to stop cooperation one period later in the next super-game and vice versa, if he cooperated longer than the previous opponent. Such (counter) reactions result into longer cooperation phases before the end effect of defection kicks in. These observations formed the starting point of the learning direction theory, later refined and applied by Selten and other researchers in various economic models (e.g., Camerer & Ho, 1999; Mitzkewitz & Nagel, 1993; Selten & Buchta, 1999).

VII G.L.S. Shackle. The paradox of rationality

In Epistemics and Economics, Shackle (2009) discusses the "paradox of rationality" (p. 246). The paradox is that, on the one hand, rationality concerns itself only with things fully known, i.e., perfect knowledge. Only then can we truly calculate benefits and costs of a thing. On the other hand, the only time we can know something fully is when we know both the past and the future in their entirety. But, we don't make choices in the (very) long run. Thus the paradox—to make a rational choice we must transcend the grasp of choice.

Unknowledge

Shackle says that a permanent part of the world we live in is the shortage or insufficiency of knowledge (Shackle, 2009, p. 3). Shackle call the shortage of knowledge "unknowledge."

Unknowledge is more than a result of imperfect information. Unknowledge implies the existence of "unknown unknowns." Some things we know that we don't know, for example, how to speak Chinese. Other things we don't know that we don't know. We can't even imagine them. Hence, we don't know what we don't know.

Economics assumes that people are rational but doesn't ask about the nature and source of knowledge. For example, what can we know and what we can't know. Shackle says that economics, instead of asking these questions asks only the questions which are "allowed" to be asked. Situations in which individuals cannot be fully informed, hence cannot be fully rational, are excluded, from conversations (Shackle, 2009, p. 85).

Intervening variables

According to Shackle, economic theoreticians assume that men apply reason to their circumstances. This is taken to mean that a person's circumstances directly affect their behavior. However, Shackle says that the relationship between circumstances and behavior involves what others such as Katona called intervening variables. Intervening variables include knowledge and thoughts. Hence, circumstances affect behavior through our knowledge and thoughts. Because we are not perfectly informed—we lack perfect knowledge—we are not fully rational.

Wall of rationality

Another thing which makes full knowledge so difficult to attain is that economists have separated economics from other aspects of life by a "wall of rationality" (Shackle, 2009, p. 4). Hence important knowledge is neglected. But according to Shackle, economics is neither inherently self-sufficient nor inherently self-contained. It must be integrated with other disciplines to be effective. But, it should not attempt an integration with either physics or chemistry. Economics is about thoughts and behavior not with the essential chemical make-up of humans. Hence there isn't any "secret of life" that would lead to a "theory of everything" about economics.

Incomplete contracts

The existence of uncertainty (and the inability to control all behaviors of all employees) implies to Shackle that contracts, through which business is organized, will be incomplete. Incomplete contracts means that surprising outcomes are inevitable. He used incomplete contracts to explain why there is not a deterministic relationship between inputs and (maximum) output. From the view point of orthodox economics, this indeterminate relationship between inputs and outputs would be "surprising." For Leibenstein incomplete contracts is a main reason why effort varies in a way which doesn't always work in the favor of minimizing costs. Thus incomplete contracts help explain the existence of X-(in) efficiency.

Satisficing and an asymmetric framing

In his 1940 article, "The Nature of the Inducement to Invest," Shackle wrote about satisficing/aspiration criteria to decision making, pre-dating Simon by 17 years. In "A Means of Promoting Investment" (1941) Shackle suggested that people consider only two options, the best possible gain plausible enough to give hope, and the worst possible loss plausible enough to create concern. Shackle, again preceding Simon, recognizes that people have a limited capacity for cognition and attention. This leads to what we can call a "2 option heuristic"—best possible gain or worst possible loss. By separating gains from losses Shackle also preceded ideas found in Kahneman and Tversky's Prospect Theory (1979) such as framing. Shackle's "reference point" could be viewed as an aspiration level which he referred to as a "neutral outcome." His analysis of gains and losses resulting in a graph is similar to Kahneman and Tversky's S-shaped utility function (Earl & Littleboy, 2014).

Probability and possibility

Shackle rejected the use of probability theory as a way to understand behavior under uncertainty. Acting as a economic philosopher critical of orthodox ideas, and based on his own introspections, Shackle offered the idea of "potential surprise," i.e., how surprised would you be if one of the possibilities occurred. Shackle saw this as more logical and more relevant to individuals who act under conditions of uncertainty. Probability makes sense for an insurance actuary considering an entire population. However, for a single individual probability is irrelevant if the person does not expect the situation to repeat. For an individual an outcome either occurs or does not occur. It does not occur with some probability distribution.

In Shackle's theory a strategy does not have an overall value as do decisions in expected utility (EU) theory. In EU theory all probable outcomes are weighted by their probabilities and summed together. In Shackle's theory a decision maker focuses on only one gain and one loss, and potential surprises are not constrained to add to any particular number. And, unlike probabilities which must sum to 1.0 and where a change in one probability affects the probability of at least one other outcome, a change in the assessment of any possible outcome does not have to affect the assessment of any other possibility. Probabilities are observable whereas possibilities can only be imagined. Probabilities are additive but possibilities are non-additive. Both Shackle (2009) and Leibenstein (1950) developed theories of decision-making which included non-additivity.

VIII Tibor Scitovsky

Tibor Scitovsky, 1910–2002, was born in Hungary and perhaps best known for his writing on the relation between happiness and consumption. This relation was most extensively presented in his 1976 book, The Joyless Economy. The Psychology of Human Satisfaction. Two years prior he published a paper titled, "Are Men Rational or Economists Wrong?" The paper was part of a volume titled *Nations and*

Households in Economic Growth. Essays in Honor of Moses Abramovitz (Scitovsky, 1974). Scitovsky begins the paper pointing out that economics began during the "age of reason" and adopted the rationality postulate as an expression of that age. However, now we are in the "age of unreason" and everyone but economists seems to have come to the conclusion that humans are motivated by irrational drives.

The economists' belief in rationality means that people weigh the benefits and costs of all available alternatives before making a decision, and equating thé MU per $ spent on each good or service. Do humans actually do this? Economists say yes while psychologists say no. Scitovsky says that sometimes the answer is yes and at other times the answer is no. Thus, humans are neither perfectly/wholly rational nor perfectly/wholly irrational. He gives an example of madmen and the insane. They might be irrational doing one or several different things, but from this you cannot infer that they always act as if they were always a madman or insane. Both Katona and Leibenstein wrote extensively about rational behavior occurring sometimes but not all the time. As an example, on a scale of 0 to 1 (100) a human's level of rationality may be 0.1 (10), 0.5 (50), or 0.9 (90), to name but three possibilities.

Money, time, and effort illusions

Scitovsky gibes economists with the question of whether they have ever come across evidence of man's irrationality. The problem with this occurring is that economists are human, and as such they sometimes find and at other times do not find what they are looking for.

However, when it comes to irrational behavior, only rarely do economists find what they are not looking for! In 1974 they were not looking for irrationality. Economists do agree that the money illusion is irrational. It is just about the only accepted exception to the rationality assumption.

Scitovsky then looks at our use of time and effort, referring to them as the "time illusion" and the "effort illusion," concluding in both cases that human behavior cannot be described as rational. Time illusion is the desire for leisure time before knowing how to use it for your own benefit. Effort illusion is about our innate capacity and ability versus what we learn from society. One such innate capacity and ability is that of being physically active. Yet what we learn from society is that the goal of technical and economic progress is a life of ease. Scitovsky says that we first learn about the value of leisure or ease, and the fact that it is a result of technical and economic progress. Only years later when we are addicted to a life of ease, and we begin to experience the effects of higher weight, diabetes and being tired too much of the time, do we realize that we made a mistake. Was too much ease irrational? This is a problem of habit formation, addiction, one which doesn't lend itself easily to the static nature of economic rationality. Are men rational? Not always. Are economists wrong? Sometimes. Humans, in general, and economists in particular are, to use Leibenstein's term, selectively rational.

Efficiency and arousal

In The Joyless Economy. The Psychology of Human Satisfaction, Scitovsky (1992) discusses the effect of arousal on the efficient performance of tasks. The term "efficient performance of tasks" suggests that this type of efficiency is not allocative—market-efficiency. It is much closer to the X-efficiency variety. Scitovsky says that efficiency requires a high enough degree of alertness and attention. Without which decision will not be made and executed properly (Scitovsky, 1992, p. 20). "Attention" is what Leibenstein called "constraint concern," the ability to pay attention to the constraints faced so that efficiency is the result. The relationship between arousal and efficiency is an inverted U: "Efficiency increases with the level of arousal at first, but it declines beyond a certain point" (Scitovsky, 1992). Unfortunately, "The arousal level often fails to provide the right background for efficient action" (Scitovsky, 1992, p. 21). In other words, X-inefficiency exists, not always, but it exists.

The Yerkes-Dodson Law. The Yerkes-Dodson Law shows the relationship between arousal and performance. The relationship is an inverted—U, with more arousal at first increasing performance, and then decreasing performance. It was originally written about in 1908 by two psychologists, Robert M. Yerkes, and John Dillingham Dodson. Leibenstein adapted this relationship between arousal and performance and talked about the relationship between pressure (x-axis) and the quality of decisions (y-axis). Pressure means the pressure from the market, market competition, pressure to survive. A monopolist faces less pressure than a firm in a perfectly competitive market. There is an optimal of pressure which produces the optimal performance, a.k.a. (close to) 100% X-efficient. There are levels of pressure which produce less than 100% rational behavior and less than 100% X-efficiency. Scitovsky calls those environments one of too much comfort. He says that "A good example of excessive comfort is the economy of effort, and the extent to which we economize effort is a striking case of irrational behavior"

(Scitovsky, 1992, p. 154).

Rationality in economics

Simon and the others wrote about the cognitive limits and the procedures used by individuals. Scitovsky's interest was more on the motivations and goals of choices. In The Joyless' Economy Scitovsky said that "…rational behavior as pictured by the economist and actual behavior as observed and explained in terms of the psychologist's motivating forces are not at all the same thing" (Scitovsky, 1992, p. 65). Are people ever rational in the economist's sense? Identical with other behavioral economists such as Simon, Katona, and Leibenstein, Scitovsky says that we are rational, selectively rational, meaning we are rational sometimes, at other times not. "Economists usually picture the consumer as rationally weighing the merits of the available alternatives before making a choice… Sometimes that is what happens, but sometimes it is not" (Scitovsky, 1992, p. 72).

Elegance vs Evidence

Camerer (1998) in a wonderfully titled article, "Behavioral Economics and Nonrational Organizational Decision Making," gives three examples of how some economists, such as Becker and Murphy, have defended "elegant theories as anomalous evidence piles up" (p. 55).

In the case of Becker and Murphy, regardless of how elegant their theories of "rational addiction," they cannot "easily explain regrettable addictions" (Camerer, 1998). Scitovsky couldn't have said it any better. Actually, he said it as well, in 1974.

Camerer makes the point that Milton Friedman's F-twist allowed economists such as Friedman, and Becker, and Murphy to ignore critics of, for example, the perfect rationality of economic-man/homo. Economicus. As if, all people are homogenous, perfectly rational.

Friedman's F-twist is not relevant for the purposes of this book. Examining, attacking economic man is not for the purpose of making the assumptions of economic models more realistic. With economic-man out of the way we can ask different research questions, such as, are their (in)efficiencies other than allocative (in)efficiency? We can make use of experiments, once so looked down upon in economics because "we don't care what people say, we only care what they do." We can extend neoclassical economics. Or replace it. But, if behavioral economists believe that we can measure or detect rationality by people sitting at a computer terminal allocating widgets between themselves and another person, then behavioral economics will eventually fail.

Certainly, many pre-Kahneman and Tversky economists questioned the assumption of full rationality, economic-man, homo economicus. The economists included in this chapter, plus the "Big 3" are only some of the "it didn't just happen overnight gang." The next several chapters are about Harvey Leibenstein, his research before X-efficiency theory, X-efficiency theory itself, and much of the empirical evidence on the x-istence of X-efficiency.

IX Final comments on this chapter, and looking ahead to chapters

Similar to the "Big 3" these first generation behavioral economists also helped knock homo economicus down to size. This group never did experiments about the status quo or any other biases but they wrote about framing, the social context of rationality, dual selves, social norms, and herding, among others. In the Appendix to this Chapter I will try to show how the topics discussed by the "It Didn't Happen Overnight Gang" were also researched by the "new" behavioral economists.

Appendix: Full rationality and the new behavioral economics

Look at Advances in Behavioral Economics, edited by Camerer, Loewenstein, and Rabin (2004). The papers in this excellent volume give the impression of having little in common with the papers of the pre-Kahneman and Tversky economists, a.k.a. the first generation behavioral economists. Even when the topics are the same, the papers appear to be "distant cousins" at best. The methodologies are different, the new group uses experiments which include empirical testing of their theories. The old group were developing theories. However, these differences is why behavioral economists are referred to as "old" and "new," not why the pre-K&T group aren't behavioral economists. Behavioral economics is, excuse the expression, a state of mind about economics. A state of mind which says that something is missing or incomplete in the economics as we know it. Katona knew this when he developed psychological economics, a.k.a., behavioral economics. Leibenstein knew it when he wrote about consumer demand, and X-efficiency theory. Simon knew it when he developed his theories of bounded rationality and satisficing. The purpose of this chapter is to show that the ideas on rationality written about by the "old" group were also written about later by the "new" group behavioral economists.

I need to be clear again about some things. The work done by the "old" behavioral economists do not resemble that of the "new" group. The point is that the "old" group wrote about topics similar to those written about by the "new" group. The methods used by both groups are different from each other. The old group by and large did not say this is herding behavior, or this is gift exchange, etc. But reading their works closely or between the lines and you can see the topics written about by the new group. This is all that I am claiming. For whatever reason, maybe it is the sophisticated-anthropomorphic sin which Paul Samuelson wrote about. Whatever it is, the first generation behavioral economists have been largely ignored. And I assert that this comes at the expense of behavioral economics. We either don't know our own history or we ignore it.

The first generation built the door and put the sign on it: Behavioral Economics, Enter Here. But because they didn't know the secret handshake, the security guard at the door wouldn't let them in. They were left with what Marshall called one of the greatest assets an economist could have, imagination. They couldn't imagine behavioral economics, understanding the behavior of human beings as we find them in this world, with homo economicus, as the main character. They couldn't imagine that humans, a.k.a. homo-sociologicus, make decisions independent of the decisions of all others. We are neither Dr. Spock or Robinson Cruscoe. They also couldn't imagine that human beings had one "big" unified Self within themselves which created harmony at every step of their lives. Rather, the Self was divided, creating tensions and "divided loyalties" within the individual.

Humans are not homo economicus

"Old" behavioral economics

XE theory is based on the assumption that individuals are selectively rational rather than homo economicus, or perfectly rational. In XE theory, rationality is seen as a variable ranging from 1.0—perfectly rational—to 0.0. James March, in his 1978 article, "Bounded Rationality, Ambiguity, and the Engineering of Choice" said that rational choice involves guessing, one guess about future preferences and the second about future consequences. But, humans are not very good guesses! Hence, rationality is limited compared to homo economicus. Rationality is also a myth which helps makes sense of our experiences and answers the question, "why did you do what you did."

Katona believed that humans are homo economicus only when they are faced with enough pressure to be willing to consider costs and benefits. Katona says that most of the time we are "ununderstandable." Shackle wrote about "unknowledge," the existence of "unknown unknowns." He believed that humans are satisficers not maximizers (rational). And, of course, Herbert Simon said that rationality is bounded. In fact, all of the economists mentioned in this chapter rejected the assumption of homo economicus. This rejection became more common as time went on.

Gabriel Tarde rejected the assumption that humans have "unrestricted" rationality, and believed that economic-man is a "mutilation" of a real human. And he considered economic-man as neither necessary nor sufficient to explain economic behavior. Ken Arrow says much of the same thing in "Rationality of Self and Others in an Economic System" (Arrow, 1986). He says that "It seems to be asserted that a theory of the economy must be based on rationality, as a matter of principle. Otherwise, there can be no theory" (Arrow, 1986, p. 201). He continues, "Not only is it possible to devise complete models of the economy on hypotheses other than rationality, but in fact virtually every practical theory of macroeconomics in partly so based" (Arrow, 1986, p. 202). Nelson and Winter, Scitovsky, and Boulding, believed that rationality is selective or bounded, and that humans are satisficers. Duesenberry believed in selective rationality, and dual selves.

Non-maximizing behavior

Related to the idea that people are not perfectly rational is the idea that people are not always maximizing because the latter is unrealistic. Selten's 1962 paper with Sauermann on the "aspiration adaptation theory of the firm" depicts managers as pursuing targets rather than profit maximization. Nelson and Winter (1973) state unequivocally that firms use decision rules which are not maximizing. Nelson and Winter, Leibenstein and Katona believe that humans maximize when the cost of non-maximizing behavior reaches a critical level. Simon's theory of bounded rationality which became the basis for a large number of publications speaks for itself.[a] Shackle in 1940 wrote about the satisficing/aspiration criteria for decision making.

A central anomaly of both X-efficiency and behavioral economics in general is that individuals are not perfectly rational. Those questioning the homo economicus assumption of perfect rationality are now a virtual whose-who in economics. To name but a few: Rabin (1998), Shleifer (2000), Mullainathan (1998), Mullainathan and Thaler (2000), Akerlof (2002), Hogarth and Reder (1987), and Aumann and Sorin (1989).

"New" behavioral economics

Perhaps the belief that humans are not always fully rational can be (efficiently) found under one cover, Rational Choice. The Contrast Between Economics and Psychology, edited by Robin Hogarth and Melvin Reder. There are chapters by Arrow, Kahneman and Tversky, Thaler, Herbert Simon, and others. Others commenting on the papers include Sidney Winter, Richard Zeckhauser, and Robert Shiller.

In "Maps of Bounded Rationality. Psychology for Behavioral Economics," Kahneman (2003) said that one thing which he and Amos attempted to do was develop an understanding of bounded rationality by understanding the differences between the systematic biases of humans and the optimal beliefs of rational agents. Most decisions, according to Kahneman are made intuitively, and while intuition can be a powerful and accurate guide for decision making it also is accompanied by the chance of biased decision making. Kahneman developed the idea of System 1 and System 2 to discuss the costs and benefits of intuition and logic. When Kahneman won the Nobel Prize in 2002, the Nobel Committee said, in part, that Kahneman and Tversky showed how human "judgments...systematically departs from the kind of rationality postulated in traditional economic theory." The main point is that Kahneman was a powerful advocate for human rationality being limited.

Rationality, what we know, remember, and notice

Matthew Rabin, in his excellent and comprehensible article, "Psychology and Economics" (1998), points out that people depart from perfect rationality when faced with the uncertainty of what we know. It is the use of heuristics which turn difficult problems into simpler problems which offer benefits but also contains costs in leading us to make systematic errors of judgment. Be that as it may, people depart from perfect rationality. Economists cling to the notion that experts repeating tasks will come closer to full rationality than studies by psychologists indicate. As reasonable as this may be, Rabin says that economists will be disappointed by the ability for experts to reduce or eliminate the biases which take us away from full rationality.

Mullainathan, in his 2002 article, "A Memory-Based Model of Bounded Rationality," concludes that repeating tasks may improve memory and decision-making rationality even among naïve decision-makers. However, both naïve and sophisticated decision makers deviate from full rationality. Another article addressing the issue of memory and rationality is that of Aumann and Sorin's 1989 article, "Cooperation and Bounded Recall." It begins with the authors asking whether the principle of cooperation emanate from the principles of individual rationality such as strategic (Nash) equilibrium? The authors say, No. They have a unique "take" on rationality. They say that "rationality in games depends critically on irrationality... rationality needs a 'noisy,' irrational environment; it cannot grow in sterile soil, cannot feed on itself only" (Aumann & Sorin, 1989, pp. 37–38). Their conclusion is rationality and cooperation can exist "when the environment is forgetful - when people in general, do not bear grudges - then there is ground to hope that rational agents will cooperate" (Aumann & Sorin, 1989, p. 38).

What we remember from the past may have a corollary in what we notice in the present. Noticing is the topic of a 2014 publication by Mullainathan, along with Rema Hanna (listed as the first author), and Joshua Schwartzstein, "Learning Through Noticing: Theory and Evidence From a Field Experiment." It expresses very well the difference between the first gen behavioral economists and those who came later. The colon in the title is more than a colon. It is the dividing line between the old and the new. The first part, Learning Through Noticing. This includes "Leibenstein 101." First, the authors use this model to show that even people with a lot of experience may be constantly off the production frontier because they fail to notice important aspects of the data they have. A minor point; the orthodox view is that it is firms not individuals which are constantly off the production frontier.

Why are firms, or individuals, off the production frontier? Because "many production functions are not known ex ante" (Hanna, Mullainathan, & Schwartzstein, 2014, p. 1311). Production functions are learned from experience. Being off of the function or frontier is used to estimate X-inefficiency. Second, the authors sound a lot like Leibenstein explaining X-efficiency in his original article. The authors state that in order to maximize product quality managers must do a variety of things including "...exactly how to monitor worker effort, what to look for to determine whether a machine needs preventive maintenance, whether to worry about the cleanliness of the shop floor, and so on" (pp. 1342–1343).

The second part, "Theory and Evidence From a Field Experiment." The first gen people developed theories but did not follow it up with empirical evidence. Leibenstein engaged in a gedankenexperiment, but not a field experiment. Mullainathan and his co-authors tested their model among a sample of seaweed farmers in Indonesia, who fail to produce with cost minimizing input combinations because of a failure to notice. They use a series of surveys to estimate the extent of non-optimizing behavior. Finally, they state that their findings help explain why "some demonstrations or agricultural extension activities are ineffective or only moderately effective in the long run" (p. 1314). They cite Leibenstein's 1966 article which included the results of some agricultural extension programs, and Kilby's (1962) article, also cited in Leibenstein's 1966 paper.

This paper by Mullainathan and his co-authors is a really good expression of the new behavioral economics. What follows here in no way reduces its value as a really good expression of new behavioral economics. Part of their theory is based on ideas of Simon and Leibenstein, a fact which Mullainathan and his co-authors freely acknowledge. Second, I have spoken with many very good academic economists who publish articles in the tradition of the new behavioral economics and in good journals. Yet, they know almost nothing about anything or anyone in behavioral economics before Kahneman and Tversky. I understand why. Still, we should know our own history.

Macro and rationality

George Akerlof' Noble lecture, "Behavioral Macroeconomics and Macroeconomic Behavior," begins with his "dream" of developing macroeconomic theory in the "spirit" of Keynes's General Theory. Keynes's spirit include a whole host of behavioral concepts, i.e., psychological and sociological factor, such as "cognitive bias, reciprocity, fairness, herding, and social status" (Akerlof, 2002, p. 411). Akerlof spent much of the space discussing rationality in the context of near rationality and near irrationality. But he also says that a "major empirical finding that casts doubt on the rationality of the stock market is the equity premium puzzle" (Akerlof, 2002, p. 425). The return to stocks has been so much higher than that for bonds since the early 19th century that "rejection of rationality is duck soup..." (Akerlof, 2002). In particular it leads to "rejecting rational consumption behavior" (Akerlof, 2002). Shleifer (2000), in Inefficient Markets. An Introduction to Behavioral Finance, speaking about the Efficient Markets Hypothesis, says that "To begin, it is difficult to sustain the case that people in general, and investors in particular, are fully rational" (Shleifer, 2000, p. 10). For example, many investors trade on "noise" rather than on information. They don't diversify, they sell winners and hold onto losers. They are too slow in changing their beliefs when new evidence becomes available. And they use heuristics such as representativeness. In short they behave as if they are uniformed, and they are subject to cognitive biases. Shleifer continues, "Investors' deviations from the maxims of economic rationality turn out to be highly pervasive and systematic" (Shleifer, 2000).

Sometimes, winning means losing

Thaler's example of the winner's curse is the outcome of oil firms bidding for the drilling rights to a piece of land. The winner of the bidding process is "cursed" because their winning bid exceeds the value of the rights to drill. The winning firm loses money. Thaler explains that "The winner's curse cannot occur if all the bidders are rational... so evidence of a winner's curse in market settings would constitute an anomaly" (Thaler, 1988, p. 192). X-efficiency theory and the Winner's Curse are consistent with each other in that both recognize that people can be less than perfectly rational and that they make systematic errors. On the other hand, as Thaler stated the winner's curse can be investigated by behavioral economics, i.e., micro theory and cognitive psychology. On the other hand, Leibenstein never attempted to make it so amenable. In fact, he wanted to see what limited rationality would mean for economic theory.

Near and quasi rationality only matters in near and quasi horse-shoes

In 1985 Akerlof and Yellen wrote a paper about "near" rationality in the context of wage and price behavior. In it they state that firms may not be optimizing but the losses will not be large, hence the word "near." In 1985 Thomas Russell and Richard Thaler wrote an article about "quasi" rationality. Since rationality is an assumption rather than a fact there is little evidence as to what would happen if people are not rational. The authors state unequivocally that "non-maximizing, non-perfectly, rational behavior is both 'common and systematic'" (Russell & Thaler, 1985, p. 1080). Second, that the notion that only rational behavior will survive is correct perhaps only in highly efficient markets such as financial markets. Third, and perhaps "channeling" Leibenstein, the authors state that "Only in less than fully efficient markets is there any penalty to quasi rationality" (Russell & Thaler, 1985, p. 1081). Russell and Thaler state that there may be little literature about the effects of non-rational behavior. However, one piece of literature was written in 1966, by Leibenstein. You can win at horse-shows if you throw the horse shoe and it hands close to the short pole. But in economics, anything less than 100% rational is, less than 100% rational. Katona, Leibenstein, and Simon called it irrational, selective rationality, and bounded rationality, respectively. Simon's position can be interpreted as meaning that given that our rationality is bounded, we maximize. Katona and Leibenstein didn't couch their idea of rationality so that it can be squeezed into a model of complete rationality.

A famous gadfly prefers satisficing heuristics

In Gigerenzer and Goldstein (1996)—Gigerenzer being a famous gadfly—the authors argue that fast and frugal heuristics which are satisficing heuristics perform better than maximizing decision making. The former assume that humans make decisions given limited time and cognitive capacity, whereas the latter assumes that the human mind is a Laplacean Demon. The Laplacean Demon is a hypothetical someone who knows the exact speed and position of every atom in the universe. The Demon can, therefore, have complete knowledge of the entire past and future of every atom. The Demon is omniscient. Gigerenzer and Goldstein discuss take the best heuristic, take the last heuristic, and the minimalist heuristic, all of which are known as "one-reason decision making." The authors test the heuristics against maximizing decision making and report that satisficing outperforms maximizing with respect to the speed and accuracy of decision making.[b]

Satisficing. Bordley and Licalzi (2000) define satisficing as a type of "take the first" heuristic as a way of meeting a target rather than maximizing a utility function. Byron (1998), in his philosophically focused article "Satisficing and Optimality" says that there exists a "satisficing conception of rationality" as well as optimizing conceptions of rationality. Hence satisficing can be maximizing. Kaufman (1990) develops a model of satisficing which integrates a needs-based theory of motivation and management's objective function. Firms are profit-maximizers until they earn adequate profits are earned which assure the survival of management. After that is attained the firm is willing to sacrifice profits for "higher order" needs. The model allows for both satisficing and utility maximizing in the same model.

Satisficing

Schwartz et al. (2002) used a sample of 1747 students in an introductory psychology class from Swarthmore College, U.C., Riverside, and the Univ. of British Columbia. Other participants were health professionals at a seminar, mostly nurses; people in a train station, and; people waiting to be called for jury duty. The authors used two scales, one measuring the extent to which a person is either a maximizer or a satisficer, and another measuring regret. Using these two instruments the authors report that as compared with satisficers, maximizers (1) regret more; (2) are less happy, less optimistic, less satisfied with their life, and have less self-esteem; (3) engage more in social comparisons; (4) are less satisfied with the results of an ultimatum bargaining game; (5) achieve more but are less satisfied with their relative achievements, and; (6) searching for the best outcome creates dismay about the opportunity costs. The overall message from the Schwartz study is that not only is being a maximizer virtually impossible, but not being a maximizer is a good thing, especially if you want to live a happy life!

Making irrational decisions

In 2003 Roy Baumeister outlined the reasons people make "irrational" decisions. The first reason is that people deliberately harm themselves. Freud and others have written that we have a "death wish," a desire to suffer at our own hands. Second, people make self-defeating tradeoffs, those where the long run costs exceed the long run benefits. We procrastinate, place too much salience on the short run benefits and not enough emphasis on long run costs. Third, we pursue self-defeating strategies for pursuing goal-oriented behaviors. Why do we do these things? First emotional stress, Second, in wanting to impress others we cloud our own judgment and make poor decisions. It is a failure of making an independent decision. Third, our inability to have self-control. Fourth, decision fatigue. And fifth, we have a need to belong to a group or "tribe," but when we can't belong to a group or tribe we can begin acting irrationally.

Leibenstein before X-efficiency theory

5

Harvey Leibenstein is perhaps best known for his theory of X-efficiency. The theory is micro-behavioral. More specifically, it is a study in industrial organization, modified by elements of psychology and sociology. More specifically, how product market competition affects the effort level of the members of the firm and hence the firm's costs and output. And more specifically how close they are to producing on their cost and output frontiers. The theory of X-efficiency first appeared in the June 1966 issue of the *American Economic Review*. The theory states that a greater amount of product market competition will pressure firm members to produce with more effort, given social norms, so that the firm is producing closer to their frontiers. At least 200 empirical studies from all parts of the world and using data from many industries supports the theory.

However, Leibenstein wasn't a flash-in-the-pan behavioral economist of the mid-1960s. Leibenstein also engaged in micro-behavioral in his 1950 Journal of Political Economy article on consumer behavior when consumers are not independent of others. He included in his study phenomena such as bandwagon or herding behavior, snob behavior, and conspicuous consumption. His 1954 and 1957 books also challenged key assumptions of neoclassical theory. Harvey was a behavioral economist from the graduate school days at Princeton.

Both the 1950 and 1966 articles questioned a basic assumption of orthodox neoclassical theory. The 1950 article questioned the assumption of independent behavior of consumers, and this makes it behavioral. What are the implications if and when consumers are not independent of each other? The implications are that the elasticity of the demand curve is more elastic when the behavior is of the bandwagon type, and less elastic when it reflects the behavior of snobs. In the case of conspicuous consumption the demand curve may actually slope upward to the right.

The 1966 article asked about the implications if and when decision-makers are not completely rational. He abandoned a basic assumption of human behavior, the assumption of complete rationality. The implication is that there is a form of (in) efficiency which is not of the allocative variety but a form which was mysterious (to Leibenstein in 1966). The mysteriousness led Leibenstein to call it X-efficiency. The inefficiency was not about the deadweight welfare loss—$[\Delta Q\ (\Delta P)]/2$—but about the effects of competitive pressure on costs (and output). As it turns out the implication is important because X-inefficiency is a multiple of allocative inefficiency, perhaps 0.04 GDP vs 0.001 GDP to 0.0001 GDP.

In the 1950s Leibenstein wrote not only about micro-behavioral, but also about macro-behavioral. Most of his writings in the 1950s were macro-behavioral—efficiency wages and unemployment, economic growth and development, population and demographic changes. In every case he questioned the orthodox theory. Some say

The Beginnings of Behavioral Economics. https://doi.org/10.1016/B978-0-12-815289-8.00005-8

that he was a heterodox economist. I say that he was a neoclassical theorist who saw the shortcomings of that theory and developed theories based on real human behavior which were at odds with the neoclassical description of human behavior. He was neither a "neoclassical denier" nor a believer that neoclassical theory was applicable to all human behavior under all circumstances. His theory of rationality was that of "selective" rationality; rationality varied from complete rationality to something less than complete rationality. His beliefs were similar, in the same "ball-park" as Alfred Marshall in his 1885 book, The Present Position of Economics. In this book he talks about the beliefs of classical economists towards human behavior. He points out their mistake in thinking that everyone responds the same way to their circumstances. Speaking of the classical economists he said that "The people whom they knew were chiefly city men; and they took it for granted tacitly that other Englishmen were very much like those they knew in the city. They were aware that the inhabitants of other countries had peculiarities of their own; but they regarded such differences, when they thought of them at all, as superficial..." (Marshall, 1885, p. 15). Leibenstein's emphasis shifted significantly from predominantly macro to micro beginning in 1960. In this chapter I will discuss his macro-behavioral and micro-behavioral work pre-X-efficiency theory.

I Efficiency wages

According to George Akerlof and Janet Yellen, Harvey Leibenstein wrote the original article on efficiency wage models and development economics (Akerlof & Yellen, 1986, p. 2). In their 1986 book, *Efficiency Wage Models of the Labor Market* (1986), George Akerlof and Janet Yellen, say that since the Great Depression the most important problem in macroeconomics is (involuntary) unemployment. Efficiency wage models, they assert, can explain cyclical and involuntary unemployment. Even with involuntary unemployment firms will pay a wage in excess of the equilibrium wage because it can reduce its production costs. This can occur because effort and hence productivity are a function of the (real) wage. Paying a wage in excess of the equilibrium wage has advantages which reduce production costs.[a] First, shirking is reduced; workers work with more effort. Second, labor turnover is reduced; turnover costs are reduced. Third, the adverse selection effect, i.e., the firm will be able to hire workers with higher ability. And, fourth, higher wages paid by the firm is reciprocated by the workers expending more effort. This is Akerlof's "gift exchange" model.

The first article on efficiency wage models in Akerlof and Yellen's (1986) book is Leibenstein's (1957) article, "The Theory of Underemployment in Densely Populated Backward Area." The article is a chapter in Leibenstein's (1957) book, *Economic Backwardness and Economic Growth*. In this article/chapter Leibenstein shows the relationships between wages, nutrition, and health problems, and; between labor productivity and real wages. Akerlof and Yellen assert that research has also shown the relevance of Leibenstein's theory for more developed economies.

[a] For example see Altman (1988).

In his 1957 article Leibenstein discusses how (disguised) unemployment is affected by the wage-productivity relationship. Disguised unemployment means that it is possible to reduce the labor force by some amount, *reorganize* in some manner the remaining employees without adding to any other inputs, and find that output does not fall. The process of reorganizing labor became a central element in the empirical work cited in Leibenstein's 1966 article on X-efficiency theory. Those workers which are now unemployed would be willing to work for a lower wage but the firm will not pay a lower wage because of its disadvantages, i.e., shirking, higher labor turnover, etc.

Efficiency wage models, including Leibenstein's model, contains a variable for effort. In these models productivity is a function of the wage rate where the two are positively related with each other. Lower wages will reduce effort and output and raise unit costs. The production function shows that output depends upon employment (n) and the level of effort (e) which itself depends on the real wage (w). The wage which minimizes labor cost per efficiency unit, i.e., output per worker per hour, or labor productivity per hour, is the efficiency wage.

In Leibenstein's model, the wage-productivity relationship has two parts. First, the relation between income or wages, and nutrition, and second; the relation between nutrition and productivity. As to the first relationship, employment is affected by work effort. Effort is determined by that person's energy level, health and vitality. These depend on his level of consumption, and hence income, and the nutrition value of the food consumed. Energy levels and income levels can be positively related with each other.

As to the second relationship he reports on numerous studies in Germany that a 21% increase in caloric intake, output rises by almost 50%. Among construction workers in Central America an "adequate" caloric intake increased worker efficiency threefold. Reorganizing labor (and other inputs) was a central point of his 1966 article. In both the empirical work cited in the 1966 article and in the data above, relatively small changes in the reorganization of labor, and/or other inputs, that is, changes in the firm's choice architecture, led to relatively larger changes in output (and cost). In 1966 as part of his original article on X-efficiency theory Leibenstein made the role of labor effort vis-à-vis labor time as one of the main ingredient in the determination of X-efficiency.

Effort also determines society's "stock of knowledge," which can't be separated from the effort put forth by the human "carriers," the people that interpret and communicate ideas and experiences to the users of knowledge. This is discussed most often with respect to entrepreneurs. However, Leibenstein says that the human carriers are much more "pervasive" than simply the entrepreneurs.

In Economic Backwardness and Economic Growth, Leibenstein shows the relation between the wage level and productivity using an average product of labor curve (APL). Higher wage payments increase health and hence APL increases for any amount of labor employed. Before the wage increase, 10 employees have an APL of 10. After the wage increase it rises to 15 (Fig. 5.1).

In the 1970s Leibenstein used the prisoner's dilemma to show this relation between wages and productivity as a determinant of X-efficiency. Akerlof discussed this relation between wages and productivity as part of his theory of "gift exchange." Their main points were similar. Akerlof used more abstract, analytical, and mathematical models. Leibenstein, the Marshallian, used mostly diagrams.

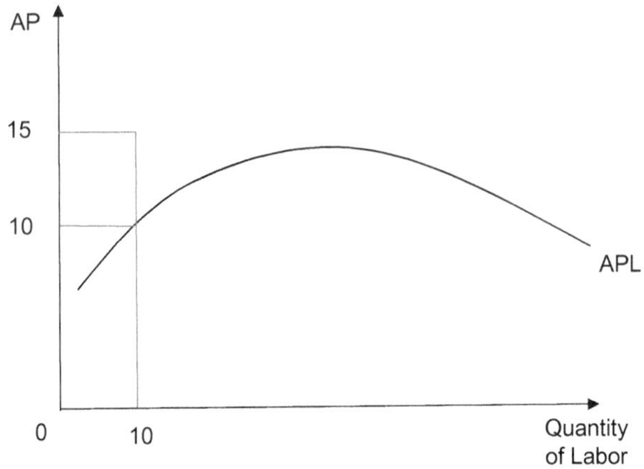

Fig. 5.1 Average product of labor, wages and nutrition.

Critical minimum effort, and zero and non-zero sum games

Higher wages can increase productivity and growth. But, can it create a sustained process of growth? Leibenstein says that the stimulation(s) to growth must be at least of a certain critical minimum size. The critical minimum size must be large enough to pull people out of their state of "inertia," or their inert areas in order that they begin to use available resources in a productive way. This is determined by attitudes toward risk taking, profits making, and monetary gains, the responses to incentives, and effort.

Effort also determines societies "stock of knowledge," which can't be separated from the human "carriers," the people that interpret and communicate ideas and experiences to the users of knowledge. This is discussed most often with respect to entrepreneurs. However, Leibenstein says that the human carriers are much more "pervasive" than simply the entrepreneurs. Leibenstein quotes Kaldor in the latter's 1954 paper, "Characteristics of Economic Development," who said that changing attitudes toward risk taking and profit-making is a major determinant of economic development. He also quotes the I.L.O. in their 1947 volume, *The Economic Background of Social Policy Including Problems of Industrialization*, where it says that a lack of enterprise is the most important explanation for a low level of economic development. The critical minimum effort must become embedded in the consciousness of a large number of people, and not only the entrepreneurs. In other words, a contagion among the population must occur. The contagion must result in economic expansion appearing rapid enough so that the critical minimum effort is achieved and the low level economic trap is transcended.

Profit-making and income earning opportunities are essential to growth. However, there are two types of such opportunities. In order to explain the difference Leibenstein uses terms from the revolutionary book of Morgenstern and Von Neumann, The Theory of Games and Economic Behavior. The terms are zero-sum (games) and non-zero-sum (games). The zero-sum opportunities allow people to make profits or income by exploiting others. Profits or income are redistributed from one person or group to another person or group. There isn't any net gain in national income from zero-sum opportunities. Non-zero-sum opportunities result in the creation of and the marshaling of resources. There may be a distributional effect but the main result is a net increase in national income. In a similar vein, zero-sum incentives lead to the holding of wealth rather than the (re)investment of wealth. Positive-sum incentives lead to an increase in aggregate output. In lesser developed economies social approval is very important and it is common for prestige to be associated with the holding of land. There is risk to the holding of land but the risk are relatively small and they are both known and certain (Leibenstein, 1957, p. 115).

Even in 1957, Leibenstein who was a neoclassical economist, was questioning neoclassical theory. He remarks that neoclassical theory market transactions result in mutually beneficial gains for both buyers and sellers and increase the national product. He adds that "counter to received theory" (p. 117) not all activities are non-zero sum. However, zero-sum activities exist.

Population and CME

There is another piece to an economy's CME: population. In 1954 Leibenstein published, A Theory of Economic-Demographic Development, in which he discusses the concept and relevance of a theory of optimum population. Leibenstein begins the book by stating that whereas economic theory is interested in the equilibrium conditions of a system, his interest is finding the conditions in which the near-Malhusian states are in disequilibrium, i.e., unstable. This is because Malthusian equilibrium is undesirable for the purposes of economic development. Economic theory's use of maximization is nothing more than a "rule of selection between alternatives" (Leibenstein, 1954, p. 140). Is the maximization principle appropriate for demographic-economic models? Under some conditions in which economic considerations are of utmost importance, the use of the maximization principle "may be an adequate rule of selection which may serve as a first approximation" (Leibenstein, 1954). One problem with maximization is that it cannot account for important determinants of (changes in) fertility and family size. Hence, "a rule of selection that would not account for such factors would appear to be inadequate" (Leibenstein, 1954). This does not mean that Leibenstein rejected outright the maximization or the rationality postulates per-se. What he rejected is maximization and rationality as the only forms of behavior. What he rejected became a central core of behavioral economics. That doesn't make him a forerunner of behavioral economics, but a first generation behavioral economist.

What is the optimal population for breaking free of the Malthusian trap? A "less often noticed" assumption of optimum population theory is that "people make the best use of the given resources and knowledge..." (Leibenstein, 1954, p. 174). That is, optimum population theory assumes that X-efficiency is perfect (X-inefficiency is zero). An optimum population means that collective action and individual choices cannot create a level of population which is preferred to the existing population. Leibenstein discusses the optimum population by discussing how many degrees of freedom there are in the equations used to determine the optimum population. If there are no degrees of freedom, there are the same number of equations and the number of unknowns, then an optimum has no policy meaning. The concept of an optimum may satisfy "idle curiosity but can hardly be of any real use" (Leibenstein, 1954, p. 182). In such a system there is only one population size and one population path consistent with the values of the variables. If the system has two or more degrees of freedom then any given population size is consistent with more than one economic state. Collective or social action can now determine not only the size of the population but the size of other variables. Hence collective or social action is necessary for the concept of an optimal population size to be relevant. In summary, the concept of an optimum is not always relevant.

In his 1957 book, *Economic Backwardness and Economic Growth*, Leibenstein claimed that "when it comes to having children, fully rational behavior, equating costs and benefits at the margin, applies only to decisions about the *n*th child. Fully rational behavior does not apply to every aspect of reproductive activity" (Leibenstein, 1957, p. 460).

The role of the entrepreneur

The zero-sum and non-zero-sum opportunities and incentives are felt and acted upon most strongly by the entrepreneurial class. What are the characteristics and qualities of an entrepreneur? Leibenstein lists four. First, they have the ability to seek the information leading to the discovery of investment opportunities. Second, They have access to the necessary resources and the ability to marshall those resources for the benefit of the firm. Third, they can promote the firm's activities. And fourth, they can organize the firm, and if they choose, assign responsibility for certain activities to others. This description of an entrepreneur is fairly common. In his 1978 book, *General X-Efficiency Theory and Economic Development*, Leibenstein's offers a different view of entrepreneurship. In neoclassical theory when markets are competitive, markets function well, production and cost functions are complete, and firms are producing on their production and cost frontiers. In this environment entrepreneurship is routine and not particularly important. This is probably why entrepreneurship is absent in much of the economic literature.

Where markets are incomplete, production and cost functions are not well defined and firms are not working on their frontier, entrepreneurship is of the innovational variety. In Leibenstein's model of economic development, entrepreneurship is important because markets are incomplete, etc. In economic theory, a complete market, also known as an Arrow-Debreu market, has two characteristics. First, transactions costs are negligible, which means that people possess perfect information. And second, there is a price for every commodity regardless of the existing supply and demand conditions, i.e., every state of the world. A complete insurance market is one where people can buy insurance to protect themselves against every possible future state of the world in every possible moment in the future. Kenneth Arrow won the Nobel Prize in 1972, and Gerard Debreu won the Nobel Prize in 1983 for their work on the theory of complete markets applied to general equilibrium. An incomplete market is one in which prices do not exist for every commodity, and not all commodities are available to be traded. An incomplete market typically fails to make the optimal allocation of assets. That is, the First Welfare Theorem no longer holds. The First Welfare Theorem states that a Walrasian equilibrium leads to a Pareto efficient allocation of resources.

If the market is incomplete the equilibrium is a constrained suboptimal equilibrium. Why would a market be incomplete? Economic theory identifies the reasons to include asymmetric information between agents, and when institutions required to guarantee that contracts are enforced are absent. When this occurs then some commodities will neither be bought nor sold.

Leibenstein's description of an incomplete market are different. An incomplete market means that using inputs are difficult because of the existence of obstacles. One such obstacle is that some inputs are available but doing other things. Someone(s) must have an imagination which can see alternative uses of these inputs. A second is that some inputs are not for sale at any known price. Third, some products and inputs are unmarketed. One such unmarketed input is knowledge. Fourth, some inputs, for example financial inputs, may be available to some but not to others. This because obtaining finance is more about family connections than the willingness to pay the going interest rate.

Markets are incomplete, in some cases completely absent. This led Leibenstein to view the economy as a net made up of nodes and pathways. The nodes are the organizations which receive inputs, and the households, which receive consumer goods. The pathways are the supply lines by which organizations receive the inputs and/or the outputs (including consumer goods to households). In a well-functioning market inhabited by X-efficient firms, the net is complete without any holes or tears. The pathways are not affected by "potholes," and the nodes do not discriminate against any other node. But in the "real world" the net has holes and tears. The entrepreneur becomes an "input completer" and a "gap filler," working between markets due to the tears and holes. If inputs are not readily available then the entrepreneur marshalls resources to make them available. As a gap filler the entrepreneur fixes the tears and eliminates the holes. They are an "intermarket operator" (Leibenstein, 1978, p. 41). "They go where no man has gone before."

II Similarities in Akerlof's and Leibenstein's behavioral economics

Akerlof and Leibenstein agreed about things such as human rationality, group, and employer-employee relations. They agreed that the maximization assumption can lead to a denial of phenomena. In Leibenstein's case the phenomena denied is non-allocative or X-efficiency. Akerlof didn't believe in homo economicus. He thought it "difficult" to believe in homo economicus as the norm of human behavior. Economists were behind the notion that homo economicus was the norm. Akerlof says this about economists' beliefs:

> *... economists have accorded the assumption of rational self-interested behavior unwarranted ritual purity, while alternative assumptions—... that psychological or sociological considerations matter, or that, heaven forbid, they act downright irrationally at times—have been accorded corresponding ritual impurity*
>
> *(Akerlof, 1987, p. 137).*

Akerlof says that any theory which is to fit the real world must be based on the assumption that humans are not homo economicus, fully rational. He adds that "It would be simply unscientific to proceed otherwise" (Akerlof, 1987, p. 138). Assuming homo economicus has resulted in economists not being able to adequately explain fairness and equity in the setting of wages, the money illusion, business cycles, and involuntary unemployment.

Akerlof and Leibenstein were similar in their rejection of homo economicus. But Akerlof utilized the idea of near rationality, Leibenstein incorporated selective rationality into his X-efficiency theory. Selective rationality means that people are simply not always perfectly rational. If perfect rationality has a value of 1.0, then selective rationality means that sometimes people may be 1.0, but at others they may be 0.75, 0.5, 0.25. Near rationality means that shifting from near rational to fully rational does not lead to significant gains in efficiency. Akerlof seems to have found it reassuring that models based on perfect rationality hold their significance when perfect rationality is replaced by near rationality. Leibenstein seems to have found it reassuring that selective rationality had significant implications, and that it could be tested empirically.

Can business cycles by explained by near-rational behavior? Akerlof says, yes. Keynes' theories of consumption, investment and money demand are based on near rational behavior. Inertia which is based on transactions costs and affects wages and prices are also based on near rational behavior. Akerlof uses a mathematical model and the envelope theorem to show that near rationality may not cost firms much, but the macro effects create business cycles. Leibenstein wasn't very good at mathematics. He once told me that not having more math skills was perhaps the largest mistake he made in his professional career.

And one big difference

Akerlof wanted more realistic behavioral assumptions in a model that showed no significant impact on the efficiency. Leibenstein wasn't trying to be reassured about neoclassical theory.

In Leibenstein's 1978 book, General X-Efficiency Theory and Economic Development (Leibenstein, 1978), Leibenstein discusses how work norms and incomplete contracts and effort discretion may result in involuntary unemployment. Akerlof acknowledged Leibenstein 1978 book in his 1982 paper, "Labor Contracts as Partial Gift Exchange," Akerlof says that his 1982 paper "carries further the work of Leibenstein." Akerlof's paper included 10 pages of mathematical modeling. Did this carry further Leibenstein's work? In at least one sense it does: economists as a group respect formal mathematical modeling. We take mathematical modeling more seriously than simply the spoken word. In the spirit of Alfred Marshall, Leibenstein relied more exclusively on the written word and graphical analysis, in coming to many of the same conclusions as did Akerlof. It carries further Leibenstein's work in substance, if not in style.

Akerlof's paper, "The Market for 'Lemons': Quality, Uncertainty and the Market Mechanism" (Akerlof, 1970) is a non-lemon of a paper. It starts out asking why it is difficult doing business in less developed countries, and tries to answer it with an analysis of how imperfect markets and asymmetric information via the new and used car markets affects market transactions and the role of entrepreneurs, in both more and less developed countries. And, he shows how these issues tie together to form an application of Gresham's law. Akerlof does not claim to be providing a theory of entrepreneurship and the effects of imperfect markets and asymmetric information in less developed countries. Leibenstein's General X-Efficiency Theory (1978) provides a behavioral theory. As was often the case, Leibenstein was more of a Marshallian in presentation, more interested in providing an alternative to NCT. Akerlof was more "rigorous" in his presentation and more concerned with integrating NCT with behavioral elements. And Akerlof deservingly won a Nobel Prize for his efforts.

III Social preferences. The psychology and sociology of demand

In 1950, the year Leibenstein published "Bandwagon, Snob, and Veblen Effects In the Theory of Consumer Demand," the theory of consumption was dominated by the Keynesian theory of consumption. The Keynesian consumption function is the relationship between aggregate real consumption expenditure and real national income. Keynes did allow for subjective factors in consumption such as attitudes, expectations, showiness, and overindulgence. However, it was argued that in the aggregate these factors would be canceled out by differences among individuals and hence need not be included in the determination of aggregate consumption.

Milton Friedman developed the permanent income hypothesis in his 1957 book *A Theory of the Consumption Function*. Friedman tries to explain consumption over a lifetime. An individual's consumption at any point in time depends on both current and expected future income. The latter is "permanent income." Modiglinai and Brumberg (1990) developed the life-cycle consumption hypothesis. The hypothesis states that individuals consumption and savings take into account their entire life-cycle. Their intention is to smooth out consumption and savings over their life-cycle so their life-style is stable over time. When they have more income then they need to maintain their life-style they save. James Duesenberry developed the relative income hypothesis. The idea is that a person's level of consumption and saving depends on his income relative to the income of others. And present consumption depends on present absolute and relative income, and by consumption in the past. Specifically, current consumption as a percent of current income depends on present income relative to their past *peak* income. Once you have a lifestyle it is difficult to live at a lower lifestyle.

What all of these theories of consumption have in common is the role of income, whether present or future, absolute of relative. Individuals, individually or collectively, are making decisions about consumption and savings based on income, all of which are relatively easily measured variables. Duesenberry introduces a comparison among people(relative income) as the basis for consumption and savings decisions. By contrast is Leibenstein's theory of consumption. His 1950 paper was written initially for a seminar at Princeton.

Leibenstein's theory consumption is not based on an objective variable such as income—current or expected future income—but on how one person reacts to what he believes that others are doing. So, objectively measured variables such as income are replaced by subjective beliefs, and by *reactions to subjective beliefs*. The inner life of a person was brought closer to a main role in an economic theory. Morgenstern's influence would seem to be clear. Thus, his 1950 paper is an early version of behavioral economics, or if you prefer, economics and psychology.

In his 1950 article, "Bandwagon, Snob, and Veblen Effects In the Theory of Consumer Demand," Leibenstein discusses three cases when a change in price affects quantity demanded and demand itself. Leibenstein refers to the three cases as the bandwagon effect, wanting to be "in style"; the snob effect, the desire to "attain exclusiveness," and; the Veblen effect, displaying your wealth or trying to convince others of your wealth via "conspicuous consumption." All three are cases of the "interpersonal aspects of utility and demand" (Leibenstein, 1950, p. 184), or social influences on consumer behavior. Leibenstein credits his ideas with his Princeton mentor, Oscar Morgenstern, who considered cases when the market demand curves are not horizontal summations of individual demand curves, i.e., there is non-additivity between individual and market demand curves. Therefore, Leibenstein describes the purpose of his article as a "reformulation of some aspects of the static theory of consumers' demand while permitting the relaxation of one of the basic implicit assumptions of the current theory" (Leibenstein, 1950, p. 184). That assumption is the independence among individuals in consumption decisions.

These three cases of the interpersonal aspects of utility and demand were discussed in the literature under three headings: sociology, welfare economics, and pure theory. The sociology of these three cases is most associated with Thorsten Veblen. However, conspicuous consumption was discussed by John Rae in 1905. "Keeping up with the Joneses" was discussed by the 18th century English poet Alexander Pope in 1905, and fashion was discussed by Caroline Foley writing in the Economic Journal in 1893.

The economic welfare approach was used by Reder (1947), A.C. Pigou, J.E. Meade (1977 winner of the Nobel Prize), and John Rae. Reder, in his *Studies in the Theory of Welfare Economics* (1947), said that, interpersonal utility and demand "is rarely, if ever, recognized in discussions of welfare economics" (Leibenstein, 1950, p. 185). Leibenstein limits his discussion of the pure theory approach to Pigou's 1913 article in the *Economic Journal*. In only six pages Pigou tries to work through under what conditions and assumptions additivity of individual demand curves conforms to the facts and when it does not so conform.

Leibenstein defines four important terms for the study of the interpersonal aspects of utility and demand. Functional demand is that part of demand derived from the inherent qualities of the commodity in question. Nonfunctional demand is that part of demand not related to the inherent qualities of the commodity, for example, how much others are buying of the commodity. Speculative demand is how much of a commodity people hold because they expect price to rise in the future. And finally, irrational demand is a "catchall category. It refers to purchases which are neither planned nor calculated but are due to sudden urges, whims, etc., and that serve no rational purpose but that of satisfying whims and desires" (Leibenstein, 1950, p. 189).

In his 1950 article, published in the Quarterly Journal of Economics, and in the context of his discussion of the bandwagon effect, Leibenstein makes a statement which points out how much the economics profession has changed since 1950 with the advent of behavioral economics. He says that "It is not within the competence of the economist to investigate the psychology of this kind of behavior. For our purposes we need only note that such behavior exists and attempt to analyze how such behavior affects the demand function" (Leibenstein, 1950, p. 196).

The bandwagon effect, the result of *herding* or the *imitate the majority* heuristic, represents a phenomena whereby an individual makes decisions based on the decisions of others. Therefore, the bandwagon phenomena occurs when someone(s) believe that others are buying more and as a response they also buy more. This is not a response to a lower price, but a response to others buying more. Therefore, a lower price directly increases quantity demand and indirectly increases demand. And, therefore, the "bandwagon demand curve" is more elastic than a demand curve for the same commodity without a bandwagon effect. And, the bandwagon demand curve is downward sloping to the right. The downward slope is caused by the "diminishing marginal external consumption effect." Due to limited income—what Leibenstein called the scarcity constraint—people cannot follow others endlessly. At some point the bandwagon effect will diminish sufficiently to maintain a downward sloping demand curve.

Leibenstein demonstrates the construction of a bandwagon demand curve by explaining in great detail the step by step process of a *gedankenexperiment*. This experiment involves several steps. In step 1 participants are asked at each hypothetical price how much would they buy. In step 2 they were asked how much they would buy, at various prices, if she believes that others are purchasing Q1. In step 3 they were told that all others purchased Q2, where Q2 > Q1. And, Q3 > Q2, and Q4 > Q3, etc. For each amount purchased by all others, each participant was asked how much they would buy at various prices. It is from this that the bandwagon demand curve is derived. The bandwagon demand curve means that participants buy more at any price when all others buy more. The process is explained without the use of mathematics and instead relies on diagrams. The same process is used to derive the snob and Veblen demand curves. Mark Perlman, who knew as much about Harvey's work as anyone, said of his gedankenexperiment that "One important contribution was Leibenstein's proposed ingenious method of iterative questioning so that dependence or independence of response could be assured. It anticipated much of what is now occurring in the…subfield of experimental economics" (Perlman, 1990, p. 13).

The snob effect

The snob effect is "negative herding." Leibenstein refers to it as a desire to "dissociate themselves from the 'common herd'" (Leibenstein, 1950, p. 189). When others buy more, snobs buy less at any price. The snob demand curve is less elastic than without the snob effect because when price falls, quantity demanded increases but demand falls as "snobs" buy less. The net effect is a less elastic downward sloping to the right demand curve.

The Veblen effect

There is one case in which a demand curve does slope upward to the right: the "Veblen demand curve." Veblen demand curve, which stems from the theory of conspicuous consumption is "a complex and subtle sociological construct" (Leibenstein, 1950, p. 202). However, as a good neoclassical economist in 1950 Leibenstein wanted to cut through the sociology so that "we can, for our purposes, quite legitimately abstract from the psychological and sociological elements and address our attention exclusively to the effects that conspicuous consumption has on the demand function" (Leibenstein, 1950, pp. 202–203).

The Veblen effect is a desire to show off your wealth by buying things others know come with a high price tag. The theory of conspicuous consumption creates a "conspicuous price" which can vary with the actual price. The conspicuous price is the price others think you paid for something. This price determines "conspicuous consumption utility" (Leibenstein, 1950, p. 203). Higher actual price reduces quantity demanded, but a higher conspicuous prices increases the numbers of buyers because conspicuous consumption utility increases. Therefore demand increases by a large enough amount to produce an upward sloping to the right demand curve. The interesting thing is that in 1950 Leibenstein was defending standard economic theory. He said that "We have tried to demonstrate that non-additivity is not necessarily an insurmountable obstacle in effecting a transition from individual to collective demand curves" (Leibenstein, 1950, p. 206).

In other words, non-additivity, a phenomena contrary to standard economic theory was not necessarily a "death sentence" for standard theory. With his X-efficiency theory Leibenstein took a step away from trying to "save" neoclassical theory. But some latter-day behavioral economists took up Leibenstein's questioning of the rationality assumption and other assumptions of neoclassical theory while for the most part ignoring Leibenstein's X-efficiency theory and his other writings containing behavioral economics ideas which would be cornerstones of latter-day behavioral economics. Life can be cruel!

Gary Becker in a 1974 article, "A Theory of Social Interactions," acknowledges Leibenstein's, 1950 paper on "the 'bandwagon' and 'snob' influences on ordinary consumption theory," (Becker, 1991, p. 1065). In his 1991 article, "A Note on Restaurant Pricing and Other Examples of Social Influences on Price," Becker shows that the bandwagon effect can result in an upward sloping demand curve. Gisser, McClure, Okten, and Santoni (2009) gather data from the Web of Science. Of the 101 economists who cited Becker's, 1991 article, 99% consider Becker's hypothesis to be beyond controversy; 87% argue against Leibenstein's theory of a downward sloping to the right bandwagon demand curve, and; not one economist cites evidence for Becker's hypothesis. Biddle in 1991 offers (the only) empirical evidence for the bandwagon demand curve in his study of vanity license plates. He reported that the bandwagon demand curve is downward sloping to the right. The dependent—price—variables were in both their current and lagged forms.

IV The nature of human knowledge

In *Economic Backwardness and Economic Growth* in which he questioned the concept of *homo economicus.* He asserted that in order to explain differences in per-capita income and economic development a researcher would have to know economic history, how to work with a large amount of data, how to develop a theory which can explain why something happens and why something else does not happen. Leibenstein has serious doubts that anyone can acquire such a broad range of expertise. "Obviously it is impossible for any individual to acquire such knowledge" (Leibenstein, 1957, p. 3). How can we, we live within a "framework of ignorance" (Leibenstein, 1957).

Hayek was writing about themes which became of interest to behavioral economists since the 1930s. One was the nature of knowledge and the limits of human nature. In, *Two Types of Mind*, Hayek (1978) Hayek distinguishes two types of minds or scientific, the "perfect master of the subject," and the "puzzler" or "muddler." The perfect master of the subject has an enormous amount of facts immediately at his disposal. This is the type of mind described by Leibenstein. The puzzler deals in "wordless thoughts," they "see" connections between things which they cannot verbalize. The result of their contemplations is the "a ha" experience. Hayek describes himself as a puzzler. Jacob Viner was the master of the subject. John Maynard Keynes was both!

For Hayek and Leibenstein, not all knowledge comes from books, classroom lectures, training programs. Some of it is simply "in the air," and we "absorb" it unconsciously. Alfred Marshall discussed this in terms of external economies, the concentration of firms in a particular locality/neighborhood. In his *Principles of Economics Marshall* said that,

> *...The mysteries of the trade become no mysteries; but are as it were in the air, and children learn many of them unconsciously...*
>
> *(Marshall, 1890, p. Book 4, Chap. 10, paragraph 7).*

Leibenstein, in *Economic Backwardness and Economic Growth* says that.

> *Many of the concepts and ideas that we usually employ are part of our professional equipment... However, some ideas, and these are difficult to acknowledge specifically, we may borrow almost imperceptibly from the intellectual climate in which we live and work*
>
> *(Leibenstein, 1957, p. viii).*

Leibenstein continues, saying what may be reminiscent of Samuelson's "sophisticated-anthropomorphic sin": "it is impossible to acknowledge one's total intellectual indebtedness...for these may well be the instances of imperceptible borrowing" (Leibenstein, 1957, p. viii).

V Organizational analysis and economic theory

In 1960 Leibenstein wrote *Economic Theory and Organizational Analysis* (ETOA). This work is perhaps the least discussed book in Leibenstein's "arsenal." Mark Perlman used 33 words to discuss the book: "I see Leibenstein's, 1960 book... as reflecting his mind in midpassage. He seems to have been organizing intellectually what others had written and what he made of it" (Perlman, 1990, p. 15). The "what others" were mainly Herbert Simon, Richard Cyert, and James March. This book represents the shift from largely macro-behavioral, to micro (and micro-micro) behavioral. Cyert and March, in their 1963 book, *A Behavioral Theory of the Firm* say that some researchers "propose…an integration of organizational theory and the theory of the firm. On occasion, such a proposal has been made explicit, and some efforts to achieve an integration have been made" (p. 16). Footnote 34 on page 16 makes it explicit that they were referring to Leibenstein's book. A lot of research in industrial organization and the theory of the firm surrounded Leibenstein's book. Some of them are summarized below.

Complex objective functions (COF)

Leibenstein was one of a number of economists in the "old days" who wrote about the firm as if profits was not the only objective of the firm. These writers were said to be writing about "complex objective functions." There is nothing in COF research which necessarily points to X-efficiency or selective rationality. These studies are simply the intellectual environment in which Leibenstein was writing.

In 1936 Chester Barnard gave a lecture at Princeton University entitled "Mind in Everyday Affairs." In it Barnard distinguished logical from non-logical, or intuitive thinking processes. He asserted that intuition was very useful under many conditions. In *The Functions of the Executive* (1962) Barnard discussed how organizations "actually" work rather than approaches which focus on narrowly focused, rigid, dogmatic, and doctrinaire principles of organizations. Simon said that he built his thesis in his 1947 book, *Administrative Behavior*, on Barnard's writing.

For Hicks (1935), the COF included profits and the "quiet life," which he said was the best "return" to monopoly power. Scitovsky in his 1943 article, "A Note on Proft Maximisation and its Implications," says that profit maximization and rationality are both fundamental assumptions in economics, so much so that it needs neither proof nor justification. However, entrepreneur's have a complex objective function which includes both profits and utility. Can they maximize profits and utility simultaneously? Yes, but only if they have a constant—independent of income—the value of which is greater than zero—the marginal utility of money This implies that the entrepreneur wants money for itself, for what it represents, and not because of what it allows you to buy. The entrepreneur's ambition is independent of income. Do entrepreneurs have such a psychology? Scitovsky believes that it applies to at least some entrepreneurs, but probably not every entrepreneur. Regardless, he says that it makes economic theory easier. Individuals are maximizing something, in this case a combination of the firm's profits and their own utility.

Rothschild (1947), in his article "Price Theory and Oligopoly," says that the entrepreneur's first objective is *long run survival*. While perfect competition leads to determinate price and output solutions, imperfect competition including duopoly and oligopoly have indeterminate solutions. The problem with indeterminate solutions is that it defies the long history of price theory centering around a long run perfectly competitive determinate price solution. Hence indeterminate solutions are "abhorrent to the 'father,' and even more to the 'mother,' of imperfect competition." The father is Edward Chamberlain, and the mother is, of course, Joan Robinson. However, an indeterminate solution means nothing more than the fact that it "cannot be suitably solved within the framework of existing price theory" (Rothschild, p. 304). It is also correct to say that the price solution under monopolistic competition cannot be solved under the conditions of perfect competition. By way of comparison, the existence of XE also defies the long history of price theory and could not be adequately explained by neoclassical theory.

Reder (1947) considers objectives other than profit maximization. The important point about which goal to pursue is that profit maximization can be ignored depending on the "market position" of the firm (p. 453). A monopolist or quasi-monopolist can tolerate inefficiency while still making "*satisfactory*" profits. (Italics added.) However, if it faces considerable competition then tolerating any inefficiency would be problematic. Under many circumstances the firm would not even know how much inefficiency they are working with. It is when their profits turn to serious losses that the firm learns how much inefficiency they were working with and begins to act in order to eliminate the inefficiency. Reder wrote this article 19 years before Leibenstein published his initial article on XE. But, it seems clear that his use of the word inefficiency is a generalized internal to the firm inefficiency, a.k.a. X-inefficiency. Or, if the reader prefers, there are aspects of Leibenstein's XE theory which are consistent with Reder's article. For example, competitive pressure and the possibility of financial ruin is what leads firms to be concerned about their (X) inefficiency and to develop a strategy for reducing or eliminating it. Second, costs are not predetermined. Firms may be off their cost frontier but they are not destined to stay there. They can lower their costs and return to their frontier.

Papandreou (1952) said that organizations replace profit maximization with that of a "preference function" (Papandreou, 1952, p. 207) which takes into account the interests of stock-holders, creditors, labor, and the government. An organization he defines as a "system of consciously coordinated activities or forces of two or more persons" (Papandreou, 1952, p. 185). According to Papandreou goals may be profits, leisure, ownership, power, prestige, and survival. For an organization to exist in the first place, the state of affairs must include three things: people must be willing to act in favor of the system, they must share a common goal, and; intentional communications must exist.

Baumol (1959) had a model of managers' behavior based on his work as a business consultant. Managers in his model of an "average" or typical oligopoly want to maximize sales revenue, constrained by a need to achieve an acceptable minimum level of profits. Sales are important because it is well correlated with the salaries of high ranking managers. If sales and profits are at odds with each other Baumol claims that managers always preferred the former. Sales maximization required sufficient funds to finance the firm's expansion and the minimum level of acceptable profits is that amount which allows for the expansion. The goal of maximum sales constrained by minimum profits was not, according to Baumol, irrational. Irrational behavior is that which makes it more difficult to attain one's own ends. It does not mean a person choosing the "wrong" end, for example, choosing to maximize something other than profits. Having worked with Leibenstein for many years my opinion is that Leibenstein would not disagree with Baumol. Leibenstein was a dedicated neoclassical economist. His only "sin" was asking what happens to neoclassical models if we assume that humans are not always perfectly rational. The result of asking that question was XE theory.

Marris (1963) sees managers of modern corporations where ownership is separated from finance as motivated by maximizing utility. Their utility function consists of their own security and the firm's growth rate. In turn, growth is measured by asset growth, and it provides things such as higher salary, more status and more power. Security is measured by the firm's (market value/book value of assets). The probability of a takeover follows a relatively low ratio. Thus, management attempts to maximize the firm's growth subject to a security constraint. Minimize the probability of a takeover and then attempt to maximize growth, which comes with it higher salary, status, and power.

Marris assumes that capital markets are not perfect—the supply of competent "raiders" is not infinite—which gives management some effort discretion. He also assumes that the productivity or efficiency of labor depends upon labor being familiar with the firm's culture. Managements are seen as best able to satisfy their own ambitions by the firm's growth rate. He agrees with Katona, that this can be expedited by identifying one's ego with the goals of the firm. In Marris's model the combination of things maximized are the firm's growth rate and their own security. Williamson (1963) says that it is both experience and insights of people such as Chester Barnard, Herbert Simon, and R.A. Gordon which lead to the following list of management goals: income, job security, performance, influence, rank, and stature. Rather than introducing any of these goals into the theory of the firm, Williamson prefers to introduce the activities which give rise to the goals. The relevant activities are "expense preferences." Expense, or cost, preference means that managers do not consider all costs as being homogeneous. Some costs are "better" than others, some add to utility while others do not. Those which add to utility include (a large) staff, which implies a higher rank, and more influence, among other things. At the time that Williamson was writing about this issue, the early 1960s, all costs were homogenous, or $1 = $1. Williamson did not completely "leave the reservation." He says that assuming self-interest and rationality allows one to introduce COF into a theory of the firm via expense preferences. So, all costs are not the same; $1 ≠ $1. Costs may exceed minimum but only because it gives the managers utility. The managers are following their self-interest and are rational, by which Williamson means fully rational. Hence, no inefficiency exists.

Monsen and Downs (1965) show that managers in large, 1000+ employees, firms do not have controlling interest in the firm. Hence, their primary goal is not the maximization of, someone else's, profits. The primary goal of the managers is the maximization of their lifetime income, while that of the owners is steady dividends and as a result rising stock prices. Finally, a steady and satisfactory increase in stock prices provides a sense of security to the managers about their jobs, and their lifetime income. Their income includes both money income, and leisure, prestige, and power. Consistent with the models of both Scitovsky and Williamson, Monsen and Downs believe that there is a conflict between maximizing profits and the maximization of the managers' "utility" (lifetime income.

The ideas of non-profit maximization and COF in general were "in the air." Leibenstein breathed in the air and when he breathed out there appeared X-efficiency theory in addition to other ideas which challenged neoclassical theory.

Herbert Simon, Richard Cyert and James March

Simon (1997a), in his 1945 book based on his PhD dissertation, *Administrative Behavior*, uses the term "organizational goal" in order to explain his ideas on COF. Simon's ideas which were also written about by Leibenstein include those of roles, equilibrium, organizational goals, inert areas, among others.

Simon wrote that an organization is a pattern of communications among people used for among other things, making and executing decisions. Sociologists refer to this pattern as a "role system" (p. 19). Organizations do not have a single goal. And the goals are not directly those of any person(s). The goals are related to the set of constraints faced by the organization. In organizations with multiple decision making "centers," different *constraints* represent the problems or concerns of different groups within the organization.

Organizational equilibrium

The groups, or participants, involved in dealing with constraints are entrepreneurs, employees, and customers. Each has a *personal motive*: entrepreneurs seek profits, employees seek wages, and customers seek attractive products in exchange for money. The organization also has its own motives or objectives. These objectives are indirectly the personal motives or objectives of one or more of the participant groups. It is through the employment contract and the contract with customers that the organization and the participants can achieve their own goals.

More specifically, there are inducements and contributions which must be considered. An inducement is what the organization offers entrepreneurs, employees, and customers. A contribution is what these groups give the organization. A contribution is the source of inducements to others. Contributions are a source of the firm's revenues, while inducements are a source of their costs. The condition for equilibrium is that $TR \geq TC$, that contributions are greater than or equal to the inducements. If this is the state of things then the organization can offer the participants sufficient inducements to continue their participation. If the contracts are not acceptable to all three groups then the contributions are not likely going to be at least equal to the sufficient inducements.

Simon defines efficiency as choosing the alternative from among two alternatives with the same costs, which achieves a greater attainment of the organization's goals. The other definition, which is essentially the same as the first is that from among two alternatives which lead to the same level of attainment of the organization's goals, the one is chosen which minimizes costs. The first definition essentially says that the organization should maximize it's output, what it attains, for a given level of costs. The second says that the organization should minimize its cost, for a given level of output. The first says that an efficient organization produces on its production frontier, while the second compares efficiency with producing on its cost frontier. Efficiency is X-efficiency.

Simon uses the concept of "balance sheet efficiency" to explain that one of the organization's goals might be to maximize and/or minimize, something(s). Efficiency, he says is a concept most related to organizations, commercial organizations, guided by the profit motive. Balance sheet efficiency means maximizing income if costs are believed to be fixed. And it means minimizing costs if income is believed to be fixed. The two criteria are dealt with simultaneously because what is really being maximized is (income – costs).

Area of acceptance/inert area

An important question is why does the employees accept the organization's requests and/or demands of their time and effort, and enter into an employment contract? The answer, according to Simon, is that employees acquiesce if the demands of the organization contributes to their own personal goals. Are within the employee's "*area of acceptance*" (p. 15). Outside this area disobedience follows. In *The Functions of the Executive*, Barnard (1936) asks how lasting cooperation is possible? One reason is the existence of a "zone of indifference." Within this zone people accept authority without question. The authority is not questioned because when the individual began an association with the organization they anticipated a certain range of orders which will be made. Hence they have already accepted authority within that range. Barnard gives the example of a soldier who expects that the military may ask him to move to A or B, or C or D. A through D are in the zone of indifference. The greater is the difference (inducements – burdens) the wider will be the zone of acceptance. Ceteris paribus, the organization's efficiency will be greater the wider the zone of acceptance. Barnard adds that the width also depends on "feeling in the ranks," "group attitude," "public opinion" (p. 169). This is how Barnard includes peers in the width of the zone of acceptance. The zone is not only a function of authority but also peers. This is one way in which Leibenstein's inert area is similar to Barnard's zone of acceptance. The "inert zone" is affected by supervisors and peers.

In XE theory the "inert area" is a concept central to the theory. The inert area is a range of effort within which the employee(s) will acquiesce to the demand of management and/or peers, even though that level of effort does not maximize their own utility. If the demands fall outside the inert area then the employees will seek to be inside the inert area. This may mean working with more effort—too little effort is boring—or less effort—too much effort can be injurious to one's mental and/or physical health.

Roles

The concept of a role is a *sociological* explanation of behavior. A captain "goes down with the ship" because that is the role of a captain which the person has accepted. A role is related to the goals of an organization. The shipping company wants the ship and all the people on the ship to arrive safely and on time at the port. The captain is ultimately responsible for these goals. Simon finds that the concept of a role is limited because it limits the pattern of behavior. The captain might get into a lifeboat while others are scrambling because he can't bear to never see his family again. He was still the captain until that moment, and is the captain even after his lifeboat moves away from the screams coming from on board the ship. Thus, a role tends to neglect idiosyncratic behavior. The interesting problem with the concept of a role is that the error it makes is "just the opposite of the one committed by economic theory – it does not leave any room for rationality" (Simon, 1997a, p. 25). An actor is neither rational nor irrational because the actor is simply reading lines. The person the actor is "playing" may make truly heinous decisions, but the actor is just reading lines. Simon says that rather than the concept of a role, the preferred concept is that of "decision premises." A role specifies some of the premises upon which behavior is based. Social influences affect our decision premises. A role stipulates some but not all of our decision making premises. *Idiosyncratic* behavior is a premise which is not part of the *role* being played. The word premise forces the actor to think and solve problems. Therefore, idiosyncratic decision makers can be either rational or irrational. Over an above all of this, the concept of a role is of particular importance here because the concept of a role was central in Leibenstein's, 1960 book, *Economic Theory and Organizational Analysis*, and because a comparison of Leibenstein's and Simon's concept of the role is part of my role as a writer/researcher.

Cyert and March, in their 1963 book *A Behavioral Theory of the Firm* define an organization as a set of coalitions and having approximately five goals. First, a production goal which includes a "smoothing goal"; production should remain within a certain range from one period to the next. It also includes a "level-of-production" goal; production should be ≥ a certain level. This goal affects employment, costs, and growth, and indirectly all those who are affected by each part of the goal. Second, an inventory goal which is that that inventories should be a certain level or within a certain range. Meeting this goal affects salespeople and customers. Third, a sales goal expressed as an aspiration for a sales level. Fourth, a market share goal measures the effectiveness of the sales department, and hence a substitute for the sales goal. Those members interested and affected by comparative success are concerned about this goal, e.g., top (sales) management. And, fifth, the profits goal. At least a minimum amount of profits provides the organization with available resources to be distributed to various groups. There is an aspiration level for profits measured by dollars. Owners, creditors, top management, and those needing capital investment are particularly interested in the profits goal. These goals may not be consistent with each other, but because goals are dealt with sequentially, and because organizational slack can change, inconsistent goals are not cause for great alarm.

Leibenstein's ETOA

Reading Harvey Leibenstein's, 1960 book, Economic Theory and Organizational Analysis (ETOA) seems both confusing and enlightening at the same time. The confusion comes from the fact that the book is more organizational theory than economic theory, and so the topics seemed somewhat "foreign" to me. The writing seemed to be "all over the place," and amorphous. Then there is the enlightening part, the part which came to me in a kind-of "ah ah" experience, that ETOA was a precursor of XE theory. This 1960 book, 6 years before his seminal article on XE theory, is actually a discussion of XET before there was XET. I do not believe that Harvey was consciously writing a precursor to XE theory. The book was part of the evolution of his writing. Since his dissertation in 1951 Harvey was challenging the orthodoxy. It all led to 1966. What appears again and again in the 1960 book is discussions about effort discretion, imperfect knowledge, non-marketed inputs, and inert areas, all of which are foundation concepts for XET.

For example, he says that microeconomic theory deals with the inducements of being hired, but not those for performance. Performance is assumed to be maximized, something Leibenstein rejected outright, explicitly in XE theory, partly because it assumes that XE does not exist (pp. 176–77). Second he explains that performance could be maximized if everything worked perfectly, if communication was perfectly effective and if everyone had all the information needed to make optimal decisions (p. 178). But alas, effort is a variable and not a constant at maximum effort. Effort discretion and performance maximization can be like oil and water. Third, costs are not determined mechanically, but depend on the human factor. These three elements explain why things don't always go the way they were planned. The result of the actual not being equal to planned performance is, X-inefficiency: (Pp − Pa = X-inefficiency). Leibenstein to going to build a theory of an organization or firm based on both neoclassical theory (NCT) and organizational analysis (OA). Here is the beginnings of XE theory (1966), but at this juncture wrapped in the sheath of OA.

He discusses effort discretion stating that individuals lack discretion only when the organization is managed by a "dictator with perfect control" (p. 275). But this rarely if ever exists. Hence the book focuses on the role of humans in the process of production.

The role of roles

In ETOA Leibenstein is concerned with the formation of an independent organization, an organization in which there is a set of related roles carried out by a somewhat durable coalition—connected roles—pursuing common aims. Leibenstein defines a role as involving doing bundles of activities which define what activities constitute the job, the pace at which the activities will be performed, and the tempo of work—the stop and start rhythm of the job. In XE theory this is the APQT bundle. Of crucial importance is that a role is an abstract concept. Individuals must interpret what the role constitutes and this implies effort discretion.

ETOA tries to explain how to create an organization so that the different people and roles move in sync with the other pieces. In other words, the purpose of ETOA is to find way to create a well-organized firm, one with a shared purpose and connected parts, which minimizes its costs. By contrast NCT assumes that the pieces do not fly off in their own direction, so that the roles are related and the pieces connected. Thus, the organization is assumed to be operating on both their cost and output frontiers. ETOA tries to create what NCT assumes to exist In short, ETOA explains how to create sync among diverse pieces which would fly off if left to their own devises, whereas NCT assumes that the sync exists and the pieces never move in a disjointed separate "orbit." Leibenstein, in effect, is attempting to integrate a theory of minimizing disorganization (ETOA) with a theory which assumes that disorganization does not exist (NCT).

Leibenstein's theory of the firm in ETOA

Leibenstein's theory of an organization or firm covers four important issues. First, how the separate pieces of the organization/firm fit together. Second, the role of limited knowledge. Third, the role of specialization. Fourth, the equilibrium of the organization/firm.

Fitting the pieces together when there is effort discretion

Leibenstein's asks the question how the separate parts of an organization fit together because he believes that one of the main problems an organization faces is organizing "lumpy" agents into a coalition which meets the organization's goals. This is the goal of ETOA.

How are the "lumpies" organized to fit together? As did Coase and Simon before him, Leibenstein says that organizations function by authority. Authority means that there are supervisors and non-supervisors, and that the supervisors tell the non-supervisors what needs to be done and the non-supervisors do it. With absolute authority communication is effective because the non-supervisor does what the supervisor tells him he wants done. And at one specified effort level. At the same time, the problem is that authority is not always "complete." That is, the authority does not have complete control over the work and effort choices of the non-authority employees. The latter have effort discretion, a main point in both ETOA and XE theory.

The Machine Analogy. If the organization is a "machine" then productivity would be maximized and costs minimized. In other words, XE would be (close to) 100%. However, neither Leibenstein, nor March and Simon in the 1958 book, Organizations, believe that an organization is a "machine." For Leibenstein this conviction held true in both ETOA and XE.

Incomplete knowledge, including that of the entrepreneur

Leibenstein assumes that humans have incomplete knowledge, including the knowledge possessed by the managers or coordinators. Therefore, the co-ordination of resources is limited because co-ordination ability is limited. Simply put, the brain of any one entrepreneur is not enough to co-ordinate a firm of any size. Nicholas Kaldor, in his 1934 article "The Equilibrium of the Firm," discusses the condition for a firm being in equilibrium. In that context he discusses knowledge and the firm's production and cost functions. On the demand side what is required for equilibrium is that buyers respond to price changes in the expected way. However, the assumption that firms (supply) are just as predictable in their behavior is questionable. This is because there is no definitive cost function, meaning that costs can vary for any output rate. Kaldor denies the existence of a definite cost function, if for no other reason than the limited co-ordinating ability for any "one brain."

The Entrepreneur, the Firm's Optimal Size, and Non-Marketed Inputs. If the production and cost functions are completely known in a perfectly competitive market, and all firms have the same technical knowledge, then long run costs and the optimal size for all firms should be the same, and the actual size should be the same. In this environment entrepreneurs would be routine-entrepreneurs and would not be very important. By contrast non-routine entrepreneurship is important for reasons which became part of XE theory: markets are not perfect, firms may not have the same knowledge, or the same access to all inputs. And, not all inputs are available or marketed.

Equilibrium of the firm

Why does an organization change? What determines the equilibrium of the firm? In ETOA Leibenstein associates equilibrium with role equilibrium. Remember that in Leibenstein's view employees at all levels of the organization have effort discretion. Meaning that employees must fill-in the details of what constitutes their job tasks. In part they get the information to fill-in the details from the supervisors, but also from individual peers and from the peer-group as a whole. A particular job role is in equilibrium, "if in the absence of external changes its nature does not change. In this condition the role will have a fixed set of interpretations, and none of the interpretations will result in organization reactions to the interpretation or its consequences such that the player cannot continue with that interpretation" (p. 200). In other words, workers interpret their job and in equilibrium those perceptions of the job and the actions performed on the job will remain constant. There is another part to equilibrium. In equilibrium the organization could not choose a new role-player for the job who could come up with a better job interpretation from the one already in existence.

Leibenstein received his PhD from Princeton in Economics in 1951; John Nash received his PhD in mathematics from Princeton in 1950. One wonders if they interacted because Leibenstein's definition of equilibrium seems similar to Nash's. Nash defined equilibrium as "A configuration of strategies, such that no player acting on his own can change his strategy to achieve a better outcome for himself." An elaboration is that no employee will change their interpretation given the interpretations made by others of their own role. In other words if others do not change their interpretations then no individual will benefit from changing their own interpretation.

What creates disequilibrium? A role may be in a state of disequilibrium because it is evolving or not fully settled. In this case knowledge about the full scope of alternative interpretations is not known. And the firm may not know the full capabilities of the individual performing the role. Second, the role may be in conflict with other roles. That is, the roles are not compatible with each other. They may be geared toward satisficing different conflicting firm goals. Third, the role structure may be in a state of disequilibrium. The role structure is the "web of role relations" (p. 203). (NET) In this case at least one role must be changed to bring it into consistency with all other roles. The roles must be well "connected" or the organization is a "paper organization." In equilibrium "all permissible interpretations of roles by representative players, and all possible choice sets by such average players do not lead to any change in any role within the structure" (p. 205).

What Leibenstein will call XE in 6 years "usually requires a great deal of constancy in the role relationships. Day-to-day internal performance often involves much role interdependence. And this suggests the desirability of a lack of change in role relationships if performance is not to be interrupted unduly" (pp. 205–206). Equilibrium with respect to role structure according to Leibenstein is not necessarily an optimal role structure. In other words equilibrium may be sub-optimal. Sub-optimality may exist for several reasons. First, individuals may have had too narrow a view of the roles because of a lack of knowledge or experience. Perhaps not enough experimentation with different role interpretations took place. Second, a fear of disequilibrium may have "frozen" roles in place even though they were not optimal. Third, the cost of changing the role structure may be too high or perceived as being too high. Fourth, a division or conflict among supervisors about roles and firm objectives may keep a sub-optimal situation in place.

Multiply Equilibriums. In XE theory multiple equilibria is called an inert area. A range of activity and role interpretations which are suboptimal and not utility maximizing, but which is the norm and followed by the members of the firm. Within this inert area there may be many equilibriums, many role interpretations which are acceptable to both supervisor and non-supervisor, and which do not cause any frictions. However, if the supervisors are X-efficient, and if their authority is complete, and if their communications are clear then the non-supervisor does what the supervisor asks to be done, and there aren't any inert areas.

XE theory

ETOA was about the firm analyzed from the perspective of organizational analysis. XE was about the firm and the market. Organizational analysis played a very minor role in Leibenstein's writings after 1960. The entrepreneur became an inter-market actor not a paper-organization actor. In XE theory the concept of the role, so central in ETOA, is absent. In his 1987 book, Inside the Firm, the concept of the role is again absent. The effect of authority, good communication, lumpy resources, to name just three, are replaced by the pressure from the market, and the human personality on the firm.

Inert Areas and Multiple Equilibriums. In ETOA an inert area is a range of role interpretations acceptable to all persons involved, and implies that an unacceptable role interpretation exists leading to a non-maximizing level of work effort being supplied. The important variables include authority relations, and communication styles. In XE theory an inert area is about inertia. It is about a comfortable range of effort, A to B, meaning that within this range the individual will put forth any level of effort within the range A to B. Any level of effort within this range is an equilibrium level of effort. Clearly there are many possible equilibriums. When more than one person is involved then the inert area is the comfort level for all members of the group. Leibenstein also showed the existence of multiple equilibrium states of pay and productivity levels using game theory. The prisoner's dilemma solution—minimum effort given pay levels, and minimum pay given productivity levels—leads to low pay and low productivity. A convention about productivity and pay levels, for example, "a good days work for a good days pay," increases both pay and productivity levels. Treating others as you would want to be treated leads to the Pareto optimum. Any one of the three states is an equilibrium state because unless something changes the productivity and pay level will have no tendency to change. Roles, role interpretations, authority, communication styles are absent from the discussion. Micro theory has replaced organizational analysis.

Both ETOA and XE theory are about inefficient firms. However, ETOA is an attempt to make the firm efficient while XE theory is concerned with the effect of inefficiency on costs and welfare. Working out details of creating workable constellations is not part of XE theory. Neither are the problems of lumpy resources, poor authority and communications part of XE theory. The degrees of specialization are not part of XET. The effect of less than optimal productivity on costs is part of XET. Details about the skills of the managers/co-ordinators is also not part of XET. The extent of managerial skills on costs is part of XET, Simply stated, XET is an economic theory, not a part of OA. The use of average cost curves shifting according to the degree of external market pressure demonstrate this as well as just about anything. The language of organizational analysis is absent, the effect of competition on the level of an ATC replaced it.

VI Final comments on Chapter 6, and looking ahead to Chapter 6

Prior to Leibenstein's seminal article on X-efficiency theory he published articles on efficiency wages, population and demography, consumer behavior, organizational theory, and fertility. Only the last was not discussed in this chapter. Leibenstein was the first person to publish on efficiency wages and economic development in his 1957 book. Why, he asks would a firm pay a wage above equilibrium when there is involuntary unemployment? Because effort and productivity, and hence costs, depend on real wages. Leibenstein's model shows the relationship between wages and nutrition, and nutrition and productivity. In his 1954 book he discussed the critical minimum effort needed for a society to escape from them Maulthusian trap. Part of his analysis used game theory, something Harvey leaned from his Princeton mentpr, Oskar Morgenstern. Leibenstein wrote an article on the effects of interdependence among consumers on the demand curve. One effect, the bandwagon effect has overlaps with a "new" behavioral economics concept, herding. Leibenstein used a technique for estimating the effects of interdependence which has similarities with what would become experimental economics. His 1960 book on organization theory and economic analysis was in many respects a preview of X-efficiency theory, and a bridge between Harvey's neoclassical side and his X-efficiency/behavioral economics side. Chapter 7 will present his X-efficiency theory.

X-efficiency. An intervening variable

6

Oliver Hart, the 2016 winner of the Noble Prize for his work on the theory of (incomplete) contracts spoke about what seems to be a plausible variant of XE theory. In particular I refer to his 1983 article, "Market mechanism as Incentive Scheme." He says that there is an important shortcoming in the concept of Pareto optimality. On the one hand a competition equilibrium is considered to be Pareto optimal. On the other hand, what is missing from the concept of competitive equilibrium is that competition not only helps to achieve an efficient allocation of resources but is also a source of discipline helping firms to reduce slack.

Slack can be thought of as a situation leading a firm to not minimizing costs and not being on their output or cost frontiers. That is, slack is a possible cause of X-inefficiency. Slack has been stressed in firms in which there is a relative lack of competitive pressure from the market, and managers and owners have different goals. Unfortunately for the owners, the firm is run by managers whose main goal seems to be to work with less than maximum effort. Asymmetric information may be the cause of owners not being able to monitor managers sufficiently enough to increase their effort. To "nudge" the managers to supply more effort, the owners supply an incentive system for managers which they hope will increase effort and reduce X-inefficiency. Leibenstein's XE theory and Hart's theory have (at least) one thing in common: they assume that contracts are incomplete.[a]

I In the beginning...

At the Univ of California, Berkeley, one of Leibenstein's graduate assistants worked with varying degrees of effort. This graduate assistant had effort discretion, one of the basic assumptions of the theory. The graduate student had effort discretion because the labor contract between the graduate student and the Economics department was incomplete. In this case Harvey did not have complete control over his graduate assistant's every action. One day this graduate student would work with great effort, and the next day he would, as if, sleep walk through the day. After observing this for some time Leibenstein had an aha moment. He wondered whether this pattern of behavior was the pattern expressed by many people other than his graduate assistant. Almost 20 years later Harvey told me about this, and he remembered every detail of the student's behavior patterns as well as his, Harvey's, reactions. Thus began X-efficiency theory.

[a] Chen and Tang (1990) use Hart's theory in their paper on exports and productivity growth in Taiwan between 1968 and 1982.

The Beginnings of Behavioral Economics. https://doi.org/10.1016/B978-0-12-815289-8.00006-X

In 1966, the year Leibenstein wrote his seminal article on X-efficiency theory, the economics profession seemed to be approaching an apex, maybe a local apex, maybe the global apex, in the utilization of "tight" analytical models and reliance on mathematics and econometrics. Leibenstein utilized neither "tight" analytical models, nor mathematics or econometrics. Leibenstein wasn't engaging in more narrowly focused experiments. He was writing a broader and a more encompassing "vision." That was the focus of the first gen behavioral economists. Broader is not better than narrower, it is simply different. And it was more characteristic of the "old" version of behavioral economics than the "new" version.

What is first generation behavioral economics? Extoll the value of neoclassical economics while examining and explaining its shortcomings. Incorporate theories from other disciplines when offering alternative theories and/or models. If it pleases, then use data to test your theories. Otherwise, leave that to others.

Bull's Eye Painting

Leibenstein never tested his X-efficiency theory. Others began doing that in 1967. His focus was showing that neoclassical economics was valuable and that homo economicus described human behavior some of the time, but not all the time. In denying that humans are always homo economicus, Leibenstein felt the wrath of many economists, including George Stigler. One of Leibenstein's responses to his critics was his article dripping with sarcasm: "Bull's-Eye Painting Economics." It tells a story about a small town in Tsarist Russia in which there was a great marksman. On barn walls throughout the town there was a picture of a bull, and a bullet mark right between the bull's eyes. When asked how he became such a good shot, the man said, "... it's not so hard. First I shoot, then I paint the bull's eyes" (Leibenstein, 1982b, p. 460). Some neoclassical economists, Leibenstein says, are practicing bulls-eye painting economics. To them, every theory and every set of empirical results can be explained in terms of, and consistent with neoclassical economics. If you think that someone is not homo-economicus, then they will write an objective function with explanatory variables which "prove" you incorrect. In Leibenstein's view this approach is not scientific and hence not of value to economics. Furthermore, making every theory and every set of results consistent with neoclassical theory makes that theory a tautology, correct by definition. The theory is not falsifiable, and potential falsifiability is a cornerstone of science.

Richard Thaler, in The Winner's Curse Paradoxes and Anomalies of Economic Life (1991), seems to agree with bull's-eye painting as being a part of neoclassical economics. For example, he says that economic theories are often "difficult to pin down... that some theories are simply not testable... they are true by definition..." (Thaler, 1991, p. 2). Theories are not testable if there is no set of data which can refute the theory. Utility maximization is not refutable because, by assumption, a person only does what increases their utility. The two key assumptions of economics is rationality and self-interest. Rationality is assumed, and whatever a person does is, by assumption, in their self-interest. But, there are, he says, few HUMANS included in economic models. Economic models have become more sophisticated, but there continue to be only a few HUMANS (Thaler, 1991, p. 2, p. 121). As opposed to homo economicus's brain, Thaler describes the human brain, and his own. "Think of the human brain as a personal computer, with a very slow processor and a memory system that is both small and unreliable. I don't know about you, but the PC I carry between my ears has more disk failures than I care to think about" (Thaler, 1991, pp. 2, 3).

My 'favorite' argument against X-efficiency theory which leaves neoclassical theory as non-falsifiable, nothing but a tautology, is the notion that on-the-job leisure is part of the firm's output. It is non-traded output but output none-the-less. Traded + non-traded output always places the firm on their output frontier. Non-traded output—on-the-job leisure is a benefit not a cost. The costs of traded output may be above minimum. However, the costs of traded output minus the benefits of non-traded output always places the firm on their cost frontier. Hence, there cannot be any X-inefficiency. Parish and Ng (1972) argue that because entrepreneurs are rational, entrepreneurial leisure is part of the social product but adds nothing to social costs. Hence X-inefficiency is actually a benefit because it means more leisure relative to costs. The best, and 'weirdest' theory is by Levin (1974) who argues that according to the laws of mass and energy, "nothing is ever lost." Hence, if the firm is producing less commodities for the market then that energy must go somewhere and that place is leisure. The firm produces more leisure and less for the market. By definition, X-inefficiency is zero because it is simply a benefit of on-the-job leisure, and not a cost.

II X vs. allocative efficiency

In 1966 there weren't any studies explicitly mentioning X-efficiency theory. So in his article on XE he presents what he interpreted to be empirical evidence for the theory. The theory asserts that there is a form of efficiency different from allocative efficiency. The theory also asserts that firms will not automatically produce on their production and/or cost frontiers. In other words, firms may be in a state of suboptimal disequilibrium. As such firms can approach their frontiers, not because of more or better capital and/or labor, but because of other factors such as better motivation, and simple changes in the 'choice architecture.' The studies cited in this chapter focused on these factors.

What are the characteristics of allocative (in)efficiency which Leibenstein believed to be deficient enough to warrant a different form of (in)efficiency? Leibenstein called it X-(in)efficiency because it was at the time an unknown type of (in)efficiency. What are the fundamental assumptions and structure of the theory? This chapter will discuss these issues.

Why a non-allocative form of (in)efficiency?

In his seminal article Leibenstein begins by discussing why a non-allocative form of (in)efficiency is important. For one thing, (allocative) efficiency is essential in economics. But empirical evidence casts doubt on the importance of allocative efficiency. Despite this doubt, efficiency in some form is important. Leibenstein gave that form the name X-efficiency.

Allocative (in)efficiency is about market (in)efficiency. When an industry is competitive it produces where P = MC, the definition of allocative, market, efficiency. When an industry is monopolized then P ≠ MC, the definition of allocative, *market*, inefficiency. Markets are inefficient because of monopolization of the industry/market. In either competitive or monopoly conditions, firms are assumed to be, internally, efficient, producing, on their production and cost frontiers.

Estimates of allocative, market, inefficiency, the welfare or Harberger triangle, depend upon the percentage of national income produced in monopolized industries, the price differential between competitive and monopolized industries, and the elasticity of demand for the product. Using any reasonable estimates for these three quantities results in very small estimates of allocative inefficiency. The original Harberger estimate was 1/13 of 1% of national income. Other estimates are as low as 1/100 of 1%. Why are they so low? The theory of allocative inefficiency assumes that firms purchase and utilize all inputs efficiently. What remains are the "net marginal effects," the difference in price and output between the competitive and the monopoly solutions. Leibenstein then says that a lack of pressure in monopolized industries could raise costs by 3/10 of one percent, but that the empirical evidence discussed in both the 1966 article and this chapter suggests that the magnitude is likely much larger. One study estimated that X-inefficiency amounts to between 2% and 4% of GNP (Bergsman, 1974). For Leibenstein, effort is better allocated studying X-efficiency. He then said that "Understandably there is considerable resistence to this viewpoint. A century of practice is not readily abandoned" (Leibenstein, 1976, p. 9).

In Fig. 6.1 below allocative efficiency is the triangle XYZ. It reflects differences in price (Mp-Cp) and output (Cq-Mq) between a competitive and a monopolized industry. Comp Cost is costs for a competitive industry. The area MpXYCp are monopoly profits, equal to (Mp-Cp)Mq. If, however, the monopolist has higher costs, predicted by X-efficiency theory, then at the extreme, monopoly costs shift up to the monopoly price, and the area MpXYCp = (Monopoly cost−Competitive cost)Mq, which are the higher costs of the monopolist. Leibenstein called X-inefficiency. Of course, if

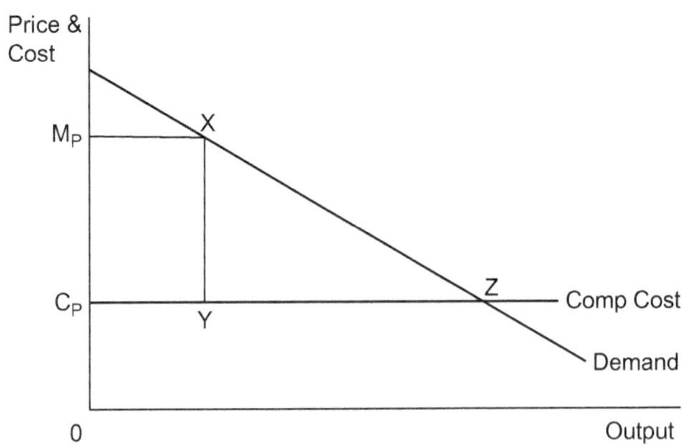

Fig. 6.1 X and allocative (in)efficiency.

the monopolist's costs increase half way between Cp and Mp, then MpXYCp would contain both profits and X-inefficiency.

Studies cited in 1966 article

In this section I will review some of the studies cited in Leibenstein's 1966 paper. The importance of these studies is they point to simple changes in the firm's environment—call it their organization, or their choice architecture—which led to relatively large increases in output, and relatively large decreases in costs for a given amount of inputs.

The "Horndahl effect" is the subject of one such study. The Horndahl effect is about the Horndahl steel works in Sweden at which there was almost no capital improvements for a period of 15 years. Despite this labor productivity increased 2% a year over the 15 year period. Eric Lundberg, who introduced the concept of the Horndahl effect to the economics profession, called it "pure productivity." Kenneth Arrow (1962) said that the Horndahl effect is due to learning by doing. Lundberg's work on the Horndahl steel works was based on interviews with managers. His conclusion is that suboptimal disequilibrium of the use of technology and existing capital x-ists and is significant (Goran Ohlin, 1962, p. 828). Leibenstein adds that if suboptimal disequilibrium exists then the proper motivations (or choice architecture) can move a firm closer to their frontier, i.e., XE will increase.

Frederick Harbison (1956) discussed the factor of production called organization as determining labor productivity, and the concept of organizational (in)efficiency. He says that in Egypt he studied two petroleum refineries which exists less than one mile apart. Labor productivity in refinery A was twice that of refinery B. New management in B led to "spectacular" increases in efficiency, due to part by better organization, which is an input in the determination of productivity and efficiency.

Peter Kilby (1962) presented the results of studies done by the International Labour Office Productivity Demonstration Missions showing that simple changes in the productive process of an organization created relatively large decreases (increases) in unit costs (productivity). The simple changes included plant layout reorganized, waste control, machine utilization and flow, payment by results, and materials handling. The studies were done in several countries India, Burma, Indonesia, Singapore, Malaysia, Thailand, Greece, and Israel. One of Kilby's conclusions is that monopolized markets tend to reduce cost savings attempts.

Laszlo Rostas (1964) in his study of British and American productivity also reported that factors other than the quantity and quality of capital have a significant increase on productivity. These "non-observable" inputs include factory lay-out—the placing of machines, materials handling, work flows, and supervisory techniques.

John Johnston (1963) studied the four largest management consulting firms in the U.K. What did these management consultants do? Things similar to that reported by Kilby: building and plant layouts, production and marketing procedures, and enhancement of general management skills. The results of these (relatively simple) changes was an average increase in productivity of 53%. Johnston says that reducing chaos and doubt can result in pushing firms closer to their frontiers.

The Hawthorne effect refers to studies done at the Hawthorne Works in Cicero, Illinois. The studies include simple changes in, for example, the strength of lighting in the workplace, keeping work stations cleaner, removing obstructions from the factory floor, and moving workstations. The result was (short run) increases in productivity of between 13 to 30%. Management simply paying attention to the workers improved their attitudes, enhanced motivations, and raised productivity (Roethlisberger, Dickson, & Wright, 1939; Landsberger, 1958).

The I.L.O.'s 1959 study of incentive systems reported the following productivity effects of payment-by-results systems. In Australia productivity increased by 69% in the first 3 months of the payment-by-results system, 95% after 6 months, and 117% after nine months. In Belgium productivity was more than 100% higher than under individual bonus systems. In the Netherlands the medium increase in productivity with the introduction of payment-by-results was 31%. In the U.K. the increase in productivity averaged 43%. Argyle, Gardner, and Cioffi (1958) focus on methods of supervising (non-managerial) employees and its effects on productivity. The results from several firm studies show that productivity is reduced when supervision is closer rather than more general, when there is pressure to produce more, when supervision is more production-centered vis-à-vis employee-centered, when supervision is autocratic and punitive. Tomekovic (1962) reports that workers who are told more about the importance of their work are more productive.

There is another group of studies mentioned by Leibenstein. The growth residual studies of Robert Solow (1957), Aukrust (1959), Edward Denison (1962), showed that "non-input" factors—changes in neither capital nor labor—accounted for between 50% to 80% of growth in more advanced economies. The non-input characterization led to the term growth "residual." Leibenstein doesn't equate "non-input" factors with X-efficiency, but he does state that there are motivational, X, elements in the non-input factors which account for some percentage of the residual. The studies mentioned above all point to non-traditional inputs having significant effects on output and productivity.

Nudging towards X-efficiency

On page 1 of *Nudge*, Thaler and Sunstein discuss Carolyn, a nutritionist, who rearranged the placing of food in school cafeterias. Simple changes in the placing of food led to an increase or decrease in the consumption different food items by as much as 25% (Thaler & Sunstein, 2008, p. 1). The important word is simple. Thaler and Sunstein used the phrase "simply by rearranging." They continue. "Carolyn learned a big lesson: school children like adults, can be greatly influenced by small changes in the context" (Thaler & Sunstein, 2008, pp. 1–2). The important word is small.

Analyzing the initial evidence and methods used for increasing XE, Leibenstein said that "The methods usually involve some simple reorganizations of the production process," already discussed in this chapter (Leibenstein, 1966, p. 399). The important word, again, is simple. The use of knowledge is based on a similar principle, that a (relatively) simple change, in this case a different inducement, changes our knowledge from vague or tacit to usable. Thus his conclusion that people live and work with intellectual "slack" However, unlike an unused or underutilized physical capital, intellectual slack is difficult to observe. (Leibenstein, 1976, p. 41). Leibenstein's evidence discussed in his 1966 paper may be referred to as "nudging towards greater X-efficiency."

X-efficiency and behavioral economics as intervening variables

According to Katona, an intervening variable comes between a stimulus and a response, or between inputs and outputs. Between income and consumption spending, the intervening variable is expectations. The intervening variable changes the response (output, or consumer spending) for a given change in the inputs (income). Thus, expectations can alter the "normal" relationship between income and consumption spending.

The optimal relationship between inputs and outputs is that firms maximize their output for given inputs, and minimize inputs for a given level of output. In other words, the optimal relationship is that firms produce on their (output and cost) frontiers. X-(in) efficiency changes that relationship. Greater X-inefficiency reduces output for given inputs and increases costs for given output. It moves the firm further from their frontiers. Greater X-efficiency pushes in the opposite direction. X-(in) efficiency is an intervening variable.

In addition to Leibenstein's graduate assistant, behavioral economics may be said to have had its beginning as a response to neoclassical economics lacking the human 'touch.' Neoclassical economics was mechanical, logical, and individuals lacked free will, which gave the engineers' blueprints a greater role. Because all relationships were optimal there was not much need for intervening variables which would affect those relationships; you cannot improve upon perfection. Many economists who enjoyed the logical nature of economics may have forgotten its limitations. Katona, Leibenstein, Simon and the others didn't forget. Not only is X-efficiency an intervening variable, but in a sense behavioral economics is one big intervening variable, explaining why things don't always follow the maximization/homo economicus story line. Leibenstein—Katona, Simon, and others—found economics to be wanting. They developed overarching theories in an attempt to reduce the want. They did not do experiments which added to a list of the ways in which human behavior violates the axioms of rational choice theory. They pre-dated all of this.

Assumptions underlying X-efficiency theory

What are the assumptions for a theory which deny that firms are always on their frontiers? And, what are the assumptions for a theory, aspects of which serves as an intervening variable in the relationship between inputs and outputs? One assumption is that a person's level of effort varies. Leibenstein says that it is obvious to everyone except some economists that people don't work as hard or as smart as they can. People don't search for information or solutions to problems as well as they can. These result in the relationship between inputs and output being indeterminate.

Why the indeterminancy? Because as Karl Marx might say, labor effort is not the same as labor time.[b] Labor time is purchased in the labor market but labor effort is not. This is because the market for effort is incomplete, it contains "gaps." In his book, *General X-Efficiency Theory and Economic Development*, Leibenstein asks how a psychological variable such as effort might affect economic development. A traditional economic model (of development) emphasizes time while Leibenstein emphasizes effort. In addition, traditional economic models assume that effort is a given, while Leibenstein emphasizes that effort varies according to the pressures felt by an individual. In a traditional model of economic development, once you assume that prices are well known, production and cost functions are well defined, markets are well functioning, then there is little if any use for entrepreneurs. Leibenstein's view of the economy is that these assumptions often do not hold in the real world. In order to express this, he uses the image of a net. The economy described by a traditional economic model of development is a well construed net, all the strands in place, and all of them in proper condition. In Leibenstein's model the net has tears and in places is completely absent.

The previous paragraph reveals three assumptions of X-efficiency theory. First, labor effort is variable or discretionary.[c] Unless the firm has a dictator who can control every movement of every employee, labor's effort is, to a certain extent, discretionary. Employees, at all levels of the firm, have their own complex objective function. Keeping their job is one, and on-the-job comfort is another. Employee effort is not allocated only to the firm's pursuit of profits and cost minimization. Second, labor contracts are incomplete. Hours to be worked, tasks to be completed, vacation time and many other aspects of the job can be specified. However, not all aspects can be specified. In fact, it is not in the firm's interests to try to completely specify all aspects of the job. Union people have always known that the way to bring a firm to a halt is to work according to the rules. Incomplete labor contracts gives employees some freedom to pursue their own complex objective function which increases costs above minimum, i.e., X-inefficiency.

Third, the production and cost functions are incomplete. This means that there is not a completely determined level of output for each level of inputs. For any level of inputs, the output rate can vary. The production function is thus a band rather than a line. Production is not the result of an engineer's blueprints being carried out to specifications. In War and Peace, Tolstoy writes that "Military science assumes the strength of an army to be identical with its numbers. Military science says that the more troops the greater the strength… In military affairs the strength of an army is the product of its mass and some unknown x . . . That unknown quantity is the spirit of the army…" (Leibenstein, 1976, p. vii). Leibenstein goes on to say that understanding the level of economic output requires more than knowing the "observable inputs" including technology. What Tolstoy calls "spirit" Leibenstein calls effort, both physical and mental. Incomplete, gaps, discretion, and spirit. These are words which demand filler-words. The fillers became behavioral economics.

[b] Showing that Harvey and Marx both distinguished labor time and labor effort may have Harvey turning over in his grave, may he rest in peace.

[c] Tong and Leung (2002) incorporate effort discretion in a "real life" game tournament.

There is a fourth assumption implied in the other three; rationality is often less than 100%/perfect/homo economicus rationality. Leibenstein claims that human beings are "selectively" rational. The basis for this is the psychological make-up of human beings. In *Beyond Economic Man* Leibenstein spells this out. The concept that an individual can contribute to X (in)efficiency arises from an individual's split or dual personality. Of course, a human personality is not literally split, but the image of a split personality conveys the intuition that individuals are torn—not literally—in their preferences. On the one hand, we want to adhere to standards, to strive for the maximum, and to strive by being calculating and attentive to details. In other words, this aspect of the personality is our rational self, the part of us that uses "tight," focused, or rational decision-making procedures. Leibenstein refers to this aspect of our personality as the "superego function." The other tendency is for each of us to "kick back," to use "loose" decision-making procedures, to follow our "animal spirits." Leibenstein refers to as the "id function." It is the id function that leads us to be "unconstrained," that is, unwilling but not necessarily unable to be calculating, attentive, rational.

XE theory assumes that, on the average, each individual is influenced by both functions in a way that leads to a compromise between the two. That is, each of us forges a compromise between the way we feel we must behave and the way we would like to behave were it not for a sense of obligation to duty or to a set of standards. In other words, each individual strikes a compromise that provides them with a sense of (psychological) "comfort." Individuals are thus selectively rational. X-E. Leibenstein assumes that, on average, each individual is pushed by their superego to maximize, and pulled by their id to kick back and watch the world flow by. That is, each of us forges a compromise between these two forces that provides them with a sense of (psychological) "comfort." The human personality is thus seen as having two end points. On the one end is an intense concern for constrained behavior—economic man—while on the other end is a complete lack of constrained behavior. The former would be a fully rational person, with others exhibiting "selective rationality."

Rationality is thus a continuous variable with an "economic person" exhibiting complete constrain concern. The economic person is thus a limiting case: a characteristic of the decision-making procedures used by some people at some times but not necessarily characteristic of all people at all times. "We assume that basically an individual effects a compromise between his desires to do as he pleases and internalized standards of behavior acquired through background and environment. Thus, we assume that individuals are influenced by others and that their psychology requires them to strike a balance between conflicting desires" (Leibenstein, 1976, p. 71). A human being lives within the needs of a dual or split personality.

Imperfect markets are a background to XE theory. A human being is affected by the needs of their dual personality, their internal environment, but also by the pressure put on them by the external environment. A basic idea of XE theory is that pressure to produce efficiently determines a human being's level of productivity. Pressure within a firm for efficiency is lower when the firm has more monopoly power. But nowhere is it assumed that the relationship is linear. Sixth, the existence of inert areas. Influenced by others, a human being will adjust their behavior to "mesh" with others around them, but only up a certain point. I may work a little harder or not work as hard as

I may prefer in order to comply with the culture. However, below or above a certain work pace a human being will not go. The range of effort "open to negotiation" is the inert area. Obviously, X-efficiency theory assumes that the firm's environment does not have a deterministic effect on ouput or costs.

Individual XE

Individual human beings are neither X-efficient nor X-inefficient. We are selectively rational. Organizations are (X) efficient, on a scale of 0 to 100 (or 0 to 1.0 depending how it is being measured). In either case, 0 is really bad. Complete X-efficiency (1, or 100) is the default position of neoclassical theory. There is an opt-out. People can choose to create X-inefficiency. What determines whether and much an individual and/or a group contribute to the (X) efficiency of the organization? I will focus on three elements discussed by Leibenstein. First, the internal, inside the mind, environment, where the super-ego and id functions of the personality push and pull the individual into different types of behavior. Second the internal to the organization environment in which the individual faces pressure by peers and others as to their level of work effort. Third, the external to the organization environment, the market.

Leibenstein adopted two terms from Freudian analysis, the super-ego and the id, to discuss how a person's dual-personality or dual-self, affects their behavior. The super-ego is that part which thrives to do things as well as possible; it aims for perfection. It represents the internalization of rules of proper behavior taught to the individual by parents. The id, by contrast, represent our impulses and instincts which seek immediate gratification and the avoidance of pain. It does not calculate, and is unresponsive to the demands of reality. The super-ego has the "fortitude" and is "forward-looking" enough to engage in the procedures necessary to contribute to (X) efficiency. The id has, well, none of the above! An individual will contribute more to the organization's level of (X) efficiency if, for whatever reason, the superego can express itself through the person's behavior. This is Leibenstein's version of a dual-self theory.

Degree of (procedural) rationality

Leibenstein placed more emphasis on procedural rationality than substantive rationality. Rationality is the outcome of behavior, not simply whether the decision maker equates at the margin, which is assumed to always be true, at least for homo economicus. Leibenstein lists specific decision making procedures which will correlate the closest with perfectly rationality. The procedures signifying a willingness and ability to be constraint concerned, to make rational decisions are as follows. First, the absence of procrastination, what Leibenstein calls the absence of "time deferral," what others call a present-bias. People who procrastinate follow "loose" procedures because they are "less irksome although the price for doing so is to defer the tightness of our procedures for a later period" (Leibenstein, 1976, p. 86). We may believe that it is safe to ignore current pressure until the future and all the while hoping that when the future comes we will have a higher capacity for dealing with pressure. Second, making independent decisions; avoid being obedient to authority or peers when you are able to make your own (inner) assessment of a situation. Avoid herding behavior, behavior characteristic of bandwagon behavior, and presentation effects. Third, being "magnitude sensitive," sensitive to small changes in the data. Fourth, not getting utility from deliberately making irrational choices. Fifth, making a realistic assessment of the environment: avoiding wishful thinking. Sixth, making reflexive assessments of an environment; avoiding a "knee-jerk" reaction. Seventh, learning (as much as possible) from experience.

When it concerns the multiple selves of the id and the superego, Leibenstein says that individuals compromise a desire to do whatever they want to do, and his internal standards of (good) behavior created by their background and the environment.

Leibenstein's view of rationality has a procedural element, and as such is consistent with Herbert Simon's view of rationality. But Leibenstein does not adhere to the satisficing view of behavior. X-inefficiency stems from sloppiness, and laziness, not satisficing behavior. Satisficing is similar to maximizing in that both are goal oriented, directed behavior. A person who satisfices does so because they do not have the degree of knowledge necessary to maximize. However, given their limited knowledge they do the best they can. An x-inefficient person may or may not have enough knowledge to maximize. However, regardless of the degree of knowledge they have, they don't use it as well as they can. One reason for not using knowledge as well as we can is that much of our knowledge is vague, not something that can be written down and fully explained. Knowledge comes from experience, it is gained from doing something over and over again. Athletes are often said to have skills developed by practice and part of their muscle memory.

Multiple equilibrium and psychological comfort at work

Leibenstein points out that we want "balance" in our life, specifically between our super-ego and id. We also want to balance utility and effort. In Fig. 6.2, utility is on the vertical axis, and effort is on the horizontal axis. The curve showing the relationship

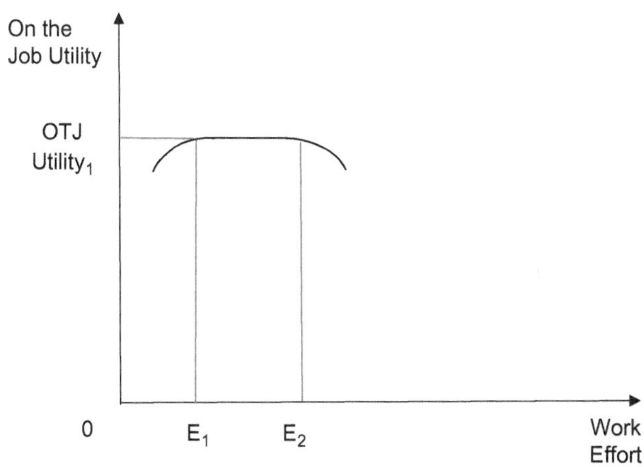

Fig. 6.2 Inert area.

between utility and effort has the shape of an inverted U, with a flat top between two levels of effort—E1 and E2. Thus between E1 and E2 the (marginal) utility is constant. Effort levels E1E2 is an inert area because within these two effort levels the individual has no preference for any single effort level. The good effect is that an individual can easily be convinced to change effort levels to help the firm (vertical relation) and/or a subset of employees/peers (horizontal relation). The negative effect is that once inside the inert area the individual will resist change. After all, the benefits of change are approximately zero, so most likely MB < MC. And as we all know if MB < MC then change is inefficient. And as we all know we don't act if it increases inefficiency. In either case every effort level between E1 and E2 is an equilibrium effort level. There is no guarantee that any effort level between E1 and E2, inclusive will lead to perfect rationality or 100% XE.

Here we have an individual doing as he pleases and responding to the internal and external pressures affecting him, with the exception that other people are not one of the pressures. How do other people affect the balancing of utility and effort, or the quality of decisions and felt pressure?

Group XE

An individual's degree of rationality can be the outcome of his or her own independent choices, or it can be influenced by others. These "significant others" may be one's peers or supervisors. These relations Leibenstein refers to as horizontal and vertical relations, respectively. The third possibility is that one is affected by what has gone on in the past, which constitutes the traditions and history of the firm. Whether formalized/conscious or not, tradition can be, and often is, a very effective influence on behavior.

The multi-person inert area comprises all effort points within the common inert areas of each group member. In Fig. 6.3, below, consider two individuals Nancy and Donald. For Nancy, Effort levels E2E4 is the inert area. For Donald effort levels E1E3 is his inert area. Effort levels less than E2 is unacceptable to Nancy. Effort levels

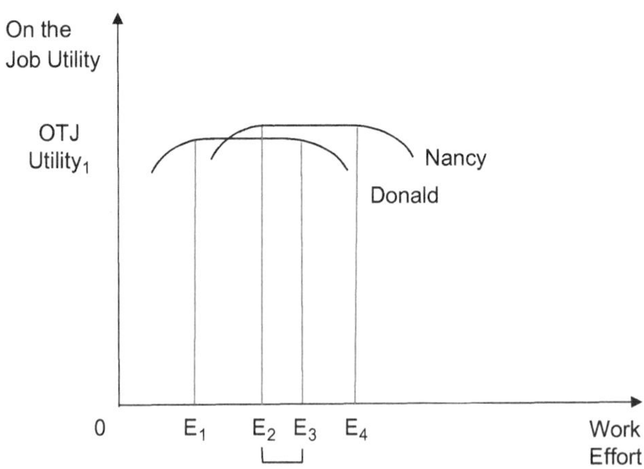

Fig. 6.3 Group inert area.

greater than E3 are unacceptable to Donald. An effort level exhibited by Nancy that is above E3 would be unwelcome and would bring a response by Donald to reduce her effort. At the same time, any effort level exhibited by Donald that is less than E2 would bring a response by Nancy to increase his effort level. However, so long as Donald does not go below E2, and as so long as Nancy does not go above E3, then neither will be motivated to change either their own or the other's effort. The 2 person inert area is E2E3, and it is smaller than the inert area for either Donald or Nancy. This does not imply that either Nancy or Donald will be at the most preferred effort level at the group inert area: they might not be happy about it, but neither will they attempt to change it.

As the size of the group becomes larger, group effort takes on the characteristics of a public good. We might expect that, ceteris paribus, an increase in the number of group members will reduce the size of the group's inert area. That is, an increase in the number of group members reduces the number of effort points that will be acceptable to everyone. On the other hand, it is not difficult to imagine that an increase in the number of group members will result in a more formalized group work ethic such as either a lower bound or an upper bound or both. In this case, each member agrees to "live and let live" so long as none of the other individuals violate the rule. The result is that the size of the inert area increases. In Fig. 6.3, this would be shown as the SE relation for each group member becoming more "satisfaction elastic." A precise result about group size and the inert area will not be attempted here. Suffice it to say that group relations affect effort.

The concept of the multi-person inert area also means that relatively low as well as relatively high effort levels will not be part of the group inert area. Thus, the effort level exhibited by the group will approach the average level of productivity of each group member. We may thus think of group effort as a "convention," an agreement. The implication of this for the determination of productivity will now be explored.

Prisoner's dilemma, gift exchange, and XE

For Leibenstein the issue was the determinant of productivity, and X-efficiency. In X-efficiency theory labor has discretion over effort because labor contracts are incomplete. Leibenstein illustrated his theory of gift exchange with his labor-management prisoner's dilemma game.[d] The prisoner's dilemma is a situation in which each individual acts according to his own self-interest and the outcome is not optimal for any one. In Leibenstein's PD model both labor and management have two options: altruistic behavior and selfish behavior, as commonly understood. Altruism means acting in accordance with the interests of the other. Selfish behavior means "looking out for # 1." These are shown in Table 6.1.

The P.D. aspect of this game is that if each side follows their own selfish, maximization strategy, both sides lose. For the firm, utility maximization/cost minimization requires that, regardless of which of the two strategies is used by the employees, the firm should give as little as possible, that is, the firm should always adopt an

[d] Incomplete contracts, effort determination, and gift exchange in a repeated game is presented in Falk, Gachter, and Kovacs (1999).

Table 6.1 Prisoners dilemma, productivity and X-efficiency

	Altruistic	Selfish
Altruistic	20 20	30 15
Selfish	18 25	10 10

adversarial strategy of selfish behavior. At the same time, regardless of what strategy the firm adopts, the employees should act selfishly, minimize their work effort for a given wage and benefits package by the firm. In both cases, maximizing one's (benefit/cost) ratio requires an adversarial strategy of individual maximization. The result, of course, is the prisoner's dilemma: a firm characterized by low productivity and poor working conditions.

In each box the number in the upper triangle is the utility for the firm, the lower triangle is for the employees. So, if both sides act altruistically, both receive 20 units of utility. If the employees act altruistically and the firm acts selfishly, then the employees are being "exploited." The utility to the firm increases to 30 but the employees receive 15. If the firm acts altruistically and the employees acts selfishly, then the firm is being "exploited." The utility to the employees increases to 25 but the firm receive only 18. If both act selfishly, then the environment in the firm is characterized by low effort and productivity, low wages, high costs, a.k.a., low X-efficiency. On the other hand, the altruistic strategy by both is Pareto optimal. X-efficiency is high because effort, productivity, and output is high, while unit cost would be kept low. The performance of humans, graduate students at Berkeley as well as others, varies, depending in part on the pressures imposed by the environment.

III Final comments on this chapter, and looking ahead to Chapter 7

Leibenstein believed that efficiency was important in economics but that allocative efficiency was very small, maybe .001 to .0001 of GNP. The other form of efficiency was of an nature, so Leibenstein called it X (efficiency). It is an efficiency of the internal workings of the firm. It has been estimated to be about .04 of GNP. One reason why X is larger than allocative is that the latter is only for Qc-Qm, while X covers all outputs.

X was developed because allocative and, in general, neoclassical theory is not the be all and end all of economic behavior. It leaves gaps between stimuluses and responses, for example, inputs and outputs. X-efficiency fills in the gaps to better understand the links between inputs and outputs, or output and costs. This makes X-efficiency theory an intervening variable. The assumptions of the theory are those which help explain the links between inputs and outputs, things such as effort discretion incomplete contracts and production functions.

Leibenstein used X-efficiency theory to explain the effect of group norms on effort, and game theory to explain productivity. He favored procedural rationality over substantive rationality and listed numerous procedures which lead to rational behavior. No experiments were done, which makes him a first generation behavioral economist, an "old" behavioral guy.

The next several chapters are a summary of empirical research on X-efficiency theory. They cover all regions of the world and many different industries.

Appendix: Dual-selves, herding, gift exchange, framing and the new behavioral economics

Look at Advances in Behavioral Economics, edited by Camerer, Loewenstein, and Rabin (2004). The papers in this excellent volume give the impression of having little in common with the papers of the pre-Kahneman and Tversky economists, a.k.a. the first generation behavioral economists. Even when the topics are the same, the papers appear to be "distant cousins" at best. The methodologies are different, the new group uses experiments which include empirical testing of their theories. The old group were developing theories. However, these differences is why behavioral economists are referred to as "old" and "new," not why the pre-K&T group aren't behavioral economists. Behavioral economics is, excuse the expression, a state of mind about economics. A state of mind which says that something is missing or incomplete in the economics as we know it. Katona knew this when he developed psychological economics, a.k.a., behavioral economics. Leibenstein knew it when he wrote about consumer demand, and X-efficiency theory. Simon knew it when he developed his theories of bounded rationality and satisficing. The purpose of this chapter is to show that the ideas on rationality written about by the "old" group were also written about later by the "new" group behavioral economists.

I need to be clear again about some things. The work done by the "old" behavioral economists do not resemble that of the "new" group. The point is that the "old" group wrote about topics similar to those written about by the "new" group. The methods used by both groups are different from each other. The old group by and large did not say this is herding behavior, or this is gift exchange, etc. But reading their works closely or between the lines and you can see the topics written about by the new group. This is all that I am claiming. For whatever reason, maybe it is the sophisticated-anthropormorphic sin which Paul Samuelson wrote about. Whatever it is, the first generation behavioral economists have been largely ignored. And I assert that this comes at the expense of behavioral economics. We either don't know our own history or we ignore it.

The first generation built the door and put the sign on it: Behavioral Economics, Enter Here. But because they didn't know the secret handshake, the security guard at the door wouldn't let them in. They were left with what Marshall called one of the greatest assets an economist could have, imagination. They couldn't imagine behavioral economics, understanding the behavior of human beings as we find them in this world, with homo economicus, as the main character. They couldn't imagine that humans, a.k.a. homo-sociologicus, make decisions independent of the decisions of all others. We are neither Dr. Spock or Robinson Cruscoe. They also couldn't imagine that human beings had one "big" unified Self within themselves which created harmony at every step of their lives. Rather, the Self was divided, creating tensions and "divided loyalties" within the individual.

"Old" behavioral economics

Dual self

Economists have usually considered the Self to be a single integrated unit. This was especially true when the first generation of behavioral economists were writing. The individual self knows their preferences, they have a well-defined preference function. Their choices are consistent with their preferences, and they are rational. Economic person is one well-integrated and "together" "dude." By contrast, dual-self models assume that the Self or personality is fragmented and containing conflicting parts.[c] Leibenstein's X-Efficiency theory included the individual as having two selves which were in conflict with each other. Leibenstein used the multiple self model to explain why individual's are selectively rational and contributing to X-inefficiency. The two Selves are the superego and the id.[d] When it concerns the multiple selves of the id and the superego, Leibenstein says that "an individual effects a compromise between his desire to do as he pleases and internalized standards of behavior acquired through background and environment" (Leibenstein, 1976, p. 71). Gabriel Tarde (1902) "divided" humans into two, one being materialistic-egoistic, and the other being spiritual. Tarde believed that competition was about a conflict within an individual, a conflict within the human mind. The conflict is between belief and desire, the two main determinants of value. According to Duesenberry (1949) one of our selves wants to increase our current standard of living while the other self wants to increase our future standard of living by saving more now. The idea of two selves continued into the "new" behavioral economics.

Herding

Leibenstein's bandwagon effect is an example of herding behavior. Tarde wrote that extra-logical imitation results in herding as people talk about ideas. Tarde says that herding is part of "inter-spiritual actions," individual minds interacting with other minds. Tarde calls this "inter-psychology." Duesenberry's demonstration effect is that others watch and imitate what we do, i.e., herding behavior. But it also states that preserving self-esteem is a strong motive for consumption and that self-esteem is related to the consumption of high quality status goods, i.e., the Veblen effect. Herding has been a way for the "new" guys to incorporate social influences on individual behavior.

Gift exchange

Leibenstein implied gift exchange in his article on game theory and productivity/X-efficiency. In Beyond Economic Man (1976), Leibenstein discusses how effort conventions affect productivity. He used a prisoner's dilemma framework. While this is not a theory of gift exchange per-se, it contains enough elements that a gift exchange interpretation is possible to make. Leibenstein shows that both the firm and employees benefit if they can agree to give more and get more. Employees give more effort and get higher wages and benefits. The firm gives higher wages and benefits and gets more effort. Hence the idea of a gift exchange.

In Leibenstein's efficiency wage model, there is a variable for effort in the determination of productivity, output, and wages. In this model productivity and wages are positively related with each other, as are wages, effort and output. Hence higher wages (effort) leads to higher effort and higher output (wages): a gift exchange, albeit an implied gift exchange. Framing. March referred to framing as stories which help firm members to place new experiences within an existing frame of reference. Shackle separated gains from losses in investing and created an S-shaped utility function resembling Kahneman and Tversky's graph of gains and losses.

"New" behavioral economics

Dual-selves

Shefrin and Thaler (1981), and Meardon and Ortmann (1996) developed a dual self or dual process model consisting of a farsighted "planner" and a short-sighted myopic "doer" who maximizes short run utility. Bernheim and Rangel's (2004) model is one of addiction in which a person either operates in a "cold" or "hot" state. The cold state utilizes more of logical analysis while the hot state is more emotional. Benhabib and Bisin (2005) use a dual process model consisting of "automatic processes" (System 1/intuition) or by "controlled processes" (System 2/logic). System 1 gets the first "crack" at influencing behavior, but when the costs become too high then System 2 steps-up to "save the day." This is similar to both Katona and Leibenstein who say that people may use System 1 until the pressure and costs of using System 1 become too high. At that point, people use more rational, System 2, processes. Other dual self or dual process models were developed in the era of the new behavioral economics. These include Kirkpatrick and Epstein (1992), Sloman (2002), Metcalf and Mischel (1999), Damasio (1994), and LeDoux (1996).

Our current and future selves

One reason for the existence of two selves is people's perceptions of themselves today and their future selves. In 1991 George Akerlof wrote "Procrastination and Obedience" in his Richard T. Ely Lecture. Procrastination and obedience are considered to be "pathological" forms of behavior because individuals make choices today without fully appreciating how current actions will affect future actions and beliefs. Hence pathological behavior means that "The standard assumption of rational, forward-looking, utility maximizing is violated" (Akerlof, 1991, p. 1). Procrastination occurs because of the "undue salience or vividness" of current costs and benefits relative to benefits and costs in the future. It leads people to live by the rule "put off for tomorrow what you don't want to hassle with today." What is not realized is that tomorrow never comes because at 12:01 am tomorrow is one day away, again. Over time, the small losses from procrastination on any one day escalates until the losses are large. "Irrational disobedience to authority" is a form of procrastination if disobedience yields negative utility. It occurs when the salience of current behavior deviate from past actions. Obedience to gang or cult leaders are given as examples.

Akerlof illustrates procrastination and obedience with examples of crime, drug use, savings, cults, and organizational culture and performance. Procrastination delays beginning and completing projects. Akerlof says that "proper management" can prevent procrastination, ignoring the idea that management would have to have complete control over all human behaviors at work in order to do this. Leibenstein's position is that effort discretion exists because management is not an all powerful controller of others' behaviors. Leibenstein also denied the existence of complete rational, utility maximizing behavior, but didn't call procrastination pathological. Rather he used the dual self concept to explain why part of our personality wants us to procrastinate and part goes not want to procrastinate. At work, it is the degree of product market competition as well as peer and supervisor pressures which determine how much superego and how much id is in charge.

In a paper, Murphy, Correia, and Barnett (2007) discuss procrastination, magnitude sensitivity, and salience in the context of college student drinking. Their review of the literature reveals certain things. First, students are sensitive to changes in cost or price in some studies but insensitive in others. Second, students tend to devalue the future, what he terms myopia. Third, among students the salience of the presence over future academic, career and other future rewards encourages (binge) drinking. Student advising about the future could help reduce (binge) drinking.

In Fudenberg and Levine (2006) posit a short run and long run self as a way to explain time inconsistency and quasi-hyperbolic discounting, and risk aversion. In a 2011 paper Hershfield, et al. used a sample of 42 students, each given a $15 Amazon gift card for participating. How much did students consider savings for retirement? The authors took a then current photo of the student was digitally scanned so that it would resemble their face at age 65. Therefore, the students would see their future self at retirement age. Upon seeing their future self the students revealed a much greater willingness to save for retirement, i.e., a lower tendency for procrastination.

In 1974 Gary Becker's "rotten kid" theorem sought to explain intra-family behavior and intra-family resource (parental wealth) resource allocation when one of the kids is rotten. Thus he posits an individual who is both loving and rotten. The rotten-self wants it all, even at the expense of siblings. But the rotten self theorizes that were he to hurt his siblings then his parents would not allocation resources to him. Thus the incentive to be loving now, for the sake of his future self.

Herding behavior

Pollak (1976) develops models of interdependent demand curves in both the short and long run. Kapteyn, Wansbeek, and Buyze (1980) develop a model which shows that individual preferences are explained by preference interdependence and habit formation, with the former explaining 67% and the latter 33% of individual preferences. Woittiez and Kapteyn (1998) explain female labor supply decisions with interdependence and habit formation, showing that habit formation plays a larger role than interdependence on female labor supply. They also show that explaining female labor supply with a variable for preference formation leads to a large decrease in the effect of having young children in the home on hours worked.

In finance herding behavior is related to the presumed collective irrationality of investors which contribute to stock market bubbles (Banerjee, 1992). Herding has also been related to "information cascades" (Bikhchandi, Hirschleifer, & Welch, 1992). The authors define an informational cascade as such: "An informational cascade occurs when it is optimal for an individual, having observed the actions of those ahead of him, to follow the behavior of the preceding individual without regard to his own information" (p. 992). An informational cascade may be seen as the cause of the bandwagon effect. Robert Shiller (2005), in Irrational Exuberance, says that herd behavior can be rational behavior when taking into account the judgments of others. However, "The behavior, although individually rational, produces group behavior that is, in a well-defined sense, irrational" (Shiller, 2005, p. 159).

In their 2008 book, Nudge, Thaler and Sunstein discuss "herd behavior," a.k.a. the bandwagon effect in the context of experiments conducted by Solomon Asch. Asch found that people almost always gave correct answers to easy questions when they had no information about the answers given by others. When they knew others' answers, even when they knew the answers were incorrect, about one-third knowingly gave the wrong answers. In other words, they engaged in herding, they jumped on a bandwagon. Thaler and Sunstein say that "social scientists generally find less conformity… when people are asked to give anonymous answers. People become more likely to onform when they know that other people will see what they have to say" (Thaler & Sunstein, 2008, p. 57).

In a paper, Baddeley, Burke, Schultz, and Tobler (2012) estimate herding in financial behavior, e.g., choosing to buy stocks. Their sample is 17 students 11 females and 6 males, at the University of Cambridge with an average age of 24.3 years. Their results include the observation that the probability of choosing to buy is positively related to the herd buying the stock. Groups less likely to engage in herding are males, older individuals, extraverts, people with greater cognitive abilities, people who are sensitive to both rewards and punishments, and people who are less socialized. People with impulse control issues, and people who are empathetic are more likely to be engaged in herd behavior. Evidence from functional magnetic resonance imaging (fMRI) analysis shows that when individuals are engaged in herding decision making that there is activity in the amygdala, an area of the brain associated with social decision making.

In their papers, Burke, Tobler, Schultz, and Baddeley (2010) and Burke, Baddeley, Tobler, and Schultz (2010), used a sample of 17 students and tested whether herding behavior activated the part of the brain called the ventral striatum, a part of the brain associated with both social (herding) and economic (stock prices) information. Herding and the activation of the ventral striatum were positively correlated with each other. And when the herd bought a stock the probability that the participants would buy was 73%. In a 2010 paper, Baddeley discussed the theory and the social, psychological, and neurological determinants of herding behavior. And, in a 2015 working paper, Baddeley discussed Leibenstein's contributions to bandwagon and herding behavior, beginning with Leibenstein's, 1950 QJE article.

Jain and Gupta (1987) [Some Evidence on "Herding" Behavior of U.S. Banks. Journal of Money, Credit and Banking, Vol. 19, No. 1: 78–89.] investigate herding behavior among small banks, whether they "blindly" followed large banks from 1977 to 1982. The authors conclude that only "weak" herding exists, because small banks were followed by large banks, as well as following the large banks. Ivaov, Levin, and Peck (2013) found that investors exhibit rational behavior but also systematic biases, including herding behavior rather than the optimal valuation of relevant information about observed investment endeavors. One result is deviations from Nash equilibrium.

Becker (1974) article, "A Theory of Social Interactions," Gary Becker acknowledges Leibenstein's, 1950 paper on "the 'bandwagon' and 'snob' influences on ordinary consumption theory," (Becker, 1991, p. 1065). In his 1991 article, "A Note on Restaurant Pricing and Other Examples of Social Influences on Price," Becker shows that the bandwagon effect can result in an upward sloping demand curve. Gisser, McClure, Okten, and Santoni (2009) gather data from the Web of Science. Of the 101 economists who cited Becker's, 1991 article, 99% consider Becker's hypothesis to be beyond controversy; 87% argue against Leibenstein's theory of a downward sloping to the right bandwagon demand curve, and; not one economist cites evidence for Becker's hypothesis. Biddle (1991) offers (the only) empirical evidence for the bandwagon demand curve in his study of vanity license plates. He reported that the bandwagon demand curve is downward sloping to the right. The dependent—price—variables were in both their current and lagged forms.

Gift exchange

George Akerlof wrote a classic article on gift exchange in 1982. His motivation was the impact of above market clearing wages on involuntary unemployment. The key variable affecting involuntary unemployment is labor effort, which depends on group norms and the definition of a fair days work. To increase the definition of a fair days work requires wages in excess of the market clearing wages. Akerlof integrates economic theory with a model imported from sociology. According to the sociology literature, interaction among workers creates sentiments for others and the firm. As a result "gifts" are exchanged. Effort in excess of some minimum standard is the gift given by the workers, and wages in excess of the market wage if the firm's gift to labor. These gifts are "rarely, if ever, in accord with the standards of the efficiency engineers" (Akerlof, 1982, p. 549). In XE theory, neither the the production function nor labor contracts are complete, meaning that inputs are not converted into outputs with the precision of an engineer's set of blueprints. Rather, performance and involuntary unemployment depends on custom.

Gneezy and List (2006) tested the concept of gift exchange using field experiments. They use two field experiments, both involving undergraduate students. One is a task of computerizing the books in a small library at a university. Students were told they would be paid $12 an hour. In the no-gift treatment they were paid $12, as promised. In the gift treatment they were paid $20 an hour once they finished training. The $20 an hour workers achieved more computerization during the first 90 min. After that the effort of the two groups were indistinguishable from each other. The second task was raising money door-to-door to support the Natural Hazards Mitigatio Research Center at a large university. The methodology and results were the same as in the first task.

Falk (2007) conducted a field experiment on gift exchange and donations to a charitable organization which works with children. Approximately 10,000 letters were sent asking potential donors for donations. Approximately one-third of the letters contained no gift, while one-third included a small gift and one-third a large gift. The small gift was a postcard and an envelope while the large gift was four postcards and 4 envelops. The postcards showed paintings done by children. A statement was added stating that the paintings were a gift from street children of Dhaka (Bangladesh). Would the gift of paintings on postcards be exchanged for the gift of donations. As compared to the no gift letters, the potential donors receiving the small gift had a donation rate 17% higher, while the potential donors receiving the large gift had a donation rate 75% higher than the no gift potential donors. Their results are consistent with the gift exchange theory.

Framing

Kahneman and Boulding agree that our image or frame of reference affects our behavior. In Thinking Fast and Slow, Kahneman uses the term image to discuss the effects of rare events on framing. He says that the rare event is in your mind and the image of the outcomes live in your mind even if the probability of the outcome is low. George Katona (1951), in talking about our gaining and using knowledge said that our frame of reference gives information its meaning to us, and that our frame of reference is a relative frame rather than an absolute frame. Kahneman and Tversky said that the reference point is, e.g., current wealth and that people evaluate gains and losses relative to this reference point.

List (2004) uses a sample of more than 375 persons operating in a well-functioning market. The participants make decisions according to neoclassical theory if those persons have a lot of "intense" market experience. For inexperienced consumers, behavior is more adequately explains by prospect theory, framing, non-fully rational behavior, than with the fully rational model of neoclassical theory. In a similar paper, Slovic et al. (2002) find that the affect heuristic allows a person to be a fully-rational decision-maker, as described by neoclassical theory if they have enough experience to correctly anticipate the effects of their decisions. However, neoclassical theory's fully-rational actor does not apply when the effects of one's decisions are different from what they anticipated. In this case, the "rational actor becomes the rational fool" (Slovic et al., 2004, p. 329). Both studies point out that people are selectively rational rather then fully-rational homo economicus.

Hossain and List (2012) used a sample of employees in the Wanlida Group Company, a high-tech Chinese manufacturer of consumer electronics, in order to measure the effect of framing on labor productivity. They have more than 20,000 employees. Their findings include the following. Framing improves productivity by individuals and team by about 1%. Second, teams respond to negative framing, i.e., losing income if productivity doesn't reach a particular level, more than they respond to positive framing. Third, the effect of framing does not decline with time.

Levin, Schneider, and Gaeth (1998) claim that the reason that the results of framing studies is mixed is because there is actually three types of framing. First, risky choice framing is the standard definition of framing introduced by Kahneman and Tversky. Second, attribute framing affects how we evaluate characteristics of an object. Third, goal framing affects how persuasive are communications. The authors summarize each type, the theory which can explain each, and give examples of each type.

Empirical research on XE: c.1967–1990

7

"... descriptions of the way managers actually behave show that they spend very little time on problem-solving, decision-making, or making choices, and when they do ... they tend to display considerable irrationalities"

(Brunsson, 1985, p. 3)

I Some issues surrounding X-efficiency

"Is Cost-Cutting Evidence of X-Inefficiency?" Borenstein and Farrell (2000) state that "X-inefficiency is surely among the most important topics in microeconomics. Yet, economists have found it difficult to study" (Borenstein & Farrell, 2000, p. 224). They test the "fat hypothesis," that financial pressure leads firms to cut costs, reduce X-inefficiency. They find that cost-cutting announcements among U.S. oil companies tend to come after oil price declines. They conclude that this is qualitative evidence for the fat hypothesis, for evidence of X-inefficiency. In their 2007 article, "Do investors forecast fat firms? Evidence from the gold-mining industry," the authors say that firms are not cost minimizers, except when economic distress is sufficient to push them to cut the "fat," reduce X-inefficiency. The next several chapters will show that many economists and others have studied X-(In)efficiency and have been able to report quantitative estimates.

In their 1990 book, Efficiency in U.S. Manufacturing Industries, Richard Caves and David Barton state that "Leibenstein contributed the name *X-inefficiency* to what is called technical inefficiency in this study" (Caves & Barton, 1990, p. 2). They estimate X-efficiency among 347 four-digit manufacturing industries basing their estimates on value-added, and; 191 industries using gross output to measure X-efficiency. The average level of X-efficiency based on value-added, and gross output are 0.28, and 0.63, respectively. Another set of estimates among 162 industries shows average X-efficiency of 0.28 (value-added), and 0.6 (gross output). Among small plants the figures are 0.28 (value-added), and 0.61 (gross output). Among large plants the two estimates are 0.33, and 0.64, respectively. The authors believe that the value-added measure is the better of the two and, hence the results showing such low estimates with value-added left them "somewhat dismayed" (Caves & Barton, 1990, p. 51).

This was not the first time that an economist(s) was dismayed over empirical results. Arnold Harberger's (1954) estimates of the welfare impact of market power in the United States were very small, on the order of 0.001 of GNP. Robert Mundell (1962) responded to the studies asserting that the welfare effects of efficiency and production are small. He expressed his own sense of dismay, saying that "Unless there is a

The Beginnings of Behavioral Economics. https://doi.org/10.1016/B978-0-12-815289-8.00007-1

thorough theoretical re-examination of the validity of the tools on which these studies are founded, some one inevitably will draw the conclusion that economics has ceased to be important" (Mundell, 1962, p. 622).

Harvey to the rescue

Estimates about the macro impact of X-inefficiency is that it is about 4% of GNP. The micro impact is that firm's are on average, around the world in many industries, about 20% off their frontier.

From 1967 until c.2015, about 200 empirical studies on the existence of XE have been published, virtually all of them in support of the theory. Yet, it has been largely ignored in the ("new" behavioral) economics literature. Leibenstein's assumption about rationality was the basis for the rejection. It was Leibenstein rejection of the assumptions that individuals are always perfectly rational, always engaging in maximizing behavior, and the firm is always producing on their output and cost frontiers which led to the rejecting of his ideas.

Especially when Leibenstein was writing in the mid-1960s employees were considered robotic, working with 100% effort and were 100% rational. They were in short, homo economicus. Firms were nothing more than a "black box," a set of engineering blueprints in which the firm produced on their production and cost frontiers. Capital produced to its technological potential. Therefore, by definition XE was zero, not because the results of empirical tests revealed that it was zero, but because XE was assumed not to be able to exist. And the science about the non-existence of XE was declared settled!

It is important to add that almost every study discussed in this book is empirical evidence about XE theory according to the authors themselves. There are hundreds, maybe thousands of studies framed in terms of technical efficiency. Rather than 200 empirical studies on the x-istence of XE, there would be several hundred more studies. Despite how similar XE and TE are, if the authors do not mention XE then, with a few exceptions, they are not discussed in this book. In Leibenstein's 1987 book, Inside The Firm: The Inefficiencies of Hierarchy, he says that technical inefficiency as used in the literature is similar to his concept of X-inefficiency. (Leibenstein, 1987a, p. 261).

One other important and/or interesting point. Many articles on X-efficiency do not even list Leibenstein's 1966 article or any other relevant article in their references. I assume that this is because the X-efficiency concept is common enough that the originator is overlooked.

X vs allocative (in)efficiency

X-efficiency (XE) theory implies that there is a form of (in)efficiency which is not allocative. Allocative inefficiency is caused by market power. It is shown by the welfare triangle. X-inefficiency is an inefficiency within the firm. It is shown as cost above the estimated cost frontier and output below the estimated output frontier. Homo economicus will place the firm on their frontiers. Homo x-inefficicus, or as Mises said, homo agens,

[a] Hollas and Hereen (1982) estimate X and allocative (in)efficiency among electric utility firms for 1972, finding that X exceeds allocative inefficiency as a percentage of the firms' revenues.

will place the firm above their cost frontier and below their output frontier. X-inefficiency means that it is possible for a firm to increase their output without any change in inputs, or decrease costs without any change in output.[a] X-efficiency can be increased through better management, better organization, a "moderate" amount of pressure from the market to increase effort, and eventually X-efficiency. The factors of management, organization, and pressure influence the degree of rationality of the organization members. Two examples of research estimating X and Allocative efficiency follow.

Joel Bergsman (1974) discussed an important difference between allocative and X-efficiency by saying that allocative efficiency is the traditional concern of economists, and X-efficiency is assumed to be zero. Bergsman estimates the relative cost of allocative market and X- inefficiency (plus "monopoly returns") due to trade protection, as a percent of Gross National Product for Brazil, Malaysia, Mexico, Norway, Pakistan, and the Philippines. His estimates of the cost of protection in terms of allocative-market-inefficiency for the six countries listed above averaged 0.12%. X-inefficiency (plus monopoly returns) averaged 3.2%. As in other estimates of X and allocative inefficiency Bergsman finds X-inefficiency considerably larger than allocative-market-inefficiency, approximately 27 times larger. Then Bergsman states, however, that results showing the X-inefficiency effects of protection are *surprising* in a model which assumes that firms are cost minimizers, and that the only inefficiency is due to misallocations due to the effect of protection on relative prices.

Pittman (1990) estimates the allocative and non-allocative effects of a proposed merger between the Sante Fe and the Southern Pacific railroads in 1983. Assuming an elasticity of −0.75 and a price increase of 22.5%, gross deadweight losses, allocative inefficiency, are $98.6 million, X-inefficiency and/or rent-seeking is $336.9 mil. X-inefficiency exceeds allocative inefficiency.

What does the estimate of X-(in) efficiency mean?

Pustay (1978) measured X-efficiency among a group of 11 airlines over the years 1965–74. Average X-efficiency was in the 0.85 to 0.88 range. Pustay recognizes that the most X-efficient airline, the airline on the frontier, is given a score of 1.0. What if the 1.0 is only a relative score, rather than an absolute score. Then the 12–15% estimate of X-inefficiency—the average firm is 12–15% off their frontier—is an underestimate of the true degree of X-inefficiency.

Rationality

X- (in) efficiency is a reflection of an organization's performance. Rationality is a reflection of a person's thinking. There is a weak and a strong sense of rationality. The strong sense is used by cognitive scientists and they use the term in a normative sense. There is a standard for complete rationality and anything which falls short is irrational. The weak sense comes from Aristotle and this use of the term is the categorical sense. Behavior is either based on thinking or it is not so based. If it is then behavior can be either rational, or arational. Being rational only applies to behavior which involves thoughts and choices. An object in space moving according to the laws of gravitation is not rational; a person who accidently falls is not irrational. But "when we say that an agent has acted rationally, we imply that it would have been a mistake in some sense to have acted in certain different ways" (Stanovich, 2011, p. 4). Therefore, if humans, with our thoughts and choices, are the only rational animals then we must be the only animals capable of being irrational (Stanovich, 2011, p. 7). However, there have been (at least) two reasons for shying away from using the term irrational; irrationality has been associated with mental illness, and with people being less than "human," i.e., civilized. However, rather than saying that we are irrational, we could also say that humans are capable of being less than perfectly, 100%, rational. Rationality and irrationality come in degrees, like 90% rational or 10% irrational, 50% and 50%, etc. Rationality is selective, being able to vary between 0% and 100%. The alternative to this is that we take the position that all of our thoughts and actions are consistent with 100% rationality, regardless of what we think and do. But this would be a (very) weak sense of rationality.

The "Great Rationality Debate" is about how much irrationality can be attributed to human cognition. There are three points of view about this, the Panglossian view, the Meliorists, and the Apologist views. The Panglossian view takes the position that maximum human rationality is the default position. That is, whatever reasoning competent people are shown to possess is also the norm against which to measure rationality. Thus, "whatever is, is rational." Irrationality ain't possible. Critics of XE theory, mostly in the 1970s and 1980s were Panglossian. XE could not exist. They offered no proof that it didn't exist, they offered an assumption that it could not exist.

More than these critics, economists in general tend to be Panglossian. Faced with research showing that people fall short of the norm of complete rationality Panglossian respond with two arguments. First, that the individual's interpretation of the task is different from what the researcher thinks it is. The result, change the norm, called "reject the norm strategy" (Stanovich, 2011, p. 11). Second, that the modal response to rationality tests is the product of evolution. The Meliorists assume that human rationality is not perfect, but can be improved through education and better information.

The Apologists believe that there is a gap between perfect and actual levels of rationality. However, they are not quick to term the gap irrationality. They believe that cognitive limits which create the gap also means that a single normative standard may not apply to every individual, especially those with low algorithmic capacity, vis-a-vis conceptual understanding. Apologists believe that there is a gap but people are doing about as well as they can. Apologists see little in the way of improving rationality. The Meliorists believe that there is a gap but that they can do better. Meliorists believe that education can enhance rationality. Panglossians, many orthodox economists, believe that everyone is doing as well as they can.

Brunsson, in, The Irrational Organization (Brunsson, 1985) accepts the x-istence if irrationality and says that there are three explanations for irrationality. First, the people studied are not smart enough to act rationally. Second, some forms of irrationality are inherent in human nature. Third, cognitive limits/limited information. Panglossians might say that the problem is not with human rationality but with theories of why it supposedly exists.

Harvey the Meliorist

Meliorists assume that human rationality is not perfect, but can be improved through education and better information. Leibenstein's theory of selective rationality speaks to the first part of the Meliorist philosophy. As to the second part, Leibenstein did not emphasize education and better information. He emphasized pressure. Pressure does come from the super-ego function of the human personality. Pressure which is stressed the most is pressure from the product market. A moderate amount of pressure is believed to be the optimal amount.

II Early studies on X-efficiency using questionnaires and/or interviews

Most of the earliest studies on XE were also the least "sophisticated." Many of the earliest studies gathered data by either questionnaire and/or interviews,[b] while simple averages were often presented as the evidence. Especially after c. 1990 and especially in studies of financial institutions, the statistical analysis became considerably more sophisticated. But first, the first empirical study on XE theory was whether franchisee-owned single restaurants as part of a restaurant chain are more (X-) efficient than a single restaurant which is part of the same chain but managed by an employee of the parent company. In this 1967 study by John Shelton the statistics used were simple averages about sales and profits. Shelton hypothesized that the franchisee-managed restaurants will be more efficient, i.e., lower costs and higher profits. The sample contained 22 restaurants. Twenty-one underwent ownership changes at least once leading to 53 restaurant "units." When any one "unit" changed ownership from company-managed to independent entrepreneur Shelton found that profits and sales increased. A manager of the parent company said that "...franchisee-owners just watch the little things closer… they reduce waste" (p. 1247). Shelton concluded that this creates an incentive system to increase X-efficiency.

What will keep health care costs lower, large outpatient clinics or solo practitioners? Joseph Newhouse (1973) gathered data on private solo practitioners using questionnaires, and data on large outpatient clinics using Newhouse's own estimates. Newhouse tested the hypothesis that solo practitioners will keep costs lower and operate with greater XE. Two reasons were given. First, doctors in large outpatient clinic have fewer incentives to control costs, and second, the large outpatient clinics are less likely to feel the pressure of the market, vis-à-vis the small solo practitioner. Large outpatient clinics may benefit more from economies of scale, but suffer from X-in-inefficiency. Newhouse examined data for 1969 among 20 solo or small groups in private practice, and three large outpatient clinics. Overhead costs per visit were over

[b] This was at a time when both were considered unacceptable, and before behavioral economics made greater use of questionnaires and interviews.

300% higher for the clinics. Using OLS regression Newhouse reports that total salary costs per visit are positively and significantly related to cost sharing among the clinics. The same basic result was found for appointments costs, billing costs, and medical records costs per visit Newhouse concludes that for large outpatient clinics, the benefits of economies of scale are exceeded by X-inefficiency.[c]

Is there such a thing as a modernization attitude? Attitudes are intervening variables between inputs and outputs, or outputs and costs. If the modernization attitude exists, then does it affect productivity? Shapiro and Muller (1977) believe that a modernization attitude exists. They collected data on modernization through questionnaires and interviews for 26 cotton farms in Tanzania for the period 1970–71. A Cobb-Douglas frontier production function with labor and land as independent variables was estimated. From this they could estimate X-efficiency, actual relative to maximum output (Q/Q*). The correlation between X-efficiency and modernization was 0.566, significant at the 1% level. Regression results show that the most X-efficient firms have higher labor productivity rather than capital productivity. The results also show that greater XE is gained by both more knowledge and a greater willingness to use that knowledge.

What has a stronger impact on labor productivity, better technology (capital stock) or a higher level of X-efficiency? Gregory and James (1973) tried to disentangle these two causes by testing the vintage capital model. Data on capital vintage was collected by a questionnaire. Vintage capital models assume that technical change is embodied in the latest technology and that technology is being used to its capacity. Therefore, older capital should be associated with a lower level of labor productivity. However, if production functions are incomplete, then the vintage capital hypothesis may be shown to be incorrect. Gregory and James tested the vintage capital model with a sample of 116 new factories operating between 1953 and 1958 from 46 Australian industries. The authors compared differences in labor productivity/industry average labor productivity among new factories in each industry. Evidence showed that differences among new factories was larger than what is predicted by the vintage capital model. And, labor productivity among new factories exceeded the industry average in only about half the cases. In both cases the evidence is inconsistent with the vintage capital model. X-efficiency, created by management quality, is seen as a reason for the failure of the vintage capital models.

X-Efficiency among the famous Mondragon cooperatives of northern Spain, as compared with that of non-cooperatives in the same region was estimated by Bradley and Gelb (1981). The data was gathered by questionnaires and interviews. The authors investigated how external and internal factors affect performance. External factors include job security, while internal factors include working conditions. Mondragon employees considered wages to be less important, but the cooperative nature of the Mondragon cooperatives more important. Mondragon employees also feel a smaller

[c] Baron (1974) estimated the effect of XE—"managerial innovations"—technological change, the hospital's case mix, the hospitals inputs and outputs among 218 hospitals over the period 1968–71. The hospital production function estimated was a Cobb–Douglas. Hospitals were divided into six groups according to their case mix, and their inputs. Costs were estimated separately for cost per patient day, and cost per admission. Twelve equations were estimated. In all 12 equations the variable which included XE were negative and statistically significant. Higher levels of XE were associated with lower costs.

gap between labor and management, they support unions to a lesser degree, support a hard work culture, and sees their work effort affecting the performance of the firm. All of these help explain the XE of the cooperatives.

Scherer, Beckenstein, Kaufer, and Murphy (1975) and his colleagues used interviews to estimate labor productivity in eight industries among firms in the U.S., United Kingdom, Canada, Sweden, France, and West Germany. For purposes of comparison, they define U.S. labor productivity as having a value of 1.0. Then, by comparison, the labor productivity, labor productivity for the other five countries was 0.47, 0.87, 0.75, 0.68, and 0.58, respectively. Why the differences? The orthodox explanation would emphasis (K/L), output, and technology. About X-(in)efficiency the authors say that cartels reduced pressure for performance and management's effort. The dissolution of the cartel increased management's effort. In the paint industry in Europe, cartels reduced management's effort which reduced everyone's effort.[d]

C. Diaz-Alejandro (1973) compared productivity and costs—X-efficiency—among cement plants in Latin (LA), with those in Australia, Canada, and the U.S. (NLA). Data came from the World Cement Directory of 1963, and data obtained from questionnaires in 1963–65. In terms of employment per plant, LA plants employment approximately 228% more than NLA plants. The output of LA plants was about 58% of NLA plants. Output per employee in LA plants was 24% that of NLA plants. As compared with the most efficient plants, the K/O ratio in LA plants was 12% higher than in NLA plants, but the L/O ratio in LA plants was about 400% higher than in NLA plants. X-efficiency is not neutral but mostly labor-using. Custom, and intervening variable between inputs and output, and other socio-economic institutional practices are given for the relative X-inefficiency among LA plants and especially for the labor-using X-inefficiency.

III Early studies not using questionnaires and/or interviews

If hospitals can be automatically reimbursed for higher costs then how will this affect health care costs? If the reimbursement policy changes suddenly, then how will this affect costs? Davis (1973) tested the effect of cost reimbursement on hospital inflation for 1965, 1967, and 1968. Cost reimbursement is measured by (costs reimbursed/ total costs). This includes plans such as Medicare and Medicaid. His estimated cost function with average cost as the dependent variables, with the cost reimbursement plans and yearly dummies as the main dependent variables. The cost reimbursement variable is statistically significant, interpreted as an increase in X-inefficiency as the percent of patients covered increases. The yearly dummies are statistically significant meaning that the introduction of Medicare and Medicaid had a one-time "announcement" or shock effect. Davis asserts that the results are consistent with XE theory.

[d] Erickson (1976) studied a cartel in the gymnasium seating industry which existed from 1944 until 1960. Using company data and "best guess estimates" Erickson concludes that the dissolution of the cartel had a "shock effect" which led to a 23% reduction in costs. Erickson does not mention XE theory. His results, however, are consistent with XE theory.

Anderson and Frantz (1985) estimated X-efficiency among 24 textile firms in Mexicali, Mexico. Average X-efficiency was 0.469. Higher levels of X-efficiency was caused by higher wages for the technicians who fix the machines. Second, firm age and X-efficiency are positively related only until the firm's age is about nine years old. Third, X-efficiency is higher among firms which faced sudden changes in the environment, i.e., demand for their product. Under the condition of a greater fluctuation in demand, managers must keep a "closer eye" on the day-to-day workings of the firm. Higher quality management can do that, reducing X-inefficiency.

Another example of high wages and X-efficiency is a 1988 paper by Morris Altman. Altman focuses on wage levels and economic development of Quebec and Ontario between 1870 and 1910. Arthur Lewis (1954) argued a "high wage—slow growth" thesis. Altman argues that high wages pressures or encourages firms to increase X-efficiency as a way of offsetting higher wages. His "high wage—high X-efficiency" thesis is supported by data from the manufacturing sector of high-wage Ontario and low-wage Quebec. In terms of current dollar value-added per capital, low wage Quebec produced 87% of high wage Ontario in 1870 and 75% of Ontario in 1910. The constant dollar figures were 87% and 73%, respectively. The growth of constant dollar value added, per-capita growth, constant dollar savings per employee, and employment growth were higher in high wage Ontario. Unit labor costs which was 10% lower in Quebec in 1870 was 5% higher in Quebec by 1910. XE is a variable and higher wages can induce higher XE, as the data shows in Quebec and Ontario.

Don Lecraw (1977, 1979) provides estimates of both allocative and X-inefficiencies during the years 1962–74. His sample is 400 light manufacturing firms in 12 four-digit industries. Data were collected by interview. A CES production function was estimated in order to estimate X-inefficiency. The estimated parameters then allowed Lecraw to estimate [(actual output/maximum output)], and [(actual (K/L)/cost minimizing (K/L))]. He called these D1 and D2. D1 less than 1.0 means that the firm is producing inside its output frontier. The average value for D1 for all firms and industries was 0.74, meaning that on average firms were producing about 25% less than maximum. If D2 is greater than 1.0 then the firm is too capital-intensive. The average for D2 was 1.71. Finally, D3 is (actual total cost/cost minimizing total cost). The average D3 was 1.60; firms were about 60% above their cost frontier.

His interviews with company managers lead to his conclusion that they are profit maximizing and interested in the satisfaction derived from using modern Western technology, The latter is known as "engineering man satisfactions." He concludes that allocative inefficiency is caused in part by engineering-man satisfactions. He also concluded that X-inefficiency was significant.

IV Ownership form

Monsen, Chitj, and Cooley (1968) studied the relationship between profits and ownership form among 72 firms from 12 industries listed in the "Fortune 500." Data on these 72 firms were for the entire period 1952–1963. For each industry, owner-controlled and manager-controlled each accounted for 50% of the firms.[e] The profit rate for manager and owner-controlled firms was 7.3% and 12.8%, respectively. The authors attribute this difference to different incentive systems causing differential XE.

William McEachern (1978) used a sample of 16 firms from each of three industries for the period 1964–73 in order to estimate the relationship between ownership form and the growth of sales. The sample included eight owner-managed firms (OM), 26 manager-controlled firms (MC), and 14 externally-controlled (EC) firms.[f] McEachern's hypothesis is that the dominant stockholder in an externally controlled firm—the stockholder is not a manager—is less likely than a manager in either an OM or MC firm to have a strong preference for the firm's growth. Therefore, growth is least likely to be pursued by an EC firm. McEachern uses an OLS regression equation where the dependent variable is the average growth of sales between 1964–68 and 1969–73. The most important independent variable is the ownership form measured as dummy variables, OM, MC, and EC. The results show, as predicted, that OM and MC firms have higher growth rates than EC firms. McEachern says that OM firms may have the highest growth rates because of lower levels of X-inefficiency.

Which is a greater incentive for enhanced X-efficiency: ownership form or competition per se? Vining and Boardman (1992) show that allocative and x-efficiency is significantly influenced by ownership form. The authors estimated a relationship between market structure and come to this conclusion by estimating a structure and organizational performance for 1986, using data on the largest 500 non-financial corporations in Canada. Ownership form is either state-owned, cooperatives, private companies, or mixed firms.. Other independent variables include market share, assets, sales, and number of employees measuring firm size. Performance measures are profits, and X-efficiency (or technical efficiency). X-efficiency is measured as sales per employee and per asset. Profits are return on both assets and sales, and net income. Cooperatives are the most X-efficient and the most profitable, while state-owned are the least x-efficient. The four-firm concentration ratio was not related to either X-efficiency or profits.

Timmer (1971) compared technical (or X) efficiency among U.S. farmers by state. Timmer's main interest was whether ownership form—owners vs tenant farmers—created different motivations which led to different levels of XE. The time period under investigation was 1960–67. Timmer used a two stage process. In the first stage he estimated a Cobb-Douglas frontier production function, where output is a function of the inputs—labor, capital, land, fertilizer, seeds, and livestock—and where the random error term captures XE. After eliminating the 2% most efficient farms (Q/Q*), the results of the frontier function is very similar to the average (OLS) production function. Timmer reports that South Dakota had the highest efficiency at 0.991, while West

[e] An owner controlled firm was defined as one in which either an owner who was actively engaged in the business owned at least 10% of the voting stock, or in which a nonactive owner owned at least 20% of the voting stock. A manager controlled firm was defined as one in which no owner owned 5% of the voting stock and for which there was no evidence of recent owner control.

[f] McEachern defined an owner managed firm as one in which the dominant shareholder owns at least 4% of the voting stock and is also a manager. A manager-controlled firm does not have a dominant share-holder. An externally-controlled firm has a dominant share holder who is not a manager.

Virginia had the lowest ranking at 0.810. The average XE ranking was 0.934, or about 6.6% below the frontier. In the second stage, Timmer used these efficiency rankings as the dependent variable regressed against several independent variables. The number of tenant farmers as a percentage of all farmers was a crucial variable. The results showed that the state's efficiency ranking increased when the percentage of tenant farmers increased. Timmer commented that this might "...be associated with the extra effort and motivation, an intervening variable, of the young farmers... attempting to save enough to buy their own farms" (p. 791).

Junanker (1976) examined the relationship between farm size and ownership form on X- efficiency for farms in India for the years 1968–70. (Land leased/total land size) was the measure for ownership form. A Cobb–Douglas was used to estimate X(in) efficiency. The dependent variable was the value of wheat produced. The independent variables included the ownership form—owner or tenant farmer—farm size, labor hours worked, the value of fertilizers, tractors and oxen. His statistical analysis was done for small (less than 25 acres) and large (more than 25 acres) farms. His results showed that among large farms, greater ownership increases X-efficiency, they produce more wheat from a given quantity of inputs.

V Protection

The effect of competition on XE among 26 Swedish manufacturing industries was estimated by Bo Carlsson for 1 year, 1968. competition on x-inefficiency in what has been described as a small open economy—Sweden. He uses a two stage process. In the first stage a linear programming technique was used which yielded a frontier production function, a potential (y*) and an actual output figure (y). The ratio (y/y*) is the degree of X-inefficiency. In stage 2, (y/y*) was the dependent variable. The independent variables includes the four-firm concentration ratio and the nominal tariff level. The average industry XE index for 26 industries was 0.78, with a range of 0.91 to 0.58. Furthermore, the industries most protected from foreign competition due to, for example, high tariffs, were the least efficient industries. On the other hand, the largest exporters among Swedish manufacturing were also among the most X-efficient industries. Manufacturing goods.

Tyler (1979) fit a Cobb Douglas function and reported that among 16 plastics firms in 1971 the average level of XE was 0.48; for the foreign firms it was 0.58. Among 22 steel firms, the average level of XE was 0.62, 0.56 for publically owned firms, and 0.72 for foreign firms. At the time of the research both the plastics and steel industries enjoyed a relatively large amount of effective protection from foreign competition. Tyler considered the average XE figures as "evidence of substantial X inefficiency" (p. 486). These X-inefficiencies are larger for both domestic and government-owned firms, vis-à-vis foreign firms. Better management is the stated reason for higher XE among foreign firms. Tyler ends the paper with one suggestion: "it would be useful to develop more explicit models of economic behavior relating to efficiency" (p. 491).

Green and Mayes (1991) reported levels of XE among 72 British manufacturing industries for 1977. They achieved their results by fitting a translog stochastic frontier production function. XE estimates ranged from 0.89 (cement) to 0.39 (broadcast and receiving equipment). Overall, the industries which engage in more international trade have higher levels of XE. Lee (1986) estimated and distinguished two major explanations for X or technical efficiency among a group of 51 Korean manufacturing industries. Data was from the Bank of Korea for 1970. Lee's results show that industries which were protected from foreign competition to a greater extent have higher average XE levels. On the other hand, those with access to subsidized credit were less X-efficient. Lee also reports that more protected industries are more profitable unless their profits leads them to become more X-inefficient.

The effect of exports and protection from international trade on per-capita GDP growth from 50 countries over the period 1950–80 was carried out by Heitger (1987). The results of his regression analysis are that protection from international trade reduces per-capita GDP growth by approximately 2% per year. Some of this loss is due to higher levels of X-inefficiency caused by protectionist policies. Heitger concludes that "competition through trade is the best anti-monopoly policy to... reduce X-inefficiencies" (Heitger, 1987, p. 251).

Kalirajan and Tse (1989) measure X or technical efficiency among 115 Malaysian food manufacturing firms for 1974–76. X-efficiency, they say reflects intrafirm entrepreneurial skills and talents. These skills and talent they consider as important as the "material" factors of production. Their estimates of XE are accomplished by fitting a translog production function. The reported average XE ranged 0.82 (cocoa manufacturing) to 0.60 (rice mills), with a mean grade of 0.73. The first and third (tapioca and saga) most X-efficient groups are heavily engaged in international trade and face stiff competition from foreign competitors. The authors' comment that "Empirical findings... indicate ... differences in efficiency of factor use is attributable to differences in the entrepreneurial talents of firms" (p. 183).

McFetridge (1973) views the structure-performance relationship (SPR) as including both static allocative efficiency, and dynamic X-efficiency, where the latter has larger effects than the former, even though X-efficiency is "less amenable to analysis" (McFetridge, 1973, p. 345). His study of the SPR is for 43 Canadian industries for the years 1965–69. He measures SPR with the price-cost margin, a measure of allocative inefficiency. He regressed the P-C margin on several variables including the tariff rate. The tariff rate and the P-C margin were inversely related, rather than positively related as expected. McFetridge philosophizes that the result is due more protection increasing costs, X-inefficiency, rather than profits.

VI Level of competition

According to William Shepherd (1972a), neoclassical theory expects that market share and profits are positively related with each other, and perhaps in a linear way. However, if X inefficiency increases with market share then the relationship may be curvilinear.

Shepherd's data showed that the relationship was curvilinear. Shepherd estimated a profits function for the largest 500 or 1000 firms in the Forbes Directory for 1956–69. Firms in older industries were included to test the theory that dominant firm eventually begin to slack-off, or suffer from "organizational sclerosis." The dependent variable was rate-of-return as a proxy for profits Independent variables included market share, the square of market share, the four firm concentration ratio, barriers to entry, and firm size (net assets). Regressions showed that firm size and profits are inversely related, especially in older industries with dominant firms. Shepherd comments that the inverse relationship is caused by X-efficiency.

In a second study, Shepherd (1972b) estimates a profits function for 1963–67 among 336 industries. Profits are measured by the P-C margin. He reports that firm size and profits are positively related except among older industries. Shepherd attributes this to increasing X-inefficiency among larger firms in older industries. He also reports that profits and the industry 4FCR are shown as an inverted U. Two possible explanations are offered. First, large monopoly firms voluntarily reduce their profits in order to avoid government anti-monopoly regulations. The other is that large firms are more X-inefficient (or unions extract higher wages) which reduces profits.

Katrak (1980) in his study of Indian manufacturing measured the P-C margins for 1963. Results show that P-C margins increase with concentration until the concentration rate is 50%, declining after. He attributes higher levels of X-inefficiency with increased power for the result. Higher P-C margins are also shown to be positively correlated with protection from foreign protection.

Primeaux's (1977) study of the effect of U.S. electric utility monopolies and duopolies on costs was done by estimating a cost function. Electric utility monopolies enjoy economies of scale which is why they are considered to be a "natural" monopoly. At least this has been the theory since the early 1900s. However, if their monopoly status raises costs above the technological minimum, then the effect of regulation on costs depends on the relative strength of economies of scale and x-efficiency. Using FPC data he reports that duopolists have lower costs than monopoly firms, ceteris paribus. At the average output rate for all firms, unit costs were 10.75% lower for the duopolist. This is primeaux's estimation for the degree of X-inefficiency caused by monopoly power. At the same time, unit costs decrease with output, meaning that economies of scale among monopoly public utilities exist.[g]

Rodney Stevenson's (1982) studied the effects of competition among gas and electricity utilities on costs for 1970 and 1972. His sample consists of 25 "combination" utilities and 54 "straight" utilities. "Combination" utilities receive at least 15% of its total revenues from gas. "Straight" utilities receive less than 5% of its total revenues from gas. Combination utilities serve customers who use both gas and electricity, while straights serve customers who use electricity. Therefore, combination utilities have more monopoly power and the prediction from XE theory is that they will have higher costs. For 1970, straight utilities had 6.5% lower costs. For 1972 the figure was 8.5%. Combination utilities have the advantage of economies of scope, but the disadvantage of X-inefficiency. The disadvantage of power exceeds the advantage of power.

[g] Chen and He (2013) argue for the positive X-efficiency effects of competition in the electricity market in China.

If utilities get reimbursed for higher costs, then will that affect (X) efficiency? Gollop and Karlson (1978) measured the effects of cost reimbursement for higher costs called the Fuel Adjustment Mechanism (FAM). The sample was privately owned electric utility firms in the U.S. for 1970 and 1972. The U.S. was divided into three regions: the Northeast, Coal Belt, and Gulf States regions. The percentage of costs covered by FAM is the measure of FAM. The utility commission set a base rate against which they evaluated market prices. When market prices exceed the base rate than the utility can be reimbursed, varying from 0% to 100% reimbursement. The research reveals that changes in FAM had no affect on X-inefficiency in the Gulf region. In the Gulf region FAM was changed more frequently than in the other regions. By adjusting FAM more frequently, by changing the environment more often, regulators were better able to keep the base prices close to market prices, thus minimizing cost reimbursement, i.e., X-inefficiency.

Water utilities face rate of return regulation, with its cost-plus feature. Bruggink (1982) argues that water company managers work in an "unfriendly private enterprise environment" and must prove their worth by being X-efficient. Bruggink uses a sample of 77 public and nine privately owned water utilities in 1960 to test the relative X-efficiency of public and private water utilities. Data is from the American Water Association. Variable costs per million gallons of water produced was the dependent variable. The result shows that publically-owned firms have average variable costs 24% lower than private firms. However, the slope of the cost curves are the same for both private and public firms. Bruggink offers no evidence that managers of public firms face more pressure due to the hostile environment factor.

Schive (1988), studied X-efficiency among the 23 sugar mills of the Taiwan Sugar Company (TSC) for 1976 to 1983. The Taiwan Sugar Company (TSC) was a government owned monopoly which accounted for about 50% of Taiwan's exports during the 1950s. Fitting a frontier production using direct labor, and fixed capital as inputs, Schieve reports that one mill operated at 80% to 90% efficiency, while seven were between 40% and 49%. The efficiency levels then became the dependent variable. His results include that X-inefficiency increases when TSC owns more land used for sugar production, and when managers have less education,

Button and Weyman-Jones classified organizations as either being under "high" or "low" pressure. The former were private sector, competitive and not highly regulated firms. Low pressure are bureaucratic and/or state-owned firms. The organizations were financial institutions in the U.S. and Europe, and government public service s organizations. For all firms in the studies the average level of XE was 0.78. For high and low pressure environments the averages was 0.80 and 0.74, respectfully. In addition the low pressure environments had lower individual firm values, and higher dispersions around the mean.

VII Government (regulations)

When a government suddenly stops supporting its currency in favor of the market, a sudden change which can create inflation, how does this affect labor effort (productivity)? In February 1982 the Mexican government not supporting its currency.

The peso-dollar exchange rate fell from 27 pesos = $1 in February 1982, to 45 pesos per dollar on February 19, 1982. Inflation followed. Given the use of dollars on border communities such as Mexicali, Mexico, which are about 100 miles east of San Diego, the real per-capita income fell by about 25% overnight. Anderson and Frantz (1982) collected daily output rates on 46 piece rate workers in two textile plants in Mexicali. Average weekly output increased by about 15%. The two firms had contracts with U.S. companies for their products denominated in pesos, but loans from U.S. banks denominated in dollars. The two firms were "between a rock and a hard place." A shock effect occurred. The Presidents of both firms said that they needed to pay closer attention to all the little things if they were going to increase their X-efficiency. This is not the only article on productivity among piece rate workers Kiyokawa (1991) identified the effect of piece rate wage system on the silk-reeling industry in Japan.

Craven, Dick, and Wood (1986) investigated how changes in per-student funding for non-university higher education in Britain, one polytechnic, affected X-efficiency. The sample period was 1979 to 1984. Eliminating "need" based funding was believed to reduce resources for education, which in turn would increase pressure and X-efficiency. Between 1978–79 and 1983–84 expenditures in the number of full-time equivalent (FTE) students increased, while FTE expenditures and academic staff fell. The quality of education—measured by the percentage of students passing their exams, the number of students graduating with honors, and faculty publications—did not fall. Increases in XE caused by a "shock effect" was the reason given for the results. Duncombe, Miner, and Ruggiero (1997) used the non-parametric Data Envelope Analysis (DEA) to study X-efficiency among 585 school districts in New York State between 1990 and 91. The average level of X-efficiency was 0.784 for all school districts. Twelve percent of school districts were on the frontier. Among the other 88% the average level of X-efficiency was 0.756. Using tobit regression analysis the authors report that a greater percentage of public school students, vis-à-vis private school, less wealth (property and gross income), and fewer teachers who are tenured as a percent of all teachers increases X-efficiency. A greater percent of adults with a college degree also increases X-efficiency of school districts. Ruggiero, Miner, & Blanchard, 2002 used the DEA and 1991 New York State data on 631 school districts to estimate X-efficiency. Their findings include average X-efficiency equal to 0.67, ranging from 1.0 to 0.16. They also investigated variations or equity in school spending according to cost and inefficiency differences among the school districts, but not how these differences affect educational outcomes. When costs and inefficiency are controlled for, equity in school spending is reduced by about 50%. In other words it is cost and inefficiency differences and not only educational outcomes which affect spending differences.

Register (1988) studied a shock effect among 275 (mostly nonprofit) hospitals in 13 MSAs, and 114 hospitals from Ohio. The cause of the shock was unionization and higher wages. The effect was productivity, and XE. The data come from the American Hospital Association's 1984 survey of hospitals. Register shows that productivity was 16% higher, and 10% lower costs than non-union hospitals. Register and Grimes (1991) studied "shock effects" of unions among 2360 secondary school students in

61 U.S. school districts. The data came from the National Assessment of Economic Education database. Empirical results show that unionization increased SAT scores by about 5%. The authors see the result as unions creating a shock effect and higher XE to control their budgets. Fiorito and Hendricks (1987) discuss the degree of X-efficiency among unions.

Does crony capitalism affect the X-efficiency of firms involved in a cozy relationship with government? Globerman and Book (1974) investigated this relationship with a sample of 33 symphony orchestras and 23 theater groups in Canada during 1971–72. The dependent variable in the cost function was the per performance cost. The key independent variable is the age of the performing arts group. Age is believed to be correlated with important (tacit and other forms of) knowledge of the grants process, and is favored by government, ceteris paribus, because government has already "invested" in the group. A statistically significant relationship between age and per-performance costs is the result of the OLS regressions for both groups. The authors conclude that monitoring grant applications more closely, especially of the older groups, would reduce X-inefficiency.

Does spending other people's money affect the way the money is spent? Silkman and Young (1982) studied this by studying whether the cost of local school transportation in 1317 school districts, and 749 local libraries is affected by who is paying for the service, local, state, or federal sources. XE theory predicts that costs will be higher the further from the users of the service is the source of the funds. The authors estimated separate cost frontiers for school transportation and library services. Regressions reveal that the school transportation district and the libraries on the frontier had per-student bus costs, and per volume costs of $67.07, and $0.24, respectively. The average transportation district and library had costs of $142.72, and $0.78, respectively. When the local source of school district transportation costs increased by 10%, the per-capita deviation from the cost frontier falls by 2.8%, or $0.74. For local libraries, deviations from the frontier are reduced by 3.4%. Thus, costs, XE, are affected by whose money is being spent.

When the break-up of the AT&T company occurred in 1982, did the level of XE among the telecommunications firms change? Majumdar (1993) investigated X-efficiency among 40 telecommunications firms between 1973 and 1978. This included 22 firms of the AT&T Bell system, and 18 independent companies. DEA was used to estimate X-efficiency. The before and after deregulation X-efficiency was estimated in 1973, 1978, 1981, 1984, and 1987. The mean sores for each of the 5 years was 0.5, 0.5, 0.58, 0.83, and 0.88. The lowest scores increased from 0.33 (1973) to 0.53 (1987), and the percentage of firms at the frontier increased from 5% (1973) to 40% (1987). XE increased due to deregulation.

Cook, Kazakov, Roll, and Seiford (1991) estimated X-efficiency among Ontario, Canada highway patrols, using the Data Envelope Analysis method. DEA revealed that X-efficiency ranged from 1.0 (working on the frontier) to 0.616. A total of 14 patrols constituted the sample. Average X-efficiency rating among more privatized patrols was 0.946, while lesser privatized patrols had an average of 0.959. The authors thus note that grouping the 14 patrols by the degree of privatization did not significantly affect X-efficiency.

Another DEA study was Leibenstein and Maital's (1992) study of measuring X-efficiency among Boston Bruin hockey players during the 1989–90 season. X-efficiency was estimated by maximizing (outputs/inputs), measured by (goals + assists per game)/(salary + shots on goal). Surprising to no hockey (sports) fan, the forwards had a higher X-efficiency score than the defense-oriented players—0.747 vs 0.464. One thing is clear, the ability of the DEA technique for estimating X-efficiency has many opportunities. There are two other papers about X-efficiency in sports. One is by Kashian and Pagel. It was published in 2016 but is included here because of it being only one of three papers on the subject. The sample consists of NCAA Division 3 schools over the period 2007–12. Until the Leibenstein and Maital paper, this one uses the parametric SFA method. Estimates of XE use the Director's Cup Score. If a school comes in first place in a sport then it gets 100 points in the Director's Cup Score (DC). The total score is from 20 sports with men's and women's teams given the same number of points for a first, second, third place, etc. One set of results showed that if women (men) athletes increase by 10% then DC points increase by 5.3% (3.8%). Smaller schools, enrollment less than 2000 earn 18% fewer DC points. Private schools earn 3% more DC points. XE scores by schools shows that Calvin College was # 1 at 0.86. Claremont McKenna was # 10 with a score of 0.66. The # 1 conclusion is that the largest increase in DC points is gained by increasing women participants in sports. Jones (2013) used a sample of Division 1 schools and found that expenditures by the athletic department is positively and statistically significant department expenditures and DC points are positively correlated in a statistically significant manner for FBS schools ("Big 5" conferences) but not other Division 1 schools.

The other is about Moneyball, the Major League Baseball draft, and its relationship with X-efficiency, and Hayek's theory of knowledge. The authors are Caporale and Collier (2013). Moneyball, written by Michael Lewis, is about (X) inefficiency in the MLB draft (labor market). Caporale and Collier state that one cause of X-inefficiency in the MLB draft is that baseball scouts do not place a premium on college baseball players. The authors ask whether college baseball players are more productive than high school players. Their data is the first round of the draft in the years 1995–99. Are baseball scouts ignoring relevant information, i.e., the superiority of college baseball players? The authors' empirical analysis finds that college players do not perform better in the major leagues than do high school players. Thus the rejection of X-inefficiency in the draft. However, it suggests the importance of baseball scouts who spend thousands of hours gaining information about potential draft picks. In particular it points to the value of localized knowledge written about by Hayek.[h]

[h] Massey and Thaler present evidence for the inefficiencies of the NFL draft. Their result are inconsistent with rational expectations theory but supportive of concepts from psychological research such as overconfidence, and judgment under uncertainty.

VIII Management

Medford's (1986) paper is about completing the incomplete production function by adding management and quality-adjusted labor and capital inputs. Mefford says tests the role of management in influencing the firm's output by fitting three forms of a production function—Cobb–Douglas, CES, and the translog forms—to data from 30 industrial plants in Australia, Europe, Asia, Latin America, and Canada for the years 1975–82. Regardlesss of the form of the production function there is a "large" error. Medford believes that differences in management quality is a major reason for the error. In the current (1986) study differences in management quality account for about 50% of efficiency differences among firms. Labor and capital inputs were adjusted for quality of the input, labor by skill level, and capital by technology used. The output variable is constructed by industrial engineers using time-and-motion studies. Higher quality management was ascertained by their higher relative plant performance. The criteria was meeting output goals, costs relative to budget, and quality of output (defects as a percentage of total output). Mefford's regression analysis showed that better management increases XE by 13.9–17.5%.

Page (1980) estimated XE with a Cobb-Douglas production function and OLS, for the logging, sawmilling, and furniture manufacturing industries in Ghana for the period 1972–1973. The average level of XE for all three industries was 0.8. Higher levels of XE are shown to be caused by (correlated with) managers who have more training and experience, firms with a larger percent of managers who are expatriates, and fewer workers per supervisor. A greater percentage of managers who are expatriates, and a smaller number of production workers per supervisor. The final conclusion was that X-efficiency reflects the quality of management which unfortunately is often excluded from the production function.

Martin and Page (1983) estimate X-efficiency in the logging and sawmilling industry in Ghana using firm-level data, and a translog production frontier. Their estimating technique is the translog production frontier. Their hypothesis is that X-efficiency is the result of managerial effort and the amount of information possessed by managers. The average level of X-efficiency among the firms in the logging and sawmilling industries are 0.724, and 0.844, respectively. The level of X-efficiency was then the dependent variable. One of the independent variables was a dummy variable = 1 if the managers had formal education and/or prior experience in the industry where they worked. The coefficients on both were positive and statistically significant. Second, firms which receive government subsidies (loans) were less X-efficient. The authors state that this effect could be either the result of government subsidies on management's ability to prefer the "quiet life," and/or the firm engaging in rent-seeking activities.

The role of managers in maximizing X-efficiency includes utilizing the optimal K/L. According to Howard Pack (1974, 1976), searching for the optimal (K/L) is important in MDCs and LDCs because input substitution, in both are "alive and well." Pack (1974) reports that elasticity of substitution ranges from 3.7 to 0.24. The inefficient firms use inappropriately high (K/L). How inefficient are the firms in this sample? Using the optimal (K/L) and maximizing output would increase output by 41% (bicycles) to 270% (paint production). Doing so also increased employment ranging from 15% (cotton spinning) to 445% (wool processing). Thus, there is no tradeoff between output and employment growth.

Pack (1976) reports that among manufacturing plants in Kenya, there is considerable ex ante choice about the K/L. It is managers with technical training who are most likely to search and choose labor intensive input ratios. Managers with sales or finance backgrounds are more likely to adopt the (K/L) favored by Western businesspeople.

In his paper on allocative and technical efficiency among firms in Bangladesh, the author, Shaikh Hossain (1987) uses a sample of 1207 firms in rural Bangladesh for the years 1979–80. Firms were either cottage industries using 0 to 1000 taka per worker, cottage industries using between 1001 and small industries using more than 4000 taka per worker. He derives estimates of XE using a Cobb-Douglas and CES production functions. His regressions show that proprietors with formal education and/or experience in financial record keeping produce greater XE.

White (1979) studied the effects of competition and "engineering man satisfactions" on (K/L) in 31 Pakistani industries during 1967–68. Industries facing foreign competition were those who exported at least 10% of their output. Those who exported less than 10% were classified as being sheltered from competition. Using OLS White finds that higher capital/labor ratios in the U.S. lead to higher capital/labor ratios in Pakistan. Thus engineering man satisfactions exist among Pakistani entrepreneurs. However, the (K/L) in Pakistan lags further behind that in the U.S. as the latter increases. Second, (K/L) in Pakistan increases as industry concentration increases. Third, (K/L) in Pakistan is higher if the industry is sheltered from competition. These results are consistent with his hypothesis that less competitive pressure gives firms more discretion to be X-inefficient. In Pakistan, cost consciousness means using more labor-intensive technologies.

How does XE, input substitution, technological change and diffusion affect output? Shen (1973) used a sample of 4000 manufacturing plants in Massachusetts for the period 1947–59 in order to gain evidence for the determinants of output (mentioned above). The results show that the best-practice plants have both a higher Q/L and K/L than other plants of the same size. Second, X-efficiency increases labor productivity more than capital intensity. And, only the most X-efficient firms take the most advantage of technological diffusion. Capital intensity is more the result of technological change. Factor substitution is of limited significance. The results, according to Shen, are consistent with technological diffusion that includes the X-efficiency. Finally, Shen says that the production function should include behavioral factors, as well as technical factors.

Price fixing conspiracies in the gymnasium seating and structural steel industries in the U.S. was estimated by Erickson (1976 X-efficiency theory is not referred to by name in the article). In gymnasium seating, price fixing lasted from 1944 to 1954. Prices during the price fixing was 40% above the non-price fixing eras. Per-foot costs during the price fixing were approximately 60% higher than during the non-price fixing eras. The price fixing resulted in less innovation and higher costs of middle and upper management. After the price fixing costs fell about 25%. The end of price fixing created a shock effect on prices and costs or X-inefficiency. The price fixing era in structural steel was between 1950 and 1962. Prices were about 25% higher during this period, while costs were 10% higher. Inertia apparently set in and two post conspiracy entrants quickly expanded their market share at the expense of the already established and conspirator firms.

The relationship between prices, profits, and market power among 17 U.S. food chains in 36 metropolitan areas for the period 1970–74 was studied by Bruce Marion and the Food Systems Research group (1977) at the univ. of Wisconsin. Their research shows that profits and prices rise with the firm's market share and the industries concentration rate. At the same time prices rise faster than profits. And the data showed that 36.5% of the higher prices led to higher profits. The remaining 63.5% of the price increases was absorbed in higher variable costs. Thus, higher market power raises costs more than prices such that profits rise at a decreasing rate. The authors believe that XE theory accounts for a good explanation of the data. The difference between the increases in prices and profits is a measure of X-inefficiency.

Chen and Tang (1990) explained the relationship between exports and productivity growth. One possible explanation is scale economies. Larger firms allow for many advantages which increases (Q/I). The other explanation is the "competitive forces" theory. Exports increases competition which pressures management to reduce "slack" of X-inefficiency. X-(in)efficiency is the result of worker morale, management quality, and competitive pressures. Less X-inefficiency means lower inputs per unit of output, or higher (Q/I). They use data on 16 Taiwan industries for the years 1968–82. The main results are that scale economies increases productivity in 10 of the 16 industries. On the other hand, export growth increases productivity in 1 of 16 industries. Second, export growth increases both XE and scale economies which increase productivity. The role of XE is as a force which increases scale economies and then productivity.

IX Final comments on this chapter, and looking ahead to Chapter 8

This chapter looked at empirical studies on X-efficiency theory from c.1967–90. The year 1990 is important in that beginning in 1990 many of the studies were done on the financial sector, Before 1990 there were very few studies on the financial sector. In addition, the empirical studies became more sophisticated in terms of the econometrics beginning in 1990. The earliest studies gathered data from questionnaires and interviews. Studies during this period eventually used econometrics, but not as sophisticated as it would be after 1990. The studies in this period covered the topics the degree of X-efficiency as affected by ownership form, protection from international trade, the degree of competition in the market, government regulations, and the role of management. Chapter 8 is the first chapter of empirical studies covering the years c.1990–2014. Specifically, it covers studies of the financial sector in the U.S.

XE among US financial institutions: c.1991–2017

8

The studies mentioned in this chapter use parametric and non-parametric approaches. Parametric approach include stochastic frontier analysis (SFA), distribution-free approach (DFA), and thick frontier analysis (TFA). The non-parametric include data envelope analysis (DEA), and the free disposal hull (FDH). The studies cover banks and other financial institutions.

I Parametric and non-parametric approaches

Estimating XE can be done with a cost function such as $C = C(w, y, z, \mu, \mathcal{E})$, where w are variable input prices, y are variable outputs, z are amount of fixed inputs or outputs, μ is that part of the residual representing inefficiency, and $\mathcal{E}$ is that part of the residual representing random error (measurement error and other data problems, and luck, good or bad. The non-parametric approaches do not allow for random error so the entire residual is assumed to be X-inefficiency. The parametric approaches allow for both X-inefficiency and "noise." As a result the non-parametric approaches are likely to report higher levels of X-inefficiency—lower levels of XE—than would the parametric approaches. Among US banks in the studies reviewed by Berger and Humphrey (1997), the average level of XE using non-parametric and parametric approaches was 0.72 and 0.84, respectively. The range of levels for the non-parametric and parametric studies is 0.31 to 0.97, and 0.61 to 0.95, respectively.[a]

The estimation of the level of XE exhibited by a particular economic agent, be it a firm, industry, country or otherwise, is typically conducted using one of two approaches: (i) stochastic frontier analysis (SFA), and (ii) data envelope analysis (DEA). In this chapter, we will describe both approaches, sketching out basic formulations of the underlying models, while highlighting key assumptions and implications of both approaches, as well as surveying uses of both approaches in the broader XE literature.

Overview

As noted by Kumbhakar and Lovell (2000) in their widely cited review of stochastic frontier analysis, there is a long history of economists approaching the estimation of production, cost, and profit functions under the assumption that firms produce according to those functions. On this view, deviations from the estimated function are random noise drawn from symmetrical distributions. The insights provided by XE theory, however, suggest this assumption may not be realistic. Instead, we may suspect that deviations away from the expected quantity produced according to a firm's

[a] X-inefficiency has been calculated in two ways. First (1-xe level). Second, (1-xe level/xe level). If XE is 0.8 then X-inefficiency is either [0.1–0.8 = 0.2, or (1–0.8)/0.8 = 0.25].

The Beginnings of Behavioral Economics. https://doi.org/10.1016/B978-0-12-815289-8.00008-3

production function are more likely to be the result of *under*-production as compared to over-production.

This intuition underscores Kumbhakar and Lovell's suggest that we "recast the analysis of production, cost, and profit away from the traditional functions towards frontiers." From this perspective, we define an efficient frontier for a firm's production—the minimum quantities of various inputs required to achieve a certain level of output. Firms which deviate from this production frontier are said to be inefficient. While this approach offers clear advantages over the assumption that all deviations from efficient production are simply statistical noise, we are presented with several immediate questions. The most pressing of these questions is how exactly does should best go about defining an efficient frontier? Once we have identified this frontier, we may want to know if the aforementioned random noise in production levels plays any role in our new formulation. Are all deviations from the production frontier inefficient by definition, or is there some natural variability in production levels? These questions provide valuable framing for the discussion of the approaches to XE estimation described below. We will see that these various estimation approaches provide differing answers to these questions, and that these differences can play an important role in interpreting the conclusions derived from empirical studies.

Data envelopment analysis (DEA)

Farrell (1957) is generally cited as the first to introduce the DEA approach to frontier estimation. Intuitively, DEA seeks to define an optimal or "best practices" production frontier. This goal is accomplished by using data on the observed combinations of inputs used by each firm in the sample and constructing a piece-wise linear optimal production frontier. Specific points along this frontier are defined by the firms within the sample that most efficiently use a given mix of inputs to produce some level of output. The efficiency of individual firms may then be measured by comparing deviations from this frontier.

We can introduce a simple formulation of the DEA model developed by Coelli et al. (2005). For the sake of consistency with the discussion of stochastic frontier analysis conducted below, we will describe an output-oriented variation of the DEA model. We begin by introducing the following notation—for firm i, let x_i represent a vector with length N of inputs to production and q_i represent a vector of outputs of length M. We can then aggregate these measures across all I firms by letting $X_{N\times I}$ denote the matrix of all input vectors (with each column corresponding to x_i for firm i) and $Q_{M\times I}$ denote the matrix of all output vectors. Finally, let $1'$ denote a vector of one of length I. We can then define the following linear programming problem:

$$
\begin{aligned}
&\min_{\phi,\lambda} \phi \quad \text{such that} \\
&-\phi q_i + Q\lambda \geq 0 \\
&x_i - X\lambda \geq 0 \\
&I1'\lambda = 1 \\
&\lambda \geq 0
\end{aligned}
\tag{8.1}
$$

where $\phi_i \in [1, \infty)$, and $\phi_i^{-1} \leq 1$ defines the efficiency level of firm i relative optimal production frontier defined by the linear program.

Stochastic frontier analysis (SFA)

Developed after DEA, SFA was pioneered by Aigner, Knox Lovell, and Schmidt (1977) and Meeusen and van den Broeck (1977). SFA models as a general class attempt to formulate a best practices production frontier that defines what a 100% efficient firm's output would be given a certain input mix. This best practice frontier is hypothetical— it may or may not be the case that any of the firms in a given sample exhibit 100% efficiency.

A basic formulation the SFA model, following Aigner et al. (1977) and the treatment given by Coelli et al. (2005) is given by

$$\ln Y_i = X_i'\beta + \in_{it} \tag{8.2}$$

where Y_i denotes the output of firm i given a set of inputs to production X_i. The key innovation in SFA is the specification of the error term u_{it}, which can be written:$\in_i = v_i - u_i$

So that u_i is defined in terms of two components: (i) v_i, a mean-zero i.i.d. error term which captures random statistical noise in the data, and (ii) u_i, a disturbance term which is greater than or equal to zero and which reflects the level of inefficiency exhibited by firm i. We can interpret this inefficiency term u_i in light of Eq. (8.2) as follows—if $u = 0$, then log production $\log Y_i$ of firm i is equal to the sum of the level of production implied by its efficient production frontier, $X_i'\beta$, and the white noise disturbance term v_{it} (which is symmetric and mean-zero). Deviations from efficient production which are not caused by statistical noise in the measurement of variables, natural variation in production processes, the exigencies of weather, etc.—namely, those factors which are captured by v_i—are driven by elevated levels of inefficiency, that is, $u_i > 0$.

Given Eq. (8.1), we can identify the level of inefficiency exhibited by a particular firm. Following the discussion provided by Coelli et al. (2005), perhaps the most common measure of efficiency is the ratio of observed output produced by the firm to its stochastic frontier level of output:

$$\text{Efficiency}_i = \frac{Y_i}{\exp\left\{X_i'\beta + v_i\right\}} = \frac{\exp\left\{x_i'\beta + v_i - u_i\right\}}{\exp\left\{X_i'\beta + v_i\right\}} = \exp\left\{-u_i\right\} \tag{8.3}$$

The value of $\text{Efficiency}_i \in [0, 1]$ gives us the ratio of output produced by the firm relative to the value it could have produced along its efficient frontier (net of the white noise v_i disturbance term). Efficiency values of 1 imply an efficient firm.

Estimation of β in Eq. (8.1) is generally conducted using maximum likelihood estimation (MLE) and iterative optimization techniques. Estimation requires making assumptions about the distribution of the disturbance terms, in particular about the distribution of ν_i. Commonly selected distributions for this term include the half-normal, truncated normal, exponential, and gamma distributions. As noted by

Coelli et al. (2005), the distributional choice for ν_i speaks view that researchers take of the extent inefficiency across firms. Distributions such as the half-normal which are centered around 0 imply generally small levels of inefficiency, with substantial departures from efficiency being an exception to the rule, while distributions which are centered away from 0, such as the truncated normal, make such departures more likely. Finally, the choice of specific distribution used in a given analysis has the ability to influence estimated efficiency levels, the rankings of firms by efficiency level is generally significantly more robust to alternative specifications.

Comparison of methods

Drawing on the summary provided by Coelli et al. (2005) and the preceding discussion, we may compare the relative strengths and weaknesses of the various approaches to estimation described above. Stochastic frontier analysis (SFA) offers researchers several key advantages at the expense of requiring additional assumptions over and above what data envelope analysis (DEA) requires. SFA allows researchers to decompose observed deviations from optimal production levels into (i) random statistical noise and (ii) inefficiency. This ability to incorporate statistical noise is a clear strength of SFA, given the massive scale and complexity of large firms in modern economies, in particular the firms and industries most of interest to researchers concerned with XE, such as those in the finance and healthcare sectors, and the measurement issues involved in tracking inputs and outputs in such firms accurately. In contrast, DEA allows for no such decomposition and we are left attributing all deviations from efficient production to inefficiency. Analyses conducted by DEA, then, may be especially susceptible to measurement error and statistical noise in the underlying data. Finally, SFA facilitates the calculation of conventional confidence intervals and the implementation of standard statistical inference.

Compared to SFA, DFA offers the advantage of requiring fewer assumptions on the part of the researcher. While both methods identify an efficient frontier against to evaluate the performance of individual firms or decision-making units (DMU's), Rosko and Mutter (2011) note:

> *DEA calculates relative efficiency based on observed best practices, while SFA measures efficiency in terms of an estimated or theoretical best practice frontier. As a result, in DEA studies, there are always DMUs that are 100% efficient. In contrast, SFA studies can have no DMUs that are 100% efficient.*

Likewise, DEA does not require the assumption of particular functional forms for the production functions of firms. Whether these considerations outweigh the drawbacks of DEA described above depends on the specific application and goals of the analysis.

II Frontier analysis

The research on XE uses frontier analysis, estimating the frontier cost or production function, and then comparing the costs or output rates between the most efficient, frontier, firm with other firms within the industry. The XE level of the most efficient firm(s) is 1.0 and that for the other firms is between 0.99 and 0.0. Frontier analysis is used for many issues including deregulation (Elyasiani & Mehdian, 1992), management quality (DeYoung, 1998), problem loans and Granger-causality (Berger & DeYoung, 1997), market power (Berger & Hannan, 1998) mergers (Peristiani, 1997), organizational form, e.g., ownership form (Berger & Meister, 1997), and intercountry and/or interindustry efficiency differentials (Ruthenberg & Elias, 1996).

Berger and Humphrey (1997) reviewed XE research among financial institutions—commercial banks, S&Ls, credit unions, as well as insurance firms covering 130 empirical studies in North and South America, Europe, Asia, the Middle East, and Africa.[b] Among US institutions, the average level of XE for banks was 0.79, 0.79 for insurance firms, 0.83 for S&Ls, and 0.88 for credit unions.

III Bank studies

Berger and Meister (1997). Profits efficiency

Berger and Meister estimate both a cost efficiency and profits efficiency functions for about 6,000 US commercial banks for the period 1990–95. The cost efficiency function is identical with the one above. Profits efficiency measures a firm's profits relative to the maximum possible profits given output and input prices, and other factors—(actual profits/maximum profits). The standard profits efficiency can be written as $\ln \pi = f(w, p, z, v) + \ln u + \ln \beta$, where w are prices of variable inputs, y are the quantities of outputs, z are the quantities of fixed inputs or outputs, v are other factors which affect efficiency, μ is that part of the residual representing inefficiency which raises (actual costs/minimum costs), and c denotes an inefficiency factor that may raise costs above the best-practice level, and β represents that part of the residual representing random error.

The authors use the parametric DFA approach. It assumes that each firm has a core or an average efficiency level which persists over time. Second the core efficiency is distinguished from the random error which is assumed to average out over time. Third, parametric is preferred to non-parametric approaches because the latter cannot account for misallocations due to relative prices, thus making it impossible to estimate allocative (in)efficiency.

The results of their estimations is that average cost efficiency with 5% truncation is 0.87,[c] so that average inefficiency is either 1–0.87 = 0.13, or (1–0.87)/0.87 = 0.15. Profit efficiency is 0.55. In other words, approximately 50% of profits are lost to inefficiency. The average scale efficiency is 0.8. Finally they estimate (efficient scale/actual scale) and call it t^*. If $t^* > 1$ then firms are not taking advantage of all economies of

[b] The average cost efficiency with a 0%, 1%, 5%, and 25% truncation is 0.69, 0.78, 0.87, and 0.9, respectively.

[c] None of the studies are included in the other empirical research covered in this book. Berger, Hunter, and Timme (1993) also have a long review article on the efficiency of financial institutions.

scale. If $t^* < 1$ then the firm is operating in the area of diseconomies of scale. The average t^* was 2.7, meaning that the firm needs to be about three times larger—producing about as much as they do—in order to take advantage of all economies of scale.

Akhavein, Berger, and Humphrey (1997)

The authors studied 57 mergers for banks with assets in excess of $1 billion for 1980–90, and found that average X-efficiency was 0.46 for the two merging banks before the merger and 0.73 for the merged bank after the merger. Profits efficiency rose from 0.74 to 0.90.

Jordan, Rice, Sanchez, and Wort (2011). Bank's market to book value and TARP

Did receiving TARP funds affect a bank's stock price and their level of XE? The authors investigated these questions using a sample of 576 banks receiving TARP funds and 6028 banks not receiving TARP funds, and a smaller sample of 283 publically held banks receiving TARP funds. The period under investigation was 2006–09. Their two hypotheses are, (1) receiving TARP funds will reduce the ratio (market-price/book-value), and (2) a higher level of XE will increase the (market-price/book-value). The authors use a translog cost function and Seemingly Unrelated Regressions to estimate XE. A bank's outputs were their loans and deposits, and the inputs were labor, physical capital, and the price of the bank's liabilities. Their data using the larger sample of banks reveal that hypothesis 2 is supported at the 0.01 level of significance: XE supports a higher ratio of a bank's (market-price/book-value). Doing an ANOVA analysis and a Random-effects GLS panel regression analysis the data using the smaller sample shows that hypotheses 1 and 2 are supported: a bank receiving TARP funds has a lower (market-price/book-value) ratio, and a bank with a higher level of XE has a higher ratio of (market-price/book-value) (Table 8.1).

McAllister and McManus (1993). Scale efficiency

Much research on economies of scale in banking show that increasing returns to scale exist for small banks with assets less than $100 million, and decreasing returns for larger banks. (Berger and Humphrey, 1997). The level of assets which separates increasing and decreasing returns depends on the size of the banks in the sample, the econometric techniques used, single translog cost function, the logic used in the model. The current authors state that once those are accounted for, increasing returns occur until assets are $500 million, and then constant returns to scale exist for all other (larger) banks.

A problem with a single translog is that most small banks produce an output mix which is different from the mix produced by large banks. The number of small banks which produce the same mix are very small so using a single translog will bias the results about scale efficiency. The author shows that the cost functions of small and large banks are different; using a single translog cost function is simply inappropriate.

Table 8.1 US financial sector

Authors	Yr pub.	Yrs studied	(Non) para	Average XE
Berger and Humphrey	1997	1980–90	Para	0.8
Berger and Meister	1997	1990–95	Para	0.85
Akhavein, Berger, and Humphrey	1997	1980–90	Para	0.74
Jordon et al.	2011	2006–09	n.a.	n.a.
McAllister and McManus	1993	1989–90	Non-para	0.65
Pi and Timme	1993	1988–90	Para	0.9
Bauer and Hancock	1993	1979–90	Para	0.67
Bauer and Hancock	1993	1979–90	Non-para	0.7
Berger and Humphrey	1992	1981–89	n.a.	n.a.
Berger and Hannan	1992	1987–88	Para	0.68
Peristiani	1997	1980–90	Para	0.7
Shaffer	1993	1984–89	Para	0.8
Rhoades	1993	1981–86	Para	n.a.
Berger	1993	1980–89	Para	0.81
Berger, Leusner, and Mingo	1997	1989–91	Para	0.94
Berger, Leusner, and Mingo	1997	1989–91	Para	0.79
Berger	1995	1980–89	Para	0.58
Berger and DeYoung	1997	1985–94	Para	0.92
DeYoung	1998	1991–92	Para	0.71
English et al.	1993	1982	Para	0.75
Meister	1993	1991	Para	0.89
Gardner and Grace	1993	1985–90	Para	0.17
Yuengert	1993	1989	Para	0.6
Fried, Lovell, and Eeckaut	1993	1990	Non-para	0.8
Rai	1996	1988–92	Para	0.73
Rai	1996	1988–92	Para	0.5
Choi and Elyasiani	2011	1992–98	Para	0.8
Choi and Weiss	2005	1992–98	Para	0.8

The authors use the kernel regression technique, a non-parametric approach. Their results show that banks with $10 million in assets have scale efficiency about 65%, whereas banks with $500 million have scale efficiency of about 98%. This difference is statistically significant. For banks with assets between $500 million and $1 billion scale efficiency is constant. Thus, below but up to $500 million in assets banks experience increasing returns to scale. From $500 million to $1 billion they experience constant returns to scale. Mergers among smaller banks increases cost efficiency. Mergers among large banks can't be justified on cost efficiency grounds.

Pi and Timme (1993). Corporate control and XE

The authors investigate how the management structure of a bank affects its level of XE. They look at structures when the CEO is and is not the Chair of the Board. The CEO is at the center of investment decision making. The Board of Directors, led by the Chair is the chief monitor of internal goal setting and achievement. When both roles are in the same person the principal-agent problems are deepened. How does this affect performance? The authors use three measures for performance: ROE, ROA, XE. The Econometric Frontier Approach (EFA), a parametric approach, is used to estimate XE. The average ROA for the CEO is Chair of Board group is 0.51%. For the CEO is Not the Chair the average ROA is 0.66%. The difference between the two groups is not statistically significant. The average level of XE for both groups is approximately 0.9 (or 90%), and not statistically difference between them. The difference between 0.9 and 1.0 was statistically significant. The average bank had costs which were about 11% higher than the bank on the frontier. The average bank's excess costs was about $180 million. At a tax rate of 34% this amounts to $120 million in after-tax profits. With average total assets of $18 billion this amounts to an increase in ROA of approximately 67 basis points, e.g., 5% to 5.67%.

Bauer and Hancock. Federal reserve check processing

The authors used quarterly data for the period 1979–90 on costs, output, input prices, and other variables from 47 Federal Reserve check-processing centers in order to estimate their XE. Before 1980 the FED provided payment services, e.g., check processing, to their members at a zero price. The Monetary Control Act of 1980 provided cost control measures including a positive price for check processing services. The authors used several techniques for estimating XE among check processing offices of the FED. The authors looked at the machine error-rate, number of end points, and whether an IBM or a Unysis was used to process checks. The error-rate was the number of errors per 100,000 checks. End points are the number of locations to which checks are delivered. IBM vs Unysis is what it sounds like. The item-pass ratio is the number of times a check must pass through the check reader. Did pricing affect economies of scale and XE? In terms of economies of scale, a 1% increase in the machine error rate increased costs by 0.01%. A 1% increase in endpoints increased costs by 0.1%. IBM sites had higher costs than Unysis sites. The relationship between the log of costs and the square of the item-pass ratio was statistically significant; the relationship is non-linear. Average XE levels were different depending on the statistical approach used. The average for Maximum Likelihood was 0.9, Generalized Least Squares was 0.71, Free Disposal Hull was 0.7, Thick Frontier Analysis was 0.67, and the WITHIN EFFICIENCY estimate was 0.54. XE is higher when labor productivity and population density are higher, and where the density of endpoints is lower. Density of endpoints is square miles per endpoint. A lower density means that checks must be sent to a larger area and this will increase costs (reduce XE).

Berger and Humphrey (1992). Megamergers

Do bank mergers between banks with at least $1 billion in assets—“megamergers”—improve X-efficiency? Berger and Humphrey tested this with a sample of US banks for the period 1981–89. The authors found three main results. First, in about 75% of the megamergers studied the acquiring bank was more X-efficient than the acquired bank, and the merging banks had some market overlap. These are the ex-ante conditions “*conducive* to improving X-efficiency” (p. 545). Second, the average increase in X-efficiency for 57 megamergers was between 1.9 and 4.7 percentage points, and was not statistically significant. And because the merged banks often operated in the area of diseconomies of scale, the net X-efficiency effect was negative, but not statistically significant. Third, the successful mergers did not satisfy the ex-ante theoretical conditions mentioned above.

Three data sets were analyzed separately. Data set 1 did not include data for the year of the merger to define the ex-ante and ex-post merger periods. Data set 2 excluded excluded the merger year plus the following year in defining the ex-post period. Data set 3 excluded the merger year plus two additional post-merger years. The authors use the distribution-free approach, five outputs and four inputs in estimating X-efficiency.

The estimate of 1.9 to 4.7 percentage points means that if the merging banks’ X-efficiency scores were the 50th best out of 100, then after the merger they would be between the 45th and 48th most XE bank. The fact that the result is not statistically significant means that the post-merger rank could be the same as before the merger or even lower. The most successful mergers led to about an 80 percentage point increase in rank, while the least successful led to about a 50 to 70 percentage point decrease in rank. Total efficiency, which is XE × SE declined by 2.5 to 11.3 percentage points, and statistically significant in two of the three data sets.

Peristiani (1997). Bank mergers

Peristiani investigated the post-merger performance of *acquiring* US banks during the period 1980–90, a period of unusually high amount of mergers and industry reorganization. Performance measures were profits, scale efficiency, and X-efficiency. Peristiani equates X-efficiency with “managerial efficiency.”[d] Three types of mergers are considered: intrastate, bank holding company (BHC) consolidations, and those assisted by the FDIC. He used the distribution-free approach. X-efficiency is measured as a bank’s X-efficiency rank. Scale efficiency is measured as the difference in average costs between scale-efficient and scale inefficient banks. The time period considered is between 1 and 2 years before the merger and 2 to 4 years after the merger. Analysis is also done separately for banks who engaged in one merger, or more than one merger. The average size (assets) of the acquiring bank and the target bank was $1.8 billion and $0.13 billion.

[d] Cyree, Wansley, and Boehm (2000) in their study of bank takeovers use as synonyms for X-efficiency methodology event study and operating performance.

Results show that X-efficient banks earn higher profits, have lower operating costs, are seen as being less of a credit risk, and receive a higher managerial efficiency rating (M) on the CAMEL score, vis-à-vis other banks. The author estimates the actual change in XE and SE as well as the "control-adjusted change," (the change in efficiency of the merging banks)—(the change of the matched control). The overall actual change in XE as a result of the merger was −0.8% among banks in more than one merger, and −0.7% for banks with one merger. The corresponding control-adjusted changes were −0.9% and −1.3%, respectively. This is the loss of merging banks vis-à-vis the control group. Among BHC consolidations the actual change in XE for multiple mergers was −0.9% and for one merger −1.5%. The corresponding control-adjusted figures were −1.4% and −2.9%, respectively. By contrast with these figures mergers increased scale efficiency, the overall figures for multiple and one time mergers being +4.5% and +6.2%, respectively. The control-adjusted figures were 2.2% and 2.8%, respectively. In sum, mergers do not increase average XE, but they do create a modest increase in scale efficiency.

Shaffer (1993). Bank mergers

Shaffer uses a sample of commercial banks with assets of greater than $1 billion during the period 1984–89. Data is from Call Reports. In 1988 these banks had 57% of all US banking assets. At the mean level of output the scale elasticity of cost is between 0.9674 and 0.9992; if output increases by 100%, then costs increase in the range of 96.74% and by 99.92%. Thus, banks have virtually exhausted economies of scale.

Mergers in which both banks had assets in excess of $10 billion saw a 6–7% increase in costs. The average merger resulted in an approximately 1% decrease in total costs, as compared with non-merging banks. X-efficiency was estimated using a "thick frontier" method. In this method the sample is divided into quartiles according to average cost. The lowest cost quartile is the frontier. A different form uses the residuals of the estimated cost function. Banks are placed in one of the quartiles depending on the residuals in the cost function. Quartile 1 is the most X-efficient, while quartile 4 is the most x-inefficient. Four asset sizes were employed: $1–$3 billion, $3–$10, $10–$30 billion, and above $30 billion. Mergers by quartile 1 banks reduce costs by about 21%. Hence the X-efficiency score of 0.8. More than 90% of mergers would result in lower costs, and two-thirds of mergers would reduce costs by more than 10%. If quartile 4 banks merge, then costs would rise by about 21%. Again, hence the X-efficiency score of about 0.8. About 80% of mergers would increase costs and about half would increase costs by more than 10%. Finally, as in most studies, potential gains in X-efficiency dominates those from economies of scale.

Rhodes (1993). Bank mergers

Rhoades analyzes the effects of 898 horizontal mergers and acquisitions during the period 1981–86. Testing the effects was done with data beginning in 1978 and ending in 1990 or 992. (X) Efficiency was measured by several (expense/asset) ratios of the merged firms relative to other firms. Using OLS and logit, the results show that merged banks do not have a decrease in their (expenses/asset) ratios relative to non-merging banks. meaning that mergers do not increase (X) efficiency. The variable for market overlap is also not statistically significant meaning, again, that mergers do not increase (X)-efficiency. Of particular note is that the acquiring banks were more X-efficiency than the acquired banks, a fact which is considered a prerequisite for a successful merger, i.e., one which increases X-efficiency.

Berger (1993). Bank regulatory environment

Berger used the DFA on annual data on US commercial banks for the years 1980–1989. Banks were categorized according to three regulatory environments: unit banking states, limited branching states, and statewide branching states. Total observations were 9000 to 10,000 per environment. For UNIT banks the average level of XE for no truncation, 1%, 5%, and 25% truncation was 0.68, 0.77, 0.85, and 0.93, respectively. For LIMIT banks the averages was 0.58, 0.76, 0.84, and 0.94, respectively. For STATE banks the averages were 0.59, 0.62, 0.75, and 0.90, respectively. Scale efficiency for the three bank types was 0.96, 0.97, and 0.93, respectively. XE is less than scale efficiency meaning that "X-efficiencies or managerial differences in banking are important and dominate the effects of scale efficiency differences" (Berger, 1993, p. 289).

Berger, Leusner, and Mingo (1997). Branch level X and scale efficiencies

The authors use a sample of 760 branches of a US commercial bank for 1989–91 in order to estimate X and scale (in)efficiencies. They use the parametric distribution-free approach (DFA). DFA unscrambles X-inefficiency from the random error assuming that inefficiencies are stable over time and random errors tend to average out over time. They report their results using two approaches to efficiency for a commercial bank: the intermediation approach, and the production approach. Costs with the intermediation approach are total operating expenses, and interest expenses. Output is measured as the number of dollars intermediated, and physical and financial input prices. Costs with the production approach include total operating expenses. Outputs are completed transactions and physical input prices.

Average X-efficiency among branches with a 5% truncation is 0.942 for the inter-mediation approach, and 0.788 for the production approach. X-inefficiency is about 6% for the intermediation approach and 22% with the production approach. Scale efficiency for the two approaches is 0.960 and 0.843, respectively. X-inefficiencies are larger than scale inefficiencies for both the intermediation and production approaches. This result is commonly found for bank-level analysis, and in other industries.

Berger (1995). Bank profits and market structure

Berger (1995) uses annual data on US commercial banks for 1980–89 to test the relationship between profits and market structure among commercial banks.

He tests two explanations within the market-power theory (MP): the structure-conduct-performance hypothesis (SCP), and the relative-market power hypothesis (RMP). He also tests two explanations within the efficient-structure hypothesis (ES): XE (ESX), and SE (ESS). Why is the market structure—profit relationship positive? SCP states that power allows banks to set prices less favorable to consumers—higher loan rates and lower deposit rates—but which raise the banks profits. RMP states that high market share and clearly-differentiated products raises the banks profits. ESX states that better management or better technology lowers costs and raises profits. Finally, ESS states that firms have equally good management and technology as per ESX firms, but produce at a more efficient scale, which lower their costs and raise profits. The MP hypotheses imply that banks set prices less favorable to their consumers which lowers consumers' surplus. Those who believe in the MP hypotheses see anti-trust as socially beneficial. The ES hypotheses view mergers as caused by efficiency considerations, thus increasing total surplus, and they view anti-trust as socially costly. Berger says that distinguishing among these four hypotheses is difficult because "efficiency variables, particularly X-efficiency of managerial efficiency measures, have generally been excluded from the analysis" (Berger, 1995, p. 405).

Berger tests the four hypotheses by regressing profits on concentration (CONC), market share (MS), XE (X-EFF), and scale efficiency (S-EFF). CONC is measured by the Herfindahl index, and the 3FCR. MS is measured by the banks share of bank deposits. Profits are measured by return on assets (ROA) and return on equity (ROE). S-EFF is measured as predicted average costs of the scale efficient firm with the predicted costs of another firm. His definition of XE is differences in costs between the most efficient and another bank not explained by differences in scale or other observable bank characteristics.

For Unit, Limit and State branch banking environments the average XE with 1% truncation are 0.62, 0.59, and 0.52, respectively. Average SE for the same truncation and branch banking regulations are 0.82, 0.82, and 0.83, respectively. As in most research, XE presents a greater opportunity for improvement than does SE.

The XE coefficient in the profits equations is positive and statistically significant in 59 of 60 equations. X-EFF isn't as significant when explaining its effects on MS or CONC. The S-EFF coefficients are both positive and negative. Statistical significance is found in 26 of the equations where S-EFF is positive, and 15 times when the coefficient is negative. There is no conclusive evidence for S-EFF.

Berger and DeYoung (1997). Bank loans and capital and X-efficieny

Berger and DeYoung test four hypotheses concerning the relationship between cost or X-efficiency, the quality of bank loans, and the bank's capital using Granger-causality methods. The four hypotheses are "bad luck," "bad management," "skimping" behavior, and "moral hazard" problems. Under the "bad luck" hypothesis problem loans occur are the effect of "external events" such as a plant closing. The increase in bad loans increases operating costs from dealing with the bad loans. Non-performing loans (NPL) "Granger-cause," to precede in time, decreases in cost or X-efficiency.

The expenses of NPL enhances the appearance but not necessarily the reality of lower cost or X-efficiency. Even banks on the frontier will appear to be less X-efficient.

Under the "bad management" hypothesis, low X-efficiency is caused by poor management. Low X-efficiency is expected to occur *before*, or Granger-cause, higher non-performing loans. Note that this hypothesis has the opposite temporal ordering from that predicted by the bad luck hypothesis, but both hypotheses predict that non-performing loans will be negatively associated with cost efficiency.

Under the "skimping" hypothesis, NPL and XE are affected by the amount of resources used to underwrite and monitor loans. The decision the bank makes is between short run variable costs and longer run loan problems. Long run profits may be achieved by reducing variable costs in the short run by skimping on monitoring and underwriting loans. The bank may *appear* to be more X-efficient in the short run but it is only an appearance. Long run profits may suffer if the longer run loan problems are large enough. Under the skimping hypothesis, the Granger-causality is that higher measured efficiency leads to more NPL. Under the *moral hazard* hypothesis, banks with relatively little capital increase the riskiness of their loans when faced with moral hazard inducements. This increases their future NPLs. Thus relatively little capital will Granger-cause high NPLs.

Their Granger causality model consists of three equations. The dependent variable in one of the equations is either XEt, CAPt, or NPLt. The independent variables include the lagged variables of the other two variables above. They use the sum of the lagged coefficients because the sum measures the total effect of past values on current values, e.g., past NPL on current XE. These three equations are estimated separately with OLS for the years 1985–94. The number of observations ranged from 46,000 to 70,000. The average XE was 0.93, higher than most estimates which average about 0.8.

In the equation in which *XE* was the dependent variable, the sum of the lagged values for NPL was −0.06, and significant at the 1% level. An increase in NPL raises costs, reduces XE. This is consistent with the *bad luck* hypothesis. The economic impact is not large, e.g., a one standard deviation increase in NPL reduces XE by 1.7% over a 4 year period. In the *NPL* equation, the lagged coefficients on the XE variable was −0.007, and significant at the 1% level. This means that a decrease in XE results in an increase in NPL, consistent with the bad management hypothesis. And, the economic impact is not large, e.g., a reduction in one standard deviation in XE reduces NPL by 1.8% over a 4 year period. The *CAP* equation shows that low XE banks have low or negative earning which Granger-cause lower amounts of capital.

The results show that increases in NPL result in (precede) lower amounts of XE, and that decreases in XE lead to (precede) increases in NPL. Reductions in capital at banks which have relatively little capital precede increases in NPL. And, the level of XE may indicate future NPL problems, and in general, bank problems. These support the bad luck and bad management hypotheses. The moral hazards hypothesis was tested among banks with relatively little capital. The results show that thinly capitalized banks take more risks leading to more NPL. A reduction in the CAP standard deviation from say 0.071 to 0.058 leads to a 3.8% increase in NPL over a period of 4 years. Finally, the results show that XE is an important type of efficiency.

> *While scale and scope efficiencies have been extensively studied... relatively little attention has been paid to measuring... a much more important source of efficiency differences—X-inefficiencies... differences in managerial ability.*
>
> *(Berger, Hunter, & Timme, 1993, p. 222)*

DeYoung (1998). Management's role in X-efficiency

DeYoung estimates the role of management on 3523 national bank XE using a subjective measure of bank and management quality, the CAMEL rating system. CAMEL stands for capital adequacy (C), asset quality (A), management/administration (M), earnings (E), and liquidity (L). Each of the five elements is rated on a scale of 1 to 5, with one being the best. CAMEL as a whole is also rated on a one to five scale. The number of banks receiving a 1, 2, 3, and 4 or 5 among the sample banks is: 477, 2085, 630, and 331, respectively. The CAMEL analysis showed that banks with rated as above average quality also have large M-scores. Banks with better management also have higher ROA, ROE, assets, but lower NPLs.

The actual M score for any bank was then adjusted using an ordered logit model. The adjusted M score was the predicted M score from the logit model. If the actual M was greater than the predicted M then the bank is considered well managed. A poorly managed bank is those for which the actual M was less than the predicted M.

The author uses the thick frontier analysis (TFA) to estimate X-efficiency. In the TFA cost efficient banks are in the lowest quartile while cost inefficient banks are in the highest quartile banks. A separate cost frontier for each quartile is then estimated. The error terms in each frontier reflects luck and error, while cost differences reflect X-inefficiency and exogenous market forces. Management quality and hence X-inefficiency is shown by the difference in the *parameters* between the high and low quartile. Differences in the *regressors* are out of the control of management and hence not reflected in X-inefficiency. TFA assumes that the quality of management leads to a different use of technology and differences in X-inefficiency.

For the years 1991 and 1992, poorly-managed banks are shown to have unit costs which were 3.9% lower than unit costs in well-managed banks. This counterintuitive result is due to the fact that well-managed banks operate in higher cost environments.

These higher cost environments came about because well-managed banks (1) hold more assets as loans vis-a-vis securities and cash balances and making and monitoring loans is more expensive than holding securities (2) have larger and had more branches, and as a result, less likely to be operating at suboptimal scale. (3) Paid higher deposit interest rates, (4) statistically more likely to be affiliates of bank holding companies—higher organizational overhead.

The author shows that when the average values for the well-managed bank's economic conditions are identical with those of the poorly managed banks, the former have unit costs which were 33% lower than the latter. Banks in the upper quartile of accounting costs had unit costs which were 29% higher than banks in the lowest accounting cost quartile. These cost differences are considered measures of X-inefficiency. The authors provide evidence for a common sense idea—that better management produces with lower unit costs than lower quality management teams. The authors conclude that "an active market for corporate control of banks, which supposedly identifies bad managers and replaces them with better managers, should be a potent weapon for reducing X-inefficiency" (p. 19). How much X-inefficiency? The average bank has costs which are 20% to 25% higher than that of the most efficient banks.

English, Grosskopf, Hayes, and Yaisawarng (1993). Banks' asset size

The authors estimate X and allocative efficiency among 442 US banks whose output and input data is taken from the Fed's Functional Cost Analysis program. They use a parametric technique. The average dollar value of all outputs, investment income plus loans, was $135 million: the banks are relatively small. The average level of X-efficiency was 0.75. Average X-efficiency among banks with state charters, national charters, unit branch banks, and branching banks was 0.74, 0.77, 0.75, and 0.76, respectively. Banks with total assets less than $40 million, the smallest asset group, was 0.72. Banks with total assets greater than $300 million, the largest asset group, was 0.86. The authors also show that banks are on the whole allocatively inefficient. Specifically, banks offered too many consumer and commercial loans, and did not have enough investment income. Second, they should increase real estate loans at the expense of investment income. Third, more real estate loans and fewer consumer loans. The result of allocative inefficiency is that banks were not producing the revenue maximizing output mix.

IV Non-bank studies

Mester (1993). S&Ls

The S&L industry went through a crises and a reorganization during the 1980s. One of the changes was that a large number of mutual ownership form S&Ls were converted to the stock form of S&Ls. Depositors, and sometimes the borrowers, own the mutual form, which increases its capital via retained earnings. On the other hand, the shareholders own the stock form which increases its capital by issuing new stock.

In mutual S&Ls, small claimants whose deposits are insured have little opportunity or incentive to oversee the managers. In other words there is a larger gulf between owners and managers in mutual than stock S&Ls. This agency problem predicts that mutual will be less (X) efficient than stock S&Ls. Evidence bears this out. In 1986 interest rates were deregulated. Before 1986 mutuals were less (X) efficient than stock S&Ls. After 1986 interest rate deregulation and increased competition made bankruptcy and job losses a more likely result of (X) inefficiency which reduced these agency problems. Mutual and stock S&Ls (X) efficiency differences were reduced and in fact mutual (X) inefficiency became lower than that for stock S&Ls.

Meister's sample of banks is for 3 years, 1986–88. The authors uses the parametric technique—Stochastic Frontier Analysis (SFA). Being parametric the error contains two parts, the random error (v) and (X) inefficiency (u). X-inefficiency is measured by the error term residual u. The S&L with the smallest u is considered to be on the frontier. Each S&L's level of X-inefficiency is then the difference between the minimum u and the S&L's u.

Four models are calculated of which two will be discussed. Model 1 allows the cost structure and the error term to differ between mutual and stock S&Ls. Model 4 assumes that the cost and error structures are the same for mutual and stock S&Ls. S&Ls are assumed to have three outputs, mortgage loans, other loans, and securities and other investments. They also have three inputs, labor, physical capital, and deposits and other borrowed funds. The author's analysis of Models 1 and 4 show that Model 1 best fits the data; mutual and stock S&Ls do not have the same cost and error structures.

Model 1 shows that scale economics are slightly increasing returns to scale. The S&L's are almost of the optimum size. Second, there are large economies of scope for the three outputs. Third, average X-inefficiency for mutual is between 8% and 10%. For stock S&Ls it is between 12% and 16%. Fourth, uninsured deposits raises X-inefficiency for both types of S&Ls. The authors speculate that these depositors are not pressuring management for greater X-efficiency. Fifth, higher profits are correlated with lower X-inefficiency.

Gardner and Grace (1993). US life insurance industry

Gardner and Grace examine X-efficiency among US life insurance companies. Studies of XE among life insurance firms were few and far between. However, one study was contained in a report by the US Congress (1990) which put part of the blame for insolvencies among life insurance firms expressed its concern about poor management practices. The authors examine XE among life insurance companies including their rent-seeking expenditures and monitoring activities as explanations for X-inefficiency.

Their data is for 561 firms for the period 1985–90. The output of these firms is "intangible" and difficult to measure. The authors measure their output by the dollar amount of life insurance premiums, annuities, health and accident premiums, and securities investments. Their inputs are labor, physical capital, and other inputs.

The authors seek the answers to three issues. First, estimate the cost function for the industry. The authors use a parametric estimating technique, the distribution-free approach (DFA). Being parametric, the residual has a random error component (v) and an X-inefficiency component (u). The firm with the lowest X-inefficiency residual is assumed to be on the frontier. Other firm's degree of X-inefficiency is (Umin—U).

Second, whether management is affected by things such as organizational ownership form—mutual or stock life insurance company—regulation by the State of New York, the firm's distribution system, and regulating monitoring activities. A mutual insurance company is owned by the policy holders and any profits are either paid to the policy holders or retained in the firm. A stock insurance company is owned by the stockholders. However, the policy holders share in neither the profits nor the losses. And the managers may not have any ownership interest.

Third, does rent-seeking activities affect (X) efficiency. Three types of rent-seeking expenditures are studies: advertising (advertising expenditures/net premiums), bureau and association fees, and legal services (unrelated to claims). The authors distinguish rent-seeking which raises costs from those which increase output. And the distinction between rational and irrational rent-seeking. The former are the expenditures which increase profits.

X-inefficiency is measured by comparing the firm with the smallest residual representing X-inefficiency. With truncating the data 1%, 5%, and 10%, average X-*efficiency* is 26%, 42%, and 47%. These figures are, compared with other studies of financial firms, very low. The New York State dummy variable reflecting monitoring is positive and statistically significant for both X-efficiency and returns on equity. Among the rent-seeking expenditures, only advertising increases X-efficiency and is statistically significant. For the equation with returns on equity as the dependent variable, all three rent-seeking variables are positive and statistically significant. Overall, "there is evidence the efficiency measure is related to the external environment and that is consistent with Leibenstein's X-efficiency story" (p. 509). An important point is that the authors discuss rent-seeking as a reason for the existence of X-efficiency. Critics of XE theory used rent-seeking expenditures as the reason why costs were above minimum, but which were inaccurately referred to as X-inefficiency (Crain & Zardkoohi, 1980; Schap, 1985).

Yuengert (1993). Life insurance

Discussing the two part residual reflecting random error or white noise, and X-inefficiency, Yuengert says the X-inefficiency part is due to "differences in the quality of management, and costly adjustment to changing technology and markets, may push firms above the cost frontier" (p. 485). Data was gathered on 1147 companies for the year 1989. The author used the parametric thick frontier approach. Average X-efficiency ranged from about 50% to 70% depending on the size (assets) of the firms. These estimates are higher than those for Gardner and Grace. The random error or white noise exceeds the size of X-inefficiency by about 20%.

Fried, Lovell, and Eeckaut (1993). Credit unions

The authors investigate XE (= radial efficiency + slack) among almost 9000 US credit unions for 1990. The credit unions are not-for-profit cooperatives owned operated by members for the benefit of the members. This makes the profit maximization motive unlikely. Almost all credit unions have assets of less than $100 million, making economies of scale and scope limited. XE is estimated using the non-parametric approach, Free Disposal Hull (FDH), which is a variation/substitute of the Data Envelope Analysis. FDH assumes that there isn't any substitution among inputs so the isoquants look like a step function. Firms are assumed to be X-efficient unless other firms can be shown to produce more at lower costs. In this study two inputs, labor and other inputs are used. Six outputs are also used: loan and saving quantity, loan and saving price, and loan and saving variety. X-inefficiency or what he calls "total slack" is estimated for all inputs and outputs. The average level of X-inefficiency for all inputs and outputs averages to approximately 20%, a number very close to that for other financial institutions.

Rai (1996). Life insurance among 11 nations

Rai studied X-efficiency among 11 nations for the period 1988–92. Using the parametric stochastic frontier approach (SFA), he reports that for all nations the average level of X-efficiency is 0.73. For the United States and Japan the average is 0.74. For European firms the average is 0.71. The least X-efficient firms are large European firms with an average of 0.68. The most X-efficient firms are small US and Japanese firms, and small specialized European firms, i.e., firms which sell either life or non-life services and which have assets below the medium level of assets among the insurance firms I n the nation where you operate.[e] Using the parametric distribution free approach (DFA) he reports that the average level of X-efficiency for all 11 nations is 0.5, as is the US, and Japan, and European firms. By nation and firm size the most X-efficient firms are large Finnish firms (0.84) and specialized French firms (0.84). The least X-efficient are large firms in the United Kingdom (0.6) and combined firms in the United Kingdom (0.58).

Choi and Elyasiani (2011). Property management insurance

The authors study foreign-owned and domestically-owned property-liability insurance companies in the United States. These two groups are known as FOPLICs and DOPLICs, respectively. The time period is 1992 to 2000. The measure inefficiency using the parametric SFA. What researchers refer to as X-efficiency they call cost X-efficiency; they also measure cost scale efficiency. This measures how far a company is from the point of constant returns to scale. The authors measure other forms of efficiency but I am limiting myself here to these two forms.

Average X-efficiency for foreign-owned, domestically-owned, the full sample are 0.808, 0.797, and 0.798, respectively. Average cost scale efficiency for the three groups are 0.860, 0.876, and 0.874, respectively. As is shown in most studies X-efficiency is less than either scale or allocative efficiency. In other words, there is a large "upside" to increasing X-efficiency than either of the other two.

Choi and Weiss (2005). Property management insurance

The authors examine efficiency among property-liability insurers over the period 1992–98. They use the parametric SFA technique. For firms not part of a group and those part of a group the average X-efficiency was 0.8, and 0.79, respectively. Scale efficiency for firms not part of a group and those part of a group averaged 0.86, and 0.85, respectively. Scale efficiency exceeds cost efficiency, meaning that the larger

[e] Rodney Stevenson (1982) found the same result for straight (specialized) public utilities vis-à-vis combination (combined) public utilities.

gains are from increasing cost or X-efficiency. The data also supports the efficient markets hypothesis, that more (X-) efficient firms charge lower prices and gain market share and market power.

V Final comments on this chapter, and looking ahead to Chapter 9

In this chapter, we have surveyed the two primary approaches to the estimation of X-efficiency: (i) stochastic frontier analysis (SFA), and (ii) data envelope analysis (DEA), while emphasizing the relative strengths and weaknesses of both approaches. We conclude by emphasizing the inherent linkages between X-efficiency theory and the empirical techniques described in this chapter.

In the decades following Leibenstein's ground-breaking work in 1966, over 200 empirical studies relating to XE theory have been published, most of which use SFA- or DEA-based analysis of operational inefficiency. In this chapter we focused on the financial sector in the United States. Under the umbrella of the financial sector we include banks, insurance companies, credit unions, and property management insurance. Average X-inefficiency is significant. In my reading of X-efficiency worldwide, I would say that perhaps the best research has been done by Alan Berger, a former member of the Federal Reserve Board in Washington, DC. Berger's research has researched X-efficiency among financial institutions worldwide. His conclusion is that the average level of X-efficiency is 0.8, meaning that firms on average are 20% off their frontier(s). If the average number was 2%, then, no big deal. However, 20% is significant.

Is 20% constant? In the next chapter I will review studies on China. Here it becomes clear that when the environment changes, ex., China enters the WTO, average X-efficiency changes. Following studies on China's financial institutions I will review studies on the financial and non-financial sectors in other Asian nations, then on Europe, the Middle East, Latin America, Australia, and New Zealand.

XE among financial firms in Asia: c.1991–2017

9

In this chapter I will review studies on X-efficiency among financial institutions in China Hong Kong, Taiwan, Singapore, Korea, Japan, Philippines, Indonesia, India, Bangladesh, and among the ASEAN nations. I am including Hong Kong and Taiwan as part of China.

I China

Mainland China

There are five papers discussing XE among private and publically-owned banks. These are Fu and Heffernan (2007), Fu and Hefferman (2009), García-Herrero, Gavilá, and Santabárbara (2009), Yao, Jiang, Feng, and Willenbockel (2007), and Jiang, Yao, and Zhang (2009). These studies except Jiang et al. use the parametric approach. Kwan is about the same topic but is for Hong Kong. It uses the parametric approach.

Fu and Heffernan (2007) investigate X-efficiency among 4 state-owned (SOCB) and 10 privately-owned joint-stock commercial banks (JSCB) between 1985 and 2002. Average X-efficiency for all banks was between 0.4 and 0.6. For SOCBs X-efficiency ranged from 0.35 and 0.46. For JSCBs the range is 0.44 to 0.55. These X-efficiency estimates of 0.4 to 0.6 mean that X-inefficiency, (1-XE) also from 0.4 to 0.6. X-efficiency among JSCBs was approximately 23% higher than that of SOCB. The causes of X-inefficiency are a lack of incentives for managers, state lending policies which affected those incentives, and a lack of knowledge about bankruptcy. For all intents and purposes state banks which are insolvent continue to operate. Another factor is state-control of interest rates. Others include a high rate of non-performing loans, the underreporting of bad loans, and poor management quality. The results also show that listing shares of a bank on an exchange improves XE because managers become answerable to owners.

Fu and Hefferman (2009) test both the market-power and the efficient-structure hypotheses and the effect of bank size and ownership form on X-efficiency for the period 1985–2002. Their sample included JSCB, and six other types of banks. Analysis is divided into two time period. The period 1985–92 is Stage 1. This is when the Chinese government allowed for small and medium size banks to be established. The average level of XE was 92.3% for Stage 1. Stage 2 covered 1993–2002. This is when privately-owned banks could coexist alongside state-owned banks. During Stage 2 average XE was 90.3%. JSCBs were about 7% more x-efficient than the SOCBs. The reasons given for the decline in XE was a rising amount of debt, and an increasing amount of pressure on state banks to lend money to state-owned enterprises who were losing more money. Managers of state-owned enterprises knew that the state would

The Beginnings of Behavioral Economics. https://doi.org/10.1016/B978-0-12-815289-8.00009-5

bailout the banks and hence they lacked the incentives to repay their loans or practice good management techniques. These agency and moral hazard problems contributed to X-inefficiency.

García-Herrero et al. (2009) investigated low profits among 87 Chinese banks which accounted for more than 80% of total assets for the period 1997–2004. The average level of X-efficiency is 0.5; state-owned banks were between 8% to 18% less x-efficient than non-state owned banks. Higher levels of XE was positively related to profits and negatively related with non-performing loans.

Yao et al. (2007) used data from 22 banks over the period 1995 to 2001, the 5 years prior to China joining the WTO. For all 22 banks, average bank XE was approximately 0.65. The average XE of state-owned banks is 0.6 and that of privately-owned joint-stock banks is 0.78. The range of individual bank XE was 0.91 to 0.49. For China's "Big 4" banks the range was 0.92 to 0.25. Using Maximum Likelihood they report that privately-owned banks averaged 8% more efficient than state-owned banks when output is measured in loans, and 18% more efficient when output is measured in profits.

Jiang et al. (2009) estimated XE using an Output Distance Function for commercial banks in China which control more than 85% of bank assets for the period 1995–2005. The average level of X-efficiency was 0.72. JSCB were the most x-efficient with an average level of 81%. JSCBs are 9% more X-efficient than SOCB. The JSCBs used their lower costs to increase their profits. The more X-efficient banks were privately-owned, were listed on a stock exchange and hence subject to all the pressures which come from needing to raise funds in the private market (Table 9.1).

Table 9.1 Chinese financial

Author(s)	**Year pub.**	**Yrs of the study**	**Av. XE**	**(Non) para**
Fu and Hefferman	2007	1985–2002	0.5	Para
Fu and Hefferman	2009	1985–2002	0.91	Para
Garcia-Herrero et al.	2009	1997–2004	0.5	Para
Yao et al.	2007	1995–2001	0.6	Para
Yao et al.	2007	1995–2001	0.77	Para
Jiang, Yao, and Zhang	2009	1995–2005	0.72	Non-para
Kwan	2006	1992–97	0.77	Para
Fung and Cheng	2010	1993–2002	0.58	Para
Fung and Cheng	2010	1993–2002	0.69	Para
Rezvanian et al.	2010	1999–2008	0.85	Non-para
Yao, Han, and Feng	2011	1998–2006	0.87	Non-para
Jiang, Yao, and Feng	2013	1995–2000	0.76	Para
Luo and Yao	2010	1999–2008	0.85	Non-para
Chen, Skully, and Brown	2005	1993–2000	0.77	Non-para

China and the WTO

A little history of China's banking reforms. China joining the WTO in 2001 created the latest, at the time, reforms in China's banking system. The reform of the Chinese banking system has progressed favorably since 1978. Before 1978, the Chinese banking system was a Soviet-style system. China had virtually one bank: the People's Bank of China (PBC). The PBC wasn't a "real" bank. Instead it was the handmaiden of the government and a part of the Ministry of Finance (MOF). The PBC was created in 1948. The People's Republic of China was created in 1949. All banks were nationalized under the PBC which in turn was controlled by the MOF. The PBC issued currency and provided the finances for all economic plans. In 1978 Mao died, and the reform policy was to rid the Chinese economy of the communist type of financial system. The creation of a "two tier" banking system was a primary policy goal. The two tiers consisted of, (1) the People's Bank of China, which became the central bank in 1983, and (2) the four big state-owned banks (called "Big 4 banks"). The PBC separated from the MOF and began to function as a modern bank. The PBC's banking functions were transferred to three new state-owned banks, the Agricultural Bank of China (ABC), the Bank of China (BOC), and the People's Construction Bank of China. The latter's name changed to the China Construction Bank (CCB). The PBC's commercial banking activities ended and was transferred to the Industrial and Commercial Bank of China (ICBC), which originated in 1984 and became the fourth state-owned bank. By 1984 the "Big 4" banks became independent of the People's Bank of China (PBC), and became commercial banks. As the Communist Party better understood the need for the economy to be more efficient, regulations of the "Big 4" were reduced. In 1995 these banks were required to be governed with efficiency, safety and liquidity in mind. They had to take responsibility for risk, profits and losses, and self-governance.

In 1986 private joint-stock commercial banks (JSCB) banks began functioning. JSCB's have stockholders and are allowed to pursue profits (maximization). These banks initially offered banking services to households and firms, mainly in the regions and cities. The majority of JSCB shareholders are SOEs and/or local governments. But, government regulations of JSCBs are less than for other economic organizations. The level of competitiveness of JSCBs is greater than it is for other commercial banks. Another characteristic of JSCBs is their funding comes from bank loans which come with a positive interest rate, rather than grants from the central government. In general, banks have evolved from being a distributor of government grants to a lender of credit for borrowers.

With the emergence of China's stock market in 1990, Shenzhen Development bank did an IPO in April 1991 in Shenzhen Stock Exchange. Beginning in the early 2000s the largest banks began being listed on stock exchanges. In October 2005 the China Construction Bank initiated an IPO on the Hong Kong stock exchange. This was the first time that Chinese stock was listed in an overseas stock exchange. By 2007–09 Chinese banks were the largest commercial banks in the world.

The banking system opened considerably after China entered the WTO in 2001, and had to open their economy to the international markets by 2006. Joining the WTO in 2001 led Chinese leaders to the realization that they were about to face intense competition in the financial (banking) sector. This created the motivation to restructure the financial sector so they would be more competitive. WTO membership required that China make significant reduction in tariff and non-tariff barriers to the entry of foreign goods into Chinese markets. In addition sectors that were long closed to international trade were opened to such trade. These included banking, asset management, and insurance. Foreign banks were required to have unrestricted access to the Chinese financial sector. Total asset of foreign banks in China grew from RMB 415.97 billion to RMB 2.56 trillion between 2003 and 2013. Net profits of these banks increased from RMB 1.67 billion to RMB 14.03 billion during the same period. By 2014 foreign banks maintained presence in 69 cities with 947 outlets. Citibank was the largest foreign bank with total assets of USD 2.5 billion and net profits amounted to USD 2.1 million in China in the year 2000. The history of financial reform is increased economic freedom and increased responsibility for their own performance. Increased market pressure had led to increased competitiveness.

Three studies focus on the effect of China joining the WTO: Rezvanian, Ariss, and Mehdian (2011), Yao, Han, and Feng (2008), and Jiang, Yao, and Feng (2013). All three papers use a non-parametric approach. Rezvanian, Ariss, and Mehdian, is about how X-efficiency, total factor productivity, and technological change were affected by China's entry into the WTO. Their sample is 62 domestic and foreign banks operating in China over the entire 9-year period between 1998 and 2006. In 1998, 2001, and 2006 X-efficiency for all banks averaged 0.97, 0.96, and 0.98, respectively. After China entered the WTO, X-efficiency increased for all banks. Among foreign banks, X-efficiency in 2001 was 0.96. For domestic, the "Big 4,"and JSCBs the figures for 2001 were 0.96., 1.0, and 0.97, respectively. For 2006 the figures were 1.0, 0.98, 1.0, and 0.99, respectively. Among all banks, X-efficiency, technological progress and total factor productivity increased by 10.4%, 2.3%, and 12.4% after WTO admission. Only the Big Four failed to increase any of the three components of efficiency. In many cases allocative efficiency (AE) was higher than XE.

Yao et al. (2008) studied X-efficiency among Chinese commercial banks pre- and post-WTO. The period of study is 1998–2005; China entered the WTO in 2001. Average X-efficiency for all banks and all years was 0.85. Average XE score from 1998 through 2001 was 0.82. From 2002 to 2005 the score was 0.90. Total factor productivity increased by 5.6% per annum over the entire period. The growth of X-efficiency was 2.88% per year, the growth of technical change was 2.64% per year. The growth of X-efficiency shows to what extent a bank(s) approach their frontier. The growth of technological change shows how fast the frontier shift outward. The majority of productivity growth among state-owned (joint equity) banks was the growth of X-efficiency (technological chanf). After China entered the WTO, total factor productivity grew at an annual rate of more than 10%.

Jiang et al. (2013) investigated X, profit and interest-income and non-interest income efficiencies, among Chinese banks for the years 1995–2010. They used the parametric SFA. The sample consisted of 49, four state-owned, 13 private joint stock, and 32 large city commercial banks. Average X and profit efficiencies were 0.76 and 0.78, respectively. The average X-efficiency among JSCBs, SOCBs, and CCBs was 0.87, 0.84, and 0.72, respectively. Average profit efficiency among JSCBs, SOCBs, and CCBs was 0.75, 0.55, and 0.85, respectively. Interest-income and non-interest efficiencies, the efficiency with which they maximize both, are 0.8, and 0.33, respectively. China joined the WTO in December 2001. In 2002 average X-efficiency was 0.7. By 2010 it was about 0.9. Finally, when foreigners are minority owners in the bank, efficiencies fall in the short run but increase in the long run. The authors surmise that the benefits from technology transfer takes time.

Being listed on a stock exchange provides different pressure. Low and falling levels of XE puts pressure on stock prices, the ability to raise capital, and raises the possibility of a takeover. Luo and Yao (2010) use a non-parametric approach on data for the period 1999 to 2008 for 14 commercial banks listed on a stock exchange. The private banks are only about 10% the size of state-owned banks. Average XE for the private banks was 0.89 while that of state-owned was 0.79. Thirteen banks had an XE rating of 1.0 and all of them were private banks. Average XE increased by about 5% after being listed on a stock exchange.

Chen, Skully, and Brown (2005) used a non-parametric approach on a sample of 43 Chinese banks to study the effects of the 1995 deregulation of the financial system on XE (and allocative efficiency) over the period 1993–2000. For the entire period average XE was 0.77. Before deregulation, 1993–94, the average XE for all banks was 0.78. Post-deregulation, 1996–00, it was 0.75. From 1996 through 2000 average XE fell every year. For the state-owned banks the average XE from '96 to '00 was 0.95. For the privately-owned banks average XE in the pre-deregulation and post-deregulation periods were 0.86 and 0.95, respectively. For the entire period it was 0.93. For all banks the highest level of XE and allocative efficiency occurred in the post-deregulation period.

Hong Kong

Kwan (2006) studies the causes of x-(in)efficiency among Hong Kong (HK) banks from 1992 to 1999. X-efficiency averaged between 0.7 and 0.85. X-efficiency increased over the period among large and small banks all, from 0.63 to 0.76 among large banks, and from 0.69 to 0.77 among small banks. Small banks tended to be privately-owned; large banks were more likely to be state-owned. Large banks more X-inefficient, and their X-inefficiency was more persistent over time. An interesting result is that whereas X-efficiency increased from 1992 through 1997, the year China gained independence from England, in 1998 and 1999 XE decreased. For large and small banks the decrease was from 0.77 to 0.75, and from 0.84 to 0.78, respectively. Small banks, the more privately-owned banks, were more negatively affected by the change-over from a more laissez-faire administration to a Communist nation.

Fung and Cheng (2010) investigated X-efficiency and convergence in total factor productivity among Hong Kong banks. The sample period is 1993 to 2002. Their definition of X-efficiency includes both technical and allocative efficiencies. Using a parametric approach the estimates of X-efficiency ranged from 0.58 and 0.69. The authors find no support for "absolute convergence," that is productivity differences among banks is not disappearing. However evidence does support the "conditional convergence" hypothesis: productivity levels and differences are contingent upon the firm's initial level of XE.

Taiwan

Liao (2009) uses DEA to investigate the effect of managerial ability on relative XE and productivity of domestic and foreign banks in Taiwan for the years 2002–04. Taiwan joined the WTO in 2001. Liao measures managerial ability by the ratio (operating expenses/operating income). The average XE score for the Taiwanese banks for all 3 years averaged 0.87, while foreign banks averaged 0.82. The authors also investigated the determinants of XE and find that larger firms, measured by assets, reduces XE, as does greater market concentration, and lower quality management. At the same time, a higher market share increases XE.

Liu and Chang (2013) use a sample of nine state-owned banks in Taiwan that began privatization in 1998 along with a sample of foreign banks with similar size for 1995–2007. The non-parametric DEA was used. The results show that before privatization, the state-owned banks had a level of XE significantly lower than foreign banks. After privatization there was no statistical difference in XE between the two groups, meaning that privatization enhanced government-owned banks more than private banks. In the case of the Chiao Tung Bank, XE before and after privatization was 0.63 and 0.97, respectively. Their analysis also showed that when government is the largest bank shareholder, XE is lower by a statistically significant amount.

Chen (2002) uses DEA and the bank manager's opinion about the bank to estimate the bank's XE for 1998 among a sample of 41 Taiwanese banks. The manager's opinions was based on the FED's CAMEL measurement: Capital adequacy, Asset quality, Management Capability, Earning, and Liquidity. Management Capability includes (deposits + loans)/employees, and revenue/employees. The average XE score using is 0.996, a very high level of XE. Of the 41 banks 36 had an XE rating of 1.0, with the lowest score being 0.933. Chen introduced the CAMEL scores into the DEA process to try and get a better distribution of scores. The average score for Management Capability was then 0.93. The introduction of CAMEL reduced the average XE score to 0.83 (Table 9.2).

Hu and Fang (2010) investigated X-efficiency, or what the authors call managerial efficiency—management's ability to implement an efficient plan—among integrated securities firms (ISF) in Taiwan. The question was how does being a subsidiary of a financial holding company (FHC) affect XE. Government regulations in Taiwan encouraged the formation of FHCs with the Financial Holding Company Act of 2001. The goal was larger financial conglomerates which was assumed to mean more (X) efficient financial organizations which could compete internationally. However, the 2001 law allowed only integrated securities firms (ISFs) to join as subsidiaries of FHC's. Thus, the 2001 law provided the opportunity to investigate the effects of managerial ability on X-efficiency.

The data includes 12–14 ISFs in Taiwan for the period 2002–05. The authors estimate XE for each year of 2002–05 using the non-parametric DEA. The average level of XE for all firms, non-FHC firms, and FHC firms was 0.95, 0.98, and 0.92, respectively. Thus, the FHC has the effect of reducing the XE of the ISF. They also find that larger firms measured by assets reduces XE.

Hsiao, Chang, Cianci, and Huang (2010) use DEA to study the effect of the "First Financial Restructuring" (FFR) on XE among 40 commercial banks in Taiwan for

Table 9.2 Taiwan financial

Author(s)	Year pub.	Yrs study	Av. XE	(Non) para
Chang-Sheng Liao	2009	2002–04	0.75 to 0.87	Non-para
Liu and Chang	2013	1995–2007	0.63 to 0.97	Non-para
Chiu, Ma, and Sun	2010	2001–03	0.95	Non-para
Chen	2002	1998	0.97	Non-para
Hu and Fang	2010	2002–05	0.96	Non-para
Rezvanian and Mehdian	2002	1991–97	0.86	Non-para
Hsiao et al.	2010	2000–05	0.85	Non-para
Liao	2009	2002–04	0.84	Non-para
Chen and Hsu	2011	2005–10	0.74	Non-para
Huang	2000	1981–95	0.71	Non-para
Peiyu, Yu, and Bac Van Luu	2003	1985–97	0.78	Para
Yeh	2010	1997–2004	0.33	Para
Lin	2005	1997–99	1.1	Para
Lin	2005	1997–99	1.15	Para
Mohanty, Lin, and Liu	2013	1995–99	0.73	Para
Chen, Chiu, and Huang	2010	2004–06	1.21	Non-para
Chen, Chiu, and Huang	2010	2004–06	0.89	Non-para
Chen and Yeh	2001	1996	0.93	Non-para

the period 2000–05. The FFR was passed in 2002 and had two main goals: increase operating efficiency, and reduce NPLs as a percent of all loans. The authors use three time periods, pre-FFR (2000–01), the FFR period (2002–03), and the post-FFR period (2004–05). For the three periods average XE is 0.86, 0.80, and 0.89, respectively. DEA tests plus others including the Mann-Whitney show that XE is statistically significant between the FFR periods and both the pre- and post-FFR periods. OLS and Tobit regressions showed that XE is reduced by a higher percentage of NPLs, and by the FFR reform period of '02–'03. Using the Malmquist productivity index, results show that productivity increased by 23.2% from pre-FFR to the FFR period and then by 20.8% from the FFR period to post-FFR. Technical change increased by 27.8% from the pre-FFR period (2000–01) to the FFR period, and increased by 7.6% from the FFR period to the post-FFR period. The FFR reform program seemed to increase important economic variable, including XE.

Chen and Hsu (2011) use the non-parametric DEA and data on 21 Taiwanese securities firms listed on an exchange over the period 2005–10 in order to investigate XE. Their time period covered the GFC of '07–'09. Two models are used. Model A, takes operational risk (OR) into account as an input. Model B does not include OR. Several important points. First, XE in Models A and B is 0.77, and 0.72, respectively. The authors state that this means that excluding operational risk underestimates the effects of XE. The most important source of efficiency gains is XE (vis-à-vis allocative efficiency). Larger firms as measured by assets reduces XE/firms size, measured by asset size, reduces XE.

Huang (2000) investigated the deregulation of the Taiwan banking sector which began in 1991 in order to enhance efficiency and meet the requirements of membership in the WTO, which it joined in 2001. Their data is for the years 1981–95. They investigated how deregulation affected profits with the level of X-inefficiency being the intervening variable. Their sample included 22 Taiwanese domestic banks, including 11 public banks. Using the non-parametric DEA, Huang shows that X-inefficiency reduced profits among public, private and all banks by 66.4%, 76.3%, and 71.4%, respectively. These results are similar to those found for US banks. Huang (2005) estimated X-efficiency for 34 of Taiwan's banks for the years 1996–2003. He distinguished two types of capital and labor: IT and non-IT. Taiwan joined the WTO in 2001. He used the parametric SFA. Average X-efficiency was 0.88. He also found that IT capital and IT labor had higher levels of productivity than non-IT capital and labor. Chang and Gurbaxani (2013) investigate the relationship between X-efficiency, IT, and competition among US firms. The data, 1987–94, comes from the US Bureau of Economic Analysis, and Fortune 1000. IT intensity, is defined as IT/L. IT is known to be associated with higher levels of competition, but the relationship is moderated by the degree of competition. Competitive environments lead firms to use IT more intensely and more efficiently. The remainder of the explanation is "pure" X-efficiency theory. A competitive market makes the firm's performance more sensitive to management's effort. Competition leads owners to more easily recognize poor performance and leads managers to strive for greater (X) efficiency. The authors measure IT intensity with the HH index. HH index is either low concentration/high competition, or high concentration/low competition. Average X-efficiency for the high and low levels of competition are 0.82, and 0.72, respectively. The expected relationship between competition and X-efficiency is as expected. Among manufacturing firms average X-efficiency is 0.81 for high competition environments, and 0.73 among low levels of competition. Among non-manufacturing firms the figures are 0.84, and 0.69, respectively.

Yu and Luu (2003) investigate the effect of bank mergers and government reforms using three different theories: scale and scope economies, cost or X-efficiency, and the market-power and efficient-structure hypotheses. Their sample consists of 38 domestic commercial banks for the period 1985–97. Two sub-periods are distinguished: 1985–91, and 1993–97. Bank reforms began in 1992 and hence it was excluded. 1985–91 is the pre-reform period, and 1993–97 is the post-reform period. In the pre-reform period average XE was 0.77. After the reforms it was 0.78. After the reforms XE increased among all bank groups with the exception of government-owned commercial banks.

Mohanty, Lin, and Lin (2013) studied Taiwanese commercial banks both before and after the economic-financial crisis of 1995–99, for the entire period of 1996–2011. Specifically they studied the effect of firm and environmental factors on cost or X-Efficiency (and profit efficiency). Their main findings is that government-owned bank and larger banks measured by assets are less X-They estimated XE using two models. One was a standard parametric stochastic frontier analysis (SFA). The other is the heteroskedastic stochastic frontier analysis (HSF). The latter allows firm-specific variables such as ownership forms (private vs state-owned) and non-performing loan ratio, and macro variables such as the money multiplier, bank reserves, and (imports/GDP). The HSF accounts for heteroskedasticity in that part of the error term which reflects (X) inefficiency. Because of these characteristics the authors believe that HSF is more unbiased than the standard SFA model. The average XE for SFA and HSF were 0.75, and 0.70, respectively. Their empirical results also showed that government-owned firms are more X-efficient than private-sector firms, but that firms with a higher ration of NPLs and larger firms measured by assets are less X-efficient.

II Korea and Japan

Shin and Kim (2011) use the non-parametric DEA to study the effects of bank restructuring in 1997 on commercial bank performance over the period 1992 to 2005. Restructuring followed the beginning of the Global Financial Crises (GFC) and resulted in mergers and acquisitions, and a reduction of commercial banks from 26 to 13. The economy recovered, and profits increased while NPLs decreased. Average XE was 0.64. The range of values for XE was 1.0 to 0.25. In a regression with ROA as the dependent variable, XE increase ROA and are statistically significant. Higher values of XE are also shown to increase both market share and industry concentration, and both are statistically significant. Finally, higher amounts of XE improve MS, a result consistent with the efficient markets hypothesis (Table 9.3).

Table 9.3 Other Asian financial

Nation	Author(s)	Yr. pub.	Yrs. studied	Av. XE	(Non) para
Korea	Shin and Kim	2011	1992–2005	0.64	Non-para
Korea	An et al.	2007	1987–97	n.a.	Non-para
Korea	Choi and Hasan	2005	1998–2002	0.45	Para
Japan	Hosono, Sakai, and Tsuru	2006	1984–2002	0.44	Para
Japan	Barros, Managi, and Matousek	2012	2000–07	0.67	Non-para
Bangladesh	Uddin and Suzuke	2011	2001–08	0.79	Non-Para
Indonesia	Hadad et al.	2011	2003–07	0.97	Non-para
Indonesia	Hadad et al.	2011	2003–07	0.34	Non-para
Philippines	Chelo and Manlagnit	2011	1990–2006	0.75	Para
Philippines	Dacanay	2010	1992–2004	0.87	Para
Philippines	Chiang and Tsaih	2015	2005–10	0.82	Non-para
India	Lall and Rodrigo	2001	1994	0.55	Para
India	Patibandla	1998	1983–84	0.37 to 0.59	Non-para
India	Kuman and Vincent	2011	1994–2007	0.9	Non-para
ASEAN	Chan and Karim	2011	2001–08	0.76	Para

Japan

Hosono, Sakai, and Tsuru (2006) examine the causes and effects of the consolidation of Shinkin banks for the period 1984–2002. Shinkin banks take deposits from small and medium sized businesses in a specific region who are members of the cooperative. The stock of the bank is not traded on a market. Consolidation, M&A, of Shinkin banks will have limited benefits to shareholders. Maximizing the value of the stocks of shareholders may not be the motive of the managers of Shinkin banks. Average X-efficiency for all banks was 0.44. Target banks had a slightly higher XE score than acquiring banks, 0.46 to 0.45. Some results for X-efficiency in this study are summarized below. First, for the entire period banks which are more X-efficient are more likely to be target bank. Seconds, the XE of acquiring banks fell the first year after an M&A, but not after. Third, higher XE is shown to increase ROA.

Barros, Managi, and Matousek (2012) examine XE among Japanese banks during a period of bank restructuring from 2000 to 2007. The sample of banks includes City Banks, Long Term Credit Banks, and Trust Banks. The analytical method was the non-parametric DEA. Average XE from 2000 to 2007 fell from 0.72 to 0.63. The cause was an increase in non-performing loans among Japanese banks.

III Other Asian nations

Singapore

Rezvanian and Mehdian (2002) use the non-parametric DEA and a translog cost function to investigate XE among 10 Singapore commercial banks during the period 1991–97. The importance of XE in Singapore is that because of deregulation and new technology banks are under pressure for greater efficiency, including economies of scale and scope. For all banks average XE was approximately 0.75. Chu and Lim (1998) investigate XE among six Singapore banks for the period 1992–96. They use the DEA. The average level of XE is 0.95. Range was 1.0 to 0.85.

Bangladesh

Uddin and Suzuki (2011) investigate the effects of financial reform in Bangladesh. Banking reforms in Bangladesh began in 1982–83 when banks began being privatized and denationalized. Uddin and Suzuki use the DEA method for the period 2001–08. The sample consisted of (de)nationalized and government owned commercial and specialized banks, domestic and foreign private commercial banks, and Islamic and non-Islamic banks. Average XE was 0.79. The range was 1.0 to 0.54.

Indonesia

Hadad, Hall, Kenjegalieva, Santoso, and Simper (2011) use the non-parametric DEA technique to examine the monthly profit-based technical efficiency and productivity of listed Indonesian banks and their market performance. The period of study was 2003–07. The sample consists of state-owned, private national, regional government-owned, joint venture, and foreign banks. The two most efficient banks over the studied period, with average efficiencies exceeding 95%. The three least efficient banks, with average efficiency levels less than 50%—between 23% and 49%. The efficiency estimates reveal a wide dispersion in average efficiency scores—from 34% to 97%.

Philippines

The Philippines, similar to other nations undertook banking reforms in the 1990s via the General Banking Law in an attempt to increase the efficiency of that sector. Manlagñit (2011) use the parametric SFA method to estimate cost efficiency among commercial banks over the period 1990 to 2006. Data consists of 387 observations from 31 commercial banks who control 63% of the somestic commercial banking system. For the entire period average XE was 0.75. And, banks who were more X-efficient in 1990 remained more X-(in)efficient over the 16 year period studied. However, X-inefficiency fell in the wake of reforms, reaching its lowest level in 2005. Larger banks were shown to be more x-efficient than smaller banks. From 1990 to 1995 the difference was eight percentage points. By 1999 the gap closes when both record X-efficiency levels of 0.73.

Dacanay (2010) shows the evolution of cost and profit efficiency for Philippine commercial banks during the period 1992–2004. Liberalization in the banking system began in 1994. Thus there are two sub-periods, 1992–94 which is the pre-liberalization period, and 1995–2005 which is the post-liberalization period. The parametric SFA method and maximum likelihood estimation are used. The empirical results show that XE declined from 0.89 to 0.86 over the 1992–2004 period, averaging 0.87. Theoretically, liberalization should increase XE. The results are inconsistent with XE theory. Two hypotheses were offered to explain the results. First, increased competition increased the quality of bank services and this increased costs enough to reduce XE and profits efficiency. Second, the "quiet life" hypothesis. The effect of new competitors could have been the use of defensive strategies-increase market share through M&As. rather than reducing costs and increasing XE. Both enhance the "quiet life," increase costs and reduce XE. A final consideration is that state-owned banks can be directed toward a social mission but they are "efficiency depleting" (Dacanay, 2010, p. 141). The most X-inefficient bank in the sample was the state-owned Land Bank of the Philippines.

Chiang and Tsaih (2015) used the non-parametric DEA approach to estimate XE among 18 Universal and 17 Commercial banks in the Philippines for the period 2005–10. The years 2007–08 were a period of an economic crises in the Philippines. The years 2005–07 were used as the pre-crises period, and 2009–10 the post-crises years. The average XE score for all banks and all years was 0.82. The maximum scores were in excess of 0.99 for all years while the minimum ranged from 0.17 to 0.41.[a] The average XE value

[a] In 2006 was average value was less than 0, which is left out because a negative value is difficult to evaluate.

for Universal banks was 0.9 while for commercial banks it was 0.68. Universal banks perform the functions of a commercial bank plus others things including the buying and selling of securities. As a result Universal banks are much larger. By size, the average XE of large, medium, and small banks were 0.96, 0.87, and 0.56, respectively. Many of the foreign banks were small, branch banks to larger banks rather than subsidiaries. Average XE of foreign, private, and government-owned banks was 0.65, 0.91, and 0.97, respectively. The authors do say that the addition of foreign banks in the Philippines put pressure on the domestic banks to be more X-efficient. Average XE before, during, and after the crisis was 0.81, 0.81, and 0.82, respectively. The GFC had little effect on the XE of banks in the Philippines.

India

Lall and Rodrigo (2001) use the parametric SFA on plant level data on four Indian industries at the three-digit level of aggregation for 1994 in order to estimate XE. The years 1981–91 were years of strong liberalization. The industries and the average XE scores are leather products (0.44), motor vehicles (0.59), machine tools (0.57), and electronics and computers (0.53). The overall average is 0.53. The low technology-intensive industry, leather products has an average XE of 0.44 and a higher variance than the higher-technology-intensive industries—autos and electronics. Among these two industries the average XE is 0.59 (autos) and 0.53 (electronics). Higher XE is also the result of better energy-intensity usage, higher quality managers, fewer factory workers as a proportion of total employment.

Patibundla (1998) estimates XE using DEA among cutting tool industry in 1983–84. The data show that average XE is 0.59 using DEA. It was 0.37 estimated with a two-input production function, and 0.50 using a three-input production function. He also reports that XE is highest for medium sized firms and lower for small and large firms. The coefficient for size is positive and statistically significant while the coefficient for size squared is negative and statistically significant. Small firms suffer from outdated technology and low labor skills. Large firms suffer from, being large.

ASEAN (Indonesia, Malaysia, the Philippines, and Thailand)

Chan and Karim (2011) estimated XE among foreign banks in the ASEAN network of nations, Indonesia, Malaysia, the Philippines, and Thailand. The data covers the period 2001–08. The average XE level for all banks was 0.76, with a range of 0.92 to 0.06. The average XE level among foreign banks which started off in developed countries was 0.77, while it was 0.71 among banks initiated in developing countries. By nation, the average, the maximum and minimum level of XE was Malaysia: 0.83, 0.9, 0.72; Indonesia: 0.75, 0.92, 0.06; Philippines: 0.74, 0.87, 0.007; and Thailand: 0.73, 0.81, 0.67.

IV Final comments on this chapter, and looking ahead to Chapter 10

The results for China (PRC) demonstrates X-efficiency theory. First, the big state-owned banks were less X-efficient than privately-owned banks. Second, after China loosened up on regulations and used markets more, X-efficiency increased. Third, after China joined the WTO, X-efficiency increased. More competition means more pressure for X-efficiency leads to enhanced levels of X-efficiency. In all the Asian nations X-inefficiency is significant.

In Chapter 10 we focus on several nations and industries. Agriculture in China; telecommunications, hotels, police, firm size, the port industry, and life insurance in Taiwan; manufacturing, cutting tools and government ownership in India; and seaweed farming in Indonesia.

XE among Asian non-financial institutions: c.1991–2017

10

I China

Agriculture

Lin (1992) examined the effect of the "household responsibility system" on Chinese agricultural growth, Tibet excluded, covering the years 1970–87. The individual based "household responsibility system" began replacing collective ownership in 1978. Lin fitted a Cobb-Douglas function with four conventional inputs—land, labor, capital, and fertilizer—and others to capture the period's reforms, including the change in ownership form. All of the statistical models used—OLS, GLS, and stochastic frontier specifications—show that the shift to the individual-based ownership had a positive and statistically significant effect on the constant-dollar value of agricultural output. Lin concludes that production is not an engineering relationship whereby inputs are automatically converted into maximum outputs, but that factors such as ownership form affect the intensity with which inputs are used, and hence affect technical or X-efficiency. What determined the output growth rate in Chinese agriculture? Lin also shows that changes in ownership form contributed more towards growth than the other conventional inputs by changing XE levels. Lin offers no estimates of X-efficiency.[a]

II Taiwan

Telecommunications

Liu, Chen, and Pai (2007) use DEA and four categories of performance to investigate the effects of mergers on XE among 60 telecommunication firms in Taiwan for the period 1993–2003. Average XE ratings for firms with and without any merger activity was 0.9 and 0.96, respectively. Average XE before and after merger activity was 0.98 and 0.94, respectively. Management capability (measured as output per employee and net profits per employee) is shown to be lower after merger activity and is statistically significant at the 1% level.[b]

[a] Marchand and Guo (2014) estimate environmental efficiency of organic and non-organic rice production in southern China.

[b] Lestage, Flacher, Kim, Kim, and Kim (2013) use the OECD countries to test the relationship between public and private telecommunication firms and investment in infrastructure.

The Beginnings of Behavioral Economics. https://doi.org/10.1016/B978-0-12-815289-8.00010-1

Hotels

Lin (2011) examined X-efficiency among 62 international tourist hotels over the period 2002–06. The model uses three inputs and one output. The three inputs are labor, food and beverage (F&B) expenditures, and other operating costs. The hotel's output is its total revenues. Finally it used two control variables: room occupancy rate and the production value of the catering space. Lin tests for the effect of the type of hotel guest, hotel size, and the management's framework, on X-efficiency. Type of hotel guest is either international traveler staying at a hotel in the Taipei metropolitan area, or a domestic traveler staying in a hotel in a metropolitan area outside of Taipei. Hotel size is either hotels with fewer than 300 rooms (small hotel), and those with at least 300 rooms (large hotels). Management framework is whether the hotel is part of a domestic chain, part of an international chain, or is an independent hotel. The author's results show that type of hotel guest or management framework does not have a statistically significant effect on XE. The mean level of XE for hotels in metropolitan Taipei and areas outside Taipei was 0.9. Among domestic chains the average level is 0.92 (statistically) significantly higher than for independent hotels (0.91), which in turn is significantly higher than it is for international chains (0.88). XE is higher in a statistically significant manner among small hotels (0.93) than large hotels (0.89) (Table 10.1).

Chen (2007) uses a parametric stochastic cost frontier on 55 international tourist hotels located in Taiwan. An international tourist hotel is defined as a four-star or five-star hotel. Thirty-three of the hotels are located in a metropolitan area and 30 are part of a chain operation. The data covers 2002. The hotel cost function contains three inputs—labor, food and beverages, and materials. There is one output—total revenue—and two control variables—room occupancy and the production value of the hotel's catering area. Using a stochastic frontier (SFA) cost function approach, the average level of XE for the entire sample is 0.8. The range of XE was 0.98 to 0.35.[c] Results show that nether hotel size nor location (metropolitan area or non-metropolitan area) created a difference in XE. The only factor which was associated with a statistically significant difference was whether the hotel was part of a hotel Chain or is independent, with hotel chains have a higher level of XE than independent hotels, 0.84 and 0.77, respectively.

Wu and Chen (2012) used DEA and tobit analysis among chain and independent tourist hotels in Taiwan between 2006 and 2007. They have 4 input variables and six output variables. Among chain hotels the range of XE scores was 1.0 to 0.56. Among independents the range was 1.0 to 0.63. Tobit analysis showed that hotels which are part of a chain have higher XE scores, as do hotels in Taipei.

Lin and Yang (2014) use data envelope analysis (DEA) to estimate XE among a sample of 25 five-star hotels in Taiwan between 2006 and 2011. They use a two-stage DEA approach. In stage one, the three inputs are number of rooms; operating expenses; and; food and beverage floor space. The outputs are revenues from room

[c] The average XE score for US tourist hotels is 0.90. By contrast, Portugal, which according to Chen has too many state-owned hotels, has an average XE score of 0.22.

Table 10.1 X-efficiency among non-financial institutions in Asia

Nation	Industry	Author(s)	Yr pub	Yrs studied	Av XE	(Non-para)
Taiwan	Telecomm	Liu, Chen, and Pai	2007	1993–2003	0.95	Non-para
Taiwan	Hotels	Lin	2011	2002–06	0.90	Para
Taiwan	Hotels	Chen	2007	2002	0.8	Para
Taiwan	Hotels	Wu and Chen	2012	2006–07	1 to 0.6	Non-para
Taiwan	Hotels	Lin and Yang	2014	2006–11	0.90	Non-para
Taiwan	Hotels	Hua et al.	2010	1997–2006	0.91	Para
Taiwan	Hotels	Tsaur	2001	1996–98	0.87	Non-para
Taiwan	Hotels	Shieh, Hu, and Gao	2014	1998–2007	0.75	Non-para
Taiwan	Hotels	Shi and Zhao	2012	2002–08	0.85	Para
Taiwan	Hotels	Anderson, Fok, and Scott	2001	1994	0.87	Non-para
Taiwan	Police	Wu, Chen, and Yeh	2010	2006	0.97	Para and non-para
Taiwan	Firm size	Yang and Chen	2009	2001	0.71	Para
Taiwan	Firm size	Hu and Schieve	1998	1954–91	0.82	Non-para
Taiwan	Life ins	Hao and Chou	2005	1977–99	0.66	Para
India	Industry	Lall and Rodrigo	2001	1994	0.5	Para
India	Various	Chhibber and Majumdar	1998	1989–94		
India	Cutting tools	Patibandla	1998	1983–84	0.37	Para
India	Cutting tools	Patibandla	1998	1983–84	0.59	Non-para
Taiwan	Port industry	Yang	2013	2001–07		
Indonesia	Seaweed farmers	Hanna et al.	2014	2007–08	n.a.	n.a.

occupancy, and revenues from food and beverages. The conversion of inputs into outputs measures operational efficiency. In stage 2, the outputs from stage 1 become the inputs, and the outputs are the occupancy rate and average output value per employee. The conversion of these inputs into output measures management efficiency. Stage 1 operational efficiency results show that XE for the years 2008–11 are 0.94, 0.93, 0.76, and 0.95. Stage 2 managerial efficiency results show that XE for the years 2008–11 are 0.49, 0.67, 0.66, and 0.64, respectively.

Hu et al. (2010) use the parametric SFA approach on 66 international tourist hotels in Taiwan for the period 1997–2006. The average X-efficiency score for the entire sample was 0.91. The range of scores was 0.98 to 0.71. The results for the environmental variables showed that four of the variables increase X-efficiency: being located in a metropolitan area, being part of a hotel chain, increasing the number of tourist guides, and reducing the distance to either airport increase X-efficiency. All are significant at the 1% level. The authors note that tourism is a very competitive industry and hence higher amounts of X-efficiency is essential for profitability and survival.

Tsaur (2001) investigated 53 international tourist hotels in Taiwan for the years 1996–98. They used DEA, with 6 output variables and 7 input variables. Average XE score was 0.87, with a range of 1.0 to 0.54. Chain hotels had an average score of 0.90. Independents had an average of 0.86. Hotels catering more to individual visitors had an average of 0.92 while hotels catering more to groups had an average of 0.86. The author's analysis shows that total operating expenses among the hotels with an XE score <1.0 could be reduced by 10.6%. The number of employees could be reduced by 19.45%, the total number of rooms by 24.8%, and total floor space utilized by catering by 23.6%.

Shieh, Hu, and Gao (2014) use DEA and tobit analysis to estimate XE levels and correlates of XE among 61 Int'l Tourist Hotels in Taiwan for the period 1998–2007. They use three output variables, total revenues from room, food and beverages, and other sources of hotel revenues. The three inputs variables are rooms, employees, and floor space. The four external or environmental variables are number of tourists by nationality, scenic spots close to the hotel, distance to the airport, and whether the hotel is part of a chain or is independent. Average XE was 0.75. Similar to other studies the authors find that hotels which are part of a chain are more cost efficient than independents. Hotels which are closer to an international airport, and have more visitors who are locals, North Americans and Japanese will also be more XE, as will hotels which are closer to scenic attractions.

Shi and Zhao (2012) use SFA model and panel data to estimate technological, X, efficiency for Taiwanese hotels of at least 200 rooms in 31 Chinese provinces during the period 2002 to 2008. They use three inputs—number of rooms, physical capital, and number of employees. They have one output: sales revenue. They also use three environmental variables: the ratio of state-owned enterprises, the number of tourists arrivals, and GDP per capita. XE ranged from 0.95 (Shanghai) to 0.47 (Xizang). The three most XE provinces are in the Eastern region: Beijing (0.92), Shanghai (0.95), and Tianjin (0.93). In addition, the Eastern region includes # 5, Jiangsu (0.89), # 6, Liaoning (0.87), and # 8, Guangdong (0.86). The authors theorize that regions with higher per-capita GDP and more tourists spurs the hotel industry to greater efficiency. Xizang province, the lowest XE ranking is in Tibet. Over time the average XE for the entire nation, the eastern, central, and western provinces merged between 0.8 and 0.9. In addition, state-owned hotels are significantly less X-efficient than others including hotels with foreign investment.

Anderson, Fok, and Scott (2000) use the DEA to estimate X and allocative efficiency, and economies of scale among 48 hotels in Taiwan. The period covered by the data is 1994. Average X, allocative, and economies of scale are 0.87, 0.51, and 0.9, respectively. Allocatively inefficient hotels spend too much on rooms, employees, and hotel operations, and not enough on food and beveridge.

Police

Wu, Chen, and Yeh (2010) study the relative XE of police units in 22 of Taiwan's administrative districts for the year 2006. The authors use DEA and SFA processes. In stage 1 output and input data was used to estimate XE among each police unit. In stage 2 the Stochastic Frontier Analysis (SFA) the XE measures from stage 1 was the dependent variable and regressed against environmental variables: population, population density, housing units, unemployment rate, level of education, percent with a college education or above, household income. None of the variables were statistically significant. In stage 3 adjustments were made in stage 1 results and the statistical noise from second stage. The DEA method used six outputs and three inputs. The outputs were the resolution of the (1) number of burglaries, (2) number of violent crimes cleared, and (3) number of other crimes. (4) number of road traffic accidents resulting in death or serious injury, (5) number of general and special services in response to residents' requests, and (6) residents' satisfaction with the public security. The inputs are (1) cost of labor, (2) general operating costs, and (3) costs of purchased equipment. Overall efficiency is the product of technical or X-efficiency and scale efficiency: $OE = TE \times SE$. The average score for all police units using DEA method is 0.97.

Life insurance

Hao and Chou (2005) estimated X-efficiency among 26 of Taiwan's life insurance companies, using the parametric distribution free approach (DFA), covering the period 1977–99. Average X-efficiency using the DFA was 0.66, ranging from 0.78 to 0.53.

Firm size

Yang and Chen (2009) studied the firm size—XE relationship for Taiwan's electronics industry using cross section firm level data and SFA for 2001. The firm size distinction is between small and medium sized firms (SMEs) and large firms (LEs), 200 employees separating the two groups. Controlling for size. among all two-digit electronics firms, average XE among MSEs (0.72) is higher than for LEs (0.70) and statistically significant at the 1% level. The maximum average level among MSEs (LEs) is 0.75 (0.78). Among both groups of firms the variables which increase XE are the firm's age, welfare-expenditures per employee, export/sales, and R&D/Sales.

Hu and Schieve (1998) used data on small and medium size firms (SME) and large firms (LE) in Taiwan for the period 1954–91. SMEs are firms with fewer than 100 employees while LEs have 100 or more employees. Their data show that SMEs in seven of nine industries studied have larger elasticity of substitution than LEs between labor and capital. The authors state that this means that SMEs vis-à-vis LEs have more flexible technology and are more sensitive to the external environment than are SMEs. SMEs are had a higher level of XE in the same seven of nine industries. The average

XE among SMEs was 0.83. Among LEs the average was 0.80. These results are similar or identical with many other XE studies; large firms tend to be too bureaucratic to be as X-efficient as smaller firms.

Port industry

Yang (2013) estimates the opportunity cost of environmental regulations (OCER) and the cost of X or productive inefficiency (PIE). The data covers the years 2001–07. DEA is used to estimate OCER and PIE. Their results show that OCER amounted to NT $385 million, or 1.8% of revenues generated by the Port industry. X-inefficiency or PIE amounts to NT $1763 million. The bigger problem is X-inefficiency not environmental regulations.

III India

Machine tools, and electronics and computers

Lall and Rodrigo (2001) use the parametric SFA on plant level data on four Indian industries at the three-digit level of aggregation for 1994 in order to estimate XE. The years 1981–91 were years of strong liberalization. The industries and the average XE scores are leather products (0.44), motor vehicles (0.59), machine tools (0.57), and electronics and computers (0.53). The overall average is 0.53. The low technology-intensive industry, leather products has an average XE of 0.44 and a higher variance than the higher-technology-intensive industries—autos and electronics. Among these two industries the average XE is 0.59 (autos) and 0.53 (electronics). Higher XE is also the result of better energy-intensity usage, higher quality managers, fewer factory workers as a proportion of total employment.

Government ownership

Does government ownership always reduce (X) efficiency? Chhibber and Majumdar (1998) test this hypothesis on ROA and ROS as dependent variables and a spline regression technique on 1100 firms listed on the Bombay Stock Exchange. Most studies investigate publicly or state-owned firms versus privately-owned firms. Chhibber and Majumdar's unique approach is to create three groups of firms according to how much government ownership exists; firms with less than 26% state shareholding, firms with 26% but less than 50% of shares owned by the state, and firms in which the state is a majority shareholder. Other independent variables are age, sales, (exports/sales), (imports/total variable costs), sales/advertising, and wages and salaries paid. Exports and imports are included because pressure from international trade is expected to reduce X-inefficiency. In the regression with ROA and ROS as dependent variables, all three government variables are negative, but only government as majority shareholder is statistically significant. Exports and imports are both positive but only exports is statistically significant.

Patibundla (1998) uses 1983–84 data for 76 firms in India's cutting tool industry. They used both the parametric SFA and the non-parametric DEA. Average X-efficiency was 0.37 with the SFA and 0.59 with the DEA. Data was gathered by extensive surveys. As reported by Shepherd, X-efficiency increases with size before it begins falling; the highest level of X-efficiency are in medium sized firms. The lower levels among small firms are due to outdated technology and low labor productivity. The low levels among large firms is due to the fact that access to better technology and information is not enough to guarantee higher levels of X-efficiency.

IV Indonesia

Hanna, Mullainathan, and Schwartzstein (2014) use a model of "learning through noticing." The authors use this model to show that people with a lot of experience are off the production frontier people fail to notice important aspects of the data they have. They can be off the production frontier because "many production functions are not known ex ante" (p. 311). Production functions are learned from experience. (Being off of the function or frontier is used to estimate X-inefficiency.) The authors sound a lot like Leibenstein explaining X-efficiency in his original article. The authors state that in order to maximize product quality managers must do a variety of things including "...exactly how to monitor worker effort, what to look for to determine whether a machine needs preventive maintenance, whether to worry about the cleanliness of the shop floor, and so on" (pp. 1342–1343). They test these ideas among 489 seaweed farmers in Indonesia who fail to produce with cost minimizing input combinations because of a failure to notice. Finally, they state that their findings help explain why "some demonstrations or agricultural extension activities are ineffective or only moderately effective in the long run" (p. 1314). They cite Leibenstein's 1966 article, and Kilby's, 1962 article also cited by Leibenstein in his 1966 paper.

V Final comments on this chapter, and looking ahead to Chapters 11 and 12

Taiwan has a very high average X-efficiency level for its industries. The average level of X-efficiency for its hotels is 0.85. Telecommunications and the police averaged 0.95 and 0.97, respectively. In India average X-efficiency is 0.53 for several manufacturing industries; 0.37 for X-efficiency measured with a parametric technique, and 0.59 with a non-parametric technique. The next two chapters, which are the final two chapters on the empirical studies of X-efficiency, are for Europe (Chapter 11), and Australia, New Zealand, Latin America, the Middle East, Africa, and The World.

XE in Europe: c.1991–2017

11

The end of Communism in Europe, the deregulation of the banking systems, and the rise of the EU increased competition among European firms. The prediction is that X-efficiency should increase. In this chapter we summarize firms from Eastern Europe, and Western Europe, and firms which are in nations which joined the EU early in its development and from nations which joined the EU later on.[a]

I Eastern Europe and post-communist

Mertens and Urga (2001) use a sample is 79 Ukrainian banks for the year 1998. For all banks, the average XE was 0.68.18 XE among large and medium banks, small, and very small banks averaged 0.63, 0.69, and 0.73, respectively. On the other hand, large and medium sized banks have higher level of profits-efficiency than (very) small banks. Large banks earn "profits without efficient production."

Kyj and Isik (2008) use a sample of all Ukrainian commercial banks in order to measure technical efficiency (TE); pure technical efficiency (PTE), and scale efficiency (SE) for the period 1998–2003. TE and PTE have both been used as a measure of XE, and hence I will focus on these two variables. The authors estimate all three efficiency concepts assuming that a common frontier exists among all banks, as well as when the frontier is estimated separately for banks of different sizes, measured by assets. The overall average level of XE was 0.61. When estimated with a common frontier, TE, and PTE, were 0.47, and 0.62, respectively. When estimated for banks of different sizes the estimates were 0.62, and 0.74, respectively. Larger banks are more X-efficient but less scale efficient than smaller banks.

The authors conjecture that the extreme uncertainty in the Ukrainian environment gave large banks an advantage and accounts for their higher XE for several reasons. People believe that large banks are more stable, and government would not allow them to fail. Second, large banks made economic profits and used it to hire more productive employees and invest more in technology. Thus unit costs and X-inefficiency is reduced.

Andries and Capraru (2013) use a sample of 17 countries from CEE for the period 2004–08, using the parametric SFA method for estimating XE. Average XE was 0.9. The nation with the highest and lowest levels of XE were the Czech Republic at 0.97, and Serbia at 0.83, respectively. By bank size measured by total assets, small (less than 1000 mil EUR), medium (greater than 1 bil EUR and less than 10 bil EUR), and large banks (greater than 10 bil EUR) had XE averages of 0.9, 0.89, and 0.93, respectively. By status within the EU, EU members, and EU non-member nations had average XE levels of 0.9, and 0.88, respectively. Finally, the authors report that more reforms of the banking system, and a greater level of inter rate freedom increases XE. The result is that the banking system can offer banking services to customers at lower prices.

[a] A review of the effects of the EU Single Market Programme on X-efficiency in banking can be found in Gardener, Molyneux, and Moore (2001).

The Beginnings of Behavioral Economics. https://doi.org/10.1016/B978-0-12-815289-8.00011-3

Andries and Capraru (2013) estimate X-efficiency and the convergence of X-efficiency levels among 10 banking systems from Central and Eastern European countries for the period 2004–10. The average level of X-efficiency for all nations in all years was 0.9088, with a standard deviation of 0.0616. Hungary had the highest average at 0.92, while Lithuania had the lowest average at 0.89. The authors also report that X-efficiency levels converge among high and low X-efficiency banking systems. Average X-efficiency levels for all nations fell in 2009–10, the years of the financial crises.

Kasman and Yildirim (2006) use the parametric stochastic frontier Approach to analyze cost and profit efficiencies in commercial banking among the eight Central and Eastern European countries (CEEC's) that became new members to the European Union. The period of study is 1995–2002). The average cost inefficiency for the entire period was 0.207. The average level of cost inefficiency ranged from 0.17 (Estonia) to 0.21 (Czech Republic). By bank size, measured by assets, banks with assets of at least $10 billion, and assets of between $200 and $300 million had average cost inefficiency of 0.222. Banks with assets of between $4 and $5 billion had average cost inefficiency of 0.174. The smallest bank size, $1 to $100 million had average cost inefficiency of 0.215. Domestic and foreign banks had average cost inefficiency of 0.210 and 0.203, respectively. Average profit inefficiency was 0.367. The Slovak Republic's profits inefficiency level was highest at 0.417. The Czech Republic level was the lowest at 0.322. By bank size, the smallest banks' average was 0.394 while the largest banks' average was 0.351. Domestic and foreign banks' average profits inefficiency was 0.386 and 0.351, respectively. Clearly, banks are closer to the cost frontier than to the profits frontier. And domestic banks were more inefficient than foreign banks.

Kraft and Tirtiroglu (1998) estimate XE for a sample of Croatian banks for the years 1994 and 1995. Deregulation and liberalization of the financial sector began in the late 1980s. The year 1989 is the cut-off date for old and new banks (Table 11.1).

Table 11.1 X-efficiency in Europe

Financial institutions	**Europe**				
Author(s)	**Yr pub**	**Yrs study**	**Nation(s)**	**Stat method**	**Average XE**
Mertens and Urga	2001	1998	Ukraine	Para	0.68
Kyj and Isik	2008	1998–2003	Ukraine	Non-para	0.61
Drake, Semper (Police)	2002	1992–97	Ukraine	Non-para	0.86
Hefferman and Fu	2009	1993–2004	Ukraine	Pars	0.47
Kasman and Yildirim	2006	1995–2002	CEE (8)	Para	0.79
Kraft and Tirtiroglu	1998	1994–95	Croatia	Para	0.79
Kenjegalieva et al.	2009	1999–2003	EE	Non-para	0.75 to 0.88
DeJonghe and Vennet	2008	1997–2004	EU-15	Para	0.83

Table 11.1 continued

Financial institutions	**Europe**				
Author(s)	**Yr pub**	**Yrs study**	**Nation(s)**	**Stat method**	**Average XE**
Beccalli et al.	2006	1999–2000	W. Eur. (5)	(Non) para	0.82
Huang et al.	2011	1993–2004	E. Eur (14)	Para	0.66
Altunbas et al.	2001	1989–97	EU-15	Para	0.78
Fenn et al.	2008	1995–2001	EU-14	Para	0.8 to 0.93
Kasman and Turgutlu	2011	1995–2005	EU-23	Para	0.88
Maudos and deGuevara	2007	1993–2002	EU-15	Para	0.86
Isik and Hassan	2003	1992–96	Turkey	Non-para	0.72
Kasman and Turgutlu	2009	1990–2004	Turkey	Para	0.63 to 0.82
DeGuevara and Maudos	2007	1986–2002	Spain	Para	0.93
Maudos	1998	1990–93	Spain	Para	0.79
Tourtosa-Ausina	2002	1985–95	Spain	Non-para	0.74
Coccorese and Pellecchia	2010	1992–2007	Italy	Para	0.89
Girardone et al.	2004	1993–96	Italy	Para	0.86
Chortareas et al.	2007	1998–2003	Greece	Non-para	0.87
Delis et al.	2009	1993–2005	Greece	(Non) para	0.84
Bikker and van Leuvensteijn	2008	1995–2003	Holland	Para	0.72
Rossi et al.	2009	1997–2003	Austria	Para	0.91
Haynes and Thompson	1999	1981–93	United Kingdom	Para	0.8
Cowie and Loynes	2012	1980–2009	England	n.a.	n.a.
Drake and Simper (Bldg Soc)	2002	1992–97	England	Para	0.91
Altembas et al.	2001	1989–96	Germany	Para	0.77 to 0.99
Feijoo et al.	2002	1995	Spain	Para	0.6
Havrylchyk and Jurzyk	2013	1993–2004	CEE	Para	0.65
Andries and Capraru	2013	2004–08	CEE	Para	0.91
Barros et al.	2010	1994–2003	Greece	Non-para	0.88
Berg et al.	1993	1990	Nordics	Non-para	0.41 to 0.78
Barros and Antunes	2011	2004–08	Portugal	Para	0.9
Kalb Germany	2014	1990–2004	Germany	Non-para	0.68
Kalb Germany	2014	1990–2004	Germany	Para	0.76
Andries and Capraru	2014	2004–10	CEE	Para	0.91

The average XE score for all banks was 0.79. Average XE for sub-sections of the sample are as follows: old state banks, 0.84; all old banks, 0.83; all state banks, 0.82; privatized banks, 0.82; New state, 0.79; all Private banks, 0.78; all New banks, 0.75; New private, 0.74.

Old banks and state banks are more XE than private sector and newer banks. Since private banks are both new (post-communist) and private, it would seem intuitive that they would be the most, not the least X-efficient. What explains this result? First, new private banks offer better and more costly services and hence their costs are higher. Second, new banks have start-up costs. Third, state banks were insolvent, and borrowed large amounts of money to stay in business. This raised interest rates. The new banks and the private banks could make profits without being very (X) efficient: so they engaged in "free-riding" behavior and were relatively X-inefficient.

Kenjegalieva, Simper, and Weyman-Jones (2009) estimate XE among banks in Central and Eastern Europe for 1999–2003. The paper focuses on banks in former socialist countries as they began attempting to join the EU. The authors use the non-parametric DEA method and find that average XE for all nations and years was 0.82. Results show that XE is negatively affected by corruption. Foreign banks have the effect of increasing XE. Average wages in the early years—1999–2000—decreased XE. However, in 2001–03 higher wages increased XE. The change is significant. In the early years of restructuring productivity of labor may still have been hamstrung by the old rules under socialism. Thus, higher wages simply meant higher costs and lower XE. As restructuring continued higher wages created higher productivity. Higher costs were offset by higher productivity, and XE increased (Altman, 1988).

Huang, Shen, Chen, and Tseng (2011) sample consists of banks in 14 transitional countries from Eastern Europe and the former Soviet Union over the period 1993–2004. The average XE score was 0.66. The average level for foreign owned banks, state-owned banks, and domestic private banks were 0.78, 0.72, and 0.65, respectively. Average allocative efficiency among the same three sets of banks was 0.94, 0.92, and 0.92, respectively. Allocative efficiency is considerably higher than X-efficiency. Thus, transition nations needed better managers more than a better input mix.

Havrylchyk and Jurzyk (2011) estimate X-efficiency among 418 banks operating among CEE nations between 1993 and 2004: Bulgaria, Croatia, the Czech Republic, Estonia, Hungary, Latvia, Lithuania, Poland, Romania, the Slovak Republic, and Slovenia. In their estimation of bank efficiency they measure bank output as loans, securities and deposits. Inputs are labor and capital. Average X-efficiency among domestic and foreign banks were 0.62 and 0.68, respectively. Among domestic banks state and private banks' average X-efficiency were 0.6 and 0.63, respectively. For foreign banks the average among takeover banks, and greenfield banks was 0.6 and 0.73, respectively. Among all banks, those which are more X-efficient, and those which are greenfield banks have higher return on assets.

Andries and Capraru (2013) studied the impact of banking reforms on X-efficiency among 17 CEE countries for the period 2004–08. They used the parametric SFA. Average X-efficiency among small, medium, and large banks was 0.91. For countries which were and were not EU members average X-efficiency was 0.91, and 0.88, respectively. Their results also show that banks in countries with a higher degree of banking reforms, more market oriented liberalization, and more financial openness, were more X-efficient.

Aristovnik, Seljak, and Mencinger (2013) measure X-efficiency among 11 police directorates in Slovenia in 2010, and compared with 2005. They use the non-parametric DEA. Police performance is measured using the following activities: crime prevention, detection and investigation; public order and overall safety of people and property, and; road safety Using the geometric mean, average X-efficiency in 2010 was 0.82, with a range from 1.0 to 0.655. In 2005 the average level of X-efficiency (using the geometric mean) was 0.84, with a range from 0.96 to 0.65.

II EU members

Delis and Papanikolaou (2009) use a sample of banks from 10 new EU members for the years 1994–2005, and a non-parametric method to estimate XE. The average level of XE was 0.66. The highest and lowest levels of XE were 0.77 in Estonia, and 0.52 in the Czech Republic, respectively.

De Jonghe and Vennet (2008) use data from nations of EU-15 for the period 1997–2004 and measure XE, and "X-asset efficiency." The average level of XE for all years and nations was 0.83. Average "X-asset-efficiency" is 0.74. Thus the average bank could increase the market value of their assets by 26% if they were the best-practice bank. Hence higher levels of XE increase the firm's long run market value, i.e., long run profits.

Beccalli, Casu, and Girardone (2006) use data from among European banks in France, Germany, Italy, Spain, and the United Kingdom to estimate XE for 1999 and 2000. The results show that XE averaged 0.82 for all nations and both years.

Altunbas, Gardener, Molyneux, and Moore (2001) measure XE with a sample of banks in *15 European nations* for the period 1989–97. *XE* for all banks *averaged 0.78*. For the smallest bank group XE was 0.79. XE for the largest group is 0.75.

Fenn, Vencappa, Diacon, Klumpes, and O'Brien (2008) estimate XE among a sample of insurance companies from EU-14 nations for the period 1995–2001. Financial markets in Europe underwent deregulation beginning in the early 1990s. There were more than 2500 M&A among insurance firms, of which about 1700 involved a change in corporate control. The authors use the parametric SFA method. They divide insurance firms into three categories, life, non-life, and; composite firms offering both classes of insurance. Average XE for life, non-life, and composite firms were 0.67, 0.88, and 0.97, respectively. In each category the smallest firms measured by assets was the most X-efficient group, while the largest firms were the least X-efficient. Non-life and composite average XE was stable over the period 1995–2001. However, average XE for life insurance companies declined from 0.86 to 0.8. M&A activity was very high among these companies. As a result firm size became considerably larger. The authors conclude that the inability to manage larger firms caused the decline in average XE.

Kasman and Turgutlu (2011) use a sample of 685 life insurance companies from EU-15 nations in order to estimate XE for the period 1995–2005. The development of a single European insurance market increased competition and put pressure on firms to become more (X-) efficient. They use the parametric SFA method. Average XE for all firms in all years was 0.88. The most X-efficient firms by nation was Portugal at 0.96. The least X-efficient was Finland at 0.72. By size, the most X-efficient were the smallest firms, $1–$100 million, at 0.9. The least X-efficient were the largest firms, $5,000,000,000, at 0.8. From 1995 to 2002, average XE fell; from 2002 to 2005 XE increased. The move to a single market accelerated in 1999 with the adoption of the Euro, and the Financial Services Action Plan. This was followed by the Lisbon Summit in 2000, and the Stockholm Summit in 2001. The shift in XE in 2002 is, therefore, consistent with this acceleration.

De Guevara and Maudos (2007) use a sample of banks in the EU-15 for the period 1993–2002 in order to estimate XE, and the relationship between market power and XE. The average level of XE was 0.86 for the entire period. Another result of their analysis is that market power, measured by the Lerner Index is positively associated with the level of XE. Thus, managers do not slack off when the market power of their firm increases. Managers do not use market power to pursue the "quiet life."

III Individual nations

Kalb (2014) estimated X-efficiency among local government's provision of highway maintenance in the German state of Baden-Württemberg for the period 1990–2004. The authors uses both the parametric SFA, and the non-parametric DEA. However, they use two versions of each. They use both the "regular" SFA and the SFA one-step. They also use the "regular" DEA and the DEA bootstrap technique. In the SFA one-step, Maximum Likelihood estimates simultaneously the parameters of the stochastic frontier and those of the exogenous variables. Average X-efficiency for SFA and SFA one-step is 0.75, and 0.76, respectively. For DEA and DEA bootstrapping the averages are 0.64, and 0.72, respectively. The parametric results in higher average levels of X-efficiency.

Maudos (1998). The author estimates XE and their effects on market power among Spanish banks for the years 1990–93. Average XE is 0.79. In regressions with return on assets (ROA) and return on equity (ROE) as the dependent variables, XE is positive and statistically significant in all equations. However, industry concentration is not statistically significant in all but one equation. Maudos concludes that, "These findings suggest that bank regulatory decisions based on concerns for their impact on changes in concentration may be inappropriate and should focus instead on bank efficiency" (p. 199).

De Guevara and Maudos (2007) use a panel of Spanish commercial and savings banks for the period 1986–2002 to study XE and market power. Average XE among all banks in the sample is 0.93. The Lerner Index (p-mc/p) served as a proxy for market power. Results show that a 1% increase in XE increases market power (Lerner Index) by 7.3%. The authors propose that the meaning of this relationship is that more efficient banks have better management which use their efficiency as a barrier to entry which gives rise to market power. In the environment surrounding the banking industry the saying that only the strong/efficient survive is even more correct than at other more "normal" times.

Tortusa-Ausina (2002) examines the effects of deregulation among Spanish banks which were among the most regulated banks in Europe. The period of investigation was 1985–95. I will report here the results for what the author calls Approach 1, the intermediary approach to banking. First, the figures for simple means. Among commercial banks average XE in 1985 and 1995 was 0.6 and 0.77, respectively. Among savings banks the averages are 0.44 and 0.80, respectively. Among all banks the averages were 0.53 and 0.79, respectively. The effect of deregulation was clearly to enhance XE. Second, using weighted means which controls for bank size. Among commercial banks the averages for 1985 and 1995 are 0.83 and 0.88, respectively. Among savings banks the figures are 0.57 and 0.86. For all banks they are 0.75 and 0.87. Again, consistent with XE theory, deregulation enhanced XE.

Feijoo, Franco, and Hernandez (2002) measure X-efficiency and energy efficiency among 66 sectors and 9984 Spanish firms in 1995.The authors use the parametric SFA. Average X-efficiency was 0.6. Energy efficiency was 0.766, meaning that the use of energy could decrease by 23.4%. By contrast, labor, capital, and advertising could decrease by 41%, 35.8%, and 70.4%, respectively.

Barros and Antunes (2011) measure X-efficiency among 65 Portuguese wind farms during 2004–08. The authors use the parametric SFA. Average X-efficiency was 0.9, with levels ranging from 1.0 to 0.74. Wind farms which are part of an energy company are more X-efficient than wind farms which are not part of an energy company. Larger farms are also more X-efficient than smaller farms. Finally, management skills are considered unique skills and differences in management skills are considered to be a significant source of X-efficiency differences.

Coccorese and Pellecchia (2010) investigated the extent and causes of XE among Italian banks for the period 1992–2007. The average XE score was 0.89. Increases in market power, measured by the Lerner index, reduces XE. The elasticity of XE with respect to changes in the Lerner index varied from −0.1013 to −0.0608. Thus, if the Lerner index increases by 10%, XE would decrease between about 1% and six-tenth of 1%. The response of XE to changes in market power is small.

Girardone, Molyneux, and Gardener (2004) investigate the main determinants of Italian banks' X-efficiency over the deregulation period 1993–96; the Single Market Programme began in 1992. Bank size was measured by total assets, and divided into four asset size groups. Average XE levels from the smallest size group to the largest size group were 87.7, 85.7, 86.3, and 83.7, respectively. XE increased over the entire period for all bank sizes suggesting that deregulation and the Ues 1992 Single Market Programme had positive effects on XE over time.

Delis, Koutsomanoli-Fillipaki, Staikouras, and Katerina (2009) estimate XE among a sample of Greek banks during the period 1993–2005. Pressure from joining the EMU and the Single European Market during the late 1980s and 1990s led to a more market oriented sector including deregulation of interest rates, M&A activity, the increased presence of foreign banks, and the adoption of newer technologies. The average level of XE among all banks was 0.81. Over time, under the pressure of deregulation in all its forms, XE increased from 0.62 (1993) to 0.9 (2005).

Chortareas, Girardone, and Ventouri (2009). Covering the period when Greece entered the EMU, XE averaged about 0.87, and increased by 4.3% over 1998–2003.

Given the pressure for efficiency during these years an increase in XE is expected. Boucinha, Ribeiro, and Weyman-Jones (2013) used a sample of Portuguese banks from 1992 to 2006 to estimate XE, and scale efficiency (SE). This 14 year period coincided with Portugal entering the Euro-area, and hence banking liberalization, M&A activities, and technological changes. The authors use the parametric SFA method. Average XE for all years was 0.83. Average SE was 0.97. Improving efficiency has a larger upside from increasing XE than scale efficiency.

Halkos and Tzeremes (2013) used a sample of 18 Greek banks and about 45 mergers for the years 2007–11 in order to estimate the X-efficiency effects of bank mergers. Between 1 year before the 2007–08 Greek financial crises, and 1 year after mergers had no effect on X-efficiency. For 2011, mergers had a positive short run effect on X-efficiency. Average X-efficiency for all banks using Variable Returns to Scale model was 0.98 in 2007. Using a boot-strapping technique, the average level of X-efficiency for 2007, and 2007–11 was also 0.98.

Barros, Nektarios, and Assaf (2010) estimated X-efficiency among Greek life insurance companies for the period 1994–2003 using the non-parametric DEA. The Third Generation Insurance Directive of 1994 was designed to deregulate the insurance market and increase efficiency among EU countries. Their sample consisted of 71 life insurance companies. Average X-efficiency for the entire period and for all firms was 0.88.

Bikker and van Leuvensteijn (2008) estimate XE among life insurance companies in Holland for the years 1995–2003. They use the parametric SFA. Average XE was 0.72. As in many other studies economies of scale (SE) offer a smaller improvement in efficiency then does XE. In this study SE=0.82, while XE=0.72. The possible increase in SE and XE are 18% and 28%, respectively. Drake and Simper (2002a) estimate economies of scale and the relationship between firm size and X-efficiency fr a sample of U.K. Building Societies for 1992–97. Average economies of scale was 0.91; firms are producing in the downward sloping part of the long run average cost curve. They don't provide an estimate of X-efficiency. However, they do report that technological change allows larger Building Societies to become more X-efficient; X-efficiency is less than 1.0.

Manasakis, Apostolakis, and Datseris (2013) measure X-efficiency among hotels in Crete for 2008. The data is for 25 independent hotels and 25 hotels operating under a brand name. Brand name hotels are either international, national, or local. The authors use the non-parametric DEA. The authors use the term technical (in) efficiency, a term which has two parts: pure technical (in)efficiency and, scale (in) efficiency. Pure technical efficiency, a.k.a. X-efficiency, measures inefficiencies due to management's poor decision making. Scale (in)efficiency measures the firm's choosing the optimal size. Technical efficiency measures the ability to reduce their inputs for a given output, or the ability to produce more for a given amount of inputs. Part of this is producing at the optimal size.

Average technical efficiency (TE) for independent, local, national, and international branded hotels is 0.78, 0.85, 0.86, and.75, respectively. For all hotels the average is 0.82. Average pure technical efficiency (PTE), X-efficiency, for the same four groups was 0.88, 0.885, 0.9, 0.81; for all hotels it was 0.87. Scale efficiency (SE) for the same was 0.89, 0.96, 0.95, 0.93, and 0.95. As usual, scale efficiency is higher than X-efficiency. TE is the lowest of the three forms of efficiency because TE = PTE × SE. For independent hotels this means that 0.88 × 0.89 = 0.78. TE is NOT the lowest because of management errors and/or biases.

Rossi, Schwaiger, and Winkler (2009) sample 96 Austrian banks for the effect of bank diversification on XE for 1997–2003. Average XE was 0.91. Diversification is measured by the diversification of the bank's loan portfolio by both the size and volume of loans, and to different industries. They find that diversification reduces XE, and risk; but increases profits efficiency.

Altunbas, Evans, and Molyneux (2001) examine X and profits efficiency, and scale economies among 1195 private commercial banks, 2858 public savings banks, and 3486 mutual cooperative German banks. The time period under examine is 1989 and 1996. The authors use both the parametric SFA and DFA instruments. They estimate efficiency including and excluding Off Balance Sheet (OBS) items. For simplicity I will report the results for the SFA including OBS items.

Among German private commercial banks, average X-efficiency, profit efficiency, and scale economies are 0.77, 0.77, and 0.91, respectively. Among German public savings banks, average X-efficiency, profit efficiency, and scale economies are 0.85, 0.83, and 0.93, respectively. Among German mutual cooperative average X-efficiency, profit efficiency, and scale economies are 0.99, 0.86, and 0.92, respectively.

X-efficiency among private, public, mutual, and the entire banking system is 0.78, 0.84, 0.86, and 0.84, respectively. Private banks are less X-efficient than the other ownership forms. Profit-efficiency among private, public, mutual, and the entire banking system is 0.76, 0.81, 0.78, and 0.79, respectively. Private banks are less profits-efficient than the other ownership forms. Scale efficiency among private, public, mutual, and the entire banking system is 0.92, 0.91, 0.91, and 0.91, respectively. Private banks are more scale efficient than the other forms. Private banks are closer to being at the optimum size, but are less effective at keeping costs down and profits up.

Fu and Hefferman (2009) use a sample of UK retail banking firms for the period 1993–2004 to estimate the relationship between the industry's market structure and XE. Average XE was 0.47. Scale efficiency (SE) was 0.96. As is a usual empirical result, there is much more to be gained from increasing XE than SE. Their analysis shows that firms with higher market shares, and profits, are those firms with better management and higher levels of XE. This is known as the "efficient structure" hypothesis.

Haynes and Steve Thompson (1999). The authors use data from 93 UK building societies over the period 1981–93 to investigate the effects of M&A on Building Society XE. Building societies historically raised funds from retail deposits which were funneled into mortgages. The Building Societies Act of 1986 allowed building societies to expand outside of mortgages. The average level of XE among the building societies was 0.8. Their results also show that productivity growth among Building Societies was 3.4% in the year following the merger. This increases to 5.6% 5 years later. Consistent with XE theory, the results suggest that the regulatory/competitive environment affects the productivity gains (or losses) of a merger. Thus it was in the post-deregulation years, 1987 onward, when the pressure to minimize costs was the greatest that the productivity gains were the greatest.

Drake and Simper (2002a, 2002b) studied (public sector) police departments in England and Wales for the years 1992–97. They use two methods, the parametric distribution free approach (DFA), and the non-parametric DEA. The average XE for DFA was 0.84. Using DFA the average was approximately 0.82. Theoretically, non-parametric methods should report lower levels of XE because the entire error term is assumed to estimate inefficiency.

Hay and Liu (2013) discuss theory: in a Cournot or homogeneous oligopoly relative efficiency determines market share and the incentive to be more, or less (X) efficient. More competitive environments create an incentive for more (X) efficiency. The authors test this theory with data from 181 firms in 19 manufacturing sectors in the United Kingdom. The period under consideration is 1970–89. They distinguish the effects of short and long run changes in relative efficiency. In the short run changes in a firm's efficiency is determined, significantly, by the efficiency level of their rivals. In the long run, a firm's level of efficiency is determined by their rate of investment; investment is subject to diminishing returns. They don't present any estimates of X-efficiency.

Cowie and Loynes (2012) assess management in the British Rail system for the period 1980–2009. There were three separate time periods. The period 1980–94 was when the railroads were nationalized. Second, 1995–2001 was the period of Railtrack, a subsidiary of British Rail, but a private organization which had a monopoly position. Third, 2001–10, the Network Rail, a private organization but state-owned. Costs included maintenance, signaling (traffic control), and costs of management. Costs initially rose under the private but imperfect market structures. Under Railtrack the increase was 33% and another 11% under Network Rail. By 2010 costs had returned to the 1890–94 nationalized years. The only costs which kept increasing were costs of management. On a per kilometer of train travel the costs of management increased by a factor of six since the end of the British Rail years. The authors assert that this is due to X-inefficiency. Other than this the authors do not provide an estimate of X-(in) efficiency.

Berg, Forsund, Hjalmarsson, and Suominen (1993) use a sample of banks from the Nordic countries—503 banks from Finland, 150 from Norway, and 126 from Sweden for the year 1990—and the non-parametric DEA to measure X-efficiency. The sample of banks constituted almost the entire number of banks for these three countries in 1990. X-efficiency was measured using a variable returns to scale (VRS) and a constant returns to scale (CRS) model. Average X-efficiency using VRS and CRS among Finland's banks are 0.53 and 0.5, respectively. The numbers for Norway are 0.57 and 0.41. For Sweden the numbers are 0.78 and 0.69. Most of the best practice banks are in Sweden, the country among the three with the fewest number of banks.

XE in Australia and New Zealand, Latin America, the Middle East, Africa, and the world: c.1991–2017

12

I XE in Australia and New Zealand

Esho and Sharpe (1996) use the parametric SFA approach to examine X-efficiency among Australian Permanent Building Societies (PBS) for the period 1974–90. In the early/mid-1990s the government ended all restrictions on market entry by foreign banks, and foreign ownership of Australian banks. The authors separated two sub-periods: the pre-deregulation period, 1974–83, and the post-deregulation period, 1984–90. XE was approximately 0.75 both before and after deregulation. The authors reject the notion that economies of scale and scope are the best ways of increasing overall efficiency. They believe otherwise, that increasing XE is the way to increase overall efficiency.

Vu and Turnell (2011) analyze both cost and profit efficiencies of Australian banks both before and during the Global Financial Crises (GFC). Their sample is eight banks, the four "pillar" banks plus four others. The time period is 1997–2009. For the entire 13 year period the XE averaged 0.87, while profit efficiency averaged 0.88. Thus, banks could have reduced their cost by 13% while producing the same level of output. And, they could have increased their profits by 12% for the same cost level. Profits efficiency fell by 26% for the larger major banks, but by 43.5% for the smaller regional banks. On the other hand, cost efficiency did not change during the crises as opposed to the pre-crises period (Table 12.1).

Neal (2004) studied X-efficiency and productivity change in Australian banking between 1995 and 1999 using Data Envelopment Analysis (DEA). This was a period of bank consolidation and a high degree of concentration in Australian banking. In the latter half of the 1990s there was pressure from the major banks for further consolidation with the major banks pressing for the abolition of the "four pillars" policy. In part this was driven by globalization and the perceived need for a "national champion"—a bank that is large enough to compete with other transnational banks on a global scale. Average XE for all banks between 1995 and 1999 ranged between 0.75 and 0.87. The average for the five years was 0.82.

Sathye (2001) uses DEA to investigate XE among Australian banks for the year 1996. The average levels of XE was 0.67. Average XE among domestic and foreign banks are 0.9 and 0.71, respectively. The main determinant of XE among Australian banks is market power (bank deposits); the coefficient is negative. The author believes this may be due to the "quiet life." The author offers a possible explanation for this result—foreign banks do not have a wide-ranging branch network, and must rely on more expensive purchased funds in order for the bank to grow rapidly. As for antitrust

The Beginnings of Behavioral Economics. https://doi.org/10.1016/B978-0-12-815289-8.00012-5

Table 12.1 Australia and New Zealand fin

Nation	Industry	Author(s)	Yr. pub.	Yrs. studied	Av XE	(Non) para
Australia	Finance	Esho and Sharpe	1996	1974–90	0.75	Para
Australia	Finance	Vu and Turnell	2011	1997–2009	0.87	Para
Australia	Finance	Neal	2004	1995–99	0.82	Non-para
Australia	Finance	Saythe	2001	1996	0.67	Non-para
Australia	Finance	Paul and Kourouche	2008	1997–2005	0.98	Non-para
Australia	Finance	Wu	2008	1983–2001	0.985	Non-para
Australia	Finance	Ralston, Wright, and Garden	2001	1993–95	0.985	Non-para
Australia	Finance	Sterm and Williams	2008	1998–2001	0.8	Para
Australia	Finance	Moradi-Motlagh and Saleh	2014	1997–2005	0.96	Non-para
N. Zealand	Finance	Margaritis and Psillaki	2007	2004	0.62	Non-para
N. Zealand	Finance	Margaritis and Psillaki	2007	2004	0.34	Non-para

policy, the larger banks with market power are less efficient. Combining them via merger can't be good for efficiency.

Paul and Khaled Kourouche (2008) investigate XE among Australian banks during the "post-Wallis" period, 1997–2005. The 1980s and 1990s in Australia was a period of rapid change in banking. An orientation towards markets and resulting deregulation included removal of exchange controls and the floating of the Australian dollar, removal of bank deposits controls, non-financial institutions offering more financial services, and freedom of entry to foreign banks. In 1997 came the Wallis Inquiry, whose report including changes in regulations which would increase bank competitiveness and efficiency. One recommendation would be to terminate the "six-pillar" policy, that there be no mergers among the four largest Australian banks plus the two largest Australian life insurance firms. The report recommended a "four-pillar" policy, no mergers among the four largest banks. The report stated that a 10% increase in efficiency would reduce overall costs by at least $4 billion per year. For the entire period XE averaged about 0.985. And 81% of the banks had an average of 1.0. Mergers were found to increase XE.

Wu (2008) investigates whether bank mergers improve efficiency. Their analysis includes which pre-merger conditions predict post-merger efficiency. They use a sample of Australian banks for the period 1983–2001. The background to the merger question are globalization, technology changes, and deregulation which have led banks to become larger and more diversified. Liberalization also allowed for easier entry into the Australian banking industry. Banks have responded with mergers. Mergers among Australian banks are restricted in that there can be no merger between any two of the four major Australian banks: Australia's "four pillars" policy, instituted in 1997. On the other hand, foreign banks can take-over any Australian bank. Wu used DEA (Data Envelope Analysis) to estimate XE among Australian banks. The average level of XE among the acquirer bank was 0.99, while that of the target bank was 0.98. When an X-inefficient bank is acquired by an X-efficient bank, then the XE of the acquired bank increases after the merger. The greater is the difference between the x-efficiencies of the acquiring and target banks, the greater is the post-merger PTE of the bank. The more that the two banks have overlapping businesses the greater the post-merger PTE. If the target bank is a former state0owned bank, the higher is the post-merger PTE and TE.

Ralston, Wright, and Garden (2001) use the non-parametric DEA methodology to evaluate the post-merger gains in technical and scale efficiency achieved by 31 Australian credit union mergers in 1993/1994 and 1994/1995, relative to non-merging credit unions. Average XE of the acquirer firms in the '93–'94 mergers was 0.99, that of the target firms was 0.98. Their findings suggests that mergers are not associated with improvements in XE superior to those achieved by internal growth.

Sterm and Williams (2008) estimate X-efficiency using the parametric SFA for Australian and foreign banks for 1988–2001. They estimate five different models, each differing from others by the inclusion of inputs and outputs. Four of the five have very similar estimates; I will report the estimates for one, what they call Model 1. In Model 1 the inputs are employees, deposits and borrowed funds, and equity capital. The outputs are loans, and off-balance sheet activity. Average X-efficiency for all banks, and foreign banks was 0.83, and 0.8, respectively.

Margaritis and Psillaki (2007) investigated the relationship between X-efficiency and a firm's leverage. Leverage is the ratio of a company's (debt/equity) ratio. They use the non-parametric DEA, and a sample of New Zealand small and medium sized firm, those with 19 or fewer employees, for the year 2004. They test Jensen and Meckling's agency-cost theory (1976). According to this theory the separation of ownership from control leads managers to place the value of the firm second to their own utility. Managers can't be forced to place the firm's value first because *complete contracts can't be written*! Higher leverage may *pressure* managers to place the firm's value first.

The authors' results include allocative and scale efficiency being 0.48, and 0.62, respectively. X-efficiency using Constant Returns to Scale, and Variable Returns to Scale are 0.34, and 0.62, respectively. Their equation for determining X-efficiency shows that both higher leverage and higher industry concentration increase X-efficiency. The positive relationship between leverage and X-efficiency is consistent with the agency cost hypothesis. Higher leverage pressures managers to be more X-efficient. On the other hand, higher firm size reduce X-efficiency. In an equation estimating the determinants of leverage they report that both higher X-efficiency and higher industry concentration reduce leverage.

Moradi-Motlagh and Saleh (2014) use the bootstrap-DEA to estimate X-efficiency among a sample of ten Australian banks on annual data for the years 1997–2005. They are particularly interested in the 2008 study by Paul and Kourouche. These authors used the same years and the same ten banks. Paul and Kourouche reported that 81% of the banks had X-efficiency levels of 1.0. Moradi-Motlagh and Saleh found that 23% of banks had 1.0. Paul and Kourouche reported an average X-efficiency level of 0.985. Moradi-Motlagh and Saleh report that the average is 0.957 for the bootstrap-DEA and about 0.97 for the original DEA.

II XE in Latin America

Chortareas, Garza-Garcia, and Girardone (2011) estimate XE for nine Latin American countries and 2,500 observations for the period 1997–2005. Efficiency is measured using DEA. Since the mid-1990s, the Latin American banking sector similar to that in other parts of the world underwent major changes as a result of financial liberalization and globalization. One result of the increased liberalization and globalization was increased concentration in the banking sector. Another was a significant increase in the presence of foreign banks, mostly from Europe and the United States, purchasing Latin American financial institutions. The results show that average XE scores ranges from 45 for Brazil to 0.84 for Chile. Of the nine countries Brazil has more than twice as many banks as any other country accounting for almost one-third of all banks among the nine countries. For all nine countries the average XE score is 0.67 (Tables 12.2A and 12.2B).

Figueira, Nellis, and Parker (2009) investigate how ownership form affects bank performance. Liberalization and privatization of Latin American banks has meant increased foreign capital injections and the privatization of state-owned banks. During the 1990s foreign ownership increased by between 20% and 50%. The sample in this paper is 204 banks in 20 Latin American countries, representing 40% of baking assets in those countries. The analysis is cross-sectional for 2001. DEA analysis and stochastic cost frontier are used. Data was analyzed aggregating all banks in all coun-

Table 12.2A X-efficiency among financial institutions in nine Latin American nations, 1997–2005

Nation	Average XE
Argentina	0.52
Brazil	0.45
Chile	0.84
Colombia	0.73
Costa Rica	0.79
Paraguaya	0.79
Peru	0.82
Uruguay	0.54
Venezuala	0.61
Average	0.67

Table 12.2B Latin America finance

Nation	Industry	Author(s)	Yr. pub.	Yrs. studied	Av. XE	(Non) para
9 in L.A.	Finance	Chortaseas, Garza-Garcia, and Girardone	2011	1997–2005	0.67	Non-para
20 in L.A.	Finance	Figueira, Nellis, and Parker	2009	2001	0.58	Non-para
20 in L.A.	Finance	Figueira, Nellis, and Parker	2009	2001	0.8	Para
Mexico	Finance	Chortareas, Garza-Garcia, and Girardone	2009	1996–2003	0.84	Non-para
Brazil	Finance	Staub, Souza, and Tabak	2010	2000–07	0.63	Non-para

tries, and then by individual countries. Average XE for all banks was 0.58 using the non-parametric DEA and 0.8 using the parametric stochastic frontier approach. All private and all domestic banks, and banks with various amounts of state-ownership, had an average of around 0.6 using DEA and 0.8 using SCF. Using DEA, banks with less than 50% foreign ownership had an average of 0.67, while banks with more than 50% foreign ownership was 0.52. This was the only category in which differences in XE scores were substantial. State ownership does not seem to be a large hindrance to X-efficiency. However, larger differences in efficiency scores are seen when comparing countries. Eight countries with enough banks to make the analysis possible were used.

Among all banks in a particular country, the highest DEA score was Chile which had an average XE score of 0.91; the lowest average was Uruguay –0.19. Among private banks, Chile had the highest average, 0.92, while Uruguay had the lowest, 0.19. Banks with 50% or more government ownership the highest and lowest scores were 0.73 (Brazil) and 0.41 (Peru). Many countries had no data for this classification. Among domestic banks Chile had an average of 0.97 while Jamaica's average was 0.46. With 50% or more foreign ownership the averages were 0.84 (Chile), and 0.19 (Uruguay). Aggregate differences which showed little variation conceal large differences by country (Table 12.3).

Mexico's 1995 financial crises ushered in a period of deregulation, but also consolidation via government and foreign ownership of Mexican banks equaling about 50% of total banking assets. The "urge to merge" in Mexico, as in other countries at this time, increased concentration levels. Between 1996 and 2003 the number of banks declined by 22%, while HHI increased by 29%, and an increase in profits. Mexican banks also benefitted from unusually high interest rate spreads—rate on loans minus the rate on deposits. For example, from 1980 to 1987 the spread in Mexico was 15.8 points while for the remainder of Latin America it was 6.8 points. The authors of this study, Chortareas, Garza-Garcia, and Girardone (2009) investigate whether market

Table 12.3 Latin America finance

Nation	Industry	Author(s)	Yr. pub.	Yrs. studied	Av. XE	(Non) para
9 in L.A.	Finance	Chortaseas, Garza-Garcia, and Girardone	2011	1997–2005	0.67	Non-para
20 in L.A.	Finance	Figueira, Nellis, and Parker	2009	2001	0.58	Non-para
20 in L.A.	Finance	Figueira, Nellis, and Parker	2009	2001	0.8	Para
Mexico	Finance	Chortareas, Garza-Garcia, and Girardone	2009	1996–2003	0.84	Non-para
Brazil	Finance	Staub, Souza, and Tabak	2010	2000–07	0.63	Non-para

power or efficiency better explains profits among Mexican banks. Their data is for Mexico's 20 largest banks. XE is measured by a bank's cost-to-income ratio. For the period 1996–2003 the average XE score was 0.84.

Staub, Souza, and Tabak (2010) use DEA to estimate XE among 127 banks in Brazil for the period 2000–07. These banks account for about 95% of banking assets. The average level of XE was 0.63. State-owned banks were more X-efficient than private sector. The opposite is the usual expectation. The authors explain this result by stating that state-owned banks had most of their bad debts written off by both PROES, and PROEF programs. PROES is the 1996 Program of Incentives to the Reduction of the State-Level Public Sector in the Bank Activity. PROEF is the 2001 Program for the Strengthening of the Federal Financial Institutions. The effect of writing off the banks' bad debts is that the banks costs are reduced, and ceteris paribus, XE is increased.

III XE in Middle East and Africa

Pakistan

Aftab, Ahamad, Ullah, and Sheikh (2011) study the effect of banking liberalization of the early 1990s on the relationship between efficiency and stock performance among a sample of seven Pakistani banks for the period 2003–07. One result of bank liberalization is that owners and investors became more attentive to XE, i.e., understanding the causes of bank and stock performance. Stock performance is measured by the cumulative annual share returns (CASR). XE is estimated by the non-parametric DEA.

Average XE score assuming constant returns and variable returns to scale was 0.60 and 0.80, respectively. CASR ranged from 6% to 13%. The regression with CASR as the dependent variable shows that XE has a positive and statistically significant effect on CASR. In other words, more efficient banks are more successful banks, providing support for the efficient markets hypothesis.

Akhtar (2002) investigates bank performance in Pakistan using a sample of 40 banks for the year 1998. For all banks average XE was 0.86. For private, government-owned, and foreign banks, the averages were 0.86, 0.85, and 0.82, respectively. Akhtar expected foreign banks to be more efficient when in fact they are less efficient. His explanation is that most foreign banks focus in volatile markets which may lead to greater (X) inefficiency.

Burki and Niazi (2009) use bank level data from Pakistan over the period 1991–2000 to evaluate how bank reforms affected XE among private domestic, state-owned, and foreign banks. In Pakistan the reforms occurred in the 1990s. They estimate a frontier separately by each bank for each of the three bank types—private domestic, state-owned, and foreign banks, and; by pooling the data for each bank type. Average XE when estimates separately, for private, government-owned, and foreign banks are 0.959, 0.956, and 0.92, respectively. When pooled the averages are 0.88, 0.82, and 0.91, respectively. Time series shows average XE equal to 0.88.

Lebanon

Ariss (2008) investigates the relationship between cost or XE and deregulation, bank size, and whether the bank is domestic or foreign. Two time periods are used: 1990–95, and 1996–2000. XE is measured using a parametric SFA. The average level of XE was 0.82 for 1990–95, and then 0.92 for 1996–2000. During the 1990–95 period the smallest banks had an average XE score of 0.74 while the largest banks average score was 0.80. For the 1995–2000 period the figures were 0.88 and 0.98, respectively. During the 1990–95 period foreign banks had an average XE score of 0.85 while the domestic banks average was 0.78. For the 1995–2000 period the figures were 0.97 and 0.98, respectively. The author attributes the increase in XE to several things including financial liberalization and regulations which increased and promoted competition.

Egypt

The authors, Poshakwale and Qian (2011), examine the relationship between competitiveness and efficiency among 45 Egyptian banks for the period 1992–2007. Banking reforms in Egypt during the 1990s ended the state's domination as a monopolist. The usual effects of state-ownership existed among Egyptian banks: Innovation was low, as was the quality of service, credit decisions were political, and management was inefficient. Between 1992 and 2007, during liberalization, the 4FCR and the HHI fell, more foreign banks entered the market, and the ROE and ROA increased. XE was estimated using the DEA, the SFA and the DFA. The DEA average was 0.78. The parametric SFA was 0.75, and the parametric Distribution-Free approach was 0.77. In the short run higher XE increased economic growth (Table 12.4).

Table 12.4 X-efficiency among various Middle East and African nations and industries

Nation	Industry	Author(s)	Yr. pub.	Yrs studied	Av. XE	(Non) para
Pakistan	Finance	Aftab et al.	2011	2003–07	0.6	Non-para
Pakistan	Finance	Aftab et al.	2011	2003–07	0.8	Non-para
Pakistan	Finance	Akhtar and Nishat	2001	1998	0.86	Non-para
Pakistan	Finance	Burki and Niazi	2010	1991–2000	0.88	Non-para
Lebanon	Finance	Ariss	2008	1990–2000	0.87	Para
Egypt	Finance	Poshakwale and Qian	2011	1992–2007	0.78	Non-para
Egypt	Finance	Poshakwale and Qian	2011	1992–2007	0.76	Para
GCC	Finance	El Moussawi and Obeid	2011	2005–08	0.86	Non-para
UAE	Finance	Al Shamsia, Alyb, and El-Bassiounic	2009	2004	0.8	Non-para
MENA	Finance	Al Shamsia, Alyb, and El-Bassiounic	2010	2000–07	0.73	Para
MENA	Finance	Olson and Zoubi	2011	2000–08	0.73	Para
Turkey	Finance	Isik and Hassan	2003	1992–96	0.86	Non-para
S. Africa	Finance	Okeahalm	2006	1999	0.83	Para
Ghana	Health	Osei et al.	2005	2000	0.91	Non-para
Eritrea	Health	Kirigia and Asbu	2013	2007	0.9	Non-para
Eritrea	Health	Kirigia and Asbu	2013	2007	0.97	Non-para
Burkina Faso	Health	Paul Marschall and Steffen Flessa	2011	2005	0.86	Non-para
Cote dIvorie	Electricity	Plane	1999	1959–99	0.83	Non-para
Ghana	Finance	Isshaq and Bokpin	2012	1999–2007		Non-para
Mozambique	Insurance	Barros and Wenke	2014	2002–11	0.94 and 0.74	Non-para
Mozambique	Insurance	Barros and Wenke	2014	2002–11	0.94 and 0.67	Non-para
OIC nations	Finance	Mobarek and Kalonov	2014	2004–09	0.8	Para
OIC nations	Finance	Mobarek and Kalonov	2014	2004–09	0.67	Non-para

GCC, MENA and OIC nations

GCC nations, or "Gulf Cooperation Council" nations include Bahrain, Kuwait, Oman, Qatar, Saudi Arabia, and the United Arab Emirates. The study by Al-Muharrami and Matthews (2009) investigated the market structure—performance relationship by considering the Structure-Conduct-Performance (SCP) hypothesis, the Relative-Market-Power (RMP), and the X-efficiency and scale-efficiency forms of the Efficient-Structure (ES) hypotheses. Whereas SCP places emphasis on market concentration as affecting profits, RMP places emphasis on market share. The authors also test the "quiet life" hypothesis. The data is for the banking sector, 52 banks, of the nations of the Gulf Cooperation Council's (GCC) over the period 1993 to 2002. They measure market concentration or market power with both the 3FCR and the HHI. The GCC banking industry is particularly concentrated. The 3FCR in Kuwait was 62% in 2002, UAE = 44%, Qatar = 81%, Saudi Arabia = 51%, Oman = 81%, and Bahrain = 79%. The authors use a nonparametric method to estimate a production frontier, measuring inefficiency as the distance a bank is from the best-practice bank. Their evidence shows that market concentration is the main source of profits. And given the level of concentration, banks which are more technically efficient earn higher profits. On the other hand, market share is not a strong determinant of profits. Their conclusion is that their evidence supports SCP but not RMP. Their results for the market concentration technical efficiency relationship is that banks in more concentrated markets do not exhibit less efficiency. The authors use this result to conclude that there is not evidence for the "quiet life" hypothesis. And, there is no consistent evidence that efficiency affects market structure as the ES hypothesis including the X-efficiency variant would suggest. To the contrary, the evidence suggests that market structure affects efficiency.

El Moussawi and Obeid (2011) used the non-parametric DEA to estimate XE among 23 Islamic banks for the period 2005–08 in the GCC region (Gulf Cooperation Council). The GCC nations are Bahrain, Kuwait, Oman, Qatar, Saudi Arabia, and the United Arab Emirates. The average level of XE among all banks was 0.86. Al Shamsia, Alyb, and El-Bassiounic (2009) used DEA approach to measuring efficiency for a cross section of UAE banks in 2004. UAE banks similar to banks in many countries world-wide are facing increased pressure due to WTO requirements for membership, plus the use of new information technology, and a wave of deregulations. The average level of XE among UAE banks is 0.8. Their empirical results show that higher levels of X-efficiency are correlated with newer banks, less government involvement in the banking sector, more experienced employees, banks with a higher percentage of female employees, and banks with a lower percentage of UAE nationals. Kobeissi and Sun (2010) test for the impact of ownership form on XE using 1550 observations among 221 banks in 17 Middle East and North Africa (MENA) region for the period 2000–07. The dependent variable of greatest importance is profit-X-efficiency (actual/maximum profits). The range of XE values is 0.65 (Iran), to 0.8 (Oman). For all 17 MENA nations the average XE value was 0.73. Profit-X-efficiency ranged from 0.65 (Iran) to 0.79 Kuwait.

Olson and Zoubi (2011) estimate cost or X-efficiency, profits efficiency and economies of scale among 83 banks in ten MENA countries for the period 2000–08. MENA countries include GCC countries (Gulf Cooperation Council countries. The authors use the parametric distribution free approach.[a] They estimated the three forms of efficiency using models which contain and do not contain dummy variables for countries. For the sake of the presentation I will report the results for the model with country dummies. Average X-efficiency for all banks was 0.73, 0.735 for GCC banks, and 0.69 for GCC Islamic banks. Among the countries, the higher level of X efficiency was for Egypt at 0.81, the lowest was for Jordan at 0.68. Average profits-efficiency for all banks was 0.63, 0.64 for GCC banks, and 0.63 for GCC Islamic banks. Among the countries, the higher level of profits-efficiency was for Kuwait at 0.70, the lowest was for Morocco at 0.51. Average scale-efficiency for all banks was 0.85 for GCC banks, and 0.77 for GCC Islamic banks. Among the countries, the higher level of scale was 0.955 for Jordan, the lowest was for Saudi Arabia at 0.72. As is often reported elsewhere, scale efficiency is higher than X-efficiency. Finally, X-inefficiency, and government as a percent of bank ownership reduces the rate of return on both assets and equity in a statistically significant manner.

Mobarek and Kalonov (2014) investigate Islamic (IBs) versus conventional banks (CBs) in 18 OIC nations (Organization of Islamic Conference) for the period 2004–09. These nations are Bahrain, Bangladesh, Indonesia, Iraq, Jordan, Kuwait, Lebanon, Malaysia, Pakistan, Palestine, Qatar, Saudi Arabia, Sudan, Syria, Tunisia, Turkey, UAE and Yemen. The authors estimate X and scale efficiency; they use both the SFA and the DEA techniques for estimating X-efficiency, and the DEA to estimate scale efficiency. Average X-efficiency among conventional banks using SFA and DEA are 0.8, and 0.63, respectively. For Islamic banks the averages are 0.63, and 0.6, respectively. The parametric SFA generates higher average X-efficiency scores than does the non-parametric DEA. Using DEA average scale efficiency for conventional and Islamic banks are 0.87, and 0.86, respectively. Banks are more scale efficient than they are X-efficient.

Turkey

Isik and Hassan (2003b) examine the effects of Turkey's 1994 financial crises by examining efficiency and productivity in Turkey's banking sector between 1992 and 1996. The four types of bank are, national public banks (NAT State) owned primarily by Turkish residents, national private banks (Nat Privt) whose ownership is at least 50% + 1 Turkish residents, foreign banks started in Turkey (For Fou Tr) whose ownership is at least 50% + 1 residents of foreign countries, and foreign banks' branches (For Brn Tr) in Turkey. For the years 1992–96 XE averaged 0.86 among all banks, 0.89 among Nat Prvt, 0.83 among Nat State and For Brn Tr, and 0.82 among For Fou Tr.

Africa

Okeahalam (2006) uses a parametric Bayesian stochastic frontier analysis to investigate the production efficiency of banks in South Africa. The data is from 61 branches is for one of the four major banks in South Africa for the year 1999. The 61 branches oper-

[a] The most popular parametric technique is the Stochastic Frontier Analysis (SFA). As compared with the SFA, DFA estimates are 5 to 20 percentage points lower.

ated with an average level of XE of 0.83. Osei et al. (2005) investigate XE among health care providers among 17 district hospitals in Ghana using DEA, for the year 2000. Of 17 health centers 14 had TE score of 1.0. The average was 0.91, with a range of 1.0 to 0.27. Among the hospitals, 47% had TE rankings of 1.0. Inefficient hospitals would become efficient if they increased maternal and child care visits by 25%, and 12% more child deliveries. Health centers would have to increase maternal and child car visits by 9%, deliveries by 11%, child immunization by 9%, and outpatient visits by 6%.

Kirigia and Asbu (2013) use DEA to estimate XE among 19 community hospitals in Eritrea in 2007. The average XE score with CRS was 0.9; with VRS it was 0.97. Scores for different hospitals ranged from 0.99 (Adikeyh) to 0.28 (Denden). What determines XE? Outpatient visits as a proportion of inpatient days reduces XE. The average length of stay in the hospital increases XE. Of the 19 hospitals, five produce with IRS, eight with CRS, and six with DRS. The authors suggest that improving health care (efficiency) means transferring inputs from DRS to IRS hospitals, either actual transfer or through "mobile pools of excess health workers" going where they are most needed (p. 13/16).

Marschall and Flessa (2011) investigated relative efficiency of primary care facilities for 2005 in Nouna, a rural health district in Burkina Faso. They use the non-parametric DEA. They report that average SE was 0.89 while average XE was 0.86. Again, average XE is less than SE. Plane (1999) investigated X-efficiency for the Cote d'Ivoire Electric Company which was privatized in 1990. For the entire period in which some form of the Cote d'Ivorie electric company existed, 1959–95, the average X-f was 0.83. From 1984 to 1989 average X-efficiency was 0.818. From 1990 to 1995, the company was privatized in 1990, it increased to 0.876. Isshaq and Bokpin (2012) measured X-efficiency among banks in Ghana from 1999 to 2007. The authors use the DEA. Their measure of X-efficiency begins at 1.0 and increases as X-efficiency increases. Until about 1980 Ghana's economy was state controlled. Deregulation and competition began in the 1980s. In 1999 average X-efficiency was approximately 1.1. By 2003 it was approximately 1.2, and by 2007 it was approximately 1.9.

Barros and Wenke (2014) estimate X-efficiency among five insurance firms in Mozambique, using DEA including a bootstrapping version of DEA. The authors also estimate X-efficiency using a constant returns to scale (CCR) model of DEA developed by Charnes, Cooper, and Rhodes, and; a variable returns to scale (BCC) model of DEA developed by Banker, Charnes, and Cooper. Since the CCR model fits a linear production technology, whereas BCC is more flexible and includes the effects of management efficiency and technical limits, BCC is expected to produce higher XE levels than will CCR. Average X-efficiency for the entire period for all five firms is 0.94 using BCC, and 0.74 using CCR. Using the bootstrapping version of DEA, the average level of X-efficiency is 0.94 using BCC, and 0.67 with CCR.

Multiple nations and regions of the world

Rosman, Abd Wahab, and Zainol (2014) estimated X-efficiency and scale efficiency among 79 Islamic banks in several countries for the period 2007–10. which includes 79 Islamic banks across a number of countries including Middle East and Asian countries.

The authors use the non-parametric DEA. For the entire period average X-efficiency among Islamic banks among all Middle East nations for all years was 0.75. Scale efficiency averaged 0.64. Average X-efficiency of 0.75 means that produced the same output with only 75% of the inputs they actually used. Among Asian nations, average X-efficiency was 0.82 while scale efficiency was 0.81.

Miller and Parkhe (2002) ask whether there is a "liability of foreignness" in banking. The time period is 1989–96, the sample covers 1300 banks from 13 host countries and foreign banks from seven other countries; 428 banks were foreign-owned. The "Liability of foreignness is defined as 'the costs of doing business abroad that result in a competitive disadvantage for an MNE subunit...broadly defined as all additional costs a firm operating in a market overseas incurs that a local firm would not incur'" (p. 56). Foreign firms are said to be disadvantaged because they are not as familiar with host country practices, and with economic, political, and cultural norms. Partly for this reason, the personnel of foreign firms will not be as adroit at entrepreneurial activities. They must also work against the "embeddedness of host country firms with suppliers and even the government" (p. 57).

In order to examine the hypotheses the authors grouped the nations into home country/host country financial system and regulations. First, The host country regulations are either high or low regulations. Second, foreign-owned banks were classified as to whether home and host country's regulations were similar with each other. Third, host countries were placed into two financial groups: capital market-oriented, and bank-oriented. Countries were placed into one of these two groups depending on their economy's "financial system orientation." This orientation is based on the following ratio: the sum of market capitalization and international bonds outstanding of a country to "the sum of market capitalization, international bonds outstanding, money supply (M2), and total bank claims" (p. 74). A capital-market (bank) oriented nation is one with a high (low) financial system orientation. A major difference between capital-oriented and bank-oriented is the source of industry finance: capital markets or banks. X-efficiency is measured using the SFA approach. A stochastic frontier allows the error term to be broken down into two parts, random disturbance and (x) inefficiency.

The authors test five hypotheses. Hypothesis 1: Foreign-owned banks will have lower average normalized X-efficiency scores than those of host country banks. Their results confirm this hypothesis: X-efficiency levels among host country banks are significantly higher than that of foreign-owned banks. However, when the sample is limited to foreign banks from high financial system efficiency—high home country competitiveness being greater than that in the host country—there is no statistical difference between X-efficiency levels of foreign-owned and domestic-owned banks: hypothesis 1 would be rejected. Hypothesis 1 was tested again by comparing X-efficiency among domestic and foreign-owned banks in four host country environments: low and high (perceived) credit risk, and capital-market and bank-oriented systems. In each case foreign banks were significantly less x-efficient than host country banks. Hypothesis 2: Foreign-owned banks from more competitive home countries than is the host country—high financial system efficiency—will have higher normalized X-efficiency scores than that of foreign-owned banks from home countries that are less competitive—low financial system efficiency—than the host country. Their results confirm this hypothesis. Hypothesis 3: Foreign-owned banks working in countries with a similar regulation regime as the host country will have higher levels of X-efficiency than banks working in countries with a different regulation regime. Hypothesis 4: Foreign-owned banks working in countries with a similar financial system orientation as the host country will have higher levels of X-efficiency than banks working in countries with a different financial system orientation. Neither hypothesis 3 or 4 are confirmed. Hypothesis 5a: The level of X-efficiency of US-owned banks will be, on average, lower than that of other foreign-owned banks. Hypothesis 5b: The average level of X-efficiency of US-owned banks will be higher than that of other foreign-owned banks. Neither hypothesis 5a nor 5b are confirmed.

The results show that foreign-owned banks do face the liability of foreignness; on average their X-efficiency scores are lower than those of host country banks. One exception is that foreign banks from high financial system efficiency countries are more x-efficient than foreign banks from low financial system efficiency. And, these more x-efficient foreign banks are not less efficient than host country X-efficiency. In other words foreign banks can overcome the liability of foreignness by maintaining higher standards of X-efficiency. Once again, X-efficiency is an important intervening variable.

Fitzpatrick and McQuinn (2008) estimate profits-efficiency for 55 large commercial banks in what the authors call "Anglo-Saxon" countries: Canada, the United Kingdom, Ireland, and Australia. The time period is 1996–2002. They use the parametric SFA. Profits inefficiency was 0.20 for large banks, 0.39 for medium sized banks, and 0.33 for small banks. Between 20% and 40% of profits are lost because of X, allocative, and scale inefficiencies. They do not provide an estimate of X-efficiency.

Lozano-Vivas and Pasiouras (2010) estimate X and profits efficiency among 752 commercial banks in 87 countries between 1999 and 2006. They use the parametric SFA. Their unique focus is including "non-traditional" activities, i.e., off-balance sheet items, and non-interest income as measures of output. Average X-efficiency in a model without non-traditional activity is 0.86. With off-balance sheet activity included it is 0.87, and with non-interest income it is 0.88. Average profits efficiency in these three situations are 0.753, 0.754, and 0.79, respectively. Non-traditional activity increases X and profits efficiency. When using different equations for Major Advanced economies, Advanced, Transition, and Developing economies, and; different regions of the world, the results are the same: non-traditional bank activity increases both X- and profits efficiency. Major Advanced economies are more X-efficient and less profit-efficient. On the other hand, Transitioning economies are less X-efficient but more profit-efficient. Industry concentration increases X-efficiency but profit-efficiency. Finally, banks which are more closely monitored by private agencies are more X and profit-efficient.

Niosi's (2002) interest is X-efficient and X-effective national systems of innovations (NSI) among all nations of the world; they list the names of the 38 nations with the highest share of mainstream journal articles in 1994, and the 22 nations with the most patents granted in the United States to United States, and foreign inventors. A NSI is a set of related institutions engaged with technical knowledge; the institutions include industry, universities, and government. X-efficiency is how close the NSI is to the frontier. X-effectiveness is how much the NSI can attain their mission. Variables used to determine X-efficiency are cost of University graduates and cost of publications and patents. Variables related to X-effectiveness include patents per industrial researcher, publications per university researcher, and number of firms conducting R&D as a measure of government effectiveness. Other than discussing the importance of X-efficiency among NSI, Niosi does not provide any numerical estimates of X-efficiency.

van Leuvensteijn, Bikker, van Rixtele, and Sørensen (2011) estimate the Boone indicator, which is a measure of competition. The authors state that significant competition is expected to force business, in this case banks, to "force banks to drive down their X-inefficiency" (p. 3155). They apply the Boone indicator to Germany, Spain, France; Italy, and The Netherlands, and compare this with the United Kingdom, Japan, and the United States. The data is for 1994–2004. The results show that the United States has the most competitive banking sector and France has the least competitive banking sector. Other than the Boone indicators, the authors do not directly estimate X-efficiency.

Aguirre, Lee, and Pantos (2008) use the parametric stochastic cost frontier (SCF), and annual data for 133 commercial banks in ten countries over the period 1986–94 in order to estimate X-efficiency and economies of scale. They also test for both the Efficient Structure Hypothesis (ESH) which assumes that more efficient banks, higher quality management, earn higher profits; profits are the effect of efficiency. The Relative Market Power Hypothesis (RMPH) sees profits as the effect of market power, not efficiency. Banks were either part of a Functional banking system or a Universal banking system. A functional banking system separates commercial and investment banking in order to minimize risk. A universal bank based is a "one-stop" for financial services. The universal banking nations are Canada, France, Germany, Italy, Spain, Switzerland, and the United Kingdom are Universal systems, while Belgium, Japan, and the United States are Functional systems.

Average X-efficiency among Universal banks was 0.84 while among Functional banks it was 0.80. Universal banks operated at about the point of constant returns to scale, whereas Functional banks operated in the area of economies of scale. In other words, Universal banks had a higher degree of scale efficiency and X-efficiency. The data also shows that more efficient banks earn higher profits. Data shows that a 1% increase in X-efficiency leads to an increase in Return on Equity of 9.7% for Functional banks and 6.7% for Universal banks. Return on Assets increased by 0.7% among Functional banks when X-efficiency increased by 1%. The data supports ESH. While there is no statistical difference in X-efficiency among Functional banks between small (less than $31 bil) and large (between $31 and $60 bil) banks, mega banks (greater than $60 bil) are less x-efficient than either small or large banks. There was no difference in X-efficiency among different sized Universal banks.

Conclusions

13

I Two beginnings and the door

I began this book talking about old and new behavioral economics, and two beginnings of behavioral economics. And there was the metaphor of the door. The old and the new group do behavioral economics so different from each other that it is understandable that the new group would discount, overlook, or even neglect the old group. But there is that pesky sophisticated anthropomorphic sin. Stated differently than it was in Chapter 2, this "sin" states that things which look different aren't necessary (all that) different. Because the old and the new are so different in terms of style, if not content, I believe that behavioral economics has had two beginnings, one for the old and one for the new. When in the future the old and the new are seen as two stages of the evolution of behavioral economics, then there will be but one beginning. In the metaphor of the Door, the first gen behavioral economists built the door and placed on it a sign saying, "Behavioral Economics, Enter Here." The second gens opened the door, and the third gens walked through. The fourth gens will build their own door in their own center for behavioral economics.

II Homo economicus

One of the foundations of neoclassical theory was homo economicus (HE). HE doesn't engage in real human behavior because HE doesn't have free will. HE made economics easier to do but it also made it an intellectually stimulating abstraction from reality. Behavioral economics needed a new image of a human being. Thaler with his comparing HE to unicorns, and his differentiating ECONS from HUMANS did a lot to diminish HE and give us a new image. But the first gens were also doing that three or more decades before Thaler. Thaler, with his huge reservoir of creativity had "subversive" thoughts that no one else did, and he was rightly awarded the Nobel Prize for changing the direction of economics. HE had to go. Thaler may have done it best, but so many made significant contributions to it.

All the first gens contributed to it. So did the early 20th century French sociologist who accused us of academic imperialism, Gabriel Tarde, a forerunner of behavioral economics. How much did the second and third gens know about the writings of the first gens? At least some knew about their writings. But they knew more without knowing where the ideas came from. Back to Hayek: most of our knowledge is implicit. Most of the rules we live by have an unknown origin. We don't know why, but we act as if we do. Back to Marshall. When people work in the same geographical area they learn skills simply by being there because the knowledge is, as if, in the air. How many books did the first gens write? How many articles did they publish? Book chapters?

The Beginnings of Behavioral Economics. https://doi.org/10.1016/B978-0-12-815289-8.00013-7

The number from these three runs into the hundreds. Citations to their works? It runs into the thousands. It was in the air. In the air from discussions at seminars and conferences, and faculty offices. Something which someone says which later appears to us as an ah-ah experience. This is in no way saying that the real source of all the ideas of the second and third generation behavioral economists are from the first gens, and transmitted to the others through unconscious processes. But, today we all live on the same "block," thanks to modern communications including the Janus-faced internet. And we don't always know where our ideas come from.

III Overlaps between the first and other generations

In the Appendix to Chapter 4, I summarized some of the publications of the later groups about the limits to human rationality. In the Appendix to Chapter 6, I summarized but a few of the publications on other topics discussed by the first gens also written about by the others. The subjects include dual selves, herding behavior, gift exchange, and framing. In both Appendices there is simply no space to adequately cover all the publications of the latter group because there are simply too many.

IV X-efficiency theory

I must admit that I always found economics to be intellectually stimulating. The reason is that it is logical such that everything "hangs" together so well that there are no "gaps" in the analysis. Everyone is maximizing something and everyone does it really well. Inputs produce the technically maximum output. Output is produced with the technically minimum inputs. Adam Smith said in the *Theory of Moral Sentiments* that gaps in the analysis creates mis-communication among people and reduces positive human interaction. But in economics if you can read a set of engineering blueprints then there is never any mis-communication.

Leibenstein studied entrepreneurship in the process of economic development and the need for entrepreneurs was that there were gaps in the market system: entrepreneurs were "gap-fillers." Leibenstein, and other first gen behavioral economists, saw gaps in economic theory. X-efficiency theory was a type of gap-filler. Katona's term, intervening variable will more than suffice. An intervening variable helps explain the relationship between two other variables, such as inputs and outputs. X-efficiency theory is an intervening variable. Behavioral economics itself is an intervening variable, a gap-filler. When the human element consists of ECONS then there are no gaps. It is just us pesky HUMANS that creates gaps and a need for intervening variables to help us understand the limits to non-behavioral economics.

V Leibenstein and the empirical studies of X-efficiency theory

Looked at correctly, Leibenstein's academic career was inadvertently and consciously devoted to the limits of neoclassical theory. What are the implications of less than complete rationality for neoclassical theory? That was the questions which Leibenstein asked himself over and over. Leibenstein didn't know much about the empirical studies on X-efficiency theory. I found it surprising when he expressed surprise that in 1982–83 when I spent the year with him at Harvard that there were about 35 studies. There are now over 200. And these are the 200 which explicitly mention X-efficiency theory. There are hundreds more which are almost identical in terms of methodology and interpretation of the data to the studies mentioned in this book except the authors never used the term X-efficiency.

The average deviation from the frontier is about 20%. If it were 2% then it would not be important. But 20% makes X-efficiency a significant concept. If this were only from one nation and one industry then there would be a lot of questions. But these studies cover numerous industries from organizations on every continent in the world. It might be interesting to contact the authors of the studies which are virtually identical with X-efficiency studies but which do not mention the term X-efficiency, and ask if their study could be included in the X-efficiency literature.

References

Abdul-Majida, M., Saal, D., & Battisti, G. (2011). Efficiency and total factor productivity change of Malaysian commercial banks. *The Service Industries Journal*, *31*(13), 2117–2143.

Aftab, M., Ahamad, S., Ullah, W., & Sheikh, R. (2011). The impact of bank efficiency on share performance: Evidence from Pakistan. *African Journal of Business Management*, *5*(10), 3975–3980.

Aguirre, M., Lee, T., & Pantos, T. (2008). Universal versus functional banking regimes: The Structure Conduct Performance Hypothesis revisited. *Journal of Banking Regulation*, *10*(1), 46–67.

Aigner, D., Knox Lovell, C. A., & Schmidt, P. (1977). Formulation and estimation of stochastic Frontier production function models. *Journal of Econometrics*, *6*, 21–37.

Ajdukovic, I., Sylvain, M., Rodolphe, P., & Spiegelman, E. (2018). The economic psychology of Gabriel Tarde: Something new for behavioral economics? *Journal of Behavioral Economics for Policy*, *2*(1), 5–11.

Akerlof, G. (1970). The market for 'lemons': Quality uncertainty and the market mechanism. *The Quarterly Journal of Economics*, *84*(3), 488–500.

Akerlof, G. (1982). Labor contracts as partial gift exchange. *Quarterly Journal of Economics*, *97*, 543–569.

Akerlof, G. (1987). Rational models of irrational behavior. *American Economic Review*, *77*, 137–142.

Akerlof, G. (1991). Procrastination and obedience. *American Economic Review*, *81*(2), 1–19.

Akerlof, G. (2002). Behavioral macroeconomics and macroeconomic behavior. *American Economic Review*, *92*, 411–433.

Akerlof, G. (2007). The missing motivation in macroeconomics. *American Economic Review*, *97*(1), 1–36.

Akerlof, G., & Schiller, R. (2009). *Animal spirits*. Princeton, NJ: Princeton Univ Press.

Akerlof, G., & Yellen, J. (1985). Can small deviations from rationality make significant differences to economic equilibria? *American Economic Review*, *75*(4), 708–720.

Akerlof, G., & Yellen, J. (1986). *Efficiency wage models of the labor market*. Orlando, FL: Academic Press.

Akhavein, J., Berger, A., & Humphrey, D. (1997). The effects of megamergers on efficiency and prices: Evidence from a bank profit function. *Review of Industrial Organization*, *12*(1), 95–139.

Akhtar, M. H. (2002). X-efficiency analysis of commercial banks in Pakistan: A preliminary investigation. *Pakistan Development Review*, *41*(4), 567–580.

Al Shamsia, F., Alyb, H., & El-Bassiounic, M. (2009). Measuring and explaining the efficiencies of the United Arab Emirates banking system. *Applied Economics*, *41*(27), 3505–3519.

Al-Muharrami, S., & Matthews, K. (2009). Market power versus efficient-structure in Arab GCC banking. *Applied Financial Economics*, *19*(18), 1487–1496.

Alos-Ferrer, C., & Strack, F. (2014). From dual processes to multiple selves: Implications for economic behavior. *Journal of Economic Psychology*, *41*, 1–11.

Altman, M. (1988). Economic development with high wages: An historical perspective. *Explorations in Economic History*, *25*, 198–224.

Altunbas, Y., Evans, L., & Molyneux, P. (2001). Bank ownership and efficiency. *Journal of Money, Credit, and Banking*, *25*, 926–954.

Altunbas, Y., Gardener, E., Molyneux, P., & Moore, B. (2001). Efficiency in European banking. *European Economic Review*, *45*(10), 1931–1955.

Anderson, R., Fok, R., & Scott, J. (2000). Hotel industry efficiency: An advanced linear programming examination. *American Business Review*, *18*, 40–48.

Anderson, J., & Frantz, R. (1982). The response of labor effort to falling real wages: The Mexican peso devaluation of February 1982. *World Development*, *12*, 759–766.

Anderson, J., & Frantz, R. (1985). Production efficiency among Mexican apparel assembly plants. *Journal of Developing Areas*, *19*, 369–378.

Andries, A., & Capraru, B. (2013). Impact of financial liberalization on banking sectors performance from Central and Eastern European countries. *PLoS One*, *8*(3), 1–9.

Angner, E., & Lowenstein, G. F. (2012). Behavioral economics. In U. Mäki (Ed.), *Philosophy of economics*: *Vol. 5*. Handbook of the philosophy of science (pp. 641–690). Amsterdam: Elsevier.

Argyle, M., Gardner, G., & Cioffi, F. (1958). Supervisory methods related to productivity, absenteeism, and labor turnover. *Human Relations*, *10*, 23–29.

Ariss, R. (2008). Financial liberalization and bank efficiency: Evidence from post-war Lebanon. *Applied Financial Economics*, *18*(11), 931–946.

Aristovnik, A., Seljak, J., & Mencinger, J. (2013). Relative efficiency of police directorates in Slovenia: A non-parametric analysis. *Expert Systems with Applications*, *40*, 820–827.

Arrow, K. (1962). The economic implications of learning by doing. *The Review of Economic Studies*, *29*, 155–173.

Arrow, K. (1986). Rationality in self and others in an economic system. In R. Hogarth & M. Reder (Eds.), *Rational choice: The contrast between economics and psychology* (pp. 201–216). Chicago: University of Chicago Press.

Ashraf, N., Camerer, C., & Loewenstein, G. (2005). Adam Smith, behavioral economist. *Journal of Economic Perspectives*, *19*(3), 131–145.

Aukrust, O. (1959). Investment and economic growth. *Productivity Measurement Review*, *16*, 35–53.

Aumann, R., & Sorin, S. (1989). Cooperation and bounded recall. *Games and Economic Behavior*, *1*, 5–39.

Axelrod, R. (1976). *Structure of decision: The cognitive map of political elites*. Princeton: Princeton University Press.

Baddeley, M. (2010). Herding, social influence and economic decision-making: Socio-psychological and neuroscientific analyses. *Philosophical Transactions of the Royal Society B*, *365*, 281–290.

Baddeley, M. (2015). *Bandwagon effects, snob effects and selective rationality: Leibenstein's contributions to the analysis of social influence, IAREP/SABE/ICABEEP joint conference, September 2015. Sibiu, Romania.*

Baddeley, M., Burke, C., Schultz, W., & Tobler, P. (2012). *Herding in financial behaviour: A behavioural and neuroeconomic analysis of individual differences*. [Cambridge working paper, number 1225].

Banerjee, A. (1992). A simple model of herd behavior. *Quarterly Journal of Economics*, *107*, 797–817.

Barberis, N. (2018). *Richard Thaler and the rise of behavioral economics* [Working paper]. Yale University.

Barnard, C. (1936). Mind in everyday affairs. In *An examination into logical and non-logical thought processes*. Princeton, NJ: The Guild of Brackett Lecturers.

Barnard, C. (1962). *The functions of the executive*. Cambridge, MA: Harvard Univ. Press.

Baron, D. (1974). A study of hospital cost inflation. *Journal of Human Resources, 9*, 33–49.

Barros, C., & Antunes, O. S. (2011). Performance assessment of Portuguese windfarms: Ownership and managerial efficiency. *Energy Policy, 39*, 3055–3063.

Barros, C., Managi, S., & Matousek, R. (2012). The technical efficiency of the Japanese banks: Non-radial directional performance measurement with undesirable output. *Omega, 40*(1), 1–8.

Barros, C., & Wanke, P. (2014). Insurance companies in Mozambique: A two-stage DEA and neural networks on efficiency and capacity slacks. *Applied Economics, 46*(29), 3591–3600.

Barros, C., Nektarios, M., & Assaf, A. (2010). Efficiency in the Greek insurance industry. *European Journal of Operational Research, 205*, 431–436.

Bauer, P., & Hancock, D. (1993). The efficiency of the federal reserve in providing check processing services. *Journal of Banking and Finance, 17*, 287–311.

Baumol, W. (1959). *The revenue maximization hypothesis*. In *Business behavior, value, and growth* (pp. 45–53). New York: Macmillan.

Beccalli, E., Casu, B., & Girardone, C. (2006). Efficiency and stock performance in European banking. *Journal of Business, Finance, and Accounting, 33*(1), 245–262.

Becker, G. (1974). A theory of social interactions. *Journal of Political Economy, 82*(6), 1063–1093.

Becker, G. (1991). A note on restaurant pricing and other examples of social influences on price. *Journal of Political Economy, 99*(5), 1109–1116.

Benhabib, J., & Bisin, A. (2002). *The psychology of self-control and consumption-saving decisions: Cognitive perspectives. Semantic Scholar, November.*

Benhabib, J., & Bisin, A. (2005). Modeling internal commitment mechanisms and self-control: A neuroeconomics approach to consumption-saving decisions. *Games and Economic Behavior, 52*(2), 460–492.

Berg, S., Forsund, F., Hjalmarsson, L., & Suominen, M. (1993). Banking efficiency in the Nordic countries. *Journal of Banking and Finance, 17*(2), 371–388.

Berger, A. (1993). Distribution-free estimates of efficiency in the U.S. banking industry and tests of the standard distributional assumptions. *Journal of Productivity Analysis, 4*, 261–292.

Berger, A. (1995). The profit-structure relationship in banking—Tests of market-power and efficient-structure hypothesis. *Journal of Money, Credit, and Banking, 27*(2), 404–431.

Berger, A., & DeYoung, R. (1997). Problem loans and cost efficiency in commercial banks. *Journal of Banking and Finance, 21*, 849–870.

Berger, A., Hancock, D., & Humphrey, D. (1993). Bank efficiency derived from the profit function. *Journal of Banking and Finance, 17*, 317–347.

Berger, A., & Hannan, T. (1998). The efficiency cost of market power in the banking industry: A test of the 'quiet life' and related hypotheses. *The Review of Economics and Statistics, 80*(3), 454–465.

Berger, A., & Humphrey, D. (1992). Megamergers in banking and the use of cost efficiency as an antitrust defense. *Antitrust Bulletin, 37*(3), [Fall] 541–600.

Berger, A., Hunter, W., & Timme, S. (1993). The efficiency of financial institutions. A review of research past, present, and future. *Journal of Banking and Finance, 17*, 221–249.

Berger, A., Leusner, J., & Mingo, J. (1997). The efficiency of bank branches. *Journal of Monetary Economics, 40*(1), 141–162.

Berger, A., & Meister, L. (1997). Inside the black box: What explains differences in the efficiencies of financial institutions? *Journal of Banking and Finances, 21*, 895–947.

Bergsman, J. (1974). Commercial policy, allocative efficiency and 'X-efficiency'. *Western Economic Review*, *8*, 409–433.

Berlin, I. (1953). *The hedgehog and the fox*. London: Orion Pub.

Bernheim, D., & Rangel, A. (2004). Addiction and cue-triggered decision processes. *American Econoic Review*, *94*(5), 1558–1590.

Biddle, J. (1991). A bandwagon effect in personalized license plates? *Economic Inquiry*, *29*(2), 375–388.

Bikhchandi, S., Hirschleifer, D., & Welch, I. (1992). A theory of fads, fashion, custom and cultural change as informational cascades. *Journal of Political Economy*, *100*, 992–1026.

Bikker, J. A., & van Leuvensteijn, M. (2008). Competition and efficiency in the Dutch life insurance industry. *Applied Economics*, *40*, 2063–2084.

Bird, D. (1981). George Katona, 79, leading economist. *New York Times*, (June 19).

Blaug, M. (1990). The evolution of Leibenstein's X-efficiency theory. In K. Weiermair & M. Perlman (Eds.), *Studies in economic rationality: X-efficiency examined and extolled* (pp. 7–26). Ann Arbor: Univ. Michigan Press.

Boden, M. (1990). *The creative mind: Myths and mechanisms*. London: Weidenfeld and Nicolson.

Bordley, R., & Licalzi, M. (2000). Decision analysis using targets instead of utility functions. *Decisions in Economics and Finance*, *23*(1), 53–74.

Borenstein, S., & Farrell, J. (2000). Is cost-cutting evidence of X-inefficiency. *American Economic Review*, *90*(2), 224–227.

Borenstein, S., & Farrell, J. (2007). Do investors forecast fat firms? Evidence from the gold-mining industry. *The Rand Journal of Economics*, *38*(3), 626–647.

Boucinha, M., Ribeiro, N., & Weyman-Jones, T. (2013). An assessment of Portuguese banks' efficiency and productivity towards euro area participation. *Journal of Productivity Analysis*, *39*, 177–190.

Boulding, K. (1945). *There is a spirit*. Nyack, NY: Fellowship Publications.

Boulding, K. (1950). *A reconstruction of economics*. New York: Wiley and Sons.

Boulding, K. (1956). *The image*. Ann Arbor: University of Michigan Press.

Boulding, K. (1961). Contemporary economic research. In D. Ray (Ed.), *Trends in social science* (pp. 9–26). New York: Philosophical Library.

Bradley, K., & Gelb, A. (1981). Motivation and control in the Mondragon experiment. *British Journal of Industrial Relations*, *19*, 211–231.

Brocas, I., & Carillo, J. (2014). Dual-process theories of decision-making: A selective survey. *Journal of Economic Psychology*, *41*, 45–54.

Bruggink, T. (1982). Public versus private enterprise in the municipal water industry: A comparison of operating costs. *Quarterly Review of Economics and Business*, *22*, 111–125.

Brunsson, N. (1985). *The irrational organization: Irrationality as a basis for organizational action and change*. New York: John Wiley & Sons.

Burke, C., Baddeley, M., Tobler, P., & Schultz, W. (2010). Striatal BOLD response reflects the impact of herd information on financial decisions. *Frontiers in Neuroscience—Human Neuroscience*, *4* [article 48].

Burke, C., Tobler, P., Baddeley, M., & Schultz, W. (2010). Neural mechanisms of observational learning. *Proceedings of the National Academy of Sciences of the United States of America*, *107*(3), 14431–14436.

Burki, A., & Niazi, G. S. K. (2009). Impact of financial reforms on efficiency of state-owned, private and foreign banks in Pakistan. *Applied Economics*, *42*, 3147–3160.

Button, K. (1985). Potential differences in the degree of X-inefficiency between industrial sectors in the United Kingdom. *Quarterly Review of Economics and Business*, *25*, 85–95.

Button, K., & Weyman-Jones, T. (1992). Ownership structure, institutional organization and measured X-efficiency. *American Economic Review, Papers & Proceedings*, *82*, 439–445.

Byron, M. (1998). Satisficing and optimality. *Ethics*, *109*(1), 67–93.

Cabantous, L., Gond, J.-P., & Johnson-Cramer, M. (2010). Decision theory as practice: Crafting rationality in organizations. *Organizational Studies*, *31*(11), 1531–1566.

Camerer, C. (1998). Behavioral economics and nonrational organizational decision making. In J. Halpern & R. Stern (Eds.), *Debating rationality: Nonrational aspects of organizational decision making* (pp. 53–77). Ithaca: Cornell University Press.

Camerer, C., & Ho, T.-H. (1999). Experienced-weighted attraction learning in normal form games. *Econometrica*, *67*(4), 827–874.

Camerer, C., & Lowenstein, G. (2004). Behavioral economics. Past present and future. In C. Camerer, G. Loewenstein, & M. Rabin (Eds.), *Advances in behavioral economics* (pp. 3–51). Princeton, NJ: Princeton Univ. Press.

Caporale, T., & Collier, T. (2013). Scouts versus Stats: The impact of Moneyball on the Major League Baseball draft. *Applied Economics*, *45*, 1983–1990.

Carlsson, B. (1972). The measurement of efficiency in production: An application to Swedish manufacturing industries, 1968. *Swedish Journal of Economics*, *74*, 468–485.

Cassidy, J. (2017). The making of Richard Thaler's economics Nobel. *The New Yorker*, (Oct 10).

Caves, R., & Barton, D. (1990). *Efficiency in U.S. manufacturing industries*. Cambridge, MA: MIT Press.

Chan, S., & Karim, M. (2011). Efficiency of foreign banks: Evidence from selected (Association of Southeast Asian Nations) ASEAN countries. *African Journal of Business Management*, *5*(14), 5617–5626.

Chang, Y. B., & Gurbaxani, V. (2013). An empirical analysis of technical efficiency. The role of IT intensity and competition. *Information Systems Research*, *24*(3), 561–578.

Chen, T. Y. (2002). Measuring firm performance with DEA and prior information in Taiwan's banks. *Applied Economics Letters*, *9*(3), 201–204.

Chen, C.-F. (2007). Applying the stochastic frontier approach to measure hotel managerial efficiency in Taiwan. *Tourism Management*, *28*, 696–702.

Chen, Y.-C., Chiu, Y.-H., & Huang, C.-W. (2010). Measuring super-efficiency of financial and nonfinancial holding companies in Taiwan: An application of DEA models. *African Journal of Business Management*, *4*, 3122–3133.

Chen, S., & He, L. (2013). Deregulation or governmental intervention? A counterfactual perspective on China's electricity market reform. *China &World Economy*, *21*(4), 101–120.

Chen, Y.-H., & Hsu, P.-P. (2011). Estimating the influences of financial crisis and diversification on efficiencies for Taiwan's listed securities firms using the two-stage DEA model. *World Academy of Science, Engineering and Technology*, *57*, 666–671.

Chen, X., Skully, M., & Brown, K. (2005). Banking efficiency in China: Application of DEA to pre- and post-deregulation eras: 1993–2000. *China Economic Review*, *16*(3), 229–245.

Chen, T.-j., & Tang, D.-p. (1990). Export performance and productivity growth: The case of Taiwan. *Economic Development and Cultural Change*, *38*(3), 577–585.

Chen, T., & Yeh, T. (2000). A measurement of bank efficiency, ownership and productivity changes in Taiwan. *Service Industries Journal*, *20*(1), 95–109.

Chetty, R. (2015). Behavioral economics and public policy. *American Economic Review: Papers & Proceedings*, *105*(5), 1–33.

Chhibber, P., & Majumdar, S. (1998). State as investor and state as owner: Consequences for firm performance in India. *Economic Development and Cultural Change*, 46(3), 561–580.

Chiang, H. C., & Tsaih, Y. C. (2015). An Analysis of the Efficiency of Philippine Financial Institutions. *The Journal of Social Sciences Research, Academic Research Publishing Group*, *1*(4), 37–40, 08-2015.

Chiu, Y.-H., Ma, C.-M., & Sun, M.-Y. (2010). Efficiency and credit rating in Taiwan banking: Data envelopment analysis estimation. *Applied Economics*, *42*(20), 2587–2600.

Choi, B. P., & Elyasiani, E. (2011). Foreign-owned insurer performance in the U.S. property-liability markets. *Applied Economics*, *43*, 291–306.

Choi, S., & Hasan, I. (2005). Ownership, governance, and bank performance: Korean experience. *Financial Markets, Institutions & Instruments*, *14*(4), 215–242.

Choi, B. P., & Weiss, M. (2005). An empirical investigation of market structure, efficiency, and performance in property-liability insurance. *Journal of Risk and Insurance*, *72*(4), 635–673.

Chortareas, G., Garza-Garcia, J., & Girardone, C. (2009). Market structure, profits, and spreads in the Mexican banking industry. *Banks and Bank Systems*, *4*(3), 43–52.

Chortareas, G., Garza-Garcia, J., & Girardone, C. (2011). Banking sector performance in Latin America: Market power versus efficiency. *Review of Development Economics*, *15*(2), 307–325.

Chortareas, G. E., Girardone, C., & Ventouri, A. (2007). Efficiency and productivity change in Greek banking: Methods and recent evidence. In P. Molyneux & E. Vallelado (Eds.), *Frontiers of banks in a global economy* (pp. 211–233). Basingstoke: Palgrave MacMillan.

Chortareas, G., Girardone, C., & Ventouri, A. (2009). Efficiency and productivity of Greek banks in the EMU era. *Applied Financial Economics*, *19*(16), 1317–1328.

Chu, S., & Lim, G. (1998). Share performance and profit efficiency of banks in an oligopolistic market: Evidence from Singapore. *Journal of Multinational Financial Management*, *8*(2–3), 155–168.

Coccorese, P., & Pellecchia, A. (2010). Testing the 'quiet life' hypothesis in the Italian banking industry. *Economic Notes*, *9*(3), 173–202.

Coelli, T. J., Rao, D. S. P., O'Donnell, C. J., & Battese, G. E. (2005). *An introduction to efficiency and productivity analysis*. New York: Springer.

Cook, W., Kazakov, A., Roll, Y., & Seiford, L. (1991). A data envelope approach to measuring efficiency: The case of highway maintenance patrols. *Journal of Socio-Economics*, *20*, 83–103.

Cowie, J., & Loynes, S. (2012). An assessment of cost management regimes in British rail infrastructure provision. *Transportation*, *16*(6), 1281–1299.

Crain, M., & Zardkoohi, A. (1980). X-efficiency and nonpecuniary rewards in a rent seeking society. A neglected issue in the property rights theory of the firm. *American Economic Review*, *70*, 784–792.

Craven, B., Dick, B., & Wood, B. (1986). The behavior of a resource reducing bureau. A case study of an English polytechnic. *Applied Economics*, *18*, 87–99.

Curtin, R. (2017). George Katona. A founder of behavioral economics. In R. Frantz, S. Chen, K. Dopfer, F. Heukelom, & S. Mousavi (Eds.), *Routledge handbook of behavioral economics* (pp. 18–35). New York: Taylor & Francis.

Cyert, R., & March, J. (2013). *A behavioral theory of the firm*. Mansfield Centre, CT: Martino Pub.

Cyree, K., Wansley, J., & Boehm, T. (2000). Determinants of bank growth choice. *Journal of Banking and Finance*, *24*, 709–734.

Dacanay, S. J. O., III. (2010). The evolution of cost and profit efficiency of Philippine commercial banks. *Philippine Review of Economics*, *47*(1), 109–146.

Damasio, A. (1994). *Descartes' error: Emotion, reason, and the human brain*. New York: Putnam.

Davis, K. (1973). Theories of hospital inflation: Some empirical evidence. *Journal of Human Resources*, *8*, 181–201.

De Guevara, J., & Maudos, J. (2007). Explanatory factors of market power in the banking system. *The Manchster School*, *75*(3), 275–296.

De Jonghe, O., & Vennet, R. (2008). Competition versus efficiency: What drives franchise values in European banking? *Journal of Banking & Finance*, *32*(9), 1820–1835.

DeAlessi, L. (1983). Property rights, transactions costs, and X-efficiency: An essay in economic theory. *American Economic Review*, *75*(1), 64–81.

Delis, M., & Papanikolaou, N. (2009). Determinants of bank efficiency: Evidence from a semi-parametric methodology. *Managerial Finance*, *35*(3), 260–275.

Delis, M., Koutsomanoli-Fillipaki, A., Staikouras, C., & Katerina, G. (2009). Evaluating cost and profit efficiency: A comparison of parametric and nonparametric methodologies. *Applied Financial Economics*, *19*(3), 191–202.

Denison, E. (1962). *The sources of economic growth in the United States & the alternatives before us*. New York: Committee for Economic Growth.

Denison, E. (1974). *Accounting for United States economic growth, 1929-1969*. Washington, DC: Brookings Institution.

DeYoung, R. (1998). Management quality and X-inefficiency in national banks. *Journal of Financial Services Research*, *13*(1), 5–22.

Diaz-Alejandro, C. (1973). Labor productivity and other characteristics of cement plants: An international comparison. In J. Bhagati & R. Eckus (Eds.), *Development and planning: Essays in honor of Paul Rosenstein Rodan* (pp. 285–315). Cambridge, MA: MIT Press.

DiLorenzo, T. (1981). Corporate management, property rights, and the X-istence of X-inefficiency. *Southern Economic Journal*, *48*, 116–123.

Dong, Y., Hamilton, R., & Tippett, M. (2014). Cost efficiency of the Chinese banking sector: A comparison of stochastic frontier analysis and data envelopment analysis. *Economic Modelling*, *36*, 298–308.

Drake, L., & Simper, R. (2002a). X-efficiency and scale economies in policing: A comparative study using the distribution free approach and DEA. *Applied Economics*, *34*, 1859–1870.

Drake, L., & Simper, R. (2002b). Economies of scale in U.K. building societies: A re-appraisal using an entry/exit model. *Journal of Banking and Finance*, *26*, 2365–2382.

Duesenberry, J. (1949). *Investment, savings, and the theory of consumer behavior*. Cambridge: Harvard Univ. Press.

Duncombe, W., Miner, J., & Ruggiero, J. (1997). Empirical evaluation of bureaucratic methods of inefficiency. *Public Choice*, *93*, 1–18.

Earl, P., & Littleboy, B. (2014). *G. L. S. Shackle*. New York: Palgrave Macmillan.

Eckel, C. (2004). Vernon Smith: Economics as a laboratory science. *Journal of Socio-Economics*, *33*, 15–28.

El Moussawi, C., & Obeid, H. (2011). Evaluating the productive efficiency of islamic banking in GCC: A non-parametric approach. *International Management Review*, *7*(1), 10–21.

Elyasiani, E., & Mehdian, S. (1992). Productive efficiency performance of minority and nonminority-owned banks: A nonparametric approach. *Journal of Banking & Finance*, *16*(5), 933–948.

English, M., Grosskopf, S., Hayes, K., & Yaisawarng, S. (1993). Output allocative and technical efficiency of banks. *Journal of Banking and Finance*, *17*, 349–366.

Erickson, W. (1976). Price-fixing conspiracies: Their long term impact. *Journal of Industrial Relations*, *24*, 189–202.

Esho, N., & Sharpe, I. (1996). X-efficiency of Australian permanent building societies, 1974–1990. *Economic Record*, *72*, 246–259.

Falk, A. (2007). Gift exchange in the field. *Econometrica, 75*(5), 1501–1511.

Falk, A., Gachter, S., & Kovacs, J. (1999). Intrinsic motivation and extrinsic incentives in a repeated game with incomplete contracts. *Journal of Economic Psychology, 20*, 251–284.

Farrell, M. J. (1957). The measurement of productive efficiency. *Journal of the Royal Statistical Society. Series A (General), 120*(3), 253.

Feijoo, M., Franco, J., & Hernandez, J. (2002). Global warming and the energy efficiency of Spanish industry. *Energy Economics, 34*, 405–423.

Fenn, P., Vencappa, D., Diacon, S., Klumpes, P., & O'Brien, C. (2008). Market structure and the efficiency of European insurance companies: A stochastic frontier analysis. *Journal of Banking and Finance, 32*(1), 86–100.

Ferber, M., & Nelson, J. (1993). *Beyond economic man: Feminist theory and economics*. Chicago: Univ. Chicago Press.

Feynman, R. (1998). *The meaning of it all*. Reading, MA: Perseus Books.

Figueira, C., Nellis, J., & Parker, D. (2009). The effects of ownership on bank efficiency in Latin America. *Applied Economics, 41*(18), 2353–2368.

Fiorito, J., & Hendricks, W. (1987). Union characteristics and bargaining outcomes. *Industrial and Labor Relations Review, 40*, 569–584.

Fishing, I. (1928). *The money illusion*. New York: Adelphi Company.

Fitzpatrick, T., & McQuinn, K. (2008). Measuring bank profit efficiency. *Applied Financial Economics, 18*(1), 1–8.

Food Systems Research Group. (1977). *The profit and price performance of leading food chains, 1970-1974*. In *U.S. congress, joint economic comm., 95th congress, 1st. sess., April 12, 1977*.

Frank, R. (2005). The mysterous disappearance of James Duesenberry. *New York Times*, (June 9) [Archives].

Frantz, R. (1997). *X-efficiency. Theory, evidence and applications*. Boston: Kluwer Academic.

Frantz, R. (2004). The behavioral economics of George Akerloff and Harvey Leibenstein. *Journal of Socio-Economics, 33*, 29–44.

Frantz, R., Chen, S.-H., Dopfer, K., Heukelom, F., & Mousavi, S. (Eds.), (2017). *Routledge handbook of behavioral economics*. New York: Routledge.

Freedman, C. (2002). The Xistence of definitional economics—Stigler's and Leibenstein's war of words. *Cambridge Journal of Economics, 36*, 161–178.

Fried, H., Lovell, K., & Eeckaut, P. V. (1993). Evaluating the performance of U.S. credit unions. *Journal of Banking and Finance, 17*(2–3), 251–265.

Friedman, M. (1953). The methodology of positive economics. In D. Hausman (Ed.), *The philosophy of economics: An anthology* (pp. 145–178). Cambridge: Cambridge Univ. Press.

Friedman, M. (1957). *A theory of the consumption function*. Princeton, NJ: Princeton Univ. Press.

Friedman, M., & Savage, L. (1948). Utility analysis of choices involving risk. *Journal of Political Economy, 56*(4), 279–304.

Fu, X., & Hefferman, S. (2009). The effects of reform on China's bank structure and performance. *Journal of Banking & Finance, 33*(1), 39–52.

Fu, X., & Heffernan, S. (2007). Cost X-efficiency in China's banking sector. *China Economic Review, 18*(1), 35–53.

Fudenberg, D., & Levine, D. (2006). A dual-self model of impulse control. *American Economic Review, 96*(5), 1449–1476.

Fung, M. (2006). Scale economies, X-efficiency, and convergence of productivity among bank holding companies. *Journal of Banking & Finance, 30*(10), 2857–2874.

Fung, M., & Cheng, A. (2010). Convergence of total factor productivity among banks: Hong Kong's experience. *Global Finance Journal, 21*(2), 201–210.

Fungacova, Z., Pessarossi, P., & Weill, L. (2013). Is bank competition detrimental to efficiency? Evidence from China. *China Economic Review*, *27*, 121–134.
Galenson, W., & Leibenstein, H. (1955). Investment criteria, productivity, and economic development. *Quarterly Journal of Economics*, *69*(3), 343–370.
Gan, A. (2016). *Das Maynard Keynes problem: Rethinking rationality*. Duke University [Economics Department Working Papers].
Gans, J., & Shepherd, G. (1994). How are the mighty fallen: Rejected classic articles by leading economists. *Journal of Economic Perspectives*, *8*(1), 165–179.
García-Herrero, A., Gavilá, S., & Santabárbara, D. (2006). Chinese banking reforms: An assessment of its evolution and possible impact. *CESifo Economic Studies*, *52*(2), 304–363.
García-Herrero, A., Gavilá, S., & Santabárbara, D. (2009). What explains the low profitability of Chinese banks? *Journal of Banking & Finance*, *33*(11), 2080–2092.
Garden, K., & Ralston, D. (1999). The X-efficiency and allocative efficiency effects of credit union mergers. *Journal of International Financial Markets, Institutions and Money*, *9*(3), 285–301.
Gardener, E., Molyneux, P., & Moore, B. (2001). The impact of the single market programme on EU banking. *The Service Industries Journal*, *21*(2), 47–70.
Gardner, H. (1985). *The mind's new science: A history of the cognitive revolution*. New York: Basic Books.
Gardner, L., & Grace, M. (1993). X-Efficiency in the U.S. life insurance industry. *Journal of Banking and Finance*, *17*(2), 497–510.
Garza-Garcia, J. (2012). Does market power influence bank profits in Mexico? A study on market power and efficiency. *Applied Financial Economics*, *22*, 21–32.
Gigerenzer, G., & Goldstein, D. G. (1996). On narrow norms and vague heuristics: A reply to Kahneman and Tversky. *Psychological Review*, *103*(3), 592–596.
Gillis, M. (1982). Allocative and X-efficiency in state owned mining enterprises: Comparisons between Bolivia and Indonesia. *Journal of Comparative Economics*, *6*, 1–23.
Gilovich, T., Medvec, V., & Savitsky, K. (2000). The spotlight effect in social judgment: An egocentric bias in estimates of the salience of one's own actions and appearance. *Journal of Personality and Social Psychology*, *78*(2), 211–222.
Girardone, C., Molyneux, P., & Gardener, E. (2004). Analysing the determinants of bank efficiency: The case of Italian banks. *Applied Economics*, *36*(3), 215–227.
Gisser, M., McClure, J., Okten, G., & Santoni, G. (2009). Some anomalies arising from bandwagons that impart upward sloping segments to market demand. *Econ Journal Watch*, *6*(1), 21–34.
Globerman, S., & Book, S. (1974). Statistical cost functions for performing arts organizations. *Southern Economic Journal*, *40*, 668–671.
Gneezy, U., & List, J. (2006). Putting behavioral economics to work: Testing for gift exchange in labor markets using field experiments. *Econometrica*, *74*(5), 1365–1384.
Gollop, F., & Karlson, S. (1978). The impact of the fuel adjustment mechanism on economic efficiency. *Review of Economics and Statistics*, *60*, 574–584.
Green, A., & Mayes, D. (1991). Technical inefficiency in manufacturing industries. *The Economic Journal*, *101*, 523–538.
Gregory, R. G., & James, D. (1973). Do new factories embody best practice technology? *Economic Journal*, *83*, 1133–1155.
Hadad, M., Hall, M., Kenjegalieva, K., Santoso, W., & Simper, R. (2011). Banking efficiency and stock market performance: An analysis of listed Indonesian banks. *Review of Quantitative Financial Accounting*, *37*(1), 1–20.
Hahn, F. (2007). Domestic mergers in the Austrian banking sector: A performance analysis. *Applied Financial Economics*, *17*(3), 185–196.

Hahn, F. (2008). Testing for profitability and contestability in banking: Evidence from Austria. *International Review of Applied Economics*, *22*(5), 639–653.

Hahn, F. (2009). A note on management efficiency and international banking. Some empirical panel evidence. *Journal of Applied Economics*, *XII*(1), 69–81.

Halkos, G., & Tzeremes, N. (2013). Estimating the degree of operating efficiency gains from a potential bank merger and acquisition: A DEA bootstrapped approach. *Journal of Banking & Finance*, *37*, 1658–1668.

Halpern, J. (1998). Bonded rationality: The rationality of everyday decision making in a social context. In J. Halpern & R. Stern (Eds.), *Debating rationality: Nonrational aspects of organizational decision making* (pp. 219–238). Ithaca, NY: Cornell Univ. Press.

Hanna, R., Mullainathan, S., & Schwartzstein, J. (2014). Learning through noticing: Theory and evidence from a field experiment. *The Quarterly Journal of Economics*, *129*(3), 1311–1353.

Hao, J., & Chou, L.-Y. (2005). The estimation of efficiency for life insurance industry: The case in Taiwan. *Journal of Asian Economics*, *16*, 847–860.

Harberger, A. C. (1954). Monopoly and resource allocation. *A.E.R.*, *44*, 77–87.

Harbison, F. (1956). Entrepreneurial organization as a factor in economic development. *Quarterly Journal of Economics*, *70*, 364–379.

Hart, O. (1983). The market mechanism as an incentive scheme. *Bell Journal of Economics*, *14*, 366–382.

Havrylchyk, O., & Jurzyk, E. (2011). Profitability of foreign banks in Central and Eastern Europe. Does the entry mode matter? *Economics of Transition*, *19*(3), 443–472.

Hay, D., & Liu, G. (2013). The efficiency of firms: What difference does competition make? *The Economic Journal*, *107*, 597–617.

Hayek, F. (1937). Economics and knowledge. *Economica*, *4*(new series), 33–54.

Hayek, F. (1943). The facts of the social sciences. *Ethics*, *54*(1), 1–13.

Hayek, F. (1945). The use of knowledge in society. *American Economic Review*, *35*(4), 519–530.

Hayek, F. (1948). *Individualism and economic order*. Chicago: Univ. Chicago Press.

Hayek, F. (1978). Two types of mind. In F. A. Hayek (Ed.), *New studies in philosophy, politics, economics, and the history of ideas* (pp. 50–56). Chicago: Univ. Chicago Press.

Hayek, F. (1979). *The counter-revolution of science: Studies in the abuse of reason*. Century Fund: Indianapolis.

Hayek, F. (1988). *The fatal conceit*. Chicago: Univ. Chicago Press.

Haynes, M., & Steve Thompson, S. (1999). The productivity effects of bank mergers: Evidence from the UK building societies. *Journal of Banking and Finance*, *23*(5), 825–846.

Heffernan, S., & Fu, X. (2010). Determinants of financial performance in Chinese banking. *Applied Financial Economics*, *20*, 1585–1600.

Heitger, B. (1987). Import protection and export performance—Their impact on economic growth. *Weltwirtschaftliches Archiv*, *123*, 249–261.

Hicks, J. R. (1935). Annual survey of economic theory: The theory of monopoly. *Econometrica*, *3*(1), 1–20.

History of economic thought website, n.d. http://www.hetwebsite.net/het/.

Hogarth, R. M., & Reder, M. W. (Eds.), (1987). *Rational choice: The contrast between economics and psychology*. Chicago, IL: University of Chicago Press.

Hollas, D., & Hereen, R. (1982). An estimate of the deadweight and X-efficiency losses in the municipal electric industry. *Journal of Economics and Business*, *34*, 269–281.

Holtman, A. (1983). Uncertainty, organizational form, and X-efficiency. *Journal of Economics and Business*, *35*, 131–137.

Hosono, K., Sakai, K., & Tsuru, K. (2006). *Consolidation of Cooperative Banks (Shinkin) in Japan: Motives and Consequences* [RIETI Discussion Paper Series 06-E-034]. Japan: The Research Institute of Economy, Trade and Industry.

Hossain, S. (1987). Allocative and technical efficiency: A study of rural enterprises in Bangladesh. *The Developing Economies*, *25*, 56–72.

Hossain, T., & List, J. (2012). The behavioralist visits the factory: Increasing productivity using simple framing manipulations. *Management Science*, *58*(12), 2151–2167.

Hou, X., Chang, K., Wang, Q., & Li, C. (2013). State ownership, foreign minority shareholders, and the efficiency of Chinese commercial banks. *Emerging Markets Finance & Trade*, *49*(Suppl. 2), 70–90.

Hsiao, H.-C., Chang, H., Cianci, A., & Huang, L.-H. (2010). First financial restructuring and operating efficiency: Evidence from Taiwanese commercial banks. *Journal of Banking & Finance*, *34*, 1461–1471.

Hu, J.-L., & Fang, C.-Y. (2010). Managerial efficiency of securities firms under the law-induced financial holding companies in Taiwan. *Journal of Information and Optimization Sciences*, *31*(1), 37–62.

Hu, M.-W., & Schieve, C. (1998). The changing competitiveness of Taiwan's manufacturing SMEs. *Small Business Economics*, *11*, 315–326.

Hu, J.-L., et al. (2010). A stochastic cost efficiency analysis of international tourist hotels in Taiwan. *International Journal of Hospitality Management*, *29*, 99–107.

Huang, T. (2000). Estimating X-efficiency in Taiwanese banking using a translog shadow profit function. *Journal of Productivity Analysis*, *14*, 241–257.

Huang, T.-H. (2005). A study on the productivities of IT capital and computer labor: Firm-level evidence from Taiwan's banking industry. *Journal of Productivity Analysis*, *24*(3), 241–257.

Huang, T.-H., Chen, K.-C., Lin, C.-H., & Chung, M.-T. (2014). Consistent estimation of technical and allocative efficiencies for a semiparametric stochastic cost frontier with shadow input prices. *Journal of Productivity Analysis*, *41*, 307–320.

Huang, T., Shen, C., Chen, K., & Tseng, S. (2011). Measuring technical and allocative efficiencies for banks in the transition countries using the Fourier flexible cost function. *Journal of Productivity Analysis, 2011*, *35*(2), 143–157.

Ihsan Isik, I., & Hassan, M. (2002). Technical, scale and allocative efficiencies of Turkish banking industry. *Journal of Banking & Finance*, *26*(4), 719–766.

Ingram, J. K. (1888). *A history of political economy*. New York: Macmillan.

Isik, I., & Hassan, M. (2003a). Efficiency, ownership and market structure, corporate control and governance in the Turkish banking industry. *Journal of Business Finance & Accounting*, *30*(9–10), 1363–1421.

Isik, I., & Hassan, M. (2003b). Financial disruption and bank productivity: The 1994 experience of Turkish banks. *Quarterly Review of Economics and Finance*, *43*(2), 291–320.

Isik, I., & Uysal, D. (2006). The sources of productivity growth in Turkish banks by ownership: The initial responses of public, private, and foreign banks to liberalization. *Turkish Studies*, *7*(3), 365–403.

Isshaq, Z., & Bokpin, G. (2012). Expansion and efficiency in banking: Evidence from Ghana. *Managerial and Decision Economics*, *33*, 19–28.

Ivaov, A., Levin, D., & Peck, J. (2013). Behavioral biases in endogenous-timing herding games: An experimental study. *Journal of Economic Behavior and Organization*, *87*, 25–34.

Jain, A., & Gupta, S. (1987). Some evidence on "herding" behavior of U.S. banks. *Journal of Money, Credit and Banking*, *19*(1), 78–89.

James, W. (1890). *Principles of psychology*. New York: Holt.

Jiang, C., Yao, S., & Feng, G. (2013). Bank ownership, privatization, and performance: Evidence from a transition country. *Journal of Banking and Finance*, *37*, 3364–3372.

Jiang, C., Yao, S., & Zhang, Z. (2009). The effects of governance changes on bank efficiency in China: A stochastic distance function approach. *China Economic Review*, *20*(4), 717–731.

Johnston, J. (1963). The productivity of management consultants. *Journal of the Royal Statistical Society, Series A*, *126*(Part 2), 237–249.

Jones, W. (2013). Exploring the relationship between intercollegiate athletic expenditures and team on-field success among NCAA Division I Institutions. *Journal of Sports Economics*, *14*(6), 584–605.

Jordan, D., Rice, D., Sanchez, J., & Wort, D. (2011). Explaining bank market-to-book ratios: Evidence from 2006 to 2009. *Journal of Banking and Financing*, *35*(8), 2047–2055.

Junanker, P. (1976). Land tenure and Indian agricultural productivity. *Journal of Development Studies*, *13*, 42–60.

Kahneman, D. (2003). Maps of bounded rationality: Psychology for behavioral economics. *American Economic Review*, *93*(5), 1449–1475.

Kahneman, D. (2011). *Thinking fast and slow*. New York: Farrer, Strauss and Giroux.

Kahneman, D., Slovic, P., & Tversky, A. (1982). *Judgment under uncertainty: Heuristics and biases*. Cambridge: Cambridge Univ. Press.

Kahneman, D., & Tversky, A. (1979). Prospect theory: An analysis of decisions under risk. *Econometrica*, *47*, 263–292.

Kalb, A. (2014). What Determines local governments' cost-efficiency? The case of road maintenance. *Economic Analysis and Policy*, *40*(1), 23–48.

Kalirajan, K. P., & Tse, Y. K. (1989). Technical efficiency measures for the Malaysian food manufacturing industries. *The Developing Economies*, *37*, 174–184.

Kalisch, G. K., Milnor, J. W., Nash, J. F., & Nering, E. D. (1954). Some experimental N-person games. In R. M. Thrall, R. H. Coombs, & R. L. Davis (Eds.), *Decision processes* (pp. 301–327). New York: Wiley.

Kang, M., & Chung, W.-T. (1998). A comparative study of X-inefficiency between Korea and Taiwan. *The Korean Economic Review*, *14*(1), 5–22.

Kapteyn, A., Wansbeek, T., & Buyze, J. (1980). The dynamics of preference formation. *Journal of Economic Behavior & Organization*, *1*(2), 123–157.

Karlo Kauko, K. (2009). Managers and efficiency in banking. *Journal of Banking & Finance*, *33*(3), 546–556.

Kasman, A., & Turgutlu, E. (2009). Cost efficiency and scale economies in the Turkish insurance industry. *Applied Economics*, *41*(24), 3151–3159.

Kasman, A., & Turgutlu, E. (2011). Performance of European insurance firms in the single insurance market. *International Review of Applied Economics*, *25*, 363–378.

Kasman, A., & Yildirim, C. (2006). Cost and profit efficiencies in transition banking: The case of new EU members. *Applied Economics*, *38*, 1079–1090.

Katona, G. (1940). *Organizing and memorizing*. New York: Columbia Univ. Press.

Katona, G. (1942). *War without inflation: The psychological approach to problems of war economy*. New York: Columbia University Press.

Katona, G. (1944). The role of frame of reference in war and post-war economy. *American Journal of Sociology*, *49*, 340–347.

Katona, G. (1947). Contribution of psychological data to economic analysis. *Journal of the American Statistical Association*, *42*, 449–459.

Katona, G. (1951). *Psychological analysis of economic behavior*. New York: McGraw-Hill.

Katona, G. (1953). Rational behavior and economic behavior. *Psychological Review*, *60*, 307–318.

Katona, G. (1960). *The powerful consumer: Psychological studies of the American economy*. New York: McGraw-Hill.

Katona, G. (1963). The relationship between psychology and economics. In S. Koch (Ed.), *Vol. 6. Psychology: Study of a science* (pp. 639–676). New York: McGraw-Hill.

Katona, G. (1975). *Psychological economics*. New York: Elsevier.

Katona, G. (1980). *Essays in behavioral economics*. Ann Arbor: Univ. of Michigan Press.

Katrak, H. (1980). Industry structure, foreign trade and price-cost margins in Indian manufacturing industries. *Journal of Development Studies*, *17*, 62–79.

Kaufman, D. (1990). A new theory of satisficing. *Journal of Behavioral Economics*, *19*(1), 35–51.

Kenjegalieva, K., Simper, R., & Weyman-Jones, T. (2009). Efficiency of transition banks: Inter-country banking industry trends. *Applied Financial Economics*, *2009*(19), 1531–1546.

Keynes, J. (1936). *The general theory of employment, interest, and money*. London: Macmillan.

Keynes, J. (1952). *A treatise on probability*. London: Macmillan and Co, Ltd.

Keynes, J. N. (2011). *The scope and method of political economy*. New Brunswick, NJ: Transaction Pub.

Kilby, P. (1962). Organization and productivity in backward economies. *Quarterly Journal of Economics*, *76*, 303–310.

Kirigia, J., & Asbu, E. (2013). Technical and scale efficiency of public community hospitals in Eritrea: An exploratory study. *Health Economics Review*, *3*(6), 1–16.

Kirkpatrick, L., & Epstein, S. (1992). Cognitive-experiential self-theory and subjective probability: Further evidence for two conceptual systems. *Journal of Personality and Social Psychology*, *63*(4), 534–544.

Kiyokawa, Y. (1991). The transformation of young rural women into disciplined labor under competition-oriented management: The experience of the silk-reeling industry in Japan. *Hitotsubashi Journal of Economics*, *32*, 49–69.

Kobeissi, N., & Sun, X. (2010). Ownership structure and bank performance: Evidence from the Middle East and North Africa region. *Comparative Economic Studies*, *52*(3), 287–323.

Kraft, E., & Tirtiroglu, D. (1998). Bank efficiency in Croatia: A stochastic-frontier analysis. *Journal of Comparative Analysis*, *26*, 282–300.

Kumar, M., & Vincent, C. (2011). Benchmarking Indian banks using DEA in post-reform period: A progressive time-weighted mean approach. *The Service Industries Journal*, *31*(14), 2455–2485.

Kumbhakar, S., & Lovell, K. (2000). *Stochastic frontier analysis*. Cambridge University Press.

Kwan, S. (2006). The X-efficiency of commercial banks in Hong Kong. *Journal of Banking & Finance*, *30*(4), 1127–1147.

Kyj, L., & Isik, I. (2008). Bank X-efficiency in Ukraine: An analysis of service characteristics and ownership. *Journal of Economics and Business*, *60*(4), 369–393.

Lall, S., & Rodrigo, G. (2001). Perspectives on the sources of heterogenity in Indian industry. *World Development*, *29*, 2127–2143.

Landsberger, H. (1958). *Hawthorne revisited*. Ithaca, NY: The New York State School of Industrial and Labor Relations.

Layour, B., & Lepinay, V. (2009). *The science of passionate interests: An introduction to Gabriel Tarde's economic anthropology*. Chicago: Prickly Paradigm Press.

Lecraw, D. (1977). Empirical tests for X-inefficiency. *Kyklos*, *30*, 116–120.

Lecraw, D. (1978). Determinants of capacity utilization by firms in LDC's. *Journal of Development Studies*, *5*, 139–153.

Lecraw, D. (1979). Choice of technology in low-wage countries: A non neoclassical approach. *Quarterly Journal of Economics*, *93*, 631–654.

LeDoux, J. (1996). *The emotional brain: The mysterious underpinnings of emotional life*. New York, NY: Simon and Schuster.

Lee, J. (1986). Market performance in an open developing economy: Technical and allocative efficiencies of Korean industries. *The Journal of Industrial Economics*, *35*, 81–96.

Lee, C.-C. (2009). Analysis of overall technical efficiency, pure technical efficiency and scale efficiency in the medium-sized audit firms. *Expert Systems with Applications*, *36*, 11156–11171.

Leibenstein, H. (1950). *Bandwagon, snob, and Veblen effects in the theory of consumers' demand. Quarterly Journal of Economics, 64(2), 183–207.*

Leibenstein, H. (1954). *A theory of economic demographic development*. Princeton: Princeton Univ. Press.

Leibenstein, H. (1957). *Economic backwardness and economic growth*. NY: John Wiley & Sons.

Leibenstein, H. (1960). *Economic theory and organizational analysis*. New York: Harper & Row.

Leibenstein, H. (1966). Allocative efficiency vs. "X-efficiency". *American Economic Review*, *56*(3), 392–415.

Leibenstein, H. (1969). Organizational or frictional equilibria, X-efficiency and the rate of innovation. *Quarterly Journal of Economics*, *83*, 600–623.

Leibenstein, H. (1974). An interpretation of the economic theory of fertility: Promising path or blind alley? *Journal of Economic Literature*, *12*, 457–479.

Leibenstein, H. (1976). *Beyond economic man*. Cambridge: Harvard University Press.

Leibenstein, H. (1977). X-efficiency, technical efficiency, and incomplete information use: A comment. *Economic Development and Cultural Change*, *25*, 311–316.

Leibenstein, H. (1978). *General X-efficiency theory and economic development*. London: Oxford University Press.

Leibenstein, H. (1979a). A branch of economics is missing: Micro-Micro theory. *Journal of Economic Literature*, *17*, 477–502.

Leibenstein, H. (1979b). X-efficiency: From concept to theory. *Challenge*, *22*, 13–22.

Leibenstein, H. (1982a). The prisoner's dilemma in the invisible hand: An analysis of intrafirm productivity. *American Economic Review*, *72*, 92–97.

Leibenstein, H. (1982b). On bull's-eye painting economics. *Journal of Post Keynesian Economics*, *4*, 460–465.

Leibenstein, H. (1983). Property rights theory and X-efficiency theory: A comment. *American Economic Review*, *73*, 831–842.

Leibenstein, H. (1985). On relaxing the maximization postulate. *Journal of Behavioral Economics*, *14*, 5–20.

Leibenstein, H. (1987a). *Inside the firm*. Cambridge: Harvard University Press.

Leibenstein, H. (1987b). X-efficiency theory. In J. Eatwell, M. Milgate, & P. Neuman (Eds.), *Vol. 4. The new Palgrave* (pp. 934–935). New York: Stockton Press.

Leibenstein, H. & Maital, S. (1992). Empirical estimation and partitioning of X-inefficiency: A data-envelope approach. *American Economic Review Papers and Proceedings*, *82*, 428–433.

Leibenstein, H. (1994). The organizational foundations of X-efficiency theory: A game-theoretic interpretation of Argyris' model of organizational learning. *Journal of Economic Behavior and Organization*, *23*, 251–268.

Lestage, R., Flacher, D., Kim, Y., Kim, J., & Kim, Y. (2013). Competition and investment in telecommunications: Does competition have the same impact on investment by private and state-owned firms? *Information Economics and Policy*, *25*, 41–50.

Levin, I., Schneider, S., & Gaeth, G. (1998). All frames are not created equal: A typology and critical analysis of framing effects. *Organizational Behavior and Human Decision Processes*, *76*(2), 149–188.

Lewis, W. A. (1954). Economic development with unlimited supplies of labour. *The Manchester School*, *22*(2), 139–191.
Levin, H. (1974). Measuring efficiency in educational production. *Public Finance Quarterly*, *2*, 831–842.
Lewis, D., & Webb, J. (2007). Potential cost synergies from banks acquiring real estate brokerage services. *Journal of Banking & Finance*, *31*(8), 2347–2363.
Liao, C.-S. (2009). Efficiency and productivity change in the banking industry in Taiwan: Domestic versus foreign banks. *Banks and Bank Systems*, *4*(4), 84–93.
Lieu, P.-T., Yeh, T.-L., & Chiu, Y.-H. (2005). Off-balance sheet activities and cost inefficiency in Taiwan's banks. *Service Industries Journal*, *25*(7), 925–944.
Lin, J. (1992). Rural reforms and agricultural growth in China. *American Economic Review*, *82*, 34–51.
Lin, P.-w. (2005). An empirical analysis of bank mergers and cost efficiency in Taiwan. *Small Business Economics*, *25*(2), 197–206.
Lin, Y.-H. (2011). Estimating cost efficiency and the technology gap ratio using the metafrontier approach for Taiwanese international tourist hotels. *Cornell Hospitality Quarterly*, *20*, 1–13.
Lin, S.-C., & Yang, Y.-H. (2014). An analysis of the operational and management efficiency of five-star hotels in Taiwan. *International Journal of Economics and Finance*, *6*(4), 12–22.
List, J. (2004). Neoclassical theory versus prospect theory: Evidence from the marketplace. *Econometrica*, *72*(2), 615–625.
Liu, Z.-J., & Chang, J. (2013). Operating performance of public banks in Taiwan after privatization. *Information Management and Business Review*, *5*(8), 424–433.
Liu, H.-H., Chen, T.-Y., & Pai, L.-Y. (2007). The influence of merger and acquisition activities on corporate performance in the Taiwanese telecommunications industry. *The Service Industries Journal*, *27*, 1041–1051.
Lovell, C., & Rouse, A. (2003). Equivalent standard DEA models to provide super-efficiency scores. *Journal of the Operational Research Society*, *54*, 101–108.
Lozano-Vivas, A., & Pasiouras, F. (2010). The impact of non-traditional activities on the estimation of bank efficiency: International evidence. *Journal of Banking and Finance*, *14*, 1436–1449.
Luo, D., & Yao, S. (2010). World financial crises and the rise of Chinese commercial banks: An efficiency analysis using DEA. *Applied Financial Economics*, *20*(19), 1515–1530.
Machlup, F. (1963). *Essays on economic semantics*. New York: W.W. Norton.
Maital, S. (2004). Daniel Kahneman: On redefining rationality. *Journal of Socio-Economics*, *33*, 1–14.
Majumdar, S. (1993). X-efficiency in emerging competitive markets: The case of U.S. telecommunications. *Journal of Economic Behavior and Organization*, *266*, 129–144.
Majumdar, S. (1994). Market liberalization and the psychology of firm performance. *Journal of Economic Psychology*, *15*, 405–423.
Majumdar, S. (1998). Slack in the state-owned enterprise: An evaluation of the impact of the soft-budget constraint. *International Journal of Industrial Organization*, *16*, 377–394.
Majumdar, S., & Venkataraman, S. (1993). New technology adoption in U.S. telecommunications: The role of competitive pressures and firm-level inducements. *Research Policy*, *22*, 521–536.
Manasakis, C., Apostolakis, A., & Datseris, G. (2013). Using data envelopment analysis to measure hotel efficiency in Crete. *International Journal of Contemporary Hospitality Management*, *25*(4), 510–535.
Manlagñit, M. C. V. (2011). Cost efficiency, determinants, and risk preferences in banking: A case of stochastic frontier analysis in the Philippines. *Journal of Asian Economics*, *22*(1), 23–35.

March, J. (1978). Bounded rationality, ambiguity, and the engineering of choice. *Bell Journal of Economics*, *9*(2), 587–608.
March, J. (1991). How decisions happen in organizations. *Human-Computer Interaction*, *6*(2), 95–117.
March, J. (2010). *The ambiguities of experience*. Ithaca, NY: Cornell Univ Press.
Marchand, S., & Guo, H. (2014). The environmental efficiency of non-certified organic farming in China: A case study of paddy rice production. *China Economic Review*, *31*, 201–216.
March, J., & Simon, H. (1958). *Organizations*. New York: Wiley.
Margaritis, D., & Psillaki, M. (2007). Capital structure and firm efficiency. *Journal of Business Finance & Accounting*, *34*(9–10), 1447–1469.
Marris, R. (1963). A model of managerial enterprise. *Quarterly Journal of Economics*, *77*, 185–209.
Marschall, P., & Flessa, S. (2011). Efficiency of primary care in rural Burkina Faso. A two-stage DEA analysis. *Health Economics Review*, *1*, 1–15.
Marshall, A. (1885). *The present position of economics*. London: Macmillan.
Marshall, A. (1890). *Principles of economics*. London: Macmillan.
Martin, J., & Page, J. (1983). The impact of subsidies on X-efficiency in LDC industry: Theory and an empirical test. *The Review of Economics and Statistics*, 65(4), 608–617.
Mason, R. (2000). The social significance of consumption: James Duesenberry's contribution to consumer theory. *Journal of Economic Issues*, *34*(3), 553–572.
Massey, C., & Thaler, R. (2013). The loser's curse: Decision making and market efficiency in the National Football League draft. *Management Science*, *59*(7), 1479–1495.
Matthews, K., Guo, J., & Zhang, X. (2008). *X-efficiency and rent seeking in Chinese banks: 1997-2006* [Cardiff economics working papers, # E2008/26]. Cardiff University, Cardiff Business School.
Matthews, K., & Zhang, N. (2010). Bank productivity in China 1997-2007: Measurement and convergence. *China Economic Review*, *21*(4), 617–628.
Maudos, J. (1998). Market structure and performance in Spanish banking using a direct measure of efficiency. *Applied Financial Economics*, *8*, 191–200.
Maudosa, J., & de Guevara, J. (2007). The cost of market power in banking: Social welfare loss vs. cost inefficiency. *Journal of Banking & Finance*, *31*(7), 2103–2125.
McAllister, P., & McManus, D. (1993). Resolving the scale efficiency puzzle in banking. *Journal of Banking and Finance*, *17*, 389–405.
McCormick, R., Shughart, W., II, & Tollison, R. (1984). The dis-interest in deregulation. *American Economic Review*, *75*, 1075–1079.
McEachern, W. (1978). Corporate control and growth: An alternative approach. *Journal of Industrial Economics*, *26*, 257–266.
McFetridge, D. (1973). Market structure and price-cost margins: An analysis of the Canadian manufacturing sector. *Canadian Journal of Economics*, *6*, 244–255.
Meardon, S., & Ortmann, A. (1996). Self-command in Adam Smith's theory of moral sentiments: A game-theoretic reinterpretation. *Rationality and Society*, *8*(1), 57–80.
Medford, R. (1986). Introducing management into the production function. *Review of Economics and Statistics*, *68*, 96–104.
Meeusen, W., & van den Broeck, J. (1977). Efficiency estimation from Cobb-Douglas production functions with composed error. *International Economic Review*, *18*(2), 435–444.
Mertens, A., & Urga, G. (2001). Efficiency, scale and scope economies in the Ukrainian banking sector in 1998. *Emerging Markets Review*, *2*, 292–308.
Mester, L. (1993). Efficiency in the savings and loan industry. *Journal of Banking and Finance*, *17*, 267–286.

Metcalf, J., & Mischel, W. (1999). A hot/cool-system analysis of delay of gratification: Dynamics of willpower. *Psychological Review*, *106*, 3–19.

Mill, J. S. (1836). *On the definition of political economy, and on the method of investigation proper to it*. In *Vol. IV, 1967. Collected works of John Stuart Mill* (pp. 309–339). Toronto: University of Toronto Press.

Miller, S., & Parkhe, A. (2002). Is there a liability of foreignness in global banking? An empirical test of banks' X-efficiency. *Strategic Management Journal*, *23*(1), 55–75.

Mitchell, W. C. (1914). Human behavior and economics: A survey of recent literature. *Quarterly Journal of Economics*, *29*(1), 1–47.

Mitzkewitz, M., & Nagel, R. (1993). Experimental results on ultimatum games with incomplete information. *International Journal of Game Theory*, *22*(2), 171–198.

Mobarek, A., & Kalonov, A. (2014). Comparative performance analysis between conventional and Islamic banks: Empirical evidence from OIC countries. *Applied Economics*, *46*, 253–270.

Modiglinai, F., & Brumberg, R. H. (1990). Utility analysis and aggregate consumption functions: An attempt at integration. In A. Abel (Ed.), *The life cycle hypothesis of saving*: *Vol. 2*. The collected papers of Franco Modigliani (pp. 128–197). Cambridge, MA: The MIT Press.

Mohanty, S., Lin, W., & Lin, H.-J. (2013). Measuring cost efficiency in presence of heteroskedasticity: The case of the banking industry in Taiwan. *Journal of International Financial Markets Institutions and Money*, *26*, 77–90.

Monsen, R. J., & Downs, A. (1965). A theory of large managerial firms. *Journal of Political Economy*, *73*(3), 221–236.

Monsen, R. J., Chitj, J. S., & Cooley, D. E. (1968). The effect of separation of ownership and control on the performance of the large firm. *Quarterly Journal of Economics*, *82*, 435–451.

Moradi-Motlagh, A., & Saleh, A. S. (2014). Re-examining the technical efficiency of Australian banks: A bootstrap dea approach. *Australian Economic Papers*, *53*(1–2), 112–128.

Mousa, F.-T., & Reed, R. (2017). The impact of slack resources on high-tech IPOs. *Entrepreneurhip, Theory and Practice*, *37*(5), 1123–1147.

Mousavi, S. (2017). Gerd Gigerenzer and Vernon Smith: Ecological rationality of heuristics. In R. Frantz, S. Chen, K. Dopfer, F. Heukelom, & S. Mousavi (Eds.), *Routledge handbook of behavioral economics* (pp. 88–100). New York: Taylor & Francis.

Mullainathan, S. (1998). *A memory based model of bounded rationality* [Mimeo]. Cambridge, MA: MIT.

Mullainathan, S., & Thaler, R. (2000). *Behavioral economics*. MIT Department of Economics [Working Paper].

Mundell, R. (1962). Review of L.H. Jansen, free trade, protection and customs union. *American Economic Review*, *52*, 622.

Murphy, G., Correia, C., & Barnett, N. (2007). Behavioral economic approaches to reduce college student drinking. *Addictive Behaviors*, *32*(11), 2573–2585.

Nagel, R., Bayona, A., Kheirandish, R., & Mousavi, S. (2016). Reinhard Selten, the dualist. In R. Frantz, S. Chen, K. Dopfer, F. Heukelom, & S. Mousavi (Eds.), *Routledge handbook of behavioral economics* (pp. 66–88). London/New York: Taylor & Francis.

Nash, J. (1950). The bargaining problem. *Econometrica*, *18*(2), 155–162.

Neal, P. (2004). X-efficiency and productivity change in Australian banking. *Australian Economic Papers*, *43*(2), 174–191.

Nelson, R., & Winter, S. (1973). Toward an evolutionary theory of economic capabilities. *The American Economic Review, Papers and Proceedings*, *63*(2), 440–449.

Nelson, R., & Winter, S. (1982). *An evolutionary theory of economic change*. Cambridge, MA: Harvard Univ. Press.

Neumann, J., & Morgenstern, O. (1944). *Theory of games and economic behavior*. Princeton: Princeton Univ. Press.

Newhouse, J. (1973). The economics of group practice. *Journal of Human Resources*, *8*, 37–56.

Niosi, J. (2002). National systems of innovations are 'X-efficient' (and 'X-effective'). Why some are slow learners. *Research Policy*, *31*, 291–302.

Ohlin, G. (1962). A review of E. Lundberg, productivity and profitability: Studies in the role of capital in the Swedish economy. *American Economic Review*, *52*, 827–829.

Okeahalam, C. (2006). Production efficiency in the South African banking sector: A stochastic analysis. *International Review of Applied Economics*, *20*(1), 103–123.

Olson, D., & Zoubi, T. (2011). Efficiency and bank profitability in MENA countries. *Emerging Markets Review*, *12*, 94–110.

Osei, D., d'Almeida, S., George, M., Kiriga, J., Menah, O., & Kainyu, L. (2005). Technical efficiency of public district hospitals and health centres in Ghana: A pilot study. *Cost Effectiveness and Resource Allocation*, *3*.

Pack, H. (1974). The employment-output trade-off in LDC's—A microeconomic approach. *Oxford Economic Papers (New Series)*, *26*, 388–404.

Pack, H. (1976). The substitution of labour for capital in Kenyan manufacturing. *The Economic Journal*, *86*, 45–58.

Page, J. (1980). Technical efficiency and economic performance: Some evidence from Ghana. *Oxford Economic Papers*, *32*, 319–339.

Papandreou, A. (1952). Some basic problems in the theory of the firm. In B. Haley (Ed.), *Vol. 2. A survey of contemporary economics* (pp. 183–221). Homewood, IL: Richard D. Irwin, Inc.

Parish, R., & Ng, Y. (1972). Monopoly, X-efficiency, and the measurement of welfare losses. *Economica*, *39*, 301–308.

Patibundla, M. (1998). Structure, organizational behavior, and technical efficiency: The case of an Indian industry. *Journal of Economic Behavior and Organization*, *34*, 419–434.

Paul, S., & Khaled Kourouche, K. (2008). Regulatory policy and the efficiency of the banking sector in Australia. *Australian Economic Review*, *41*(3), 260–271.

Pepper, A., Gore, J., & Crossman, A. (2013). Are long-term incentive plans an effective and efficient way of motivating senior executives? *Human Resource Management Journal*, *23*(1), 36–51.

Peristiani, S. (1997). Do mergers improve the X-efficiency and scale efficiency of U.S. banks? Evidence from the 1980s. *Journal of Money, Credit and Banking*, *29*(3), 326–337.

Perlman, M. (1990). The evolution of X-efficiency theory. In K. Weiermair & M. Perlman (Eds.), *Studies in economic rationality: X-Efficiency theory examined and extolled* (pp. 7–26). Ann Arbor: University of Michigan Press.

Persky, J. (1995). The ethology of homo economicus. *Journal of Economic Perspectives*, *9*(2), 221–231.

Pi, L., & Timme, S. (1993). Corporate control and bank efficiency. *Journal of Banking and Finance*, *17*, 515–530.

Piget, P., & Kossai, M. (2013). The relationship between information and communication technology use and firm performance in developing countries: A case study of electrical and electronic goods manufacturing SMEs in Tunisia. *African Development Review*, *25*(3), 330–343.

Pinker, S. (2018). *Enlightenment now: The case for reason, science, humanism, and progress*. New York: Penguin Books.

Pittman, R. (1990). Railroads and competition: The Santa Fe/Southern Pacific merger proposal. *Journal of Industrial Economics*, *39*, 25–46.

Plane, P. (1999). Privatization, technical efficiency and welfare consequences: The case of the Cote d'Ivoire Electricity Company (CIE). *World Development*, *27*(2), 343–360.

Pollak, R. (1976). Interdependent preferences. *The American Economic Review, 66*(3), 309–320.

Poshakwale, S., & Qian, B. (2011). Competitiveness and efficiency of the banking sector and economic growth in Egypt. *African Economic Development, 23*(1), 99–120.

Primeaux, W. (1977). An assessment of X-efficiency gained through competition. *Review of Economics and Statistics, 59*, 105–113.

Primeaux, W. (1978). The effect of competition on capacity utilization in the electric utility industry. *Economic Inquiry, 26*, 237–248.

Primeaux, W. (1985). Dismantling competition in a natural monopoly. *Quarterly Review of Economics and Business, 25*, 6–21.

Primeaux, W. (1986). *Direct electric utility competition: The natural monopoly myth*. New York: Praeger.

Pustay, M. (1978). Industrial inefficiency under regulatory surveillance. *Journal of Industrial Economics, 27*, 49–68.

Rabin, M. (1998). Psychology and economics. *Journal of Economic Literature, 36*, 11–46.

Rabin, M. (2002). A perspective on psychology and economics. *European Economic Review, 46*, 657–685.

Rai, A. (1996). Cost efficiency of international insurance firms. *Journal of Financial Services Research, 10*(3), 213–233.

Ralston, D., Wright, A., & Garden, K. (2001). Can mergers ensure the survival of credit unions in the third millennium? *Journal of Banking & Finance, 25*(12), 2277–2304.

Reder, M. (1947). *Studies in the theory of welfare economics*. New York: Columbia Univ. Press.

Register, C. (1988). Wages, productivity, and costs in union and nonunion hospitals. *Journal of Labor Research, 9*, 325–345.

Register, C., & Grimes, P. (1991). Collective bargaining, teachers, and student achievement. *Journal of Labor Research, 12*, 99–107.

Rezitis, A. (2008). Efficiency and productivity effects of bank mergers: Evidence from the Greek banking industry. *Economic Modelling, 25*(2), 236–254.

Rezvanian, R., Ariss, R., & Mehdian, S. (2011). Cost efficiency, technological progress and productivity growth of Chinese banking pre- and post-WTO accession. *Applied Financial Economics, 21*, 437–454.

Rezvanian, R., & Mehdian, S. (2002). An examination of cost structure and production performance of commercial banks in Singapore. *Journal of Banking & Finance, 26*(1), 79–98.

Rhodes, S. (1993). Efficiency effects of horizontal (in-market) bank mergers. *Journal of Banking and Finance, 26*, 311–322.

Ricciardi, F. M. (1957). *Top management decision-making simulations: The AMA approach*. New York: American Management Association.

Roethlisberger, F., Dickson, W., & Wright, H. (1939). *Management and the worker: An account of a research program conducted by the Western electric company, Hawthorne works, Chicago*. Cambridge, MA: Harvard Univ. Press.

Roger, F., & Marsh, L. (2016). *Minds, markets, and mileux. Commemorating the centennial birth of Herbert Simon*. New York: Palgrave Macmillan.

Rosko, M. D., & Mutter, R. L. (2011). What have we learned from the application of stochastic frontier analysis to U.S. hospitals? *Medical Care Research and Review, 68*(1 Suppl.), 75S–100S.

Rosman, R., Abd Wahab, N., & Zainol, Z. (2014). Efficiency of Islamic banks during the financial crisis: An analysis of Middle Eastern and Asian countries. *Pacific-Basin Finance Journal, 28*, 76–90.

Rossi, S., Schwaiger, M. S., & Winkler, G. (2009). How loan portfolio diversification affects risk, efficiency and capitalization: A managerial behavior model for Austrian banks. *Journal of Banking and Finance, 33*, 2218–2226.

Rostas, L. (1964). *Comparative productivity in British and American industry. Research Paper, # 13.* Cambridge: National Institute of Economic Sociology.

Rothschild, K. W. (1947). Price theory and oligopoly. *The Economic Journal, 57*, 299–320.

Ruggiero, J., Miner, J., & Blanchard, L. (2002). Measuring equity of educational outcomes in the presence of inefficiency. *European Journal of Operational Research, 142*, 642–652.

Ruggles, R. (1952). Methodological developments. In B. F. Haley (Ed.), *Vol. 2. A survey of contemporary economics* (pp. 408–458). Homewood, IL: R.D. Irwin, Inc.

Russell, B. (2009). *The basic writings of Bertrand Russell.* New York: Routledge.

Russell, T., & Thaler, R. (1985). The relevance of quasi rationality in competitive markets. *American Economic Review, 75*(5), 1071–1082.

Ruthenberg, D., & Elias, R. (1996). Cost economies and interest rate margins in a unified European banking market. *Journal of Economics and Business, 48*(3), 231–249.

Samuelson, P. (1949). Reviewed work(s): Theories of welfare economics by Hla Myint. *Economica, New Series, 16*, 371–374.

Sathye, M. (2001). X-efficiency in Australian banking: An empirical investigation. *Journal of Banking & Finance, 25*(3), 613–630.

Sauermann, H. (Ed.), (1967-1978). *Contributions to experimental economics (Beiträge zur experimentellen Wirtschaftsforschung, eight volumes).* Tübingen: J. C. B. Mohr.

Sauermann, H., & Selten, R. (1959). Ein Oligopolexperiment. *Zeitschirft für die gesamte Staatswissenschaft, 115*, 427–471.

Sauermann, H., & Selten, R. (1962). Anspruchsanpassungstheorie der Unternehmung. *Zeitschrift für die gesamte Staatswissenschaft, 118*, 577–599.

Savage, L. (1954). *The foundations of statistics.* New York: Wiley.

Schap, D. (1985). X-inefficiency in a rent-seeking society: A graphical analysis. *Quarterly Journal of Economics and Business, 25*, 19–27.

Scherer, F., Beckenstein, A., Kaufer, E., & Murphy, R. (1975). *The economics of multi-plant operations: An international comparisons study.* Cambridge: Harvard Univ. Press.

Schive, C. (1988). An intra-firm study of X-efficiency of Taiwan's sugar industry. *The Developing Economies, 26*, 161–171.

Schwartz, B., et al. (2002). Maximizing versus satisficing: Happiness is a matter of choice. *Journal of Personality and Social Psychology, 83*(5), 1178–1197.

Scitovsky, T. (1943). A note on profit maximization and its implications. *Review of Economic Studies, 11*(1), 57–60.

Scitovsky, T. (1974). Are men rational or economists wrong. In P. David & M. Reder (Eds.), *Nations and households in economic growth: Essays in honor of Moses Abramovitz* (pp. 223–235). NY: Academic Press.

Scitovsky, T. (1992). *The joyless economy: The psychology of human satisfaction.* New York: Oxford Univ. Press.

Seiford, M. L. (1990). *A bibliography of data envelope analysis (1978-1990): Version 5.0* [Technical report]. Amherst: Department of Industrial Engineering, University of Massachusetts.

Selten, R. (1965). Spieltheoretische Behandlung eines Oligopolmodells mit Nachfrageträgheit. *Zeitschrift für die gesamte Staatswissenschaft, 121*(301–324), 667–689.

Selten, R. (1967). Investitionsverhalten im Oligopolexperiment. In H. Sauermann (Ed.), *Vol. I. Contributions to experimental economics* (pp. 60–102). Tübingen: J. C. B. Mohr.

Selten, R. (1970). *Preisploitik der Mehrproduktenunternehmung in der statischen Theorie.* Berlin/Heidelberg/New York: Springer.

Selten, R. (1973). Equal share analysis of characteristic function experiments. In H. Sauermann (Ed.), *Vol. III. Contributions to experimental economics* (pp. 203–232). Tübingen: J. C. B. Mohr.

Selten, R. (1978a). The chain store paradox. *Theory and Decision, 9*, 127–159.

Selten, R. (1978b). The equity principle in economic behavior. In H.-W. Gottinger & W. Leinfellner (Eds.), *Decision theory and social ethics: Issues in social choice* (pp. 289–301). Dordrecht: Reidel.

Selten, R. (1983). Equal division payoff bounds for three-person characteristic function experiments. In R. Tietz (Ed.), *Aspiration Levels in bargaining and economic decision making* (pp. 255–275). Berlin/Heidelberg/New York: Springer.

Selten, R. (1990). Bounded rationality. *Journal of Institutional and Theoretical Economics, 146*(4), 649–658.

Selten, R. (1999). *Game theory and economic behaviour: Selected essays. (Vols. I and II)*. Cheltenham (UK)/Northampton (US): Edward Elgar.

Selten, R., & Berg, C. C. (1970). Drei experimentelle Oligopolspielserien mit kontinuierlichem Zeitverlauf. In H. Sauermann (Ed.), *Vol. II. Contributions to experimental economics* (pp. 162–221). Tübingen: J. C. B. Mohr.

Selten, R., & Buchta, J. (1999). Experimental sealed bid first price auctions with directly observed bid functions. In D. Budescu, I. Erev, & R. Zwick (Eds.), *Games and human behavior: Essays in the honor of Amnon Rapoport* (pp. 79–104). Mahwah, NJ: Lawrenz Associates.

Selten, R., & Stoecker, R. (1986). End behavior in sequences of finite prisoner's dilemma supergames. *Journal of Economic Behavior and Organization, 7*(1), 47–70.

Sen, A. (1977). Rational fools: A critique of the behavioral foundations of economic theory. *Philosophy & Public Affairs, 6*(4), 317–344.

Sent, E.-M. (2004). Behavioral economics: How psychology made its (limited) way back into economics. *History of Political Economy, 36*(4), 735–760.

Shackle, G. L. S. (1940). The nature of the inducement to invest. *The Review of Economic Studies., 8*(1), 44–48.

Shackle, G. L. S. (1941). A means of promoting investment. *Economic Journal, 51*(202–203), 249–260.

Shackle, G. L. S. (2009). *Epistemics and economics*. New Brunswick, NJ: Transaction Pub.

Shaffer, S. (1993). Can megamergers improve bank efficiency? *Journal of Banking and Finance, 17*(2), 423–436.

Shapira, Z. (1998). Prescriptive models in organizational decision making. In J. Halpern & R. Stern (Eds.), *Debating rationality, nonrational aspects of organizational decision making* (pp. 21–25). Ithaca: Cornell University Press.

Shapiro, K., & Muller, J. (1977). Sources of technical efficiency: The roles of modernization and information. *Economic Development and Cultural Change, 25*, 293–310.

Shefrin, H., & Thaler, R. (1980). Interpreting alpha rationality in hierarchical games. *Economics Letters, 5*(2), 109–113.

Shefrin, H., & Thaler, R. (1981). An economic theory of self-control. Journal of Political Economy, 89(2), 392-406.

Shelton, J. (1967). Allocative efficiency versus 'X-efficiency': Comment. *American Economic Review, 57*, 1252–1258.

Shen, T. Y. (1973). Technology diffusion, substitution, and X-efficiency. *Econometrica, 41*, 263–284.

Shen, T. Y. (1984). Estimation of X-inefficiency in eighteen countries. *Review of Economics and Statistics, 66*, 98–104.

Shen, T. Y. (1986). Putting X-efficiency in its place at a pinnacle. *Journal of Behavioral Economics, 15*, 29–34.

Shepherd, W. (1972a). The elements of market structure. *Review of Economics and Statistics, 54*, 25–37.
Shepherd, W. (1972b). Elements of market structure: An inter-industry analysis. *Southern Economic Journal, 38*, 531–537.
Shi, X., & Zhao, D. (2012). Technological efficiency of hotel industry in China and its influencing factors. *International Journal of Innovation, Management and Technology, 3*(4), 368–373.
Shieh, H.-S., Hu, J.-L., & Gao, L.-Y. (2014). Tourist preferences and cost efficiency of international tourist hotels in Taiwan. *International Journal of Marketing Studies, 6*(3), 35–48.
Shiller, R. (2005). *Rational exuberance*. New York: Doubleday.
Shin, D., & Kim, B. (2011). Efficiency of the banking industry structure in Korea. *Asian Economic Journal, 25*(4), 355–373.
Shleifer, A. (2000). *Inefficient markets*. Oxford: Oxford University Press.
Silkman, R., & Young, D. (1982). X-efficiency and state formula grants. *National Tax Journal, 35*, 383–397.
Simon, H. (1954). Bandwagon and underdog effects of the possibility of election predictions. *Public Opinion Quarterly, 18*, 245–253.
Simon, H. (1955). A behavioral model of rational choice. *Quarterly Journal of Economics, 69*, 99–118.
Simon, H. (1956). Rational choice and the structure of the environment. *Psychological Review, 63*, 129–138.
Simon, H. A. (1957a). *Models of man*. New York: John Wiley & Sons.
Simon, H. (1957b). Theories of decision-making in economics and behavioral science. *American Economic Review, 49*, 253–283.
Simon, H. (1972). Theories of bounded rationality. In C. B. McGuire & R. Radner (Eds.), *Decision and organization*. [Chapter 8]. Amsterdam: North Holland Pub. Co.
Simon, H. (1982). *Models of bounded rationality. Vol. 1*. Cambridge, MA: MIT Press.
Simon, H. (1985). Human nature in politics: The dialogue of psychology with political science. *The American Political Science Review, 79*(2), 293–304.
Simon, H. (1996a). *Models of the life*. Cambridge, MA: MIT Press.
Simon, H. (1996b). *The sciences of the artificial* (3rd ed.). Cambridge: MIT Press.
Simon, H. (1997a). *Administrative behavior* (4th ed.). New York: Free Press.
Simon, H. (1997b). *An empirically based microeconomics*. Cambridge: Cambridge Univ. Press.
Simon, H., & Hawkins, D. (1949). Some conditions of macroeconomic stability. *Econometrica, 17*(3–4), 245–248.
Sims, C. (2003). Implications of rational inattention. *Journal of Monetary Economics, 50*(3), 665–690.
Sloman, S. A. (2002). Two systems of reasoning. In T. Gilovich, D. Griffin, & D. Kahneman (Eds.), *Heuristics and biases: The psychology of intuitive judgment* (pp. 379–396). New York, NY: Cambridge University Press.
Slovic, P., et al. (2002). Rational actors or rational fools: Implications of the affect heuristic for behavioral economics. *Journal of Socio-Economics, 31*, 329–342.
Slovic, P., et al. (2004). Risk as analysis and risk as feelings: Some thoughts about affect, reason, risk, and rationality. *Risk Analysis, 24*(2), 311–322.
Smith, A. (1776). *An inquiry into the nature and causes of the wealth of nations*. New York: Modern Library.
Smith, A. (1976). In D. D. Raphael & A. L. Macfie (Eds.), *The theory of moral sentiments*. Indianapolis: Liberty Fund.
Smith, V. (2008). *Rationality in economics: Constructivist and ecological forms*. Cambridge: Cambridge Univ. Press.

Solow, R. (1957). Secular change and he aggregate production function. *Review of Economics and Statistics, 39*, 312–320.

Stanovich, K. (2009). *What intelligence tests miss: The psychology of rational thought.* New Haven, CT: Yale Univ. Press.

Stanovich, K. E. (2011). *Rationality and the reflective mind.* New York: Oxford University Press.

Staub, R., Souza, G., & Tabak, B. (2010). Evolution of bank efficiency in Brazil: A DEA approach. *European Journal of Operational Research, 202*(1), 204–213.

Sterm, J.-E., & Williams, B. (2008). Characteristics determining the efficiency of foreign banks in Australia. *Journal of Banking, 32*, 2346–2360.

Stevenson, R. (1982). X-inefficiency and interfirm rivalry: Evidence from the electric utility industry. *Land Economics, 58*, 52–66.

Stigler, G. (1976). The Xistence of X-efficiency. *American Economic Review, 60*, 213–216.

Sunstein, C. (2016). *The world according to star wars.* New York: Dey Street Books.

Sunstein, C. (2018). The rise of behavioral economics: Richard Thaler's misbehaving. *Journal of Behavioral Economics for Policy, 2*(1), 53–57.

Sunstein, C. R., & Sunstein, C. (2018). The rise of behavioral econonomics: Richard Thaler's misbehaving. *Journal of Behavioral Economics for Policy, 2*(1), 53–57.

Svorencík, A., & Maas, H. (Eds.), (2016). *The making of experimental economics: Witness seminar on the emergence of a field.* Cham/Heidelberg/New York/Dordrecht/London: Springer.

Tarde, G. (1902). *La psychologie economique.* Paris: Alcan.

Thaler, R. (1976). *The value of saving a life: Evidence from the labor market.* In *Household production and consumption* (pp. 265–302). Cambridge, MA: National Bureau of Economic Research, Inc.

Thaler, R. (1980a). *Judgment and decision-making under uncertainty: What economists can learn from psychology.* In: *Risk analysis in agriculture: Research and educational developments, proceedings of a seminar sponsored by the Western Regional Research Project W-149, Tucson, AZ, June 1980.*

Thaler, R. (1980b). Toward a positive theory of consumer choice. *Journal of Economic Behavior and Organization, 1*, 39–60.

Thaler, R. (1981). Maximization and self-control. *The Behavioral and Brain Sciences.* A commentary on "Maximization theory in behavioral psychology," by H. Rachlin, R. Battalio, J. Kagel and L. Green.

Thaler, R. (1988). Anomalies: The winner's curse. *Journal of Economic Perspectives, 2*(1), 191–202.

Thaler, R. (1991). *The winner's curse paradoxes and anomalies of economic life.* New York: Free Press.

Thaler, R. (2015). *Misbehaving: The making of behavioral economics.* New York: W. W. Norton & Company.

Thaler, R. (2016). Behavioral economics: Past, present, and future. *American Economic Review, 106*(7), 1577–1600.

Thaler, R., & Shefrin, H. M. (1981). An economic theory of self-control. *Journal of Political Economy, 89*, 392–406.

Thaler, R., & Sunstein, C. (2008). *Nudge.* New Haven, CT: Yale Univ. Press.

Timmer, P. (1971). Using a probabilistic frontier production function to measure technical efficiency. *Journal of Political Economics, 79*, 776–794.

Tobin, J. (1959). Liquidity preference as behavior towards risk. *Review of Economic Studies, 25*(2), 65–86.

Tobin, J. (1972). Wealth, liquidity, and the propensity to consume. In B. Strumpel, et al. (Eds.), *Human behavior in economic affairs: Essays in honor of George Katona* (pp. 37–56). Amsterdam: Elsevier.

Tomekovic, T. (1962). Levels of knowledge of requirements as a motivational factor in the work situation. *Human Relations*, *15*, 197–216.

Tong, K., & Leung, K. (2002). Tournament as a motivational strategy: Extension to dynamic situations with uncertain duration. *Journal of Economic Psychology*, *23*, 399–420.

Tortusa-Ausina, E. (2002). Exploring efficiency differences over time in the Spanish banking industry. *European Journal of Operational Research*, *139*, 643–664.

Tregenna, F. (2009). The fat years: The structure and profitability of the US banking sector in the pre-crisis period. *Cambridge Journal of Economics*, *33*(4), 609–632.

Tsaur, S.-H. (2001). The operating efficiency of international tourist hotels in Taiwan. *Asia Pacific Journal of Tourism Research*, *6*(1), 73–81.

Tugwell, R. (1922). Human nature in economic theory. *Journal of Political Economy*, *30*(3), 317–345.

Tullock, G. (1967). The welfare costs of tariffs, monopolies, and theft. *Western Economic Journal*, *5*, 224–232.

Tversky, A., & Kahneman, D. (1974). Judgment under uncertainty: Heuristics and biases. *Science*, *185*, 1124–1131.

Tyler, W. (1979). Technical efficiency in production in a developing country: An empirical examination of the brazilian plastics and steel industries. *Oxford Economic Papers*, *31*, 477–495.

Uchitelle, L. (2001). Some economists call behavior a key. *New York Times*, (February 11).

Uddin, S., & Suzuki, Y. (2011). Financial reform, ownership and performance in banking industry: The case of Bangladesh. *International Journal of Business and Management*, *6*(7), 28–39.

Ullman Margalit, E. (1977). *The emergence of norms*. Oxford: Clarendon Press.

van Leuvensteijn, M., Bikker, J., van Rixtele, A., & Sørensen, C. (2011). A new approach to measuring competition in the loan markets of the euro area. *Applied Economics*, *43*, 3155–3167.

Vining, A., & Boardman, A. (1992). Ownership versus competition: Efficiency in public enterprises. *Public Choice*, *73*, 205–239.

Vu, H., & Turnell, S. (2011). Cost and profit efficiencies of Australian banks and the impact of the global financial crisis. *The Economic Record*, *87*(279), 525–536.

Walter, I. (1997). Universal banking: A shareholder value perspective. *European Management Journal*, *15*(4), 344–360.

Warneryd, K. (1982). The life and work of George Katona. *Journal of Economic Psychology*, *2*(1), 1–31.

Warneryd, K. (2008). The psychological underpinnings of economics: Economic psychology according to Gabriel Tarde. *Journal of Socio-Economics*, *37*, 1685–1702.

Weiss, L., & Pascoe, G. (1985). *Concentration, X-inefficiency and Mr. Peltzman's superior firms* [Social Systems Research Institute Working Paper No. X501]. Madison: University of Wisconsin.

Wertheimer, M. (1945). *Productive thinking*. New York: Harper.

White, L. (1979). Appropriate technology, X-inefficiency, and a competitive environment: Some evidence from Pakistan. *Quarterly Journal of Economics*, *90*, 575–589.

Whitehead, A. N., & Russell, B. (1910). *Principia mathematica*. Cambridge: Cambridge University Press.

Williamson, O. (1963). A model of rational managerial behavior. In R. Cyert & J. March (Eds.), *A behavioral theory of the firm* (pp. 237–252). Mansfield Centre, CT: Martino Pub.

Winter, S. (1964). Economic natural selection and the theory of the firm. *Yale Economic Essays*, *4*(1), 225–272.

Winter, S. (1971). Satisficing, selection, and the innovating remnant. *Quarterly Journal of Economics*, *85*(2), 237–261.

Winter, S. (1986). Rationality of self and others in an economic system. *The Journal of Business*, *59*(4), 427–434.

Woittiez, I., & Kapteyn, A. (1998). Social interactions and habit formation in a model of female labour supply *Journal of Public Economics*, *70*(2), 185–205.

Wu, S. (2008). Bank mergers and acquisitions—An evaluation of the 'four pillars' policy in Australia. *Australian Economic Papers*, *47*(2), 141–155.

Wu, S.-I., & Chen, J.-H. (2012). Comparison between hotels and motels using CRM effect model—An empirical study in Taiwan. *International Journal of Hospitality Management*, *31*(4), 1254–1263.

Wu, H.-L., Chen, C.-H., & Lin, H.-L. (2009). Can a stock market listing help to improve the operational performance. *Journal of Economic Policy Reform*, *12*(1), 13–28.

Wu, T.-H., Chen, M.-S., & Yeh, J.-Y. (2010). Measuring the performance of police forces in Taiwan using data envelopment analysis. *Evaluation and Program Planning*, *33*, 246–254.

Yang, C.-C. (2013). A DEA approach for evaluating the opportunity cost of environmental regulations. *Asia-Pacific Journal of Operational Research*, *30*(2), 1–17.

Yang, C.-H., & Chen, K.-H. (2009). Are small firms less efficient? *Small Business Economics*, *32*, 375–395.

Yao, S., Han, Z., & Feng, G. (2008). Ownership reform, foreign competition and efficiency of Chinese commercial banks: A non-parametric approach. *World Economy*, *31*(10), 1310–1326.

Yao, S., Jiang, C., Feng, G., & Willenbockel, D. (2007). WTO challenges and efficiency of Chinese banks. *Applied Economics*, *39*(5), 629–643.

Yeh, T.-l. (2009). Bank loan loss provision decisions: Empirical analysis of Taiwanese banks. *Journal of Financial Services Marketing*, *14*(4), 278–289.

Yerkes, R. M., & Dodson, J. D. (1908). The relation of strength of stimulus to rapidity of habit-formation. *Journal of Comparative Neurology and Psychology*, *18*, 459–482.

Yu, P., & Luu, B. (2003). Banking mergers: The impact of financial liberalization on the Taiwanese banking industry. *Review of Quantitative Finance and Accounting*, *20*, 385–413.

Yuengert, A. (1993). The measurement of efficiency in life insurance: Estimates of a mixed normal-gamma error model. *Journal of Banking and Finance*, *17*, 483–496.

Index

Note: Page numbers followed by *f* indicate figures, *t* indicate tables, *b* indicate boxes, and *np* indicate footnotes.

A

ABC. *See* Agricultural Bank of China (ABC)
Acceptance/inert area, 88
Adaptive rationality, 50–51
Adorno, Theodor W., 57
Africa, XE in, 194–202, 196*t*
Agricultural Bank of China (ABC), 159
Ai, Mohammad, 18
Akerlof, George, 4, 6, 11, 15–16, 18–19
  behavioral economics
    difference, 77–79
    similarities, 77–79
Allocative (in)efficiency vs X-efficiency theory, 97–108, 118–121
  assumptions underlying X-efficiency theory, 101–104
  gift exchange, 107–108
  group XE, 106–107, 106*f*
  individual XE, 101
  non-allocative form of (in)efficiency, 97–99, 98*f*
  nudging towards X-efficiency, 100–101
  prisoner's dilemma, 107–108, 108*t*
  studies cited in 1966 article, 99–100
Arousal, 62–63
Arrow-Debreu market. *See* Complete market
Arrow, Kenneth, 18, 76–77
ASEAN, XE among, 168
Ashraf, Nava, 47
Asian financial forms, XE among
  ASEAN, 168
  Bangladesh, 166
  China, 157–165
    Mainland China, 157–158, 158*t*
    and WTO, 159–161
  Hong Kong, 161
  India, 168
  Indonesia, 166–167
  Japan, 165*t*, 166
  Korea, 165–166, 165*t*
  Philippines, 167–168
  Singapore, 166
  Taiwan, 162–165, 163*t*
Asian non-financial institutions, XE among, 173*t*
  China, 171
    agriculture, 171
  India, 176–177
    computers, 176
    electronics, 176
    government ownership, 176–177
    machine tools, 176
  Indonesia, 177
  Taiwan, 171–176
    firm size, 175–176
    hotels, 172–174
    life insurance, 175
    police, 175
    port industry, 176
    telecommunications, 171
Aspirations, theory of, 36
Asset size, 151
Asymmetric framings, 61
Atoms, 30
Attitudes, 37
Australia, XE in, 189–192, 190*t*

B

BACON program, 26
Bagwadi, Jagdish, 15
Bandwagon effect, 81
Bangladesh, XE among, 166
Bank mergers, 145–147
  branch level X, 147
Bank of China (BOC), 159
Bank regulatory environment, 147
Bank studies, 141–151
  asset size, 151
  bank mergers, 145–147
  bank regulatory environment, 147

Bank studies *(Continued)*
book value and TARP funds, 142, 143*t*
corporate control, 144
federal reserve check processing, 144
loan and capital, 148–150
management's role in X-efficiency, 150–151
megamergers, 145
profits and market structure, 147–148
profits efficiency, 141–142
scale efficiency, 142–143, 147
Ban profits, 147–148
Becker, Gary, 15, 18
Behavioral economics, 11, 13–15, 14*b*, 19–24, 45
as intervening variable, 101
similarities in, 77–79
Behavioral economics/psychological economics (BE/PE)
characteristics of, 32–33
Behavioral economists, 20–23
Behavioral macro, 35
BE/PE. *See* Behavioral economics/psychological economics (BE/PE)
Black, Fisher, 15
Black box, 52–53
BLACK program, 26
BOC. *See* Bank of China (BOC)
Bonded rationality, 44–45
Boo value, 142, 143*t*
Boulding, Kenneth, 1–3, 5, 10–11, 53–54
Bounded rationality, 14, 28–30, 50, 57–58
Branch level X, 147
Buchanan, James, 15
Bull's eye painting, 96–97
Burke, Edmund, 14

C

Camerer, Colin F., 4, 11, 47
Capital, 148–150
CASR. *See* Cumulative annual share returns (CASR)
Causal diagrams, 58
CCB. *See* China Construction Bank (CCB)
Chain store paradox, 59
Chetty, Raj, 4, 11, 31
China
agriculture, 171
and WTO, 159–161
XE among, 157–158, 158*t*, 171
China Construction Bank (CCB), 159
CME. *See* Critical minimum effort (CME)
COF. *See* Complex objective functions (COF)
Commons, John R., 40
Competition, as mental conflict, 49
Complete market, 76–77
Complex objective functions (COF), 84–87
Constructionist rationality, 15
Consumer behavior, 35–36
Consumption, 56–57, 79–80
Contextual rationality, 50–51
Conventional price theory, 39
Corleone, Fredo, 17
Corleone, Michael, 17
Corleone, Sonny, 17
Corporate control, 144
Credit unions, 153–154
Critical minimum effort (CME), 74–76
population and, 75–76
Cumulative annual share returns (CASR), 194–195
Cyert, Richard, 1–3, 5, 19–20
organizational analysis, economic theory and, 87–89

D

Das Adam Smith Problem, 43
Das John Maynard Keynes's Rationality Problem, 43–44
Data envelope analysis (DEA), 137–140, 189–190, 192–193
DEA. *See* Data envelope analysis (DEA)
Debreu, Gerard, 15, 18, 76–77
Decision premises, 88–89
Demographic transition (DT), 39
Denisonin, Edward, 41–42
Descartes, Rene, 14
DFA. *See* Distribution-free approach (DFA)
Distribution-free approach (DFA), 147, 152
Distributive justice, 58
DT. *See* Demographic transition (DT)
Dual selves, 54
new behavioral economics, 111
old behavioral economics, 110
Duesenberry, James, 1–5, 19–20, 25, 54–57
consumption, 56–57
dual selves, 54

interdependence, 55–56
Leibensteined, 54–55
social norms, 55
Dysrationalia, 19*b*

E

Earl, Peter, 20
Eastern Europe, XE in, 179–183
Ecological rationality, 15
Economic inputs, 49
Economic welfare approach, 80
ECONS, 9–10, 13, 17, 28–29, 203–204
versus HUMANS, 32
Edgeworth, F., 18
Efficiency, 62–63
wages, 72–77
Efficient Structure Hypothesis (ESH), 202
Effort illusions, 62
Egypt, XE in, 195
Einstein, Albert, 41
Elegance vs evidence, 63–64
Entrepreneur, role of, 76–77
EPAM program, 26
Equilibrium of the firm, 92–93
ESH. *See* Efficient Structure Hypothesis (ESH)
EU. *See* Expected utility (EU) theory
EU members, XE in, 183–184
Europe, XE in, 180–181*t*
Eastern Europe and post-communist, 179–183
EU members, 183–184
individual nations, 184–188
Expectations, 37
Expected utility (EU) theory, 61

F

Fairness, 58
FAM. *See* Fuel Adjustment Mechanism (FAM)
Farming, 109–116
Federal reserve check processing, 144
Financial liberalization, 189–190, 192
Firm size, 183, 186
First and other generations, overlaps between, 204
First Welfare Theorem, 76–77
Four pillars policy, 189–190
Framing, 10–11, 34–35
asymmetric, 61
new behavioral economics, 115–116
Friedman, Milton, 15, 18, 21–22, 30, 64
Frontier analysis, 140–141
Fuel Adjustment Mechanism (FAM), 129
Full rationality, 64–70

G

Galenson, Walter, 6
Game rationality, 50–51
GCC. *See* Gulf Cooperation Council (GCC) nations, XE in
Gedanken experiment, 81
Gift exchange, 107–108
new behavioral economics, 114–115
old behavioral economics, 99
Gilad, Benjamin, 12
GLAUBER program, 26
Globalization, 189–192
Government (regulations), 129–132
Granger causality model, 148–149
Group XE, 106–107, 106*f*
Guesses, 50
Gulf Cooperation Council (GCC), XE in, 197–198

H

Hagen, Tom, 17–18
Harrod, Roy, 15
Hawkins, D., 26
Hayek, Friedrich, 10*np*
behavioral economics, 14*b*
Hayek equilibrium, 41
HE. *See* Homo economicus (HE)
Herding
new behavioral economics, 112–114
old behavioral economics, 110
Hicks, J.R., 18
Homo Corleone Economicus, 17
Homo economicus (HE), 2, 17–19, 30, 203–204
humans and, 65–66
pre-eminence of, 18–19
Hong Kong, XE among, 161
Horndahl effect, 99–100
Human knowledge, nature of, 82–83

Human rationality, 14
HUMANS, 9–10, 13, 28–29, 96–97, 203–204
  versus ECONS, 32
Humans, and homo economicus, 65–66
Hume, David, 14

I

ICBC. *See* Industrial and Commercial Bank of China (ICBC)
Idiosyncratic behavior, 88–89
Image, 10–11
Imitation, 49
Incomplete contracts, 60
India
  computers, 176
  electronics, 176
  government ownership, 176–177
  machine tools, 176
  XE among, 176–177
India, XE among, 168
Individualism false, 14
Individualism true, 14
Individual XE, 101
  degree of (procedural) rationality, 104–105
  multiple equilibrium and psychological comfort at work, 105–106, 105*f*
Indonesia, XE among, 166–167, 177
Industrial and Commercial Bank of China (ICBC), 159
Ingram, John Kells, 17
Interdependence, 55–56
International Labour Office Productivity Demonstration Missions, 99
Inter-psychology, 49
Intervening variables, 37, 60
  behavioral economics as, 101
  X-efficiency theory as, 101
Irrational decisions, making, 70

J

Japan, XE among, 165*t*, 166
Jevons, William Stanley, 18
Joint-stock commercial banks (JSCB), 159–160
JSCB. *See* Joint-stock commercial banks (JSCB)

K

Kahneman, 1–4, 10–16, 18–19, 21–22, 47
Katona, George, 1–4, 9–11, 17–21, 30–38
  beginnings, 31
  behavioral economics/psychological economics, characteristics of, 32–33
  behavioral macro, 35
  consumer behavior, 35–36
  drift between economics and psychology, 31–32
  ECONS vs HUMANS, 32
  framing, 34–35
  intervening variables, 37
  law of large numbers, 36–37
  prediction and understanding, 38
  rationality, 33–34
Keynes, John Neville, 17
Koffka, Kurt, 31
Köhler, Wolfgang, 31
Korea, XE among, 165–166, 165*t*
Krugman, Paul, 15

L

Laibson, David, 4, 11, 13–14
Lange, Oscar, 26
Latin America
  finance industry, 193*t*
  XE in, 192–194, 192*t*
Law of large numbers, 36–37
Lazear, Edward, 15
Lebanon, XE in, 195
Leibenstein, Harvey, 1–4, 9–10, 12–13, 15–22, 38–45, 205
  atoms and molecules, 39
  and Austrian economics, 39–41
  behavioral economics
    difference, 77–79
    similarities in, 77–79
  and marginal productivity theory, 41–42
  theory of the firm, 91–93
  writings (1950–66), 5–7
  X-efficiency theory (*see* X-efficiency theory)
Level of competition, 127–129
Lewsin, Kurt, 34–35
Liability of foreignness, 200–201
Life insurance industry, 152–154
Limited rationality, 50–51

Loans, 148–150
Loasby, Brian, 20
Lowenstein, George, 4, 11, 47
Lucas, Robert, 15

M

Machlup, Fritz, 18
Mainland China, XE among, 157–158, 158*t*
Management, 133–135
  role in X-efficiency, 150–151
Mandeville, Bernard, 14
MAPP program, 26
March, James, 1–5, 19–20, 25, 50–52
  guesses, 50
  myths, 50
  organizational analysis, economic theory and, 87–89
  procedural rationality, 51–52
  rationality, 50–51
  stories, 50
  substantive rationality, 51–52
Marginal productivity theory, 41–42
Market reform and liberalization, 182–183
Market structure, 147–148
Marshall, Alfred, 42–43
Maximization vs reality, 52
Megamergers, 145
Mental accounting, 10–11
Methodological individualism, 40
Middle East and North Africa (MENA), XE in, 197–198
Middle East, XE in, 194–202, 196*t*
Mill, John Stuart, 17–18
Miller, Merton, 15–16
Minsky, 19–20
Mitchelle, Wesley Claire, 31–32
Mitzkewitz, Michael, 57
Modigliani, Franco, 15
Molecules, 30
Money, 62
Morgenstern-Austrian Subjectivism, 43
Morgenstern, Oscar, 39–41
Motives, 37
Mullainathan, Sendhil, 4, 11
Multiple equilibrium, 105–106, 105*f*
Myths, 50

N

Nagel, Rosemarie, 57
National champions, 95
Nelson, Richard, 1–3, 5, 19–20, 25, 52–53
  black box, 52–53
  maximization vs reality, 52
Neoclassical Models 1.0, 11–12
Neoclassical Models 2.0, 11–12
Neoclassical theory (NCT), 90–91
New behavioral economics, 64–70, 109–116
  current and future selves, 111–112
  dual-selves, 111
  framing, 115–116
  gift exchange, 114–115
  herding, 112–114
Newell, Allen, 26
New Zealand, XE in, 189–192, 190*t*
Non-allocative form of (in)efficiency, 97–99, 98*f*
Non-bank studies, 151–155
  credit unions, 153–154
  life insurance industry, 152–154
  property management insurance, 154–155
  S&L industry, 151–152
Non-maximizing behavior, 66
Non-parametric approaches, 137–140
  data envelope analysis, 118–121, 140
  overview, 137–138
  stochastic frontier analysis, 139–140
Non-zero sum games, 74–76
Normative game theory, 58
Notestein, Frank, 39–41
Nudging towards X-efficiency, 100–101

O

OIC nations, XE in, 197–198
Old behavioral economics, 65–66, 110–111
  dual-selves, 110
  gift exchange, 111
  herding, 110
Optimum population theory, 5
Organizational analysis, economic theory and, 83–94
  acceptance/inert area, 88
  complex objective functions, 84–87
  organizational equilibrium, 87–88
  roles, 88–91

Organizational (in)efficiency, 99
Organizational equilibrium, 87–88
Ownership form, 124–126

P

Pakistan, XE in, 194–195
Parable of the ant, 27–28
Parametric approaches, 137–140
  overview, 137–138
  stochastic frontier analysis, 139–140
Pareto, Vilfredo, 18
PBC. *See* People's Bank of China (PBC)
PD. *See* Prisoner's dilemma (PD) game
People's Bank of China (PBC), 159
Perlman, Mark, 42
Philippines, XE among, 167–168
Pigou, Arthur C., 42
Posner, Richard, 15–16
Possibility, 61
Post-communist Europe, 179–183
Posterior rationality, 50–51
Prediction, 38
Prisoner's dilemma (PD) game, 28, 59, 107–108, 108*t*
Probability, 61
Procedural rationality, 41, 50–52
  degree of, 104–105
Process rationality, 50–51
Profits efficiency, 141–142
Property management insurance, 154–155
Protection, 126–127
Psychological comfort at work, 105–106, 105*f*
Psychology
  definition of, 23
  inter-psychology, 49
PTE. *See* Pure technical efficiency (PTE)
Pure technical efficiency (PTE), 186–187

Q

Quiet life, 189–190, 197

R

Rabin, Mathew, 4, 11, 21–22
Rational choice theory, 50
Rational inattention, 34
Rationalistic-hedonistic decision making, 31–32
Rationality, 14, 30, 33–34, 50, 67–68, 103
  adaptive, 50–51
  bounded, 14, 28–30, 44–45, 50, 57–58
  constructionist, 15
  contextual, 50–51
  ecological, 15
  in economics, 63
  forms of, 50–51
  full, 64–70
  game, 50–51
  human, 14
  limited, 50–51
  macro and, 68–69
  nature of, 41
  near and quasi, 69
  paradox of, 59–61
  posterior, 50–51
  procedural, 41, 50–51, 126–127
  process, 50–51
  selected, 50–51
  substantive, 50–51
  wall of, 60
  X-efficiency theory, 119–120
Rausch, Edwin, 57
Ray, Donald, 11
Reality vs maximization, 52
Relative Market Power Hypothesis (RMPH), 202
RMPH. *See* Relative Market Power Hypothesis (RMPH)
Roles, 88–89
  role of, 90–91
Rosen, Sherwin, 11, 15–16

S

Salk, Jonas, 5, 41
Samuelson, Paul, 2, 18
Satisficing, 61, 70, 105
  heuristics, 69–70
Satisfying, 28–30
Scale efficiency (SE), 142–143, 147, 179, 185–187
SCF. *See* Stochastic cost frontier (SCF)
Scholes, Myron, 15
Scitovsky, Tibor, 1–3, 5, 15, 19–20, 25, 61–64
  efficiency and arousal, 62–63
  elegance vs evidence, 63–64
  money, time and effort illusions, 62
  rationality in economics, 63

Selected rationality, 50–51
Selten, Reinhard, 1–3, 5, 25, 57–59
SE. *See* Scale efficiency (SE)
SFA. *See* Stochastic frontier analysis (SFA)
Shackle, G.L.S., 1–3, 5, 19–20, 25, 59–61
  asymmetric framing, 61
  incomplete contracts, 60
  intervening variables, 60
  probability and possibility, 61
  satisficing, 61
  unacknowledgement, 59–60
  wall of rationality, 60
Shenzhen Development Bank, 159
Shenzhen Stock Exchange, 159
Shleifer, Andrei, 4, 11
Simon, Herbert A., 1–4, 9–11, 14, 16–17, 19–21, 25–30, 41
  bounded rationality, 28–30
  organizational analysis, economic theory and, 87–89
  parable of the ant, 27–28
  satisfying, 28–30
  simplicity, 26–28
Simplicity, 26–28
Singapore, XE among, 166
S&L industry, 151–152
Smith, Adam, 47
Smith, Vernon, 14–15, 20–21
Snob effect, 81
Social norms, 54–55
Social preferences, 79–82
Sophisticated anthropomorphic sin, 13, 203
Speculation, 45
STAHL program, 26
Stanovich, Keith, 19
Stigler, George, 96
Stochastic cost frontier (SCF), 202
Stochastic frontier analysis (SFA), 137, 139–140, 154
Stories, 50
Substantive rationality, 50–52

T

Tacit knowledge, 29–30
Taiwan
  firm size, 175–176
  hotels, 172–174
  life insurance, 175
  police, 175
  port industry, 176
  telecommunications, 171
  XE among, 171–176
Taiwan, XE among, 162–165, 163*t*
Tarde, Gabriel, 1–3, 5, 19–20, 25, 47–49
  competition, as mental conflict, 49
  economic inputs, 49
  imitation, 49
TARP funds, 142
TE. *See* Technical efficiency (TE)
Technical efficiency (TE), 179, 186–187
TFA. *See* Thick frontier analysis (TFA)
TFT. *See* Tit-for-Tat (TFT)
Thaler, Richard, 2–4, 9–12, 10*np*, 15–16, 18–19, 21
Theory of the firm, 91–93
  equilibrium, 92–93
  incomplete knowledge, 91–92
  pieces, fitting, 91
Thick frontier analysis (TFA), 150
Time illusion, 62
Tit-for-Tat (TFT), 28
Tobin, James, 15, 36
Tugwell, Rexford, 23–24
Turkey, XE in, 198
Tversky, Amos, 1–4, 10–14, 21–22, 47

U

Uchitelle, Louis, 3, 13–14
Unacknowledgement, 59–60
Understanding, 38
Urge to merge, 193–194
US financial institutions, XE among
  bank studies, 141–151
    asset size, 151
    bank mergers, 145–147
    bank regulatory environment, 147
    book value and TARP funds, 142, 143*t*
    branch level X, 147
    corporate control, 144
    federal reserve check processing, 144
    loan and capital, 148–150
    management's role in X-efficiency, 150–151
    megamergers, 145
    mergers for banks with assets, 142
    profits and market structure, 147–148
    profits efficiency, 141–142
    scale efficiency, 142–143, 147

US financial institutions, XE among (Continued)
frontier analysis, 140–141
non-bank studies, 151–155
credit unions, 153–154
life insurance industry, 148–150, 152–154
property management insurance, 154–155
S&L industry, 151–152
parametric and non-parametric approaches, 137–140
comparison of methods, 140
data envelope analysis, 138–140
overview, 137–138
stochastic frontier analysis, 139–140
Utility and demand, interpersonal aspects of, 80

V

Veblen effect, 82

W

Walras, Leon, 18
Wanner, Eric, 22
Wertheimer, Max, 31, 34
Williamson, Oliver, 40
Winning and losing, 69
Winter, Sidney, 1–3, 5, 19–20, 25, 52–53
black box, 52–53
maximization vs reality, 52
World Trade Organization (WTO)
China and, 159–161
WTO. *See* World Trade Organization (WTO)

X

X-efficiency theory (XET), 6–7, 41–45, 93–94, 204
Akerlof's and Leibenstein's behavioral economics, similarities in, 78–79
diffference, 77–79
vs allocative efficiency, 97–108
assumptions underlying X-efficiency theory, 101–104
gift exchange, 107–108
group XE, 106–107, 106*f*
individual XE, 104–106
non-allocative form of (in)efficiency, 97–99, 98*f*
nudging towards X-efficiency, 100–101
prisoner's dilemma, 107–108, 108*t*
studies cited in 1966 article, 99–100
among Asian financial firms (*see* Asian financial forms, XE among)
among Asian non-financial institutions (*see* Asian non-financial institutions, XE among)
among US financial institutions (*see* US financial institutions, XE among)
bull's eye painting, 96–97
critical minimum effort, 74–76
efficiency wages, 72–77
empirical studies of, 7–8, 205
entrepreneur, role of, 76–77
in Europe (*see* Europe, XE in)
government (regulations), 129–132
human knowledge, nature of, 82–83
as intervening variable, 101
issues surrounding, 117–121
versus allocative (in)efficiency, 118–121
estimate, 119
Harvey the meliorist, 121
Harvey to the rescue, 118
rationality, 119–120
level of competition, 127–129
management, 133–135
not using questionnaires and/or interviews, early studies on, 123–124
organizational analysis, economic theory and, 83–94
acceptance/inert area, 88
complex objective functions, 84–87
organizational equilibrium, 87–88
roles, 88–91
ownership form, 124–126
population and critical minimum effort, 75–76
protection, 126–127
snob effect, 81
social preferences, 79–82
theory of the firm (*see* Theory of the firm)
using questionnaires and/or interviews, early studies on, 121–123
Veblen effect, 82
zero and non-zero sum games, 74–76
XET. *See* X-efficiency theory (XET)

Y

Yellen, Janet, 6
Yerkes-Dodson Law, 63

Z

Zero sum games, 74–76

Kolibri 360 GmbH
Ferdinand-Jühlke-Straße 7
99095 Erfurt, Deutschland
produktsicherheit@kolibri360.de